Deccan in Transition, 1600 to 1800

This book presents the socio-cultural and historical trajectories of the Deccan plateau as well as the coastal areas of the current states of Andhra Pradesh, Maharashtra, Karnataka and Goa. It studies the art of diplomacy by discussing the diplomatic relations between the Marathas and various European companies, as well as the indigenous regional states. The author also probes into the Maratha naval policy, the evolution of a composite Deccani culture and the cultural flux that was taking place within the Maratha country. Through an interdisciplinary lens, the volume examines how caste and gender relations operated, how the idea of dissent was generated as well as the socio-political impact of various linguistic, ethnic and religious groups. Through a study of monuments, sculpture and paintings prevalent in the region, the book also discusses the developments in art and architecture in the Deccan.

Rich in archival sources, this book is a must read for scholars and researchers of Indian history, colonial history, South Asian history, Maratha history and history in general.

Umesh Ashok Kadam is Professor of Medieval Indian History & Early Modern History at the Centre for Historical Studies, Jawaharlal Nehru University, New Delhi, and Member Secretary, Indian Council of Historical Research, New Delhi. He specializes in History of Deccan and Western India. For the last two decades he has been visiting universities in the Netherlands, France, Portugal and the United Kingdom to promote advanced research on the History of Deccan through the 8th to 18th centuries.

Deccan in Transition, 1600 to 1800

European Dominance and Maratha Sovereignty

Umesh Ashok Kadam

Routledge
Taylor & Francis Group
LONDON AND NEW YORK

First published 2023
by Routledge
4 Park Square, Milton Park, Abingdon, Oxon OX14 4RN

and by Routledge
605 Third Avenue, New York, NY 10158

Routledge is an imprint of the Taylor & Francis Group, an informa business

British Library Cataloguing-in-Publication Data
A catalogue record for this book is available from the British Library

Library of Congress Cataloging-in-Publication Data
A catalog record has been requested for this book

ISBN: 978-1-032-42716-4 (hbk)
ISBN: 978-1-032-45548-8 (pbk)
ISBN: 978-1-003-37751-1 (ebk)

DOI: 10.4324/9781003377511

Typeset in Sabon
by Deanta Global Publishing Services, Chennai, India

Contents

Preface

The representation of the "History of the Marathas" through varied historiographic representations has always centred around the colonial discourses of the English East India Company in matters related to politics, diplomacy and interdependency in Deccan all through the 17th and 18th centuries. The gradual rise of the Maratha state (Swaraj established by Chhatrapati Shivaji) had a bearing on the politics and diplomacy across all the European powers in the Indian subcontinent, viz. the Portuguese, the Dutch, the English, and the French right from its inception. The 17th and 18th centuries in Indian history was a precursor to the developments of the 19th century. It can be seen as a marker for Deccan as longue durée since Deccan in the 17th and 18th centuries saw marked changes in terms of economic structures, diplomatic policies, etc. with the rise of the Marathas. The European Companies also brought about such changes to the Indian sub-continent in terms of social and cultural policies that over the years it became the new order. The process of acculturation did not happen overnight, it was a process of slow gradual change as the change of mentalities, traditions and customs was a process of contest and conciliation.

The purpose of this research program is to indulge in the discourse and review and reconstruct the existing generalizations about the region Deccan with a particular focus on the Maratha State and trace its relations with the contemporary European powers by underlining their art of diplomacy with the help of unpublished sources from the East India companies formed by the Portuguese, the Dutch and the French and highlighting autochthonic vernacular sources. The research has also tried to get a better sense of historical narrative without a British-centric view. Likewise, the Deccan states have been termed as successor states by various scholars; however, after re-examining the various contours of the Maratha state, it can be concluded that it was not only a trans-regional state with indefinite geographical boundaries and regional identity. The Marathas consolidated and expanded their power in the South of India in the 17th century while in the 18th century they concentrated in the North of India thus becoming the most formidable power in India. We also see the transitional shift in the authority of the state from the Chhatrapati to a powerful Confederate and lastly to the domination of the Barbhai Council which shows the resilient nature of the Marathas towards adapting to the needs of the time. The constant tussle with the Deccan powers and the European Companies shaped their ideology and domestic policy. For example, the Barbhai Council were supporters of the French, and hence they designed their state policy by employing French mercenaries in the army. Thus, when it came to trade and commerce the Marathas allowed the Europeans to set up factories in places where it benefitted them. The 18th century which witnessed a period of mercantilism saw the various interlopers of the European Companies taking part in the profitable Asiatic trade and gradually participated in creating trading posts in India in which the Western and Eastern Coasts of Deccan virtually became the nodal points for trade, commerce and investments in the world trade. Deccan was transforming into an inclusive economy, creating different, fairly open, assimilating, cosmopolitan cultures and communities. Gradually, during the 18th century, it also found an outlet in banking, which grew increasingly important in sustaining the new "mercantilist" indigenous states: the Marathas, Tanjore, Mysore, Hyderabad, Arcot, etc. Thus, Deccan became that part of the structure in which the survival of trade depended. Hence, an understanding of Deccan in totality is imperative.

Medieval Deccan has remained under-researched as a substantial amount of historiography, documentation, sources and interpretations remains unexplored yet. The region never had a stable cultural or political crater. Unlike Deccan, regions like north India, Bengal or the Tamil south, as analysed by Richard Eaton, are well placed in historical literature that were stable and were characterized by long-term political and cultural brackets. The region presented periods of imperial rules from various centres like Kalyana under the Chalukyas, Bidar under the Bahmanis or Vijayanagara under its first three dynasties. Deccan in a larger span never held a single core of politics or one imperial crater as juxtaposed to Delhi or the Kaveri delta rule. Maratha supremacy from the 16th to 18th centuries ushered in several newer parameters in the relations with the indigenous and the foreign powers, economic and socio-cultural patterns of the region. The present work undertaken explores the significance of the Maratha state in relation to the European powers, its contact, conflict and collaborations. The work clarifies the doubts of Maratha dominance in the 18th century under historiographical role of the state in the 17th and 18th centuries.

The interdisciplinary approach of the study is highlighted in the changing nature of the European dominance on the Indian coast. Locally, the work explores the caste system, religious, cultural, customs and rituals ubiquitous in the Deccan. The project distinguishes the worthiness of local magnates, small traders and pecuniary transactions taking place at the local level. Nationally, it highlights Deccan's connections with the North and South. The indigenous Maratha navy in the 16th century is a harbinger to the modern navy. Art, architecture, dress, music, cuisine and so on amalgamated the European and Central Asian cultures prevalent in the Indian society even today. Internationally, the relevance of the work recognizes the role of diplomacy in maintaining relations with neighbouring states without the need of wars. Those diplomatic skills are crucial and useful in maintaining peace internationally even today.

This research in particular deals with the Maratha interaction with the European powers. An attempt is made to evaluate and analyse such relationships. So far issues have been focused mainly on political history; with the change in nature of European influence on the Indian coast, there was bound to be a cohesion or incoherence with the Maratha Supremacy. The aim of the research is to convey the socio-economic, maritime and political intrigues of Maratha relations with the Europeans. The contemporary European powers are the Portuguese, Dutch and French. Research on relations between the Marathas and the Europeans has been a neglected study. New sources have been used and evaluated, and hence a rewriting of the Marathas-European power relations becomes imperative. This work tries to explore the diplomatic practices of the Portuguese *Estado* da India, VOC and the French in the 17th century, a period when the imperial project in the Indian Ocean faced drastic changes imposed by the aggressive competition of the European rivals. The *Estado* in particular faced antagonism from local powers, especially the Marathas. The Marathas had a vast and strong navy which has been given due importance.

Edward Said's work "orientalism" published in 1978 defines the word "orientalism," where he *traditionally refers to the field of study which studies the languages, the history and the cultures, and every other aspect about the people and the lands of the "Orient."*

Though the term "orientalism" is a patronizing term which was used to show the Westerners attitude towards Asian culture and people, it carries a negative connotation. According to Said, the "West" essentializes these cultures and people as static and undeveloped. He also manufactured the view that the Orient and its peoples can be studied, depicted and reproduced. His work implants the idea that Western society is developed, rational, flexible and superior.

This project carries a huge task of examining these orientalist perspectives and contradicting the age-old notion about the Asian communities and particularly about Deccan and establishes our own discourse through reading of indigenous sources and literature. Colonial literature manifests the perspective that the colonial administrators and its historians had already formed about the Asian communities. They already presumed to have knowledge about their culture and, accordingly, it has been represented in their writings. Portuguese have fairly been a long experience of colonization in Asia before the British expansion, but still Portuguese Orientalism has not been studied and pursued with the same vigour as the colonial orientalism. The Portuguese had developed their own framework in order to understand the Asian cultures which they encountered. In order to better understand Portuguese orientalism and how they have characterized our culture, we have undertaken a rigorous study of their existing literature. The Portuguese and the colonial writings have drawn parallels in essentialism and objectification of their subjects; however, we have tried to point out such prejudices and establish our own counter-arguments. Our study of Portuguese orientalism shows that it had variations in their intellect pursuits, their colonial goals, cultural currents and orientalist visions of the colonial power.

The foundation of the Dutch Company was structured to be a pure mercantile organization and its motives were primarily commercial, i.e., "emporialism" rather than imperialism in the Indian subcontinent. In this way, Dutch Orientalism was different from English orientalism, which focused on the traditional view of "empire" in Asia. To them, it was the command on the market instead of territories, for which the Company pursued emporialist strategy on the subcontinent. It was all geared to the single purpose of trade and commerce, more of a monopolistic nature, but on the condition that the expenses of imperial ambition be avoided. The Dutch East India Company wanted itself to be a strictly run business enterprise, organized for profit, and based on sound book-keeping procedures. They soon realized that foreign trade depended on the generosity and harmony of the native rulers who dominated the trade routes and the trade posts, and by a good combination of negotiation, consideration and religious toleration to which was added competent defence and government; the Dutch made sure that their trading interest was safeguarded from the other European rivals.

The realm of historically developing their perception of Marathas, through their craft of diplomacy, warfare, trade and working relationship, has been dealt with in this project. Their relationship underwent a significant change during the 18th century as a consequence of the rapid disintegration of the Mughal Empire and the emergence of numerous regional polities and the Anglo-French war in India. We find that Marathas were also trying to maintain a relationship with the Dutch to keep away the Mughals, Siddis and other local powers in the region. For Marathas, the arrival of the "*valendej*" (Dutch) was neither awful nor disruptive to them, and they were easily absorbed or "indigenized" in the Deccan society. Although, the Dutch were never indulged in religious persecution, which strikingly contrasts them with the Portuguese. However, in exception to this, some of them were appointed by the Company, for example, Phillipus Baldaeus, as a predicant responsible for converting the Tamils on the Coast to the Dutch Reformed religion.

French colonizing aspect was very much different from that of the British. For them colonizing a country meant including it as part of the mother country. Every colony came under the Church as the King came under it. When we look at French Orientalism, we must recognize the agents responsible for such acts. The French East India Company was endowed with two aspects of responsibilities, one is to civilize and the other was for commercialization. The civilizing aspect meant a unison was created with the natives, by assimilating with the colonies. However, some aspects of the superior authority complex dominated the minds of the administrators such as the White and Black Towns which divided the town of Pondicherry. Perhaps, it was their way of showing power. Nevertheless, their aim at segregation only led to integration with the locals, in which the architectural designs have been discussed in the project. Conceivably, one can say that the policy followed by the French was one of paternalism. The Pondicherrians could attain French citizenship and intermarry with the Europeans. Thus, they were treated as equals. The other aspect of acclimatization was the Indo-French language exchanges which gradually came to be accepted in the Tamil dialect. The various missionary groups that entered Pondicherry definitely left an impact on the Indian sub-continent. Missionaries who were also scholars did their research on the customs and traditions of the natives and therefore followed policies which would benefit the population. Thus, evidence suggests that the Pondicherrians were quite content with French rule as they only demanded independence in 1920, and it was only in 1954 that Pondicherry became part of India.

The purpose of undertaking this research is to address the transition that progressed at political, diplomatic, cultural patterns and economic spheres in the region. The presence of European powers in the Deccan alongside the other regional powers eventually altered the power dynamics of the region during the time. Deccan had emerged as a precondition for all the regional and European powers to test their legitimacy. It was the time when the dominant seat of power situated in the north of India was shifting to the south which gradually remodelled the politics of India. Economically, the idea of a free market, the emergence of newer industries and a stable supply of resources attracted trade and commerce and migration into the Deccan. Diplomacy and mercantile relations swayed the cultural statistics of the region. Deccan gradually got transformed into a fusion of multiculturalism. Sources are indicative of the economically powerful Marathas in the region of the Konkan and the Coromandel in the 17th and 18th centuries that magnetized various East India Companies into the region. Diplomatic and mercantile relations in the region were placed acknowledging the presence of the Marathas. European maritime relations with the Marathas still remain shallowly explored with loads of areas yet to be discovered and reviewed with the abundance of vernacular and European sources, especially the Portuguese, Dutch and French.

Historiographically, these relations have been understudied and ignored due to linguistic barriers. The strong economic Maratha presence on the Konkan and Coromandel in the 17th and 18th centuries was primarily responsible to have diplomatic and trade relations with the various East India Companies in the region. The first-hand primary sources record these developments in the Deccan in an era when the World Economy was blossoming due to a number of trade and mercantile partners. This work not only evaluates the relations between Marathas and the European powers at various stages but also tries to throw light on the unpublished records detailing these relations in the archives of Lisbon, Netherlands, Paris et al. Indigenous vernacular sources especially in Marathi, Kannada, Tamil, Telugu, Rajasthani and Hindi languages and documents in Modi script will be widely studied to bring out the historical ethos and essence. The project will also try to highlight the cultural dimensions and the Pan-Indian approach promoted by the Marathas. Traditional sources like *Bakhars*, *Ballads*, *Shakawali*, *Karina*, *Navadpatras*, *Mazahar*, various *Daftars*, etc. will have been used as supplementary evidence.

The data collected from different repositories have been analysed with the help of fieldwork. The research is based upon both primary and secondary sources. The primary sources include archival sources, travelogue, Persian translated works, English Factory Records and Portuguese documents, French records and Danish documents. Indigenous sources such as Marathi, Modi, Tamil and Kannada sources have been used. We visited the Directorate of Goa archives and archaeology, Panjim, and Goa university library to consult Pissulencar's works and his personal collections of books in Marathi, Portuguese and English. The sources consulted are the Marathi sources which include Bakhars, family papers and other documents, and also literary works available in Maharashtra state archives, Bombay. An ample number of Modi documents being a correspondence between the Marathas and the Europeans that are available at the Pune archives, Chennai and the Tanjore Saraswati Mahal Library have been used extensively while working on the different segments of this project.

This work has been divided into five main sections that are, Diplomacy, Sovereignty over sea, Society and culture, Art and architecture and lastly Trade and commerce.

The chapter on diplomacy is a detailed investigation of the methods of political diplomacy adopted by the Marathas towards the Deccan Powers and the European Powers in Deccan. Marathas' administrative and diplomatic strategies as well as the execution of their techniques depended on their warfare methods and espionage system. During the 17th century, Marathas made extensive use of their light cavalry and followed an attrition strategy against their enemies. Extreme mobility and the ability to make deep penetrations behind enemy lines characterized the Maratha cavalry. By the 18th century, other powers got aware of their warfare tactics, so it was now time to adopt new warfare techniques. This was the point at which they utilized French-hired fighters in their armed forces. Fortresses in the 18th century could not withstand the blow of the powerful canons and firearms, so this situation compelled them to resort to other methods of warfare. The 18th century was a time of Maratha ascendency, the change of the state itself from the Chhatrapati to the Confederacy. The Marathas were the main force that opposed the English till the end; along these lines by aligning themselves with the other European forces they felt that they could reverse the situation.

Moving on to the next topic of examination is navy; it was one of the important pillars of Maratha power. The mere establishment of the Maratha Navy had created a strong front against the European Power. With the coming of the Angrias, we see there was a constant tussle for power among the

Marathas, the European companies and the neighbouring kingdoms. The strengthening of Maratha Navy under the Angria helped them to emerge as a strong naval power, whose autonomy was tough to be challenged. The period of Angrias saw technological improvements in the fields of naval construction, shipbuilding and other sea-related skills. The construction of different types of warships and several forts gave Marathas clear supremacy in their naval engagements.

When we explore Deccan as a transitional phase in Indian history, change was happening at various levels then society becomes an important parameter to trace or map transition. Plural culture was the main ethos of Deccan and it showed assimilations of plethora of cultures and religions. It absorbed the essence of those multi-culture and diverse societies. This section of the project offers an interesting insight while studying the dynamic society of Deccan. This section examines the nature and intensity of acculturation in the Maratha country. It therefore explores the nature of the society and culture prevalent during the 17th and 18th centuries and also the response of the Europeans towards Deccan culture. This section therefore is an illustration of what Deccan symbolizes, a melting point of cultures and cultural assimilation.

As mentioned earlier, Deccan was a land of diversity when it came to religion, culture, ethnicity, beliefs, etc. It had left a strong impression on the art and architecture of that region. The influence and confluence of European and regional culture can be very well seen on paintings, architecture and sculpture. We see a conjunction of culture in Deccan. Deccan has everything on its platter which we see in the form of a rich social legacy. The study of architecture, art, sculpture and temple art provides us a wholistic approach while studying transition.

The last segment of this work engages in the study of trade and commerce prevailing in Deccan. The wide network of trade existing in Deccan made it economically viable. Deccan attracted all the European companies as well as local magnates to conduct trade. This led to the emergence of new classes of indigenous banking houses and business classes. The period of study that is the 17th and 18th centuries was witnessing a transition in configuration of a new economic model which was characterized by the change in power and structural framework.

Realization of a dream is a collective endeavour. It is an emotional moment and a moment of immense joy that this project is seeing the light of completion. It would have been difficult to complete this project without the co-operation of many people during the course of this Research Program. I take this opportunity to acknowledge all those people who have silently contributed to make this project a success.

Firstly, I would like to thank ICSSR for seeing the merit and granting me funds to carry out this Research Program. I thank the Member Secretary of ICSSR Prof. V.K. Malhotra and Mrs. Revathy Vishwanathan (Deputy Director, Research Projects). ICSSR has been kind enough to facilitate my foreign travel to procure primary sources for this project, under the category Data collection aboard. The tedious paperwork behind the foreign travel grant was smoothly facilitated by Mr. M.P. Madhukar (Deputy Director, Research, In-charge of International collaboration and National) and Dr. Ajay Gupta (Deputy Director, Publication) for making my work see the light of the day, I appreciate his efforts.

During the duration of this research program, I conducted two National seminars entitled "**Deccan in Transition: Politics and Interdependency, European Powers in relation to the Marathas.**" First, in collaboration with the Centre for Historical Studies, JNU, New Delhi and **Chh. Shahu Maharaj Center for Studies of Maratha History**, Shivaji University, Kolhapur. The hospitality provided by Dr. Neelambari Jagpat, Coordinator, CSMCSM, and Dr. Nanda Parekar, Head, Department of History is highly commendable. It was only because of their co-operation and hard work that the two-day National Seminar was an immense success. The second seminar was conducted in collaboration with the Centre for Historical Studies, JNU, New Delhi, and the Department of Defense and Strategic Studies, Savitribai Phule Pune University. For this I would like to thank Prof. Vijay Khare, Head, Department of Defense and Strategic Studies, for cooperating and making this Seminar a huge success.

Few people deserve a special mention, because they have directly or indirectly contributed to the success of this project. Prof. Dilbagh Singh who is my mentor for life has been motivating and encouraging in words and Prof. Heeraman Tiwari has been associated with this project to smoothen the administrative hurdles, and they have given their valuable inputs to enrich this project. Prof. Pius Malekandathil has been a constant friend and a huge support system during the course of this Research Program. He always lent a helping hand whenever in need.

I really appreciate the warm welcome by Dr. Lennart Bes, Lecturer, Department of History, Leiden University, Netherlands. His valuable insights on the Dutch segment of this project have enhanced the subject matter. Dr. Andre Teixeira, Faculty at Centre for Social and Human Studies, Department of History, Lisbon, Portugal, gave his valuable time to discuss this project and provided knowledge about the existing Portuguese primary sources in and around Lisbon.

I would like to thank all the staff, the librarians and the archivists of the various archives and libraries that I have visited during the course of this research program. To mention a few of them are the Arquivo Nacional Torre de Tombo (Lisbon), Nationaal Archief (Hage) Netherlands, Archives Nationale (Paris), Bibliotheque Nationale de France, National Archives of New Delhi, Nehru Memorial Museum and Library (Delhi), Indian Historical Council for Research, Dr. Bhimrao Ambedkar Central Library (JNU), Dr. Lohia Library of Centre for Advanced Studies in History, CHS/JNU, Directorate of Archives and Archaeology Goa, Goa University, National Archives of India Records Centre Puducherry, Ecole de Extreme Pondicherry,

Pondicherry University, Tamil Nadu Archives, Bharat Itihas Sanshodhak Mandal, Pune Archives, Gokhale Library Pune, Savitribai Phule Pune University Maharashtra State Archive, Mumbai, Kolhapur Archives, Chh. Shahu Maharaj Centre for Studies of Maratha History, Shivaji University, Kolhapur, Archival Cell Library section Shivaji University (Kolhapur), Satara Archive, Saraswati Mahal Library, Thanjavur, Tamil Nadu.

Lastly, I would like to thank my Research Co-investigator Dr. Rohit Phalgaonkar from Goa and Ms. Ashwini Kamble Research Assistant from the Chh. Shahu Maharaj Centre for Studies of Maratha History, Shivaji University, Kolhapur, for providing, collecting, correlating and organizing most of the information. I am truly indebted to my research students who contributed as research associates—Dr. Ankita Kumar, Dr. Shelley Christine Lamare, Dr. Dolly Purohit and Dr. Anuradha, for organizing the content of this project thematically. Maintaining the records, classifying them, corroborating them and above all keeping up the accounts and files, for conducting intensive archival work immensely contributed to shape up this project. I would also like to thank my Ph.D. students Mr. Aditya Sharma, Mr. Anwit Shahi and Mr. Abhinav Yadav for systematically arranging the bibliography. I take this opportunity to thank Shri Manoj Kumar Manuj, Shri Aditya ji, Health Centre, JNU, Shri Sameer Sharma, Finance officer, JNU, Shri Santosh and Miss Kanchan S & P Section, Director R & D, Dr. Rupesh Chaturvedi & Dr. Suneel Kateria JNU, Professor Pradipta Choudhary, Former, Dean SSS, all my colleagues at the Centre for Historical Studies for cooperating with me and extending help in all possible ways. Shri Asheesh ji and Sonu ji, Shubho Photocopying and Sonu Printing for doing all the typing, binding, photocopying, printing, etc.

I thank my awesome wife, Dr. Kaveri Kadam, for her patience and cooperation, even though she was engaged in her thesis writing for Ph.D. and she was giving me advice on drafts to keep the munchkins out of my hair so I could edit; she was as important to this project getting done as I was. Thank you so much, dear.

My happy-go-lucky son Aditya for making critical remarks with all his childish inquisitiveness and to my little darling angel, my daughter Aditi for not minding to give me time to complete the work at hand when I was home, I truly lost all that precious time full of joy with her.

I want to thank everyone who ever said anything positive to me or taught me something, I heard it all, and it meant something. I want to thank GOD for the most of all because without GOD, I wouldn't be able to do any of this.

Place: New Delhi
25/10/2020,
Dussehra (Vijayadashami)

Professor Umesh Ashok Kadam
Centre for Historical Studies, Jawaharlal Nehru University, New Delhi, & Member Secretary, Indian Council of Historical Research, New Delhi, India

Abbreviations

AV	Archive de Versailles
AMAE	Archives du Ministere des Affaires Etrangeres
AMC	Archives du Ministere des Colonies
AN	Archives Nationales
BN	Bibliotheque Nationale
BISM	Bharat Itihas Sansodhak Mandal
CUP	Cambridge University Press
DMCMW	The Despatches, Minutes and Correspondence of the Marquess of Welesley
EFI	English Factories in India
ERS	English Records on Shivaji
EEIC	English East India Company
GA	Goa Archives
GBP	Great Britain Pound or British Pound
ICHR	Indian Council of Historical Research
ICSSR	Indian Council of Social Sciences Research
IESHR	Indian Economic and Social History Review
IHR	Indian Historical Review
IHRCP	Indian Historical Records Commission Proceedings
INR	Indian National Rupee
IOR	India Office Records
JESHO	Journal of Economic and Social History of the Orient
JISOA	Journal of the Indian Society and Oriental Art
KS	Kavyetihasa Sangraha
MCCBLBL	Memoire a Consulter et Consultation, pour le Sieur de Bussy, avec des Letters de Bussy, Lally, etc.
MSHKP	Mahadaji Shinde Hyanchi Kagad Patre
MIS	Marathyanchya Itihasachi Sandahe
MSA	Maharashtra State Archives
NA	Nationaal Archief
NAF	Nouvelles Acquisition Francaise
NAI	National Archives of India
NMML	Nehru Memorial Museum and Library

OUP	Oxford University Press
PD	Peshwa Daftar
PRC	Poona Residency Correspondence
PIHC	Proceedings of Indian History Congress
SSRPD	Selections from the Satara Rajas and Peshwa Diaries
SPDD	The Secret and Political Department Diary
TNA	Tamil Nadu States Archives
TANAP	Towards a New Age of Partnership
VOC	Vereenigde Oost-Indische Compagnie

1 Instrumenting Power

Maratha Synergy and Diplomacy

The Politics of Diplomacy

Modern dictionaries like the *Webster English Dictionary* defines diplomacy as "the art and practice of conducting negotiations between nations for the attainment of mutually satisfactory terms; adroitness or artfulness in securing advantages without arousing hostility; address or tact in conduct of affairs"; while the short *Oxford English Dictionary* defines it as "the managements of international relations by negotiations; the ambassadors and envoys use this method for managing their relations."[1] Indians have been familiar with the art of diplomacy since time immemorial. The various traditions of deploying the art of diplomacy are well projected from sources like the *Sukranitisara* and *Arthashastra*; they talk about the political thought and ideas prevailing during those times. The germination of Maratha diplomacy takes its shape and form from the magnum opus *Ajnapatra*. In the 17th and 18th centuries the Maratha idea of diplomacy is depicted in the *Ajnapatra*. It lays down general rules that should guide the conduct of the King and makes observations as regards the general policy that should guide the different functions of the state. The *Ajnapatra* was against the concept of giving land grants, and thus, Shivaji's diplomatic policy towards the Europeans was limited to trade concessions.[2] Similarly, we get an idea of diplomacy practised by the Europeans from the Portuguese, Dutch and French sources. Their diplomatic ideology revolves around three aspects: territorial gains, missionary activities and commercial enterprise. Thus, the interaction of these various powers often resulted in the "politics of compromise" through court exchanges such as treaties and envoys which did not always mean undermining the other's power, but a diplomatic compromise was reached through deliberations. Thus, an understanding was reached and through these negotiations we see a transition taking place in the political arena and court culture.

Power comes when one is able to control the agents responsible for disposition of tactics in times of war; hence, diplomats play an important role. When these diplomats betray their superior authority, the whole sovereign power of the individual collapses. The loyalty of these agents then comes

DOI: 10.4324/9781003377511-1

into question. One advantage that a historian has is to be able to give a hindsight of such narratives. These diplomats often resort to betrayal which is so common in this period that it is of no surprise that when one power is established, the other breaks down. Therefore, it is important to study the mechanisms associated with these diplomats and link it with the establishment of power. Their responsibilities lie in establishing stability and taking heed that no harm is perpetrated in their territory. They are also responsible for signing treaties and conducting alliances; thus, it renders them complete masters of foreign and diplomatic affairs.[3] They diligently acquire such knowledge and information during times of war. Hence the importance of these diplomats cannot be stressed enough.

The broad themes analyzed in this segment are what was the Maratha idea of diplomacy? One needs to identify the agents responsible for executing diplomacy for the Maratha state. The causes of warfare ranged from territorial, commercial and the fight for sovereignty. The presence of freelancers and adventurers transitioned military warfare; for example, Indian sepoys were trained by European adventurers. The context of gift-giving needs to be examined in the manner of "politics of compromise." How was the pattern of diplomatic handling altered from the times of the Chhatrapatis and the Peshwas? While scholars such as V.G Hatalkar, M.A Nayeem, and Balkrishna have concentrated on the political narrative of such relations, this chapter tries to evaluate the Maratha tactics for various forms of warfare.

The political circumstance in the Deccan was set apart by political confusion and breakdown during the last two decades of the 15th century. The downfall of the Bahmani dynasty, which ruled the Deccan as a sovereign kingdom until the 16th century, resulted in the emergence of the five independent kingdoms ruled respectively by Qutub Shahis in Golconda, Barid Shahis in Bidar, Imad Shahis in Berar, Adil Shahis in Bijapur and Nizam Shahis in Ahmadnagar. These self-governing but petty kingdoms continued to fight against each other, and instead of gaining strength, they lost what was bestowed to them by the Bahmanis. In 1601 Akbar captured Khandesh and Jahangir took Ahmadnagar in the year 1633. Last years of Aurangzeb's reign were spent campaigning against the two surviving Sultanates. He defeated Bijapur in 1686 and Golconda in the following year. Soon after this accession, a new cause of resistance to Mughal political power appeared in the form of Maratha leader Shahaji Bhonsle, who was in the process of constructing a self-sufficient state within the declining shell of the Sultanate of Bijapur. They rose to prominence in the early sixteenth century when local Maratha chieftains served as mercenary captains in the armies of the Muslim kingdoms of Deccan India.[4]

Shivaji's kingdom was confined to Poona district bounded by the rivers Bhima in the North and Nira in the South. It included four major parganas, namely, Indapur, Poona, Supa and Chakan. It was from this *jagir* that Shahji assigned about 36 villages from Poona pargana to Shivaji in 1636. By 1645–46, Shivaji had become the trustee of the entire *jagir*.[5] With the disintegration of the Vijayanagar Empire, the Deccani Sultans (Bijapur and Golconda) began to encroach upon its territory. Shahji established a sound administration in the Carnatic and brought many "polegars"[6] and chieftains like Raja Virabhadra of Vidupur, Kantirava of Seringapatnam, Nayak of Kondes, Tirumala Nayak of Madurai, etc. under his sway and became their leader in advocating their cause in the Adil Shahi kingdom.[7] A.R. Kulkarni believes that Shahji was a kingmaker in Maharashtra and law giver in the Carnatic. He did not assume royal power or become a sovereign ruler himself, but he was the virtual ruler of the Nizam Shahi kingdom between 1633 and 1636. He created a feeling among the Marathas that they could also carry on an independent existence. The political condition in the Carnatic bordered on anarchy. Thus, Shahji Bhonsle under Bijapur service marched upon these territories in the Carnatic and managed to take possession of a few territories such as Ikkeri, Sira, Bangalore, Seringapatam, Jinji, Tanjore, Tegnapatam and Porto Novo. The Golconda Sultan too to profit from such a chaotic situation decided to conquer the Carnatic.

During Shivaji's time the condition of life in the Deccan was deplorable as reported by some travelogues: the Great Famine of 1630–31 struck the plateau badly, and the rising prices caused by scarcity of food made life miserable. The famine dislocated families, trade and industry had come to a standstill.[8] Shivaji therefore had to work against many odds, economic as well as political. He had to create a state which was politically and economically viable. Thus, he worked towards attaining the support of the people. Shivaji was helped in the administration by Dadaji Khondev a Kulkarni of Malthan (Poona district) and Shamrao Ranzekar. They were both trusted servants of Shahji and were responsible for imparting the spirit of independence to Shivaji. While stabilizing his position with the adjoining areas, Shivaji maintained friendly relations with the Mughals which had been administered by Aurangzeb since 1653.

Maratha Diplomacy and Indigenous Regional Powers in the Deccan: The *Swarajya's* Burgeoning Power, Negotiation and Consolidation

Shivaji's first diplomatic skill was realizing the need for integration of the Deccan; he had a clear set of goals, and therefore he envisaged the founding of the Maratha state and resolved to establish *Swaraj*. He then followed the policy of "Deccan for the Deccanis" to accomplish his desire. The integration of the Deccan was twofold: firstly, there was the task of unifying the Maratha chiefs under one umbrella; and secondly, an alliance with the Deccan kingdoms—Bijapur and Golconda–was essential.[9] He then visualized the need to unite together the scattered forces of the Maratha chiefs to form a sovereign alliance. By doing so, he hoped that it would destroy the Shahi dynasty and enable him to form the Maratha state. He began to gather a band of young faithful comrades, and he started holding secret meetings, planning to capture forts, and securing funds by attacking private and public treasures. With his persuasive tongue he moved his fellow comrades on two fronts: political and religious. The religious aspect had the moral fervour of "*Maharashtra Dharma*," to animate the people for a common purpose and sanctified by a common devotion to the country. He eventually succeeded in creating a feeling of new spirit among the people of common interest and common patriotism born of liberal religious fervour. He addressed them to realize the disadvantages of the Mughal and Bijapur governments and the position of the Maratha General under their rule. *Sabashad* records Shivaji saying

> Let us draw the sword in defence of our sacred religion, liberate our native country and acquire new lands and wealth by our own effort. We are as brave and capable as our ancestors of yore. If we undertake this sacred task, God will surely help us. All human efforts are so helped. There is no such thing as luck or ill-luck. We are the captains of our soil and the makers of our freedom.[10]

However, the representatives of the great Maratha families in the service of Bijapur proved to be bitter foes of Shivaji. They were: Baji Mohite of Supa, Baji Ghorpades, Mores of Javli, Sawants of Wadi, Davis of Konkan, Shirkes and Surves of Shringarpur. They refused to join Shivaji and were obstructive in the new movement, Shivaji through stratagem got the Mores and Sawants subordinated. However, the Nimbalkars of Paithan, Mheswad and Zunjarrao Ghadge were in Bijapur service and continued to fight Shivaji.

Shivaji sought permission from the Mughals to acquire territories and forts from the Adil Shahi kingdom, and it was granted without hesitation as they were also interested in wiping out the Adil Shahi kingdom.[11] Shivaji had by now consolidated his position in his original territory and had extended it by capturing the Javali principality of the Mores. By 1656 his domination included areas between Mahuli and Mahad, thus making himself the master of North Konkan. In 1659, he entered into a treaty with the Sawants of Wadi for the establishment of *Swaraj*. In a letter to Ghorpade, Shivaji wrote

> He [Qutub Shah of Golkonda] has placed such a high confidence in me that I am in a favourable position which I can well utilize to enhance the interests of the Marathas and to reduce the power of the Pathans of Bijapur. As soon as an agreement was reached on both sides, my uppermost idea was to take into confidence all the great Maratha nobles, to bring them for an interview with the Qutub Shah on one side and that of all the Maratha nobles on the other.[12]

Shivaji's "Deccan for the Deccanis" was a principle to fight aggression from the north, but when it came to establishing his Maratha *Swaraj*, he did not hesitate to betray Bijapur and side with Golconda. By 1661 Shivaji had moved on to Shrinagarpur (Konkan), which was under a Maratha chief, Surya Rao Surve; the chief was killed in action and Shivaji became the master of the whole Konkan.[13] In 1665, he entered into a treaty with Jai Singh which came to be known as the famous Treaty of Purandar. But this was only a diplomatic move to divert the Mughal onslaught from Maratha territory. By 1673 Shivaji had eliminated himself from Bijapur and Mughal danger and executed his grand plan of coronating himself as Chhatrapati and thus proclaiming the foundation of the Maratha state as a sovereign entity. He proceeded South towards his half-brother's (Ekoji) territory, and he even persuaded Ekoji from allying with Bijapur and offered him an equal position and *jagir* under Qutub Shah. His coronation ceremony (1674) is important because he wanted to demonstrate to the Mughals that he was not a mere zamindar or a vassal of Bijapur; he wanted complete equality of status with other sovereign powers. He felt that he could claim loyalty of the people and allegiance of the chieftains only after declaring himself as a crowned head over the Maratha dominion.

In the light of the aforementioned trajectory of the rising Maratha power and its attempts to establish itself as a sovereign polity in its own right on the Deccan's political scene, it becomes imperative to study the diplomacy between the Marathas and the other indigenous powers on the Deccan's political scene. Here we must note that the diplomatic history of the Marathas and the Imperial Mughals, particularly in its early phase in the 17th century, is a topic that has been subjected to detailed treatment in many studies and monographs, such as the monograph "Mughal-Maratha Relations" by G.T. Kulkarni, and in the works of Sir Jadunath Sarkar and G.S. Sardesai. Therefore, what this section proposes to pursue in detail is the diplomatic relations between the rising Maratha power, and other polities with regional power bases, as this is something which is deserving of treatment in greater detail. Accordingly, the regional powers within the purview of study here are the rival Maratha kingdom of Tanjore, the Siddis of Janjira, the principality of Walikondapuram, the Mughal successor-state of Hyderabad and the kingdom of Mysore.

So far as Tanjore is concerned, Shivaji, firstly, wanted a claim to his father's possession in the Carnatic. Ekoji on the other hand refused to submit to his brother's control because it would mean being submerged in the greater Maratha territory. This would also imply a loss of independence on the part of Tanjore. Thus, Shivaji returned to his home after receiving a sum for not invading his half-brother's (Ekoji) territory again. Fortunately, for Ekoji Shivaji died in 1680 and his kingdom was unbound from his brother's clutches.

As the years passed, the then Maharaja Shahu who ascended the throne in 1708 felt the need for a jovial relation with his distant cousins at Tanjore. Thus, when the Carnatic was in a political turmoil, Shahu sent help to the Marathas at Tanjore. Although Ekoji had proclaimed earlier that any relation with the Chhatrapati was not desirable, political circumstances however point to the other direction. The presence of the Chhatrapati in the Carnatic cannot be denied. His influence over the politics of Tanjore cannot be brushed aside. Thus, a direct political relation was established between the two. In 1740, the army that was sent to the Carnatic by Shahu was comprised of troops belonging to the Chhatrapati, Peshwa and Fateh Singh Bhonsle under the command of Raghuji Bhonsle. The force amounted to 50,000 men. G.S. Sardesai quotes a Nagpur Bakhar,

> As you are the trusted servants of the State, His Highness has no doubt that you will achieve success in this enterprise. The Maharaja's cousin of Tanjore is being harassed by Chanda Sahib of Trichinopoly. Fateh Singh Bhonsle is ordered to meet the Tanjore Raja and chastise Chanda Sahib.[14]

The Siddis of Janjira had carried out destructive activities from the castle of Danda-Rajapuri and on numerous occasions plundered and burnt villages. Hence Shivaji wanted to reduce the Siddis. In this connection, a dispatch from Bombay to Surat dated 13 November 1673 states that "If the French have sent down so many guns and so much lead to Rajapore, Sevagee will be able to arm out a notable fleet against the Siddi."[15] Another example of indirect correspondence that happened was when Shivaji decided to conquer the fort of Khanderi island in order to counter the Siddi English alliance; the reason that this occupation bothered the English was it was a direct threat to them in Bombay. According to the treaty Shivaji retained his hold over Khanderi islands and continued its fortifications, but on the other hand, the English consented not to shelter the Siddis at Bombay or give them arms and ammunition, gunshots and powders.

Shivaji's dealings with the principality of Walikondapuram are an important key in the chain of events. Bijapur Karnatak was ruled by two rival governors, viz Nasir Muhammad and Sher Khan who had their capitals at Jinji and Walikondapuram. Sher Khan wanted to annex Jinji with the help of the French; he had also helped the French by giving them a loan in 1674 to start a factory at Pondicherry. Nasir Muhamad on the other hand sought the help of the Sultan of Golconda. Qutub Shah had his own vested interests in interfering; his minister Madanna Pandit, a devout Hindu, thought of establishing rule in the Karnatak, and for this he looked towards the Marathas. Shivaji agreed on terms that he would get the total spoils of war.[16]

Regarding Hyderabad, the Marathas were interested in the territories of the Nizam mainly for *Chauth* and tribute. The Nizam too realized this and he did not think that the Marathas were entitled to any share in the tribute. Bajirao sensed that the Nizam's efforts were directed at keeping the south as his own preserve and tried to prevent them from dealing directly with the Rajas of Mysore, Bidnur and other regions. Thus, the Nizam decided to weaken the Marathas, and he induced Sambhaji, the Raja of Kolhapur, to come over to his side and contest the claims of Shahu to be recognized as the legal head of the Maratha state. In 1727 Bajirao campaigned in the south, and this annoyed the Nizam and led him to have an open conflict with the Marathas which ended badly for the Nizam. The Nizam was therefore forced to recognize Shahu as the head of the Maratha state, and therefore he was entitled to *Chauth* and *sardeshmukhi*.[17] The Nizam was unhappy with the power balance between him and the Marathas; he therefore diplomatically intervened in the court politics of the Marathas, and he sided with the pro-Nizam lobby (i.e., Sambhaji of Kolhapur) in Shahu's court. In a letter from the Nizam-ul-Mulk addressed to Sambhaji of Kolhapur, it says that

> Nilu Pandit is an old and trusted servant of yours. The message from me which is conveyed through him will be agreeable to you. You may act accordingly. It is hoped that with unity between us things will turn out as we desired. With your support great results will ensue from this step. This will contribute to the peace and contentment of the populace. It will also be agreeable to God. The imprint of good reputation will prevail in the world. Bonds of friendship will be strengthened. Robes and other articles are being sent separately according to the list attached. Kindly keep me informed of your welfare.[18]

However, his efforts failed due to Bajirao's effort to curtail him. The Nizam's attitude towards the Maratha changed when his own authority was challenged by his son. Syyad Lashkar Khan, an envoy of the Nizam, was sent to Balaji Rao's camp to ask for his help. Syyad Lashkar said that his master was in danger of not only losing the battle against his son but losing his life and honour as well. The Marathas at this point decided to remain neutral.[19] Thus, while dissensions happened at the Maratha court, the Nizam descended upon the Carnatic this time to strike at Tanjore. Hence, rivalries between the Marathas of Satara and the Nizam dragged Tanjore into their conflict. The Nizam directed Iwaz Khan to proceed towards the Carnatic, and he seized Trichinopoly. Trichinopoly was held by Serfoji the Tanjore Raja; he accordingly appealed to Shahu for help. Shahu was advised by Fateh Singh Bhonsle to send an expedition to the Carnatic to re-establish the rights of tributes. Fateh Singh then marched to the Carnatic to the aid of Serfoji and recapture Trichinopoly, but the resistance given by Iwaz Khan made Fateh Singh retreat.

Mysore under Nand Raj served as a tributary state to the Nizam. After the death of Muzaffar Jung, Salabat Jung was installed on the throne by the French. The new Nizam then marched on Seringapatnam and demanded a large sum of money as tribute, and at the same time the Marathas under Peshwa Balaji Baji Rao demanded a contribution for their *Chauth* of which five lakhs was paid in cash. Haider Ali during this time was summoned to Mysore owing to disputes between Devaraj and his brother Nand Raj; he found the troops in despair due to lack of funds. Haider was able to manage the situation by careful scrutiny of the accounts and disbanded 4000 men.

After the Marathas withdrew to their homeland, Haider evaded payment due to Poona. This act of Haider angered the Peshwa, and he dispatched a force in 1759 under the command of Gopal Hari. The Maratha leader attacked Bangalore and seized Chennapatnam, and Haider countered the attack by sending his favourite officer Luft Ali Beg to surprise Gopal Hari and relinquish the blockade of Bangalore. The fight between the two ensued at length, and in the end the Maratha chief decided to withdraw his troops on the condition that 30 lakhs should be paid by Mysore.[20] Haider was recognized for his endeavour by Raja Chikka Krishnaraj and received the title Fatah Haidar Bahadur.

The rise to power of Haider naturally aroused the attention of the Marathas, and this time he made sure not to sue for peace. He accordingly applied to Razi Ali Khan son of Chanda Sahib for help because of his experience in French military tactics. He sought to train and discipline his troops along these lines. The then ruling Peshwa was Madhav Rao who succeeded his father Balaji Baji Rao in 1761. This Peshwa wanted to subdue Haider and surrender the territories that he had usurped. Haider attacked the chief of Savanur because of his alliance with the Rani of Bednur, and Haider wanted to punish him, so he ravaged his state and also seized the fortress of Dharwar on the other side of Tungabhadra. Madhav Rao in order to check Haider's advance sent Gopal Rao, the chief of Miraj, but Haider emerged victorious. Soon after, the main body of Maratha troops met Haider near Rattihalli south of Savanur. Haider was routed in the event and was forced to flee to Bednur. Madhav Rao made sure he hemmed Haider on all sides and forced him to sue for peace. The Marathas were in an advantageous position, but for Haider it was an expensive peace. He had to give up the territories that he had earlier conquered from Morari Rao of Gutti (Gutty), Savanur had to be surrendered and a sum of 32 lakhs had to be paid as war indemnity.[21]

In 1767, the Marathas again descended on Mysore; this time, they were in alliance with the Nizam and the French. Madhav Rao shrewdly separated Haider Ali's brother-in-law, Mir Ali Raza Khan, who was stationed at Sira; he surrendered the fort and deserted Haider's cause and received Gurramkonda as a reward. Haider retaliated by sending Appaji Rama and the Maratha chief had to withdraw.

The Marathas, Europeans and the Expanding Influence Overseas: A Diplomatic Overview

As the Maratha power in the Deccan continued to rise, it became inevitable for the European trading companies, all of whom had also acquired territorial bases along the Eastern and Western coasts, to take note of this rising force to be reckoned with. Some of them, like the Portuguese, had been long settled in the region, while the others, like the Dutch and the French, were relatively newer arrivals in the region. Irrespective of this fact, the administrations of these trading companies and settlements felt the need to address the rising Maratha power. What this section will deal with is an overview of how the Europeans diplomatically approached the Marathas. The next section, entitled "The Marathas and European powers: politics and interdependency in the 17th and 18th centuries," will cover the diplomatic relations between the individual European powers and the Marathas in detail.

We must note that the relations between the Marathas and the English East India Company, and thereafter the Company State, right from the time of Shivaji himself down to the era of the Confederacy and their eventual culmination into the Anglo-Maratha Wars, are quite well known and have been extensively covered in many detailed studies as well as textbooks. Therefore, the major portion of this section focuses on the Marathas' relations with other European powers, namely, the Portuguese, the Dutch and the French, which have hitherto not been studied in significant detail. The English have been mentioned wherever absolutely necessary.

To begin with, let us deal with the Portuguese response. The Portuguese were great diplomats and were very unscrupulous in their dealings with the native powers. Their main concern was their own welfare; time and again they changed sides in their relations with the Marathas, the Bijapuries and the Mughals, as they wanted none of these powers to be strong enough to threaten their power and influence. They wanted to fish in the troubled waters of Deccan and achieve their ends by breaking the Indian bones by knocking them together. They adopted the "policy of subordination" with all the states such as Calicut, Kanara, Bijapur and Ahmadnagar. The Portuguese helped one state against the other while maintaining a cordial relationship with both states. The Portuguese employed a spy system to enter into a diplomatic relationship with the Indian states. The Portuguese officials tried to build alliances with the people who could provide information and any other kind of support which could damage their interests. This gave birth to the group of persons called *linguas*, who the Portuguese trusted for any kind of information.[22]

The Dutch were the second European power to arrive in India next to the Portuguese and emerged as a prominent commercial power during the 17th century. The company VOC (Vereenigde Oost-Indische Compagnie) was founded by a charter granted by the States-General, the national administrative body of the Dutch Republic, a monopoly of Dutch trade with authority to negotiate treaties of peace and alliance, wage defensive war and build fortresses in the waters between the Cape of Good Hope and the Straits of Magellan for an initial period of 21 years. In order to expand their commercial activities, they soon realized that foreign trade depended on the generosity and harmony of the rulers who dominated the trade routes and who governed the areas neighbouring these trade posts and by a good combination of negotiation, consideration and religious toleration to which was added competent defence and government.[23]

Diplomatic relations of Marathas with the Dutch were constantly changing in nature throughout the 17th and 18th centuries. This is reflected in the various incidents where the Marathas consistently favoured or used the Dutch in their designs, for example, the Marathas offer to help the Dutch in taking Goa in 1664 or the rumoured Dutch takeover of Bombay in 1673 with Maratha help. Sometimes when it came to choosing between two European powers that were neutral to Marathas (e.g. the Dutch and the French), the Marathas chose the most beneficial one to them, as with the Dutch capture of Pondicherry in 1693. Unlike the other European powers, the Dutch's contact with the Marathas was lesser during the 18th century. The Dutch activities in the Deccan were mainly commercial. They strived for friendship with the Marathas only to establish their trade and defend their territory from the other European powers. On the other hand, we see that the Marathas had an unusually positive opinion about the trade-oriented Dutch, especially when contrasted with the territorially ambitious English and the Portuguese.

Marathas maintained diplomatic relations with the French for various purposes. During the time of Shivaji, his relation with them was for commercial reasons on the French side; however, Shivaji perceived and calculated that having them as an ally would be beneficial for them because of their superiority in artillery. When the Siddis of Janjira were carrying out destructive activities from Danda-Rajapuri, Shivaji had written to the French to supply him with arms and ammunition. He purposely chose the French because he knew about their alliance with the Mughals, so if the French were on his side, he would avoid a direct confrontation with them. Thus, by manipulating the politics of the region he hoped that he would minimize war with the Mughals. He therefore kept the French at Rajapur.[24]

Another example of Maratha diplomatic skill in the 18th century was the peace treaty which was signed between Salabat Jang and the Peshwa Balajirao in 1752, famously known as the Treaty of Bhalki. The Peshwa recognized Salabat Jang as the legitimate viceroy of the Deccan and in return the Marathas got back their rights to *Chauth* and *Sardeshmukhi* in Deccan. The Marathas also signed a treaty with the French to ensure that they continue as mediators since the French were stationed at Hyderabad court. Thus, the Peshwa wanted to make sure that Salabat Jang would abide by the terms of the treaty. In return for their services the Peshwa would promote the French cause in India, help the French with troops whenever they demanded, offer protection to French merchants and not charge custom duties for goods belonging to the French.[25]

The Marathas and European powers: Politics and interdependency in the 17th and 18th centuries

For convenience and better understanding, it is pertinent to divide the 17th and 18th centuries of Maratha dominance into the following time periods:

i) 1630–1680—Period of establishment of *Swaraj* and sovereign authority
ii) 1681–1689—Period of resistance and turmoil
iii) 1690–1707—Period of Maratha independence
iv) 1707–1761—Maratha expansion and consolidation in Deccan and North India
v) 1761–1800—Post Panipat power politics: consolidation through confederacy

Keeping this periodization in mind, let us now deal in detail with the diplomatic relations between the Marathas and each individual European power within the purview of this study in the Deccan.

A. Portuguese–Maratha Diplomatic Relation

The period between 1630 and 1680 marked the period of establishment of *Swaraj* and sovereign authority in Deccan. The emergence of the Marathas in the early decades of the 17th century was a threat to the sultans of Bijapur, Ahmadnagar and the Portuguese. This period was also the deciding factor in changing the balance of power. The rise of Maratha power had begun soon after 1624 under the leadership of Shahji. Shivaji experienced many problems but still stood firm.[26]

The early success of Shivaji was not a problem for the Portuguese because his attention was on the Muslim states. The Portuguese at times supported the ambitions of Shivaji especially when he was attacking the Mughals and the Bijapuri territories, as they had adopted the policy of helping the rival princes. This period also marked the period of friendship where they were helping the Marathas. This also prevented Goa from attacks by the Bijapuri state. When Shivaji turned towards Bassein and Chaul, the Portuguese became concerned. By 1658 Shivaji had prepared his own naval force. The Portuguese tried their best to stop Shivaji from building his own navy. The main reason behind this step was that the Portuguese wanted to help Siddi Rajapuri, who was commanding the northwest hinterlands and was always on good terms with the Portuguese. Shivaji was at war with the Siddhis and was ready to send a fleet against them. The Portuguese were scared for themselves also, so they did not give permission to Shivaji's fleet to leave the port. The Portuguese were even successful in convincing *Viegas* and 300 other compatriots, who were assisting Shivaji to desert him.[27] But this did not stop Shivaji from posing a threat to the Portuguese sea power.

The Portuguese followed a mix of everything in their relationships with others depending on the circumstances and their enemies at that time. They were hostile, friendly and neutral with the Marathas accordingly. The Portuguese were always conscious about the balance of power in Deccan since it was also the time when the Dutch were very active on the western coast and the ships of the VOC were a constant threat to the Portuguese ships and the colonies. The Portuguese therefore acted very diplomatically and mostly remained inactive with the Marathas.[28] By the end of 1664, Shivaji had occupied Kudal, Perne and Bicholim in Adil Shah's territories; these areas were given to the Desais, who took shelter in Goa, and from here they made raids into the Maratha territories. Here the logic was given that the Desais were the vassals of Bijapuri kingdom so they must be supported by the Portuguese.[29]

The Portuguese were sympathetic and helpful towards Shivaji, but it changed accordingly. When the Portuguese were at war with the Dutch in the Southern ports of Malabar and Kanara and needed help on both sides on the sea and the land. They also wanted to keep the Mughals at bay, and if they would be successful in defeating Adil Shah and Shivaji, then their next target would be Goa. So, when Shivaji sought shelter in Chaul and Bassein because of fear of the Mughals, he was given shelter. Besides these two places he was also provided a place in Goa for his arms and ammunition. The Portuguese ordered the authorities in Bassein and Chaul not to supply provisions to the Mughals and they had to retreat. The Portuguese helped the Marathas when they needed the Maratha forces to protect the southern coast of Quilon, Cranganore, Cochin and Cannanore from the heavy attacks of the Dutch and the Zamorin. The Portuguese had given shelter to Shivaji secretly in their fortress of Bassein and Chaul because they wanted to gain his friendship and at the same time to be protected from the Mughals. This diplomatic move was made simply to protect their northern possessions without putting much effort.[30]

In January 1664, when Shivaji attacked and looted the city of Surat, the Portuguese authorities not only expressed their approval but also helped his forces. When the Mughals complained to the viceroy of Goa that the Portuguese soldiers were seen plundering Surat along with Shivaji, he refused to accept that they were his men.[31] There is another instance when Jai Singh, the Mughal general, requested that Shivaji's ships should not be returned and they should not help him anymore. But the Portuguese did not listen, and they provided him with food and ammunition.[32]

There was a change in the attitude of the Portuguese after Shivaji escaped from Agra. The response was not positive from their side as they were powerless to face a mighty ruler as Aurangzeb.

There were ups and downs in the Portuguese's policies towards Shivaji vis-a-vis the Mughals. They were struggling to maintain their colonies and ports in India, and in order to survive they took such diplomatic steps.

Shivaji was also interested in a diplomatic relationship with the Portuguese because of the generation of revenue and *Chauth*. In 1672, Shivaji conquered major portions of the Kingdom of Ram Nagar, to whom the Portuguese were paying the *Chauth* for some territories in Daman. But even after his defeat and Shivaji's repeated demand that he should be given the *Chauth* and not the ruler of Ram Nagar, the Portuguese preferred to give the *Chauth* to the Ram Nagar in order to equip him to continue his war against Shivaji.[33] On 9 April 1675, Shivaji surrounded Fonda, which then belonged to the king of Bijapur. Though the Portuguese publicly announced their neutrality, they secretly supported the besieged with supplies and soldiers.[34] In their dealings with Shivaji, the Portuguese were diplomatically following a policy that aimed at curtailing the growing power of the Marathas under their illustrious monarch.

The relations between the Portuguese and Shivaji ended up being stressful by 1679 over the issue of *Chauth*. When Shivaji died, the Portuguese felt a sense of relief. A report submitted by the Viceroy Antonio Paes de Sande, to the King of Portugal on 24 January 1681 says "The state of India is presently at peace with its neighbours, and the death of Shivaji has relieved us from an enemy, who was more to be feared while at peace than during open hostilities."[35]

The period from 1681 to 1689 witnessed Maratha resistance and turmoil. Sambhaji had a fluctuating relationship with the Portuguese. Portuguese gave more prominence to the Mughals in comparison with the Marathas. The Portuguese believed in playing safe and mostly tried to be neutral. After the death of Shivaji, his elder son, Sambhaji succeeded him to the throne. Sambhaji assumed the reins and got Panhala in his possession. In a very short time the fort of Raigad was captured by him in June 1680 without resistance. On 16 January 1681 he celebrated his coronation in the capital of the Maratha kingdom.[36]

The earliest politico-diplomatic relations between Sambhaji and the state of Portuguese-controlled territory dated back to the time when he captured Panhala and he was about to take possession of Raigad. He got into friendship with the Portuguese lest they would enter into an alliance with the enemy. With this in mind Shambhaji wrote a letter to the Portuguese Governor, Antonio de Sande, from Panhala itself communicating "*the news of his becoming the heir and successor of the Kingdom of his deceased father*,"[37] and requesting for every help of the Portuguese in his interests.[38] The letter was carried by Ramoji Naik Thakur who proposed to the Governor of Portuguese India the terms of peace. The Governor replied to this letter saying, "*With necessary declarations so that the cordial relations might turn to be true, firm and perpetual.*"[39] Ramoji also took back gifts from the government, a musket decorated with gold and pieces of clothes woven with gold thread. A letter was received back from the Governor of Portuguese India to Sambhaji saying that he "*assured the latter that the state would put everything in his favour against his enemies.*"[40]

Later on we see Ramoji himself turned out to be a traitor. He plotted against his own king and ran to take shelter in Goa as a fugitive where he stayed, initially, as a private individual but later as an ambassador of Sultan Adil Shah. When Sambhaji complained to Conde Alvor, he was imprisoned, but he was later released when the Bijapur Government intervened.[41]

On one occasion when the king of Marathas was at war with Aurangzeb, Sambhaji had to secure an alliance with the Portuguese as well as with other states of Deccan as it was the old practice with Deccanis during war. But

Sambhaji did not send any letter to his envoy on expediting the draft of the Luso-Maratha treaty. On the other hand, Aurangzeb took all the sympathy from the Portuguese government.[42]

Soon the Viceroy, Condo de Alvor, wrote to the Captain General of the North and also to the other captains of Chaul, Bassain and Daman advising them not to get into conflict with the powerful Mughal Emperor.

In reaction to the liberal passage given to the Mughals, Sambhaji captured some mercantile and warships of the Portuguese and over and above set fire to some of the villages of the Portuguese territories.

The viceroy wrote a letter on 24 January 1683 to the Royal Court.[43]

> An ambassador of the king Aurangzeb is here. He has come in connection with certain matters that he has not yet disclosed to me though he arrived four days back and is in the fifth, resting down the fatigue of the voyage ...

Actually Aurangzeb wanted the viceroy, Conde de Alvor, requesting him to have war with Sambhaji, and the Portuguese should not allow him to have passage and should not assist him because his fourth son Akbar had revolted against him by joining hands with Sambhaji, and when the time was right Aurangzeb might ask the Portuguese to capture and kill Sambhaji.

Here we see an excellent example of the diplomatic relationship of the Portuguese with Shambhaji in a letter written by the viceroy to his Majesty.[44] The letter was dated 16 December 1683, it said that he had got a letter from Aurangzeb and his intentions were conveyed to them. He appreciates Aurangzeb's intentions but also conveyed to him that the Portuguese could not support him in this cause because they were on friendly terms with Shambhaji. And also the Portuguese believed in peace, and they did not wage war until it was justified, and in the present scenario, it was absent.

But the Portuguese also did not completely upset the Mughals because in return for the gifts brought by the ambassador they were promised safe passage in the river which were in the Portuguese territories. Along with this they promised to protect their ships which were involved in the purchase of foodgrains. Therefore it is very clear that the Portuguese believed in playing safe and mostly they tried to be neutral. They only sided with the others if they saw any benefits or any threat. Portuguese showcased the finest example of political diplomacy.

After Shambhaji was killed, Rajaram came to the throne. The diplomatic relationship always kept fluctuating during his time. Mughals had free passage throughout the Portuguese territories, but they also allowed Rajaram's subjects access to their territories and they were treated at par with others. Governors Dom Rodrigo Da Costa and Dom Minguel de Almeida sought their assistance. They wanted to keep peace with Rajaram and put up a show of neutrality and indifference to either. Many officials of Rajaram were kept in the territories of the Portuguese. Seeing the Portuguese on friendly terms with the Marathas the Mughals attacked the fort of Bassein and set fire to a church that was situated outside the walls of the fort. The viceroy succeeded through his diplomacy by securing an order from Aurangzeb for an immediate cessation of war with conditions favourable to the Portuguese.[45]

Illustrative of the diplomatic relations between 1689 and 1707, there is an incident where Rajaram had entered the Portuguese territories and recovered a tax from the residents. The viceroy protested against this and wrote a letter dated 13 November 1694. The island of Chaul was issued an order for not allowing Kolaba to provide any foodstuff to the Marathas. They threatened to cause great damage to their land and seashore. He ordered the removal of the soldiers from Bardez; if not they would have to face the wrath of the Portuguese. The other option was to ask for peace negotiations for which they were ready.[46] They were ready for a peace agreement if Rajaram acted as a friend.[47]

Rajaram died on 22 March 1700. His minor son took over the throne. There was a friendly relationship between the Marathas and the Portuguese for at least two years after the death of Rajaram.

In the period between 1707 and 1761, if we analyse the result of the Mughal Maratha war, it was the Portuguese that took advantage and secured back most of their territories which they had lost during this war.[48] The Mughals in the Deccan were welcomed neither by the Marathas nor by the Portuguese in the later stage. Sensing the danger of the presence of the Mughals, the Portuguese started helping and giving the same facilities to the Marathas which were earlier given to the Mughals. Offers of signing a peace treaty with the Portuguese had already been made by Rajaram, and the friendly response from the Portuguese further encouraged the Marathas who now felt free to ransack the territories at free will. The Portuguese did not like the Mughals in their vicinity as they knew that they would face a similar fate after the eventful end of Bijapur, Golkunda and Raigarh.

Having gained the Konkan territory from the Mughal Empire as a *Jagir* allotment to Chhatrapati Shahu, the Marathas considered it a rightful and legitimate act to recover tribute from the Portuguese also. When he returned from captivity, he informed the Portuguese that he had gained Konkan as *Jagir* from the Mughals. Balaji Vishwanath brought Sanads of the same from the Mughals.

The Marathas' policy towards the Portuguese became more aggressive under Baji Rao. First was the capture of Vasai which led to the fall of Bacaim. The Marathas, with the help of the English, defeated the Portuguese at Bacaim in 1739.[49] They got information from the English about the planned attack of the Portuguese. The English informed them that the reinforcement came from Portugal and they were planning to attack. The English were also frightened because of their activities near Bombay. In this war the Portuguese faced defeat, and the Marathas on the other hand moved to take possession of the smaller fortifications at Tarapore, Mahim, Sirigao, Danu, Dharavi and Caranja. One important point to note here was that

Chimaji Appa who was commanding the Marathas, ordered that prisoners and their wives should be accorded due respect, and he also allowed the last rites of the deceased according to their customs.[50] With the conquest of all its subsidiaries, Bacaim, the province of the north, was incorporated into the Maratha Empire.

This siege took more than three months. According to the Portuguese chronicles, the total casualty was around 950, whereas the total number of soldiers was 1500. While on the other hand around 22000 Maratha soldiers were killed because of the superior firepower of the Portuguese.[51] As a result of the campaign, the Marathas acquired the entire northern provinces, 20 leagues in length, viz. from Versova to Damo, with their chief ports, 350 villages and a revenue of 250000 rupees.[52]

This period was marked by Maratha expansion and consolidation of power in Deccan. Marathas were struggling to maintain diplomatic relationships with the Portuguese and the Sawants of Wadi. Portuguese were also concerned about encroachment within their territories. In turn they were also playing diplomatically to safeguard their interest. One of the finest examples of diplomacy used as a tool by the Portuguese, the Sawants of Wadi and the Marathas has been discussed below.

Peshwa Bajirao I, before the beginning of the Bassein campaign, tried to forge united opposition to the Portuguese. He, therefore, asked the rulers of Savatwadi to give military help to the Maratha forces for assaulting Bassein.[53] The Sawants, therefore, sent Sultanji Rayjade, their general to Poona to negotiate with Peshwa Bajirao I.[54] The Sawants were also in conflict with the Portuguese and the Angrias.[55] Peshwas needed an ally on the Konkan coast, whereas, the Sawantwadi, too, after the recent experience with the Portuguese, who had tried to destroy their autonomy, needed a powerful ally. The hand of friendship offered by the Peshwa was, therefore, welcomed by the Sawants.

A treaty between Peshwa Bajirao and Ramchandra and Jayram Sawant[56] was signed on 11 December 1738. The treaty dealt with the mutual military help between the Peshwa and the Sawants and the islands which the Portuguese had acquired from Sawantwadi. It was agreed by the Sawants that they would give military assistance of 2000 infantry and 100 horses when the Peshwa would lead an expedition against the Portuguese in the prant Sashti, and the Peshwa agreed to give some villages in *inam* to the Sawants for this military help.

In addition to the village to be given in *inam*, the Peshwa agreed to give gold, silver and pearl ornaments to the Sawants and also assented to give five horses and 10000 rupees to equip the forces of Sawantwadi; Peshwa Bajirao, moreover, agreed to acquire the islands of Khorjuve and Paneli and village Dicholi from the Portuguese and to hand it over to Sawantwadi. The Peshwa promised military assistance to the Sawants of Wadi, if the Portuguese attacked them.[57] The Marathas were adopting the policy of appeasement in this case. They wanted to enter into a diplomatic relationship with Sawants of Wadi and simultaneously use the appeasement policy to be in an advantageous position to defeat the Portuguese.

The treaty between Peshwa and Sawantwadi (1738) was ostensibly advantageous to the Sawants because in return for military assistance to the Peshwa in the campaign of Bassein, the Sawant received presents, money and promise of help from the Peshwa against the Portuguese.

The news of this agreement between the Sawants and the Peshwa was communicated on 23 January 1739 by Narsingrao Sarasabnis, the Portuguese agent at Pune, to Goa, in the letter.[58] Narsingrao communicated that the Sawants had brought the Peshwa army in which there were 200 soldiers from the Sawants, to invade the Portuguese territory. He also communicated to the Portuguese that Ramchandra Sawant would besiege the forts of Phonda and Usgaon, and the joint forces of the Peshwa and Sawant would invade the prant Bardesh of the Portuguese.

The Portuguese, too, were aware of the preparations made against them by the Marathas. In his letter[59] to the King of Portugal (1 January 1739), the Viceroy of Goa pointed out the financial difficulties of Vyankatrao Ghorpade of Ichalkaranji, the brother-in-law of the Peshwa, who was given the command of the proposed campaign against the Portuguese. The Viceroy also communicated that Vyankatrao Ghorpade could not invade Goa without the assistance of the Sawants.[60]

In another letter to the general of Bardesh (26 January 1739), the Viceroy of Goa expressed his view that the Sawants of Wadi would not co-operate with the Marathas in the campaign, except in handing over the fort of Phonda to the Marathas.[61]

The Portuguese understood the important role of the friendship with Sawantwadi in the defence of Goa proper. Even though they received the knowledge of the treaty between the Peshwa and the Sawants, the Portuguese tried to maintain friendly relations with the Sawants in their critical condition. The Viceroy of Goa in his letter[62] to Ramchandra and Jayram Sawant (16 February 1739) communicated the news of the invasion of prant Sahti by the army of Vyankatrao Ghorpade and that this army would also enter into prant Bardesh. The Viceroy hinted at the negotiation between Vyankatrao and Sawants and thanked the Sawants for not continuing talks with Vyankatrao. The Viceroy expressed his gratitude and the hope that the friendship between the two neighbours (Portuguese and Sawant) would remain firm and honest.

The Portuguese wanted to avert the opening of a second frontier of conflict near their capital, in addition to the hostility which they were facing around Bassein. The Sawants understood this difficulty of the Portuguese and communicated to them in 1739 that if they did not want their prant of Bardesh invaded by the Marathas, they should accept three conditions.[63] One of the conditions was that the Portuguese should return the villages of Khorjuve and Paneli. Secondly, the *khandani* of 1000 Xerafines which the Sawants had accepted to give annually to the Portuguese should be condoned. Thirdly, the Portuguese should reimburse the expenditure which the Sawants had made in the defence of prant Bardesh.

The Portuguese did not accept these demands but tried to maintain friendly relations with the Sawants. The invasion of Portuguese territory by the Marathas was a good opportunity for the Sawants to reassert their position in the region. In order to increase the difficulties for the Portuguese, who had troubled Sawantvadi during the rule of Phond Sawant II, the Sawants requested Peshwa Bajirao to increase the tempo of the invasion by sending additional troops against Goa. The Sawants promised the Peshwa that they too would proportionately increase the strength of their army against Goa.

The Peshwa tried to blockade the Portuguese by asking the Sawants and the Angrias on the coastline that the supply of foodgrains to the Portuguese should be stopped. Due to this blockade, it became difficult for the Portuguese to get the supply of rice and other foodgrains which they used to receive from Karnataka. The Portuguese, thus, faced the force of military power of the Peshwa in addition to the shortage of foodgrains.

The Portuguese diverted some of their forces from the Bardesh region to Bassein, which was under the Siege of the Maratha forces led by Chimaji Appa, brother of Peshwa Bajirao. The prant Bardesh, therefore, was defenceless, and it was invaded by the Sawants, according to the instructions of Peshwa Bajirao, in the early hours on 5 March 1739. Some parts of the prant of Bardesh came under the control of the Sawants, without much difficulty.

The period between 1761 and 1800 is marked by the consolidation of the confederacy. The various pockets of power were trying their best to make their presence felt by becoming allies and entering into a diplomatic relationship. One such incident is discussed whether the house of Bhonsles played an important role. Khem Sawant had lost militarily with the Portuguese, so now he wanted to enter into a diplomatic relationship with the Peshwa in order to get back his lost provinces. He took the help of Mahadaji Shinde. In May 1783, Khem sent his envoy, and on the other side the Peshwa sent his envoy Govind Laxam to mediate between the Portuguese and the Sawants. But the meeting did not result in any conclusive talks.[64] After this, Khem wrote to the Portuguese to return his lost provinces, which were Dicholi, Sakhali and a portion of Pedne.

The Sawants suffered a setback when the envoy from the Peshwa's side died; all hopes of reconciliation with the Portuguese were lost after this. The death of Govind Laxam put an end to all the negotiations between the Peshwas and the Portuguese.[65] All the territories which were conquered were joined with the Goa territory. The Portuguese have fulfilled their long-cherished desire.

Khem was still hopeful that the Peshwa will mediate and get back his territory. The Portuguese came to know that the Peshwa was still backing the Sawants and it was also possible that Tipu sultan would attack Goa, so the plan of capturing the remaining part of Pedne was stalled for some time.

A twist took place when Khem was given the title of Raja Bahadur by the emperor Shah Alam II. The king of Kolhapur was very upset by this, and their relationship deteriorated which in turn led to a war known as the "Morchel War."[66] The Portuguese took advantage of this situation, and they supported the Khem, which led to the surrender of the remaining part of Pedne. By 1788, the Portuguese possessed the territories of Dicholi, Sakhali and Pedne.

Later when the conflict between the king of Kolhapur and Khem came to an end they both came to a conclusion that the territories of Dicholi, Sakhalia and Pedne were important to them and also economically viable. The intervention of Nana Phadnis was sought, but even he could not convince the Portuguese to return the territories.

The death of Mahadaji Shinde on 12 February 1794[67] was a great setback for Khem. After that he decided to secure his territories on his own. The troops of Bhonsles under Som Sawant and Santo Ram Akerkar attacked Pedne, fomenting a rebellion. Pedne was occupied by the Bhonsles. In September 1794, Khem attacked Phonda. There was a heavy battle between the Bhonsles and the Portuguese, and the Portuguese were forced to retreat.

Francisco Antonio da Viega had succeeded Menezes as the Governor General of Goa. He was very upset with Khem because of his relationship with the previous Governor General. He attacked the territories of the Bhonsles. Shivaji Raje of Kolhapur was also ready to help the Portuguese against Khem. The Portuguese considered the kingdom of Sawantwadi as very small, yet the Portuguese instructed Shivaji Raje of Kolhapur to secure back whatever Khem had taken from Kolhapur. Khem was defeated and the Bhonsles armies were also injured and taken to prison by the Portuguese.[68]

In the period between 1800 and 1818, Pedne remained a bone of contention between the Portuguese and Khem. After the death of Nana Phadnis on 13 February the Portuguese attacked Pedne. Bhonsles had kept Pedne in a constant state of disturbance. The Portuguese captured the esteemed persons of Khem. The Portuguese took them to fort Aguada and treated them well. The troops of Bhonsles surrendered Pedne to the Portuguese, and it was added to the Portuguese dominion. All the Desais of Pedne took an oath of allegiance to the Portuguese.

The Portuguese wanted permanent peace with Khem. Khem was asked by the Governor to pay for all the losses that the Portuguese had suffered during the war. Khem sent his envoy Zaitoji Mohite, who was accommodated in Panjim.[69] The Bhonsles could not reach a lasting settlement because the Portuguese did not accept Khem's last line of argument. All the attempts to gain friendship were turned down by the Portuguese; also they did not return the prisoners and kept them as hostages so that Khem could bow down in front of them.

In 1803, Khem Sawant died, and this year is considered to be very critical in Modern History because the powerful Maratha states like the

Peshwas, the Shinde and the Bhonsles of Nagpur had entered into a subsidiary alliance with the British. Khem's territories were taken by the British in 1818.

B. Diplomatic Relations with the Dutch

Looking at the period between 1630 and 1680, the Dutch established a factory in 1637 at Vengurla on the Konkan coast. It was during the 1660s that the Dutch had their first contact with the Marathas, and we find the earliest reference to Shivaji in a letter from Vengurla, sent to Batavia on 5 May 1660. It mentions him as "Siwasie, the son of Sahasie" and notes that "he has been revolting against his majesty (meaning Adilshah here) since last 10–12 years."[70] Shivaji's continuous activities of expansion along the chain of adjoining forts in the Western Ghats and the entire Konkan coast were not liked by the other European companies. But the nature of the contact of the Dutch with Shivaji was somewhat different as compared to the Portuguese and the English as both the Portuguese and the Dutch were rivals and had a keen competition in capturing the market of Basrur. Basrur supplied a large quantity of rice and pepper to Goa.

Instead of directly attacking Goa, which could involve him in a long campaign, Shivaji thought of cutting off the food supply from Basrur to the Portuguese.[71] In 1663, Shivaji sent word to the Dutch factory, saying that he had planned to bring Vengurla under his control and asked the Dutch's thoughts on the plan. The factors were told that they had nothing to worry about in this regard because Shivaji had nothing against them. The resident thanked Shivaji for this goodwill but added that being a mere merchant, he was unable to offer any advice regarding the matter of the capture of Vengurla. The Dutch factory at Vengurla was not disturbed by Shivaji with a view to secure a balance of power between the Portuguese and the English and keeping the Dutch satisfied and contented in his areas. He threatened the English that he would assist the Dutch in destroying Bombay, but he never fulfilled the threat.[72]

After 1664, Vengurla's trade was hampered by the rising conflict of Mughals, and Bijapur Sultanate and Shivaji's operation in the area continued to have essentially unsettling effects on the Company's factory. For example, in 1665, some goods were bought by the local merchants for delivery to the Company, along with a sum of 500 pagodas intended for investment on the Company's account. It was allegedly looted by Shivaji's men. The merchants petitioned the Company that it should agree to bear the loss, which, of course, it refused to do. The situation became worse with time, but the important thing is that the relations between the Company and Shivaji continued to be extremely cordial. In 1671, book-keeper Lefeber was sent to Raigad to greet Shivaji with a gift of 450 pagodas. The gift was graciously accepted, and it was gently hinted that a bigger gift would have been more welcome.[73]

Shivaji's diplomatic relations with the Dutch can also be seen in securing financial help from the Dutch, as they were always short of money due to continuous war in the region. Shivaji and his chancellor Anaji Pandit wanted to revive the trade at Vengurla. He started negotiating trade relations with the Dutch. Thus, in early September 1676, the *subehdar* of the region, Balaji Suri, visited the Dutch at Vengurla and enquired about the affairs of their trade. The Dutch were initially aloof, after which he mentioned that Shivaji greatly needed copper, for which the Dutch would be paid in cash and in advance, and that they would bring more than 600,000 pounds of copper. Shivaji was in dire need of copper, and so, he maintained a peaceful relationship with the Dutch perceiving their help in importing copper for him. The Dutch used to pay Shivaji a toll for allowing them free trade in all commodities at Vengurla port. It was meant for mintage. Such urgency and huge quantity point out the most likely use of coinage. After the coronation, Shivaji struck copper, gold and silver coins. The copper one was called *Shivarai* and was the most common. One reason behind his haste in obtaining copper might be his impending Karnataka campaign. He gave many other promises as well, but the Dutch were cautious, having seen how the English and French at Rajapur struggled with getting the payment from Shivaji, using the promissory notes given by him. Sensing the reluctance of the Dutch, Balaji Suri further said that "the Dutch should try to find a middle path and satisfy the Raja's desire partly, if not fully."[74] In spite of trade-related pressure between the Dutch and the Marathas, Shivaji never gave any trouble to the Dutch factory.

There were also proposals for business dealings between Shivaji and the Dutch. In 1676, for example, Annaji Pandit offered Abraham Lefeber a yearly payment of 1000 pagodas. This unexpectedly generous offer was to leave no doubt that Shivaji would buy the loyalty of Lefeber, which would have given him an insider's access to the machinations of VOC—a huge asset for an ambitious King like him. This attempt did not succeed, and Lefeber was quick to mention to his superiors that "He won't be a rascal for 4000 or even 10000 pagodas a year."[75] He wanted to underscore his honesty to his superiors at Batavia, perhaps in the hope of reward. This whole episode is very interesting where one finds the explicit mention of an offer from Shivaji. Thus we can say that Shivaji's relation with Dutch was relatively peaceful and purely commercial in nature.

Shivaji's Karnataka Expedition is an important episode in Maratha history. He captured the Adilsahi forts at Vellore and Jinji. By that time, the Dutch were also attempting to enter and set up their trade in the region, and several financial proposals were made between Dutch and Maratha authorities and how each of them was anxious to meet for their mutual interest in the region. Soon after this, the Dutch started preparations for visiting Shivaji and securing trading rights from him. A Dutch merchant, Herbert de Jager, famous for his command on oriental languages, reached his seniors at Tegenapatnam for further instructions in view of Shivaji's activities. He went to the Dutch factory, and it was decided that Nicolas Clement, the second-in-command at the factory, would accompany him and finalize the gifts, which they would give to Shivaji. Shivaji arrived on 6 August, with Raghunath Pant and Janardan Pandit. He listened to the VOC's demands and promised to be helpful and confirmed the contents of the previous *cowles*.[76]

After this, the Dutch started making headway at Porto Novo, where there was no Dutch settlement till then, despite it being an important port city. On 20 March 1678, a *cowle* was issued by the *havaldars* of Porto Novo to the Dutch and exempted them from half of the toll on the goods brought there and also permitted them to build a customs house there.[77] But Gopaldas Pandit, the governor at Devanampatinam and Porto Novo was very much displeased with this *cowle*, because "He feared that, as was their habit, the company (i.e., The Dutch) would penetrate there more & more until even the ruler of the land couldn't do anything."[78] These measures before long met with a serious backlash from the Dutch, who at that point denied to issue passports to local ships going out from Porto Novo, which resulted in the disarray of trade. Merchant Jacob Clement, a native broker, took this matter to Raghunath Pant, the Governor of Adilshahi Karnatak, and secured a *cowle* from the latter that permitted the Company to conduct trade at Porto Novo. It was the outstanding work of diplomats like Raghunath Pant, who was solely responsible for the amicable relations of Shivaji, Ekoji and the Dutch power. The service of Raghunath Pant is lauded by Shivaji by saying this:

> you have served our father and like me possess the power to correct and guide us when we cannot see our way. No other person can exercise such influence in our affairs. We look upon you fully in the place of our reverend parent and cannot too highly estimate your services.[79]

Concerning Dutch-Maratha relation in Tanjore between 1681 and 1689, Tanjore was one of the important successor states of the Vijayanagara Empire in South India. After a war between the Nayakas of Tanjore and Madurai, the former was killed, and thereafter, Tanjore was quickly seized by Ekoji, an Adilshahi general, who was also the half-brother of Shivaji. After the death of the dynamic ruler Ekoji, who had kept the Dutch at bay as well as he could, Tanjore was succeeded by weak rulers who had pressing financial problems. Tanjore recognized that the sum agreed by the Dutch for their tax-free tenure of Negapatam was to be paid annually in cash and in elephants and horses and was important to the state's revenues. The ruler often asked for advance payments, and there was disagreement on the quality of the horses and elephants. On account of this, the ruler held the Dutch to be in arrears on the delivery of elephants. There was also disagreement on the value of gifts made by the Dutch when they sent an embassy to felicitate a ruler. One such embassy in 1691 was sent back, and its gifts were held to be inadequate.[80]

In 1683, as mentioned in the previous section, the Maratha administrator began to create difficulties for the VOC; he forbade the export of rice to Ceylon and also collected a capitation tax from the inhabitants of the ten villages. Sometimes before a major change occurred in the organization of VOC. Adriaan van Rheede was transferred to Coromandel from Bengal in 1687, and he was invested with extraordinary powers by the Heren XVII because they were deeply unhappy about the poor performance of VOC's Coromandel directorate of late. He collected all the contracts and began their investigation to see which ones were still in force. He found Shahaji of Tanjore to be favourable to the company and succeeded in getting an advantageous *cowle* from him in March 1688. The VOC secured permission to build a trading lodge at Darasurpette and also received the much-coveted exclusive trading rights at the important ports of Karikal, Trimelavaas and Sadraspatnam.[81] This *cowle* helped in the improvement of VOC trade during this period.

Regarding the activities of the Marathas at Jinji between 1690 and 1707, we see that Rajaram, brother of Shambhaji (who had been captured and executed by the Mughals), became the new Maratha king. In November 1689, Rajaram arrived at Jinji and continued his war with the Mughals. The Marathas at Jinji were in urgent need of money as they had to send funds to their army in the Carnatic as the soldiers were deserting because of lack of pay. Due to their long and strenuous war with the Mughals, almost in every quarter of the Deccan, the Maratha government found all sorts of ways to extort money from the European powers on the Coromandel Coast.

As the French were in very close proximity to the Marathas at Jinji, the Marathas had initially demanded money, arms and ammunition for war against the Mughals, but the French preferred to remain neutral, and neither did they supply money and ammunition. The financial constraints of Rajaram forced him to sell Pondicherry. At first, he gave priority to the French, but they followed delaying tactics to have a better bargain. Finally, Rajaram sold Pondicherry to the Dutch, who were arch-rivals of the French only because they were ready to pay a better price. This act was not purposely crafted for revenge on the French, but due to diplomatic pressure from the disturbing political situation and financial constraints, they confirmed the Dutch possession of the fort. Regarding the issue of Pondicherry, Rajaram had initially supported the French but later on chose to support the Dutch instead. This shows that the Maratha behaviour is best characterized as being motivated by the sore need of money and the urgency of immediate survival.

Between 1707 and 1761, with the fall of Jinji in 1698,[82] there was an atmosphere of chaos immediately after the death of Rajaram, but the Marathas survived under the able leadership of Queen Tarabai. The Marathas, after the death of Aurangzeb, recovered all the possessions in Maharashtra. The relationship between the Marathas and the Dutch was very dynamic in nature. We find many ups and downs in the nature of their interactions in the prevailing political condition of the Maratha rule in the region and the clash of interests of the Dutch in and around Negapatam. During the rule of Sahuji or Kattu Raja, Chanda Sahib forced him to cede Karikal to the French. However, late in July 1738, he prevented the French from landing at Karikal, which in turn brought Tanjore the invasion of Chanda Sahib, who was an ally of the French. The Marathi inscription says that he obtained help from the Dutch at Negapatam under specious promises. In 1739 the Dutch of Negapatam wrote home as follows:

> Chanda imprisoned Shagy Maharaj in Tanjore under a pretence that he was not of royal blood. Pratap was seated on the throne against his own will. Having gone to the prison and expressing his unwillingness to ascend the throne to Sahuji's prejudice, Pratap was answered by Shagy, If you do not accept the government, both of us lose our heads, if on the other hand, we continue alive, we may watch the course of events. Hence ascend the throne.[83]

Thus in 1739, Raja Sahu ji was succeeded by Pratap Singh. This Maratha rule was often disturbed by the Nawab of Arcot. On the other hand, there were instances when we see Dutch trade was hampered due to the Maratha incursion in the Carnatic. During the Anglo-French war, when trade at Madras and Pondicherry was interrupted, at Porto Novo, it was noted to be brisk.[84] It is, therefore, no wonder that the port was often the target of neighbouring powers. When the Marathas fell upon the Carnatic in 1740, they attacked Porto Novo. A contemporary source estimated the value of the Maratha raid of the Dutch factory in 1740 at 100,000 pagodas and that of the town at 500,000 pagodas.[85] The Dutch factory was abandoned after the Maratha attack on the port in 1740. All trading activities were carried on from their base at Tegenepatnam till December 1745. The Dutch were trying to obtain a concession on the customs duty payable at the port. Finally, in 1745, they received a *parwana* from the nawab, granting them the privilege to pay 1% on the value of their export from that post, while the normal rate was 2.5%.[86] Thus, we see in the 18th century despite the written assurance and several treaties signed between them, frequent conflicts occurred between the two parties.

With the beginning of the Carnatic wars between the English and the French, these two powers were rising ahead of the Dutch in political power and influence on the Carnatic. On the other hand, we also see the emergence of the Marathas as a mighty power and a centrally located power which had the potential of manoeuvring the politics in the North as well as the South during the 18th century. As far as the Dutch were concerned in the 18th century, their factories became increasingly squeezed by the ongoing political conflicts in the interior, involving the states of Hyderabad of Arcot and the Marathas, and also by the increasing pressure from the British and the French. Moreover, the war of the period 1740–1763 was a major hindrance to the Dutch trade. The VOC was facing a financial crisis due to the fourth war between the United Provinces and Great Britain (1780–1784), and in 1800, the company was dissolved, four years after the States-General was replaced by the French-supported Batavian Republic, and restored to the French. After the defeat of the French empire, the previously privately owned East Indies territories were granted to the newly created Kingdom of the Netherlands by the Congress of Vienna in 1815.[87]

C. Diplomatic Relations with the French

If we look at the period between 1630 and 1680, we see that it was in 1668 that the French first came in contact with the Marathas, and they built their first factory at Rajapur. Francois Martin recorded in his diary that on arriving at Calicut in 1669, on his way to Surat, he met Messieurs Faes and J. Boureau, who informed him that "they have been to Rajapur and seen there Raja Shivaji who received them well and gave them permission to trade and establish in his lands."[88] Shivaji gave them "coul" (licence) to trade freely in his ports.[89] Shivaji's relations with the French were cordial, but he had political intentions as well, since the Konkan was subjected to expeditions he wanted to restore the Konkan economy. There are correspondences which show his generosity towards M. Baron the Director of the French East India Company. He writes to Colbert "the Maratha chief shows great esteem for the French company."[90]

The relation at this point of time was purely a commercial one. In 1670, Shivaji sacked the town of Surat for the second time, almost all European factories in Surat had to suffer damages, the French were spared from an assault because they had supplied him with arms and ammunition. M. Blot a Director of the French East India Company writes "If he (Shivaji) returns to sack Surat, he will have great respect to the French flag."[91]

The Marathas and the French came into close contact in Pondicherry. Pondicherry was part of the Bijapur Karnatak and it was ruled by two rival governors, viz Nasir Muhammad and Sher Khan who had their capitals at Jinji and Walikondapuram. The French were, however, very much disturbed by the escalating events in the Deccan; with the ambitions of Shivaji, they feared that the Sultan of Golconda would also march against them with the help of Shivaji. The French then sent an envoy to Sher Khan of Walikondapuram for protection to be given to them by withdrawing to the fort of Tegnapatnam (fort St David) which was close to Madras, and in case of an attack, they could escape by sea. But Sher Khan refused to give such permission on the pretext that it would invite the hostility of the Dutch. On the other hand, Sher Khan offered the French refuge in Pallamkotta which was an insult to the French as Francois Martin tells us.[92]

Circumstances determined the actions of the French during this period; the relationship with Sher Khan was based not on loyalty but on assurance of protection from the approaching army of Shivaji. At this stage, trust and loyalty no longer determined the relationship between the two. As we will see later, the French sent envoys to Shivaji to ensure their protection. With the fall of Jinji under Shivaji, Nir Muhammad concluded a treaty with him. This alarmed the rulers of the various regions who now decided to send envoys to Shivaji. The French sent a letter to Shivaji asking him to allow them to stay within his territories at Rajapur and grant them privileges, the French informed Sher Khan about their affairs. He was still bent on defeating Shivaji with reinforcements from Bijapur.[93]

As has been said earlier, the ambitious Shivaji refused to hand over Jinji to the Sultan of Golconda and started sending detachments to many villages around Valudar and Kunimedu. The troops of Shivaji patrolled the countryside and soon became masters of the entire low-lying region. Meanwhile, the envoy sent to Shivaji guaranteed the protection of Pondicherry on the condition that the French remained neutral in all affairs. He sent a havaldar to administer Pondicherry. With the combined effort of the Sultan of Golconda, Shivaji and the Deccani party, the defeat of Sher Khan was inevitable. At this time the help of the French was needed by Sher Khan but help could not be provided due to lack of men and therefore what followed was the decisive defeat of Sher Khan in July 1677.

Owing to the success of Shivaji, the French no longer had a friend to rely on because Sher Khan had submitted himself to Shivaji's service, the French tried to befriend Shivaji by sending an envoy laden with a piece of gold and silk brocade, five to six ells of white cloth, a saffron shawl, four pieces of painted cloth and a pair of double-shot rifles. The envoy had its ripples when Shivaji confirmed a *firman* ensuring the security of Pondicherry.[94] Trade had been hampered and virtually came to a stop, but Martin says that the English and the Dutch were able to carry on normal trade. The French on the other hand were too dependent on the local powers and thus, when the war occurred, the French also suffered. Francois Martin's opinion on the Hindus was that they recklessly broke promises and each one was the enemy of the other and that was the main reason for their loss of dominion.

Judging from events, if the French had reinforcements and funds, they would have helped Sher Khan defeat Shivaji and their territory would not have been administered by the officials of Shivaji. Thus, the continuous lack of funds prevented the French from taking advantage of the situation. They could not command the sequel of events due to non-cooperation from the French government. The English and the Dutch were clever enough to realize the magnitude of events and hence did not get involved in the affairs, and this did not hamper or destroy their trade in the Coromandel region. Thus, in the 17th century, we can see that the French were still in a weak position, their friendship was not desired by any local power, and hence, it was the French who needed the help and support of the indigenous powers more than the Indian powers at this period. By the 18th century, we shall see how the position of the French changed dramatically, with their superiority in cavalry and artillery, and their relationship was desired even more.

Between 1685 and 1707, we see that by 1701, we get to know that the French had firmly established themselves at Pondicherry (after the Dutch returned it with the signing of the Treaty of Riswick 1697). It looked like the wars in Europe brought peace in India too with the signing of the Treaty of Utrecht, and the French were finally able to strengthen their hold in India. A *firman* was obtained by them from the Mughal Emperor to coin money at Pondicherry on 17 August 1736. Ananda Ranga Pillai's opinion was that Pondicherry flourished under Lenior who obtained for the French Company the right to mint coins in Pondicherry.

Scholars like V.S. Kadam and U.A. Kadam have given tremendous information on the French and Maratha relations in the 18th century, and by this period the Marathas became the most formidable power in India after the disintegration of the Mughal Empire. Their conflict and expansion involved the whole Deccan. Umesh.A. Kadam opines that the period between 1693 and 1740 was a period of indirect contact between the French and the Marathas through a series of correspondence with the Portuguese, because of the prolonged war with the Marathas, the Portuguese were in an acute state and needed soldiers from the French.[95] Apart from this, after 1740, the direct contact between the two powers played a significant role in the history of the Marathas. After Chhatrapati Rajaram died, there was much chaos; however, the leadership of Queen Tarabai, the widow of Rajaram, prevented the Marathas from joining hands with the Mughals. The Mughal Emperor also died in 1707, and the Marathas recovered their lost possessions in Maharashtra.

As for the period between 1707 and 1761, after Nasir Jung, Muzzafur Jang was put on the throne by the French. The new Nizam conferred on Dupleix the title of Zafar Jang and granted the French Company the *jagir*s of Gingee, Tiruviti and gave suitable titles, mansabs and presents to Law, D'Auteuil and other French Captains.[96] From December 1750 to March 1751, Pondicherry was the political centre of Deccan politics. Dupleix in his memoir informs us of the situation. He says,

> The designs of this war were to assist the lawful sovereign of Deccan and the true Governor of Arcot in expelling two usurpers universally acknowledged to be such by the European Nations, all the Powers in India and by the Great Mogul himself-for certainty nobody could doubt but Muzaffar Jung constituted heir and success to Nizam ul Mulk his grandfather by the last will of his uncle and confirmed in the sovereignty of the Deccan by a Firman from the Great Mogul was the only lawful Subah of Deccan and Chanda Sahib nominated by that Prince to the Government of Arcot, the only true Nawab of the Province of Carnatte whereof Arcot is the capital.[97]

Thus, Dupleix was clear in his mind that the French support given to Muzzafar Jung was justified in which he was the true heir and that Chanda

Sahib was nominated by Muzzafar Jung. This support can also be seen from the grant of territories given to them in which they joined the war as auxiliaries. Dupleix had also calculated that the total sum generated from the French settlements (before 1749) of Karaikal, Yanam, Chandernagore, Patna, Ballasore, Dacca, Kasimbazar and Pondicherry only amounted to 120,000 rupees. Thus, it was necessary for him to expand French territories by engaging with the local politics. Another lingering thought that disturbed Dupleix when reading his memoir was the fact that if he did not grab this opportunity another rival European Company would swoop it away.

The Marathas obtained three imperial grants from Delhi: a) The *Chauth* of the six Subhas of the Deccan including Hyderabad, Bijapur, Karnatak, Tanjore, Trichinopoly and Mysore, b) the Sardeshmukhi over and above the *Chauth* and c) full sovereignty over the kingdom possessed by Chhp. Shivaji at the time of his death.[98]

The Confederacy that was formed after the death of Rajaram was the most important from the viewpoint of the military aspect; it even appeared as the power destined to seize the whole Mughal inheritance. The chiefs of the decentralized Maratha Confederacy were very powerful; they were Gaikwar, Bhonsle, Holkar and Sindhia. Thus, the French very much desired an alliance with the Marathas.

With the shift of French interest from the West (Surat) to the East (Bengal) due to a change in preference for commodities, the French had factories at Chandernagore, Kasimbazar, Jugdia, Dacca, Balasore and Patna. The factory at Chandernagore with Dupleix as its Governor flourished (1731–41). But the Maratha entry into Bengal disturbed the prosperity of these establishments. The pretext for such incursions was the hostility for Nawabship of Bengal between Murshid Kuli Khan and Ali Vardi Khan. Murshid Kuli Khan invited the Marathas (Bhaskarram Kolhatkar Commander-in-chief of Raghuji Bhonsle) to invade the country. The French observed hostility in the war between Ali Vardi Khan and the Marathas, and this spared the Marathas from plundering their settlement. But due to constant Maratha attacks (1744, 1747 and 1748) the French settlements in Bengal were under permanent insecurity.[99]

Having given the background on the tension that was created between the French and the Marathas. From letters of Bussy to Dupleix in March 1754, we come to know of the French victory over the Marathas in the Deccan that had been undertaken jointly with Salabat Jang. Bussy, who was the general of the French troops, had placed Salabat Jang, third son of the Nizam of Hyderabad, as the viceroy of the Deccan. The proclamation of Salabat Jang as the viceroy created a rift between the French and the Marathas as the Marathas were trying to promote the cause of Ghazi-ud-din, the eldest son of the Nizam to the Viceroyship of the Deccan. Ghazi-ud-din had promised the Marathas to cede the districts of Aurangabad and Burhanpur if they would support his cause. V.S. Kadam is of the opinion that it was due to the superiority of the French artillery they were able to protect Salabat Jang's army.[100] By January 1752, the Marathas under Balajirao and Salabat Jang concluded a treaty that was in favour of Salabat Jang. The Marathas now realized the superiority of the French and they decided to send an embassy to the French governor. But Dupleix was clever in realizing the tactics of the Marathas, and he was determined to shatter the Maratha Supremacy. This is evident from a letter Bussy wrote to Dupleix on 23 September 1751.[101]

The French were determined to reduce the Maratha power before their expedition into Bengal and Dupleix wanted to overthrow the Nawabship of Ali Vardi Khan and replace him with Salabat Jang who would be easily persuaded by the French. Preparations for war were made; for this they tried to get the help of the Portuguese who were geographically close to the Marathas. Dupleix negotiated with the Viceroy of Goa in September 1751, and he agreed to attack the Marathas by sea, while the French and the Mughals would attack by land. But the plan did not materialize because the Portuguese had become hostile. Thus, the Mughals and the French fought the Marathas at Jamgaon on 1 December 1751. The French were also joined by Salabat Jang. Bussy wrote to Dupleix in his letter in November and reported on the advances of the joint forces of the Nizam and the French on Poona; he writes,

> We are not more than 20 KOSS(64Kms) from Poona and ten from the army of Balajirao, and I hope that my forthcoming letters will inform you of the success of the enterprise as glorious for the (French) nation as advantages for Salabat Jang. War against Balajirao was officially declared only three days ago, and the circumstances which led to this declaration will delight you.[102]

This short success created fear in the Marathas who now settled for peace, but the offer was rejected by the French. Eclipsed by their short success, the French had wrongly judged the strength of the Marathas, the Maratha chiefs were united in their fight against the French. Hence, the French hope of creating dissension among the Maratha chiefs was a lost cause. As U.A. Kadam suggests, it was really the success of the Marathas; we learn from the letters of Ramdas Pant (Diwan of Salabat Jang) who was aware of Maratha tactics, had to check and prevent the French from falling into the Maratha traps.[103] The French contingent was in a deplorable state, and their co-operation with the Mughals seemed to decline. The nobles of Salabat Jang became jealous of the French influence at the court of Aurangabad.

The Treaty of Bhalki (24 November 1752), which was signed between Salabat Jang and the Marathas, determined the relationship between the French and the Marathas. The Peshwa demanded that the French should be made mediators between them and Salabat Jang. Hence the Peshwa recognized Salabat Jang as the legitimate viceroy of the Deccan. Thus, it was the Marathas who had the upper hand and dictated the terms to the French.

A treaty was also signed between the Peshwa and the French, thus the two maintained friendly relations till 1750.

By 1752, the French could not keep their position in the Carnatic without the active support of the Marathas. The French desired a permanent Franco-Maratha alliance. The Peshwa's growing influence was a serious threat to the French interests in the Deccan and also in the Carnatic. With the signing of the Treaty of Bhalki, Bussy took utmost care not to violate the treaty and to show sincere regard to the Marathas. The French were also interested to form an alliance with the Marathas because they wanted to capture the port town of Surat. For peaceful trade and commerce, the French wanted a safe passage from the Maratha territory to Surat. However, the success of this enterprise was dependent on the co-operation of the Marathas.

The year 1761 sounded the death knell for both the French and the Marathas in Deccan. The defeat of the Marathas in 1761 by Ahmad Shah Abdali (Third battle of Panipat) and the surrender of Pondicherry to the English in 1761 indicate the decline of these two powers. Pondicherry was returned in 1763 but was in shambles; nonetheless, they made their presence felt in south India till the end of the 18th century. The Maratha defeat, on the other hand, ended the attempt of the Marathas as successors of the Mughals.

Between 1761 and 1818, we see that the French colonies in India were restored by the Treaty of Paris in 1763, the political presence of the French in Deccan was not the same by 1765, and the English had obtained Bengal and the Carnatic, Awadh and the Northern Circars. The ruler of Hyderabad had been reduced to a subordinate ally of the English and the Mughal Emperor had been living as their pensioner. The French colonies were in a disgraceful state and the treaty had forbidden any fortification of the French colonies.[104] The battle of Panipat crippled the Maratha Confederacy, Peshwa Nana Saheb died of shock and most of the Maratha aristocracy was ruined. By 1763, Haider Ali had risen to power, he started to consolidate his power and later his son Tipu became the de facto ruler of Mysore. While the English, on the other hand, subjugated one state after the other. They made Muhammad Ali, the Nawab of Karnatak, their puppet prince. Pondicherry had come under the jurisdiction of Muhammad Ali. The Marathas soon started to recover their lost glory under the leadership of Peshwa Madhav Rao. They forced Nizam Ali to complete submission and inflicted severe defeats upon Haider Ali of Mysore.[105]

Keeping in mind their common enemy, i.e. the English, Peshwa Madhav Rao took the reins in his hands and had become a very skilful statesman. He realized that he needed the help of the French to destroy English power, and the rise of Haider Ali was also a cause of concern for the Marathas. Peshwa Madhavaram started negotiations with the French. In 1772, he had instructed Trimbakrao Pethe, his general operating in the south, to negotiate with the French Governor Jean Law de Lauriston at Pondicherry. The Marathas had inflicted crushing defeats on Haider but were unable to completely route him.[106] Narayanrao succeeded Madhav Rao as Peshwa, and he desired to have an alliance with the French, firstly to expulse Muhammad Ali the Nawab of Arcot and secondly to oust the English. This desire was communicated by the Maratha commandant of the fort of Gurumkonda (90 miles north of Bangalore) to Law. Law then sent a pair of pistols and a costly gun as a present to the Peshwa. The Peshwa too sent a "*sarpech*"[107] with a friendly letter. Unfortunately, before the letter could reach Pondicherry Narayanrao was assassinated by his uncle Raghunatharao. Narayanrao's commandant informed the French that he could not send the letter because Raghunatharao had stopped communication with the French.[108]

The assassination of the Peshwa Narayanrao ended Peshwa rule which transformed the Maratha state from the rule of the Peshwa to the Karbhari (or Barbhai Council), i.e. servant of the Peshwa. The Barbhai Council were a strong enemy of the English; they therefore automatically looked to the French for assistance. In 1775 a Maratha agent, Govind Raghunath, was sent to the French consul at Surat, M. Anquetil de Braincourt; according to the proposals made by the council, they were willing to cede to the French a port of their choice on the Malabar coast and the French in return should supply 200 soldiers from Pondicherry to check English activities on the coast. However, these negotiations did not materialize because the French were interested in Gheria (Vijaydurg) of Bassein.

The Embassy of Saint-Lubin (1777) at the Maratha court was an important embassy sent from France. The efforts of both these agents were concentrated on forming alliances with the Maratha Confederacy. Saint-Lubin's treaty with the Marathas contains the following:

1. The French would furnish 2400 corps of artillery troops.
2. These troops were to be divided into two regiments:
    a. One of them was composed of 1200 men and was called "The Regiment of Alliance," who would serve the Marathas and would always maintain its full strength.
    b. The other would be stationed at Pondicherry and would be utilized for recruiting the regiment of the alliance.
3. The Marathas would meet all the expenses of these corps, incurred from its leaving Europe, transport to India, maintenance, pay, etc.[109]

However, due to fear of hostility with the English, it was suggested by Saint-Lubin that the troops could be dispatched to the Marathas secretly, or under the pretext of desertion. Saint-Lubin negotiation was a conditional treaty of offensive and defensive alliance between the two powers. The other additional responsibility was the way to impress upon the Marathas the necessity of protecting French possessions in India. In return for this favour, the King of France would grant permission to his shipowners to deal in arms and ammunition with the Marathas.[110]

The reappearance of Bussy at Porto Novo on 16 March 1783 redefined his personal relationship with the Indian princes. He wrote letters to Nana Fadnavis and the Peshwa expressing his desire to co-operate and fight the common enemy. He therefore received Gopalrao the Maratha Vakil at Pondicherry, the vakil complained that the French did not keep their promise of sending arms and ammunition for the Maratha war against the English. Bussy expressed his late arrival in India, and he also warned Gopalrao not to trust the English and that an alliance between the Marathas, Nizam Ali, Tipu and the French would be fruitful in annihilating the English.[111] However, the untimely death of Bussy on 7 January 1785 only provided for the dwindling relationship of the French and the Marathas. This second attempt of Bussy to have a relationship with the Marathas failed miserably due to lack of participation from the French government. After Bussy, Vicomte de Souillac was appointed as the new Governor General; he expressed his desire to have an alliance with the Marathas solely for restoring to the Indian princes the territories conquered by the English. This change in nature of the French–Maratha alliance was due to the conclusion of the American War of Independence. Thus, it was necessary for the two European powers to settle their differences with the Indian princes.

Thus, from 1785 to 1787 the Franco-Maratha relation centred around the conflict between the Marathas and Tipu; the French on the other hand wanted an alliance with these two powers so that the English would be defeated. However, the hatred towards Mysore from the Marathas was inevitable and led to the Marathas drawing closer towards the English.

The fall of Pondicherry in 1793 ended all possible relations between the French and the Marathas; the French with their difficulties in Paris could not spare troops for the east and the Marathas and Nizam Ali joined hands with the English.[112] The fall of the Marathas however did not come all of a sudden; it was a slow process of the balance of power in the Maratha state. It started declining from 1774, and the final blow came in 1818 when the Anglo-Maratha Wars happened, the First Anglo-Maratha War (1774–1783), Second Anglo-Maratha War (1803–1809) and the Third Anglo-Maratha War (1817–1818). It is significant to note that during these wars the French power in India was already in decline and thus leaving the English with full authority and supremacy in the South.

Military Expansion through Adaptation and Innovation: The Maratha Method of Warfare

Another aspect of diplomacy of the Marathas towards their opponents can be seen through their warfare and combat strategies. With the rise of the Marathas, a new style of warfare came into existence popularly known as *bargir-giri*[113] or guerrilla tactics which were remarkably used against the enemy. The skill was initially adapted from Malik Amber when Shivaji's father was serving him in the Ahmadnagar dynasty. This consisted of not meeting the enemy's main force in the field, but cutting off supplies, manoeuvring for the best position and using superior mobility to strike vulnerable locations far from the battle side. Swiftness, speed and mobility was their specialty. Shivaji successfully challenged the Mughal army through the implementation of guerrilla tactics as an appropriate military strategy in the Maratha geo-strategic territory.[114]

The classic model of early Maratha type of warfare is provided by Santaji Ghorpade who was the perfect master of this art. This type of warfare is rightly described as Parthian warfare rather than as guerrilla tactics. He covered long distances not only swiftly but also with accuracy and punctuality which were incredible in any Asiatic army other than those of Zengis Khan and Timur.[115] The main Maratha military strength was dependent upon its infantry and light cavalry. The military culture and the diverse armies of the Marathas tell us that both matchlocks and flintlocks and a diversity of artillery were an important part of the Maratha warfare. The garrisons were concentrated in a number of fortresses which were used both as a defensive chain as well as for shelter during the rainy season. The proficiency of the Maratha military system lay in the fact that their horsemen could march long distances with extreme swiftness and secrecy, disperse for hunting or confusing their enemy and yet combine for striking a blow. A French officer gives the picture of Shivaji's army during the invasion of Madras coast in 1677. According to him the

> camp of Shivaji is without pomp, without women, without baggage. It has only two tents, both of simple coarse stuff and very small, one of them for himself and other for his prime minister. There are ordinarily three horses to every two men, which contributes to the speed that he makes. He thus surprises his enemies who believe him to be far distant when he falls upon them.[116]

Under the Peshwas, the Marathas were now in a position to carry war into their enemies land, and in these distant expeditions, designed mainly for plunder, a cavalry was more useful than infantry.[117] Later the Peshwas adopted a policy of war in the North which led to a major alteration in army organization and fighting techniques because they had to cover very long distances and thus the cavalry became more important. The introduction of non-Marathas into the army brought major organizational changes and affected the discipline in the army. Now the Marathas adopted field-battle techniques to replace the Gamini Kava.[118]

Shivaji had a regular artillery department called the *Tephkhana*, and among his state departments is mentioned the Darukhana; it is popularly known that the Indians never excelled in artillery and hence borrowed a lot from foreigners. Thus, from 1668 onwards the Marathas had contacts with the French in particular and took help from them in terms of arms and armoury. French soldiers were employed in the Maratha army and the Marathas purchased French artillery in times of war. He was dependent on foreigners for the supply of guns and cannons. The European merchant companies carried a regular trade in artillery and ammunition; it was for this reason that he allowed the French to build a factory at Rajapur. Shivaji purchased 2,000 maunds of lead and 88 iron guns in 1673 from the French.[119] Besides artillery of European manufacture, Shivaji also possessed some light pieces of Indian made called *Jejala* and *Zamburak* or *Shutarnal*. With the rise of the Peshwa, the Maratha army began to change in composition. Whereas Shivaji had relied equally on his fleet-footed Mawali infantry and light cavalry, the Maratha army under the Peshwa became a cavalry army.[120]

A. Significance of Forts

Grant Duff states that there is probably no stronger country in the world than the Deccan from the military defence point of view. The Sahyadri mountain ranges offered immense political advantages in times of war with the northern powers. Unlike the Gangetic plain, this country could not be conquered and annexed by one cavalry dash or even one year's campaign.[121]During the 16th and 17th centuries great emphasis was placed on building and capturing forts, as were designed and constructed to serve as defence in warfare and as military bases. In fact Shivaji's name is synonymous with forts, the hills of Maharashtra had offered him excellent sites. Every *taluka* under his possession was impregnated with forts.[122] Sites were selected carefully, for example, Raigad could be reached by one narrow steep and difficult footpath along an inaccessible cliff and one had to be extra careful. Valentia gives a description of the forts, he says,

> Each high side of the way forms a sheltering place, secure against all attacks from the top, whether of marquetry or their more usual weapons, large stones rolled down from above. The gateway and the parapets have the same effect. Had the whole been scalped off, and only a strong work at the top, I believe no earthly power could have taken it. [123]

Shivaji's forts were therefore defended by stone walls; the hillside was rendered more inaccessible by the usual thorny cactus which was a common feature.

In his earlier activities Shivaji realized the strategic importance of the hill forts and launched a movement to capture them as early as 1645. He first captured Torana, followed by Sinhgad, Purandar and Rajgad. Due to limited resources he had to seek the co-operation of nature in defending his territory. Thus, hill forts became of utmost importance to him.[124] Shivaji understood that these hill forts were centres of protection to his kingdom and could be used as a tool to achieve his goal of *Swarajya*. Most of the hill forts were located on the trade routes. The main purpose of the fort is to protect the political and economic interest of the area which falls under its sphere of influence. In the middle ages the old trade routes were converted into military routes. Consequently these hill forts played an important part in commanding the military routes as well.

For a fort to be rendered impregnable the commander had to ensure maximum storage of food and water supply, tanks had to be kept. Grose in his account says that Raigad was "large enough, independent of the stores accumulated there, to grow grain sufficient for the maintenance of its garrison, which, were it but a handful of men, could with pleasure defend it against the greatest that could be brought to take it."[125] Shivaji had perceived the advantage of these strongholds and therefore did not permit any person to build a fort. This precaution was not enough and hence Shivaji wanted to ensure that all forts must always be held in his own interests and should never be used against him. A cautious selection of the garrison was followed, each man must furnish a surety for his good faith before he could be enrolled.[126] Thus, one relied on trust and loyalty during this period. However, one could never be so sure of one's loyalty as a person is always subjected to betrayal, and therefore extra steps were taken by Shivaji, for example, no single officer was entrusted with the sole charge of the fort. He definitely laid down that the *Havaldar*, *Sabnis* and *Sarnobat* should be of the same status. These three should conjointly carry on the administration.[127] Capturing a fort required a breach in the walls by means of mines or cannonade and by escalating by means of rope ladders. They found another technique in which they tamed and trained the big monitor lizard or iguana called *Ghorpad* in Marathi and sent it to climb up the most difficult hillsides or ramparts with a rope around its body. It soon found a convenient cleft whereto it drove its nails and steadfastly clung and enabled a man to climb up the rope.[128]

B. Maratha Spy System

Shivaji's administrative strategy as well as the execution of his techniques depended on his spy agency. The Ramoshis and Mahars whose services were used for watch and ward duties in the village and fort administration had the potentiality of becoming good spies and messengers.[129] For example, Bahirji Naik was the Chief of his detective agency who played an important role in capturing the Torna fort. He brought all the details and planned a graph of the fort to make an attack on the same. Chhatrapati Shivaji modified his army and made an attack on the same forts and succeeded. During the battle of Pratapgarh he brought a lot of information against Afzal Khan like his height, family background, past, and also his food habits. They also brought information about Afzal Khan's cruel intentions towards Shivaji and details of his planning. Shivaji acted on this information and killed Afzal Khan and won against Adil Shahi Sultanate. Even during Shivaji's Surat sack, Bahirji

Naik was sent to the city as a folk singer to collect information. The information collected by him helped Shivaji in organizing a surprise raid on the city.[130]

To conclude, this chapter gives a detailed analysis of the art of diplomacy followed by the Marathas towards the Deccan Powers and the European Powers in Deccan. Their combat strategies and methods of deploying the art of warfare were effective in the 17th century, and they manoeuvred their enemies in the battlefields; however, by the 18th century the other powers learnt their military skills and soon the Marathas had to adopt new ways of warfare. This was when they employed French mercenaries in their armies. Forts in the 18th century could no longer be effective against the use of cannon balls and guns and thus, their method of warfare changed.

The 18th century was a period of Maratha ascendancy, the transformation of the state itself from the Chhatrapati to the Confederacy and the Barbhai state is a testimony of its resilient nature to the needs of the time. Their relation with the Europeans was based on alliances which were needed for the establishment of *Swarajya*. The Marathas were the only power which resisted the English till the end; thus by allying themselves with the other European powers they thought that they could turn the tables and fill the vacuum that was created in the balance of power.

Notes

1 *A Short Oxford English Dictionary*, Vol. I, Oxford, 1994, p. 514.
2 A.R. Kulkarni, *Ajnapatra*, Pune, Mansanman, 2003, p. 343.
3 Roving Englishman, *Embassies and Foreign Courts: A History of Diplomacy,* London, Routledge & Co., 1856, p. 32.
4 Pradeep Barua, "Military Developments in India 1750–1850", *Journal of the Royal Society of Arts*, Vol. 78, October 1994, No. 4049, pp. 604.
5 A.R. Kulkarni, *The Marathas*, Pune, Diamond Publication, 2008, p. 14.
6 A petty chieftain in South India especially in Karnataka occupying chief tracts of hills and forest, subject to pay tribute and service to the Nayak.
7 Kulkarni, *The Marathas*, p. 12.
8 Ibid., p. 13.
9 M.A. Nayeem, "Shivaji-The Integrationist of the Deccan", *National Seminar on "Chhatrapati Shivaji as a Nation Builder,* 8th–10th January 1975, p. 1.
10 Ibid., p. 2.
11 R.M. Betham, *Marathas and Dekhani Musalmans*, Calcutta, Superintendent of Government Printing, 1908, p. 21.
12 Nayeem, "Shivaji-The Integrationist of the Deccan", p. 5.
13 Kulkarni, *The Marathas,* p. 20.
14 G.S. Sardesai, *New History of the Marathas*, Vol. 2, Calcutta, The Asiatic Society, 1946, p. 252.
15 D.V. Kale, ed., *English Records on Shivaji*, Vol. 1, Poona, Shiva Charitra Karyalaya, 1931, pp. 48, 309.
16 Jadunath Sarkar, *Shivaji and His Times*, Calcutta, Orient Longman, 1929, p. 284.
17 Setu Madhav Rao Pagadi, "Maratha-Nizam Relations: Nizam-Ul-Mulk's Letters", *Annals of the Bhandarkar Oriental Research Institute,* Vol. 51, No. 1/4 (1970), p. 95.
18 Ibid., p. 103.

19 V.G. Dighe, "The Edlabad Meeting of the Peshwa and the Nizam", *Proceedings of the Indian History Congress,* Vol. 13 (1950), p. 326.
20 L.B. Bowring, *Haider Ali and Tipu Sultan and the Struggle with the Musalman Powers of the South*, New Delhi, Asian Educational Service, 1998, p. 30.
21 Ibid., p. 41.
22 Afzal Ahmad, *Indo-Portuguese Diplomacy During the 16th and the 17th Centuries*, Delhi, Originals, p. 93.
23 Owen C. Kail, "Dutch Commercial & Territorial Influence in India", *Journal of the Asiatic Society of Bombay* (henceforth JASB), Vol. 43–44 (1968–69), (new series), pp. 156–57.
24 U.A. Kadam, "French Maratha Relations: India in the 17th Century", pp. 4–7, https://www.researchgate.net/publication/236590084, accessed on 17 March, 09:30.
25 Alfred Martineau, ed., *Lettres et conventions des Gouverneurs de Pondicherry avec different Princes Hindous*, (1666–1793), Pondichéry, 1911–1914, pp. 263–64.
26 Afzal Ahmad, *Indo-Portuguese Diplomacy During the 16th and the 17th Centuries*, New Delhi, Gian Publishing House, 1991, p. 126.
27 B.S. Shastry, *Studies in Indo-Portuguese History*, Bangalore, IBH Prakashana, 1981, p. 111.
28 Ibid., p. 112.
29 P.S. Pissulenkar, *Portuguese Mahratta Relation*, Bombay, T.V Parvate, 1983, pp. 66–92.
30 Ahmad, *Indo-Portuguese Diplomacy During the 16th and the 17th Centuries*, p. 128.
31 Pissulenkar, *Portuguese Mahratta Relation*, pp. 80–89.
32 Shastry, *Studies in Indo-Portuguese History,* p. 113.
33 S.S. Desai, ed., *Marathiyanchya Itihasachi Sadhane—Portuguese Daftar* Vol. II, Bombay, 1974, p. 203.
34 Ibid.
35 Ibid.
36 Sardesai, G.S. ed., Shivaji Souvenir, 1927, p. 25.
37 Letter of Antonio Pais de Sande to Sambhaji dated 5 May 1680, *Reis Visinhos*, Book of Neighour Kings No. 1 and 2, p. 43.
38 Letter of Antonio Pais de Sande to Sambhaji Raje dated 4 June 1681, *Reis Visinhos*, Book of Neighour Kings No. 1 and 2.
39 Letter of Antonio Pais de Sande to Sambhaji dated 5 May 1680, *Reis Visinhos*, Book of Neighour Kings No. 1 and 2, p. 43. [Emphasis mine]
40 Letter of Antonio Pais de Sande to Sambhaji Raje dated 4 June 1681, *Reis Visinhos*, Book of Neighour Kings No. 1 and 2, p. 54.
41 Letter to Conde De Alvor to Adil Shah dated 26 November 1682, *Reis Visinhos*, NO. 2, p. 250.
42 Manucci, *Storia do Mongor*, Vol. II, London, Murray, p. 259, Abdul Hakim knew that the Portuguese of Goa were brave enough, so he advised Aurangzeb to be on friendly terms with the Portuguese. This would also restrict Sambhaji and he will have to fight two fronts: one in Dakhan and another one against the Portuguese. This would facilitate Aurangzeb to stop Sambhaji from all directions.
43 Letter of Viceroy to chief Captain, Manoel DeSouza Pereira, dated 20 January 1683.
44 *Livro das Moncoes*, No. 48, p. 181.
45 *Livro das Moncoes*, No. 54, p. 194.
46 *Livros dos Reis Visinhos,* No. 3, p. 18V.
47 Ibid., p. 24.

48 Rev. Alexander K. Nairne, *History of Konkan* (Reprint), New Delhi, Asian Educational Service, 1988, p. 78.
49 Luis Assis Correia, *Portuguese India, Mumbai-Chaul-Vasali*, Goa, The Golden Press, p. 425.
50 P.S.S. Pissurlencar, *Portuguese Maratha Relations*, Poona, Poona University, 1967, p. 66.
51 Ibid., p. 145.
52 F.C. Danvers, *The Portuguese In India*, vol. II, Calcutta, Asian Educational Service, 1992, pp. 411–13.
53 G.S. Sardesai, ed., *Selections from Peshwa Daftar*, Vol. II, ,Bombay Government Central Press, Bombay, 1930, pp. 16–17.
54 Ibid., p. 17.
55 G.H. Khare, ed., *Shjyacharltra Sahitya* XIII, Poona, BISM, 1965, pp. 23–24.
56 Ibid.
57 Ibid.
58 V.T. Gune, ed., *Bassein Campaign*, Pnaji, Government Printing Press, 1979, pp. 18–19.
59 Ibid., p. 17.
60 Ibid.
61 S.S. Desai, ed., *Marathyanchya Itihaaachi Sadhane Portuguese Oaftar* III, Maharashtra Rajya Sahityb Sanskriti Mandal, Bombay, 1968, p. 567.
62 Ibid., pp. 16–17.
63 Pissurlencar, *PortuqESE Marathe Sambandha*, p. 180.
64 S.K. Mhamai, *The Sawants of Wadi*, New Delhi, Concept Publishing House, 1984, p. 122.
65 Ibid.
66 Ibid.
67 Ibid., p. 124.
68 Ibid., p. 125.
69 Ibid., p. 131.
70 Bal Krishna, *Shivaji the Great,* Vol. 1, part 2, Bombay, Taraporevala Sons, 1932, pp. 474–75.
71 Kulkarni, *The Marathas,* p. 35.
72 Ibid., p. 41.
73 W.Ph. Coolhas, *Generale Missiven Van Gouverneurs-Generaal en Raden aan Heren XVII derVerenigde Oostindische Compagnie,* (1655–1674), Vol. III, February 1672, The Hague, Martinus Nijhoff, 1968, p. 819.
74 Ishrat Alam, "The Dutch East India Company Trade at Vengurla in the Seventeenth Century", *Proceedings of Indian History Congress*, Vol. 64 (2003), p. 655.
75 *Generale Missiven*, Vol. IV, November 1676, p. 150.
76 *Pieter van Dam's Beschryvinge vande Oostindische Compagnie*, Vol. 2, part 2, pp. 113–14, also in *Corpus Diplomaticum Neerlando Indicum*, Vol. 3, pp. 61–65.
77 J.E. Heeres, *Corpus diplomaticum Neerlando-Indicum*, Vol. 3, Koninklijk Instituut voor Taal-, Land- en Volkenkunde , 1907-1955 pp. 126–27.
78 Nikhil Bellarykar, "Dutch-Maratha Relations and the Porto-Novo Affair, 1678–1680", Quarterly of the *Bharat Itihas Sanshodhan Mandal*, Vol. 1–4, 57–71, Pune (June 2015–April 2016), p. 58.
79 T.T. Mahajan, *Shivaji and His Diplomats*, New Delhi, Commonwealth Publishers, 1997, p. 63.
80 *Generale Missieven*, Vol. V, 28 December 1681, p. 487. also see Sinnappah Arasaratnam, *Merchants, Companies and Coromandel On the Coromandel Coast 1650–1740*, OUP, New Delhi, 1987, p. 78.

81 Ibid., pp. 446–50.
82 Sir Jadunath Sarkar has left the question of the date of the fall of the fortress open. Thus he gives a note on the dates embodied in his sources of information: History of Aurangzeb, Vol. V, p. 108, explicitly says that Jinji was captured on 6th Shaban, 41st of Aurangzib (7 February 1698). This date cannot be accepted in the light of contemporary Madras records which refer to the capture of Gingee even early in January 1698. Scott in History of Deccan, Vol. 2, has given the date 1700 A.D. (A.H. 1112) for the capture of the fort. Cited in, History of Gingee, p. 344. Sarkar has also quoted the authority of the Diary and Consultation Book of Fort St. George, where there is an entry dated 2nd January (O.S. 1698) or 12th January (N.S. 1698), which says that information had been received that all but one of the fortresses of Gingee had fallen to Zulfikar Khan. It records a letter received from Amir Jahan from the Mughal camp which says "that the Nawab had taken all the forts except one which also doth offer to capitulate" (Diary and Consultation Book, 1697, p. 152).
83 *Press list of ancient Dutch Records 1657–1825.Catalogue,* No. 282, in Supplementary Catalogue of Dutch Records, Madras Record Office, Madras, 1952.
84 J. Frederick Price and K. Rangachari, eds., *The Private Diary of Ananda Ranga Pillai, 1736–1761,* Vol. 2, Madras, 1904, p. 126.
85 Ibid., Vol. 1, pp. 141–44.
86 B. Bhattacharya, "Porto Novo and Shipping in the Bay of Bengal in the Mid-18th Century", in *International Conference on Shipping, Factories and Colonisation*, ed. by J. Everaert and J. Paramentier, Brussels, 1996, pp. 103–18, p. 106.
87 Kadam Umesh, "Fragments of Maratha History, Luso-Dutch Presence in the Deccan", 2013, pp. 9–10. https://www.researchgate.net/publication/236590147, accessed on 17 March, 09:30.
88 Kadam, "French Maratha Relations: India in the 17th Century.".
89 V.S. Kadam, "The Foreign Policy of Shivaji the Great", *National Seminar on "Chhatrapati Shivaji as a Nation Builder,* 8th–10th January 1975, p. 3.
90 Paul Kaeplin, *La compagnie des Inde Oriental et Francois Martin*, Paris, 1908, pp. 83–84.
91 Kadam, "French Maratha Relations: India in the 17th Century."
92 Lotika Varadarajan, ed., *India in the 17th Century (Social, Economic and Political) Memoirs of Francois Martin* (1670–1690), Vol. 1, part 2, South Asia Books, 1983, p. 573.
93 Ibid., p. 601.
94 Ibid., pp. 593–95.
95 U.A. Kadam, *History of the Marathas (French-Maratha Relations) (1668–1818*), Delhi, Sundeep Prakashan, 2008, p. 72.
96 Burhan Ibn Hasan, *Tuzuk-I-Walajahi tr by Muhammad Hussain Nainar*, Madras University, 1939, p. 53.
97 Dupleix's Memoire, India Office Records, *The French in India*, Vol. 1, 1664–1810, Unpublished.
98 Ibid., p. 85.
99 K.S. Mathew, *French in India and Indian Nationalism (1700 A.D–1963 A.D)*, Vol. I, New Delhi, B.R Publishing Corporations, 1999, p. 25.
100 Ibid., p. 26.
101 Kadam, *History of the Marathas*, p. 90.
102 V.G. Hatalkar, trans, and ed., *French Records: Relating to the History of Marathas,* Vol. VIII, Bombay, 1985, p. 426.
103 Kadam, *History of the Marathas*, p. 96.

104 S.P. Sen, *French in India, 1763–1818*, University of Calcutta, Calcutta, 1971, p. 35.
105 Kadam, *History of the Marathas*, p. 133.
106 Ibid., p. 142.
107 A turban ornament worn by significant Hindu and Muslim prince.
108 Kadam, *History of the Marathas*, p. 144.
109 Ibid., p. 150.
110 V.G. Hatalkar, *Relation between the French and Marathas, 1668–1815*, Bombay, T.V Chidambaram, 1958, p. 185.
111 Kadam, *History of the Marathas,* p. 182.
112 E. Gaudart, "Catalogue Des Manuscrits des Anciennes Archives de L'Inde Française", *Tome II*, 1927, pp. 216 and 224.
113 Stewart Gordon, *The Marathas, 1600–1818,* New Delhi, Cambridge University Press, 1993, p. 41.
114 Jayanta Kumar Ray, *Aspects of India's International Relations, 1700 to 2000: South Asia and the World*, Pearson Education India, New Delhi, 2007, p. 378.
115 Raj Kumar, *Maratha Military Systems*, Delhi, Commonwealth Publishers, 2004, p. 91.
116 Ibid., p. 90.
117 Surendranath Sen, *Military System of the Marathas*, Calcutta, the Book Company Ltd., 1928, p. 77.
118 Ram Krishna Tandon, *European Adventurers and Changes in the Indian Military System*, in *Responding to the West: Essays on Colonial Domination and Asian Agency,* Amsterdam University Press, Amsterdam, 2009, p. 37.
119 Sen, *Military System of the Marathas*, p. 96.
120 Pradeep Barua, "Military Developments in India, 1750–1850", *The Journal of Military History*, Vol. 58, October 1994, p. 605.
121 Jadunath Sarkar, *Shivaji and His Times,* Calcutta, S.C Sarkar and Sons Ltd., 1984, p. 5.
122 S.N. Sen, *Military System of the Marathas*, p. 79.
123 Valentia, *Voyages and Travels to India, Ceylon, and the Red Sea, Abyssinia and Egypt*, Vol. II, Cleveland, W. Bulmer & Co., 1809, p. 169.
124 J.N. Kamalapur, *The Deccan Forts*, p. 35.
125 Grose, *A Voyage to the East Indies*, London, S. Hooper, 1772, p. 137.
126 Sen, *Military System of the Marathas*, p. 81.
127 Sen, *Siva Chhatrapati*, University of Calcutta, 1920, p. 29.
128 Sen, *Military System of the Marathas*, p. 86.
129 M.R. Kantak, "The Political Role of Different Hindu Castes and Communities in Maharashtra in the Foundation of Shivaji's Swarajya", *Bulletin of the Deccan College Research Institute,* Vol. 38, 1978–79, p. 44.
130 Vijay K. Seth, *Ascent and Decline of Native and Colonial Trading: Tale of Four Indian Cities*, SAGE Publications India, , New Delhi, 2008.

2 Maritime Frontiers—Challenges, Conflicts and Collaborations

Establishing Sovereignty at Sea

India's connection with maritime practice dates back to the ancient past. Archaeological discoveries made in Gujarat have established that India was a seafaring nation 5000 years ago. From the days of the Indus Valley Civilization, the eastern coastline was dotted with a number of ports. A number of Indus valley seals and terracotta artefacts depict a craft with a mast and a yard in the background, indicating the existence of seagoing vessels. Allan Villiers a well-known explorer regards the Indian Ocean as the birthplace of sailing in the world.

Thus, maritime trade was recognized in earlier times. Lothal dock is the earliest archaeological evidence of marine activity in India; it was built by Harappans at the head of the Gulf of Cambay on Gujarat coast not later than 2300 B.C. Indians and Arabs collaborated in the development of navigation. The Arabs acted as intermediaries in Indian trade with the neighbouring countries and then with Europe. At the time of the advent of the Portuguese, Indian rulers had their own interests, and their interests in sea were minimized. The only semblance of a centralized state in the south was that of the Vijayanagar Empire. On the west coast the zamorins of Calicut and on the south eastern coast the Cholas wielded great naval influence.

However, in the 15th century, the Portuguese arrived in India and claimed sovereignty over Indian waters and monopoly of trade in certain commodities. They changed the structure of Indian trade to a great extent. This chapter looks into the relation between the Europeans and the indigenous powers such as the Zamorins, Mughals and Marathas. The years leading to the rise of the Mughals was a period of transition in the Indian Ocean. The period had been dominated by South Indian naval powers, most notably the Chola Empire based in Tamil Nadu and the kingdom of Vijayanagar. They came as close as any medieval South Asian states to achieving an Atlantic-style command of the Ocean. Their fleets controlled commerce and suppressed piracy throughout south and southeast Asia. A number of minor states and merchant coalitions based in Arabia and Indonesia as well as India competed for the Indian Ocean trade.[1]

The idea of sea power was born when the sea was found useful as a means of transport or communication. According to B.K Apte, "*Navalism*"

DOI: 10.4324/9781003377511-2

originated among the Marathas for the control of sea, i.e. to check their neighbouring enemy who not only carried fire and sword along their coast but also hampered their trade.[2] The time when Shivaji was trying to establish his military and political authority over the Konkan Coast, he came across the maritime powers embedded at several places on the west coast. He was smart enough to understand the root of their success and domination. Therefore he decided to establish his own navy. Shivaji had realized the importance of controlling the waters of Konkan coast, and this is especially remarkable because it was during this time that the European powers were establishing their sovereignty over the sea. Shivaji chose to stand in resistance to these powers when the Mughals were opening their ports and markets to these foreign powers. The Mughals and even the Adil Shahis did not pay much attention to the establishment of naval organization as they did not come directly in control with these outsiders. He was fully convinced that he who possessed a navy ruled the sea. The foreigners therefore could refer to the Maratha fleet as Shivaji Armada in their official correspondence.[3]

The Naval Policy of the Mughals: Alliance with the Siddis

The Mughals were a land-based power, and one can argue that they did not have much vested interests in maritime occupation. It is true that their navy was no match to that of the Portuguese or the rulers of Indian Maritime states like those of the zamorins of Calicut, the Cholas of Coromandel or even the Maratha fleet. Their navigation was mostly riverine, but they also built ships capable of carrying over 500 soldiers and were mounted with guns. They fought many naval battles on the mouths of the Ganga and some of the ships ventured over the seas.[4]

There are two early references to the naval expeditions of Babur, one in 1528 when he fought a naval battle with the Rajputs on the Ganga near Kanauj and the other with the Afghans of eastern provinces on Gogra when the enemy offered a naval encounter with 150 boats. He crossed the Yamuna in March 1529 with 420 boats. Babur writes,

> A favorable wind having sprung up and flowing down the river, they hoisted the sails of a Bengali boat and made her tow the large vessel which went very quick… I embarked and sailed a little way up the river and then returning again crossed over the north side of the Ganges and brought the boats close to the bank.[5]

Akbar's desire to be a *Chakravartin*[6] prompted him to be ambitious so as to pave his way into the Deccan. The other factor was the Portuguese control over the seas which exasperated him. Therefore, by 1596 Akbar had annexed Berar, and in 1601 Khandesh, Ahmednagar too was formally annexed. Vincent Smith argues that the Mughals never showed any interest towards maritime affairs and therefore did not possess a fleet worth mentioning.[7] However, Abul Fazl says,

> In every part of His Majesty's empire, ships are numerous; but in Bengal, Kashmir and Thathah (Sind) they are the pivot of all commerce. His Majesty had the sterns of the boats made in shape of wonderful animals, and thus combines terror with amusements. Turrets and pleasing kiosks, markets and beautiful beds, have likewise been constructed on the rivers. Along the coast of the ocean, in the west, east and south of India large ships are built, which are suitable for voyages. The Harbors have been put into excellent condition, and the experience of seamen has much improved. Large ships are also built at Allahabad and Lahore, and are then sent to the coast.[8]

The first true salt water navy was assembled by Akbar; he provided the fleets area of operation, and this gave a coherent structure to the navy. The *Ain-i-Akbari* identifies four primary objectives: the maintenance of a fleet for both transport and combat, the retention of a corps of skilled seamen, the protection of civilian commerce and the enforcement of tolls and tariffs. The overall organization of the navy closely resembled that of the Mughal army. It was divided into two primary units—a western fleet based in Gujarat and an Eastern fleet based in Bengal. As the Empire further extended south it came into contact with other seafaring states Tamil Nadu and Kerala. The trade networks based in these areas extended from Africa, the Red Sea and the Persian Gulf in the west to Indonesia in the East linking India's economy with Europe, the Mediterranean and China.[9]

During the reign of Aurangzeb, Niccolo Manucci had presented him with the latest ship design; he says,

> This order was taken to my countrymen ... who made a small ship with its sails and riggings, guns and flags. When it was ready it was launched on a great tank. The King and all the court assembled to behold ... The European artillerymen accustomed to navigation went aboard the vessel and caused it to move in all directions by adjusting the sails and working the helm with great dexterity and cleverness. Then as if engaging some other man-of-war, they discharged the cannon, turning in all directions.[10]

The Siddis of Janjira (the Admirals of the Mughal Navy) rose to very high positions during the reign of Aurangzeb; after the partition treaty of 1636, the west coast became part of Bijapur which recognized the Siddi chief and conferred on him the title of *Wazir*. The Siddis maintained an efficient naval fleet. Throughout the 17th century he held the position of an admiral, first of the Bijapur Sultanate and later of the Mughal Navy. Jadunath Sarkar opines that "The Abyssinians were hardy, skillful and daring mariners and most efficient fighters at sea among the Muslim races, while their courage and energy, joined to coolness and power of command made them enjoy a high estimation as soldiers and administrators."[11] He was very keen on building a strong naval base so that ships of *haj* pilgrims going annually to Mecca are not molested or detained.[12] Aurangzeb sanctioned an annual grant of four lakh rupees to be paid to the Siddis for the maintenance of his fleet.

The Siddis had made the island fortress of Janjira 26 miles south of Bombay their stronghold. This stronghold was a threat to the Marathas. The fall of Rajgadh in 1689 and the disintegration of the Maratha State following the death of Chhatrapati Sambhaji considerably strengthened the hands of the Siddis who occasionally became bold enough to lead raids up the Ghats.[13] They even managed to take possession of the important fortresses of Raigad, Madangadh and Anjanwel. The Siddis even managed to alarm the English when they blockaded Bombay which was their strong base.

However, the Mughals left the responsibility of the sea in the hands of the Siddis, therefore losing out on vast opportunities of overseas trade. The Mughals instead of focusing on "command of the seas" established "command of the coast," and the emphasis was on littoral and riverine warfare. The Mughals focused on points of lines, controlling ports, fortresses and other strategic locations instead of patrolling the open sea.[14]

Development, Domination and Decline: An Overview of the Trajectory of Maratha Naval Power

The Deccan campaign of the Mughal Empire for outright annexation started in the mid-17th century. This was visible in the Mughal policies towards Bijapur, the most powerful southern state from 1657. Bidar, an important fort was lost to the Mughal Empire.[15] The decline in the authority of the Bijapur and the retreat of the Mughals from Deccan created an excellent opportunity for Shivaji to expand his sphere of influence in the Deccan. He thus started his expansion in the north Konkan region. Kalyan, Bhivandi, Mahuli, some parts of Thana, Kolaba, Raigad, Kangori, Sudhagad, Ghosalgad, Tala, Birwadi and Surgad were made part of the Maratha state by Shivaji. Shivaji had complete authority over the entire north Konkan by 1659 excluding the areas controlled by the Siddis, the Bijapur court and the Portuguese. The regions south of Konkan such as Dabhol, Rajapur, Pallivana, and Shrinagarpur were brought under the folds of the Maratha territory between 1661 and 1663, but the Marathas lost Kalyan and it remained under Mughal control for nine years.[16] This was the time when Shivaji mooted the idea of building a navy for the state which had an entire coastal strip under its belt.[17] By the 1660s, Shivaji had already built a small state navy, and their initial target was Basrur in south Kanara, which was attacked in 1665.[18] However, this conflict did not witness any naval engagements. The sources mention that Shivaji attacked Basrur with 85 big and small ships[19] and collected huge booty from there. Kulkarni mentions that the first known naval expedition of Shivaji was in 1664. He attacked Basrur which was the chief port of Bidnur Chief Shivappa Nayak of Karnataka. This was the time when Shivaji had already established himself as the major power in the land of the region, so the other powers carefully watched his movements in the sea.

This naval expedition of the Marathas under Shivaji was quite important in the sense that it was for the first time that King himself was leading the "*Armada*," and it made Shivaji aware of the importance of having a naval force for the state which had under its control coastal areas from Kolaba to Bhatakal. Shivaji also became aware of the different aspects associated with the navy such as the importance of having marine forts, techniques of naval warfare and other associated facts. This expedition helped Shivaji in understanding the importance of coastal ports and the geography of the coastal region.[20] James Douglas in his book says that "It was great mercy that Shivaji was not a sea-man, otherwise he might have swept the sea as he did the land … He liked the sea but sea did not like him."[21]

Gradually the centre of power of the Martha navy was shifted to Kanhoji Angre, who not only had great skills and powers in executing the navy but showed the superiority of Marathas on the Konkan waters. For defeating the foreign invaders, he improved the facilities in the navy like training his people with different skills and efficiency, introducing strict discipline and maintaining the standard administration policy of the navy. With the help of naval force, he fought those enemies. For this, his policy, management and skill of battle are very important. Kanhoji Angre was well aware of the Konkan coast. Chhatrapati Rajaram Maharaj has offered him the post of "*Sarkhel.*" He was honoured with the chief of the navy by Chhatrapati Rajaram Maharaj. He devoted his whole life to fight against the British, Portuguese, Dutch and Siddi. He got victory in many battles with these foreign enemies. Therefore, he is recognized as an immortal and the great and brave admiral.

Shivaji's main conflict in the seas was with the Siddis who could not be defeated by either Shivaji or Sambhaji. Shivaji did not achieve any major naval war and important strongholds of Siddis like Murad Janjira or Danda Rajapuri, which could not be made part of the Maratha state. But his struggle and conflict against Siddis' island fort is an important maritime event of that time. Shivaji's forces defeated the Siddis in the land war and also occupied Danda Rajapuri for a brief period of time, but they again lost it to the Siddis in February 1671.[22] Shivaji tried many times to win over Janjira and it remained unaccomplished.[23] Shivaji won an important naval battle in 1679 when his navy defeated the British and took control over Kanderi. The control over Kanderi was strategically important for the Marathas because by controlling it they could check the movements of the Siddis near

Bombay. The Siddis often used to come to Bombay with the permission of the English, which was now checked by the Marathas.[24]

As far as the career of Sambhaji is concerned, it was short but eventful. The navy under Sambhaji comprised 50 Gurabs and 120 Galbats, and their prime task was to curb the menace of the Siddis in the region. However, as mentioned earlier, their campaigns against the Siddis did not achieve the desired success. Sambhaji also renewed hostility with the English and the Portuguese as a result of their continued support to the Siddis. The question of retention and the occupation of Kanderi and Underi became the source of renewed conflict of the Marathas under Sambhaji with the Siddis. Sambhaji could not achieve success in his attack against Underi. The Marathas' fleet of 30 ships under Sambhaji also attacked Mazgaon in 1682 but did not succeed because the Siddis were waiting for this opportunity. The Marathas had to suffer heavy losses because the Siddis captured flagship and other ships of the Marathas. Faced with the defeat, Sambhaji planned fortification of the island of the Elephanta but later on changed his design and started negotiating with the English. However, the Marathas did not achieve the desired result.[25] The Marathas again attempted to defeat the Siddis in 1682, and it lasted from January to August. The island fort was not conquered, and a couple of months later the Maratha navy had to suffer a huge defeat in a naval conflict.[26]

As far as the history of Maratha navy is concerned, the contribution of the house of Angrias is immense. The first in the house of Angrias, Kanhoji Angre was one of the great seamen of his time both among the foreigners and Indians. When compared with the foreigners, there was only one shortcoming, i.e. the lack of scientific knowledge in Kanhoji Angre about the sea. Kanhoji was hardly concerned with getting himself updated with the scientific acumen such as nautical matters, manufacture of guns and other scientific development required for sea. He was neither interested in transcontinental voyages nor in the development of marine mercantile to cater to the needs of navy. Nevertheless, as far as courage, knowledge of naval warfare and organizational skill of the navy are concerned, there was hardly any other seaman of that calibre.[27] Kanhoji's early career is not available in the sources, but it is said that his rise was during the reign of Chhatrapati Sambhaji. Kanhoji Angre assisted most of the officers of Sambhaji in the seawaters of the Konkan. However, with the defeat of the Marathas against the Mughals, and the subsequent death of Sambhaji, Kanhoji defended the coast against Mughals and the Siddis. During the tenure of Rajaram, Kanhoji Angre was given the title of "*Sarkhel*" as a mark of his exemplary service.[28] Some scholars believe that Tarabai gave the title of "*Sarkhel*," but it seems far from being true because she could not give the title when Rajaram was still alive.[29] However, in one of the letters that was written by him in 1699, he named himself as "*Sarkhel.*"[30]

The release of Shahu created confusion in the minds of Kanhoji Angre as the entire nobility was divided between Tarabai and Shahu. However,

Kanhoji Angre chose to support Tarabai as Shahu was new to him. Kanhoji as the able and loyal commander of Tarabai had control over Dhanagad, Tunga-Tikona and Rajmachi and had threatened to advance towards Satara and Poona. The only option left before Shahu was to use the wisdom and political acumen of the newly appointed Peshwa Balaji Vishwanath Bhatt. Balaji Vishwanath Bhatt and Kanhoji Angre knew each other for many years. Balaji never believed in using military might as far as possible and through a series of negotiations, Balaji could win over Kanhoji Angre to the side of Shahu. This was one of the biggest achievements of Shahu and Balaji Vishwanath. It was a mutually beneficial alliance as the Marathas under Shahu got the support of Kanhoji Angre, and on the other hand, Kanhoji got the support of the biggest land power in the Konkan, which made the coasts safer. The treaty that was signed between Kanhoji and Balaji Vishwanath awarded 16 land forts and 10 sea forts to the former. He was also awarded the office of the "*Sarkhel*" upon accepting the over lordship of the Chhatrapati Shahu. Shahu also decided to initiate war against his opponents in the north Konkan region. This treaty helped the Marathas, who got in Angrias an important ally, to look after the development in seawaters.[31]

Jaysing Angria alias Sekhoji became the "*Sarkhel*" of the Martha navy after the death of his father. Peshwa awarded him with the Khillat of Sarkhelship at Alibag. It was not an easy task for Sekhoji as he had to maintain respect of his position and the contribution of his great father.[32] Sekhoji had a huge task in front of him at the beginning of his career as the English had formed an alliance with Savants of Wadi and, later on, they formed another alliance with Siddis of Janjira against him. The English were determined to crush the powers of Angrias and hence of the Marathas as they could not do this when Kanhoji was alive.[33] In retaliation, the Angrias captured the English ships, but it was handed over when the situation became normal.

Sekhoji helped the Marathas in their campaign against the Siddis in 1733. This was the campaign in which the English openly sided with the Siddis. The Mughals were appealed to by the English to help the Siddis in their struggle against the Marathas so that they can safeguard their western frontier. The Portuguese also helped the English and the Siddis and sent two ships on the pretext of mediation. However, this conflict proved to have benefited the Marathas a lot, as they defeated the combined force of the Mughals, the English and the Siddis. The Siddis surrendered all their important ports except Janjira and Ajanwel. So, the dream of the Marathas of defeating the Siddis was accomplished with the help of the Angrias during the rule of Chhatrapati Shahu. The Angrias during the reign of Sekhoji were also successful in solving their household problems. He was successful in mediating the rival brothers Manaji and Sambhaji. However, the premature death of Sekhoji was a big blow to both the Marathas and the House of the Angrias.[34]

The rivalry between the two brothers was sorted out through the timely interference and mediation of Peshwa in 1735, and an accord was signed between Sambhaji and Manaji. By this accord entire Kolaba was divided with Kolaba as the headquarter of Manaji and Suvarnadurga as the headquarter of Sambhaji. Sambhaji got the Sarkhelship while Manaji was conferred with the title of "*Vajarat-mab.*" However, this treaty was shortlived, as Sambhaji attacked Manaji's territory in 1740. Manaji Angria had the support of the Peshwa against his brother Sambhaji. Manaji had helped the Peshwa in their fight against the Portuguese in the Bassein campaign.[35] Manaji also benefited from this campaign as he got control over the island of Karanja. This was the beginning of the conflict between the Angrias and the Marathas. However, after the conquest of Bassein, the Peshwa became the masters of the Konkan.[36] In 1744, Bhairavgad fort belonging to Manaji was taken over by Peshwa's men, and in retaliation, three gurabs and 30 galbats were dispatched by Manaji to impede Peshwa's armada in Bassein.[37]

Tulaji Angria became "*Sarkhel*" of the Martha navy after the death of his brother Sambhaji. His headquarter was located in Vijaydurg. The rebel faction of Anjanwel was also brought under the administrative control of Tulaji.[38] It was one of the greatest victories of Tulaji in the Konkan, and the fort was renamed Gopalgad. Till mid-18th century, Tulaji was one of the most feared and tough administrators in the west coast region. Every ship that was passing through that region had to purchase a pass from them. Many ships belonging to European powers were blocked from sailing. Ships such as Phate Daulat of Muscat, the Benjinmali of Malabar, the Ann, the rose of Mangalore, the Augusta, the Pilot, etc. were taken over by Tulaji. But it was one of the political blunders on the part of the Peshwa that with the help of the English, they defeated Tulaji in the battle of Vidyudurga in 1756, and he was taken a prisoner for the rest of his life.

The consequent defeat of Tulaji at the hands of combined forces of the English and the Peshwa in 1755 and 1756 resulted in a glorious era of Martha navy in the Konkan. This end of Maratha navy led to the rise of the establishment of the base of the English on the west coast of India. However, some of the scholars have argued that one of the important reasons for the dispassionate relationship between Tulaji and the Peshwa was feudal tendencies within the Marathas. The entire coastal strip was divided between different Maratha nobles. The wielding authority was the Chhatrapati who also had an interest in the Konkan region. These nobles often benefitted at the cost of each other, and the mediating agency was the *daftar* of the Peshwa who also demanded a certain share. This was the case when he demanded his share and when he mediated between Sambhaji and Manaji, but it did not erode the prevailing feudal tendencies within the Marathas. The issues became more complicated with the death of Tulaji. His death brought about an inevitable destruction of the Maratha navy. It also led to the disintegration of the Marathas as a maritime power, who were now considered a mere maritime community. Tulaji's territory was taken over by Peshwa and was redistributed among the Maratha nobles.

After Manaji, Raghuji Angria succeeded and started ruling from Kolaba. Underi was wrested from the Siddis in 1760 by the joint naval expedition of the Marathas and Raghuji. Raghuji helped the Marathas in numerous ways. He was the last important admiral from the house of the Angrias, as Maratha navy had by this time become a mere myth.

Conflict, Rivalry and Cooperation: Lusso-Maratha Relation

The relationship between Shivaji and the English was not cordial. In 1660 the first conflict had taken place between them.[39] Shivaji was successful in neutralizing the threat which arose from the Rajapur factory. It was the Rajapur factory that was helping the Siddis against him. Shivaji took the treasures and also captured their soldiers.[40] The English were asked to pay the full amount in lieu of their soldiers who were held captive. Also, they were asked to help the Marathas capture Danda-Rajpuri, which turned out to be a false promise.[41] This created a rift between the English and the Marathas. The other strategic area which became a bone of contention between the English and the Marathas was the question of Khanderi. Khanderi was strategically located because having control over Khanderi meant getting easy access to the port of Bombay. This could pose a threat to the English in this region. The English opposed this move by the Marathas, but they did not get much success in this.

On the other hand, the relationship between the Marathas and the Portuguese was good in comparison to the English. The Portuguese considered the Marathas an equal power.[42] The naval conflict of the Marathas with the Portuguese and the English indicates the fact that the Maratha navy under Shivaji became a formidable power and threat at sea.

Shivaji's successor Sambhaji was not on good terms with his European counterparts. In 1682, Maratha naval admirals captured the Portuguese merchant ships. The Marathas befriended the Arabs and they were admitted to his services; they were also bitter rivals of the Portuguese. The alliance between the Marathas and the Arabs, who were seeking lost glory, became a major threat to Portuguese. The combined naval force of the Arabs and the Marathas attacked Portuguese ships plying in the region and the booty was divided between them. These episodes worsened the relationship between the Marathas and the Portuguese. The reaction was the attack and capture of Maratha ships. Sambhaji's relation with Mughals also worsened, and the focus of the Marathas shifted from the Portuguese.[43]

The hostility between the Marathas and the Mughals ended with the withdrawal of the last Mughal forces from Konkan in 1683, thus giving rise to conflict with the Portuguese. The Marathas raided the northern territories in April 1683. Marathas received heavy casualties at Tarapur and faced a tough challenge from the Portuguese. Marathas under the leadership of Sambhaji attacked Cheul, and after the decisive battle of Phonda, Goa was invaded.[44] All these battles were land battles. The two most important achievements of the Marathas in these battles were the occupation of Karanja and St. Estevas. Most of the naval conflicts between the Portuguese and the Marathas have not been recorded. All this conflict led to the signing of a mutual non-aggression treaty at sea between these two parties in 1684. This treaty re-established equal rights of Marathas vis-à-vis the Portuguese at sea.[45]

Kanhoji Angre led the Maratha navy to new heights during his Sarkhelship and fought bravely with his European counterparts. Kolaba was made the headquarters or admiralty's chief station, and this made the English unhappy. The English authorities became restless with the passing of the island of Khanderi under Maratha command. The sailing time between Bombay to Khanderi and Kolaba was a couple of hours in a favourable wind. The control over Khanderi meant that it was easy to keep an eye on European vessels moving towards Bombay. The control over these regions by Kanhoji Angre was a constant threat to English trade and commerce operating from Bombay.

The English befriended the enemies of Kanhoji Angre to counter the growing threat of the Marathas in the region because it was impossible to neutralize the threat. One important aspect of this policy was that they made an alliance with the Siddis, and it provided them all possible help to use to counter Angrias.[46] The English authorities allowed their friends to ply their ships with English flags even without a pass, but this was not acceptable to Kanhoji Angre. On the other hand, Kanhoji made it very clear to the authorities that beyond a point he would negotiate with the vessels according to his own will. In this context, any understanding or treaty was bound to fail even at the slightest imbalance of power.

The first major conflict between Angria and the English started in 1702 with the capture of an English ship which was plying on the sea, and they did not have a cartaz which was now issued by the Marathas. Four years later the Marathas under the leadership of Angrias captured three English ships which also had guns mounted on them. Marathas captured another yacht of the governor of Bombay in 1712. These conflicts concluded with the signing of a peace treaty between the Marathas and the English which brought temporary peace to the region. The peace settlement had the following clause; the English ships and crew which were captured by the Angrias were to be returned; the Angrias also promised not to harass any English ships plying in the region; the Angrias were asked not to harass any European ships coming towards the English port, i.e. the region between Khanderi and Mahim; and Kanohi was also requested to allow all those ships to enter into Maratha waters with Maratha passport. On the other hand, the English also promised that they would not allow their flags to be used on any other vessels except for the English. The English allowed Kanhoji to trade from Bombay on the payment of regular customs duties.[47]

Thus as far as controlling the sea waters is concerned, the earlier practice changes through these clauses.

The two English ships seized by Kanhoji Angre were returned in accordance with the treaty. However, the peace did not last long. This is indicated by the communication between Kanhoji and Governor Boon and how the governor was unsuccessfully trying to implicate and punish Kanhoji Angre. In retaliation, the ship named "Success" belonging to Govardhandas, an ally of the English, was captured by Kanhoji in 1717. Even when the negotiations were going on, Kanhoji captured another ship named Robert. He refused to release the ships and stated that Moors owned them. Kanhoji was very firm and clear in interpreting things even if there was the slightest of clarity. Within a few months, Kanhoji seized another English ship named Otter. In retaliation and frustration, the English captured *shibar* belonging to Kanhoji Angre. The English declared war on the Marathas in June 1718.[48] A naval expedition was carried out by the English to places like Gheria, Kolaba and Kahander, but it had little success.[49] An English ship Charlotte was lost to Kanhoji in 1720, but in 1721 they made an alliance against the Portuguese, their common enemy. The joint attack was a complete failure.[50] Over the years, his prestige increased, and he continued to be a threat to the English and their ships. The last few years of his life were spent in peace.

The relation of Kanhoji Angre with the Portuguese can be traced on similar lines. The Portuguese were greatly disturbed by the lawlessness of the Siddis. On the other hand, Kanhoji was also disturbed by the activities of Siddis who were the allies of the English. The disturbances caused by the Siddis were common ground for the coming together of both the Portuguese and the Angrias. The alliance between Angrias and the Portuguese was formed in 1701 against the Siddis. This alliance was kept a secret because on the one hand Siddis were working for the Mughals and on the other hand the Portuguese never wanted to start their hostility with the Mughals. The hostility with the Mughals would have affected the Portuguese trade and commerce in the region. The alliance between the Angrias and the Portuguese existed until 1708. However, this alliance did not last long as the Mughals attacked the Marathas and, in return, Kanhoji started seizing the Portuguese ships.

The breakdown of the alliance led to constant warfare between these two powers till 1722. Some Portuguese ships were captured by Kanhoji in 1708. Against this act the Portuguese marched up to Cheul, but they were defeated very badly by a large number of Maratha forces, 2000 against 400 of their own. Kanhoji fought two manchuas-of-war belonging to the Portuguese fleet of the north. He burnt one and captured another with 27 Portuguese.[51] They were all put to the sword, according to a Portuguese official account, except one captain who purchased his life and liberty by paying a ransom of 12,000 *Xerafins*. Many merchantmen sailing under Portuguese colours shared the same fate and contributed to Kanhoji's coffers.[52] Again in 1712 the Portuguese flagship was captured by the Marathas. But in the next two wars against the Portuguese at Cheul in 1713 and at Karwar in 1718, the Angrias were defeated very badly and suffered huge losses.[53] The Angrias attacked one ship at a time, and at times groups of ships together when their chances were high. They tried to avoid open sea fights with the Portuguese. As far as naval conflict with the Portuguese is concerned, it is more often that Marathas under Angrias suffered defeat. Nevertheless, on land, the Angrias proved their mastery and superiority even against the combined forces of the Marathas and the Portuguese. The Angrias neutralized the threat that was emerging out of the combined attack of the forces of the English and the Portuguese on Vijaydurg and Kolaba in 1720. These combined forces once again threatened Maratha territory in 1721. The combined forces reached Kolaba and tried to enter the fort by erecting batteries. Timely help was given by Shahu who sent a contingent of 6000 mounted soldiers under the command of Bajirao I to aid the Angrias. Fearing defeat against the mighty forces, a peace treaty was concluded with Bajirao I on 12 January 1722 by the Portuguese.[54]

Kanhoji's successor Sekhoji Angria tried to deal with the Europeans in a similar manner as his predecessors did. However, one important development took place, the English formed two major alliances against him, first with the Sawants of Wadi and second with Siddis of Janjira.[55] The English were not willing to leave any opportunity to defeat the Angrias. They wanted to achieve the feat of defeating the Angrias, which they were unsuccessful in doing during the reign of Kanhoji Angre. To avoid conflict Sekhoji Angria released the captured English ship named Rose.

One important reason for the strained relationship between the Marathas under Sekhoji and the Portuguese was the question of paying *sardeshmukhi*. The Portuguese sent their navy to support their army which was in action in Maratha territory and sought refuge in Vijaydurg, due to bad weather and disturbances in the sea. Sekhoji attacked the Portuguese navy. The Portuguese blamed Sekhoji that he had violated the treaty of 1722. On the other hand, the Chhatrapati had already decided to abolish the treaty. The reaction to all this development was the seizing of many Portuguese ships by Sekhoji. He also obstructed the free movement of ships plying through Goa harbour.[56]

Sekhoji also helped the Maratha forces which were led by Chhatrapati Shahu and Bajirao against the Siddis. The English supported the Siddis in their battle against the Marathas. They also appealed to the Mughals for help in their battle against the Marathas and also promised them that their interest in western coast will be protected, a task which was not fulfilled by the Siddis. The Portuguese were also involved in this conflict in the name of mediation and sent two ships to Janjira. Marathas with the help of the Angrias defeated the Siddis. The Siddis offered to surrender all important places like Raigad with the exception of Anjanwel and Janjira proper. So, the dream of the Marathas was complete with the defeat of the Siddis and it was accomplished with the help of the Angrias, the Maratha's coastal ally.

Sambhaji led Maratha navy to many successful campaigns against his European counterparts. His victories can be compared to his father's naval exploits. He continued the policy of seizing the European ships and creating troubles for them in the waters. In 1735, a severe blow was inflicted upon the European trade, the Marathas attacked the ship named *Derby* with five gurabs. After a bitter conflict, the ship was seized which was laden with valuable cargo. A few years later in 1738, nine gurabs and 13 galbats sailed from the port of Gheria along the shore. These ships were chased away by the English navy. The Maratha ships found a safe anchor at the Rajapur river to avoid further conflict. However, these pursuits by the English navy met with little success. In 1739, Sambhaji sent a clear message to the English that if they want free navigation in seas, they should pay Rupees 2,000,000 annually for purchasing a Maratha passport.[57] This testifies to the growing power of Sambhaji in the region.

In 1739, a bitter conflict started between the Marathas and the English ships mainly "*Halfix*," "*Cores*," "*Pulteny*" and "*Harrington*." The Marathas fought bravely with these English ships but found these ships powerful in built and capacity. However, the next few conflicts brought mixed fortunes to the Marathas. In November 1739, Sambhaji entered Bombay and carried away 14 fishing boats which had 84 crew on board.[58]

Manaji, Sambhaji's brother, released "*Salamander*," the English ship which was captured by Sambhaji. In another conflict, the Marathas had the prize possession of five ships of the English East India Company and a Portuguese Ketch.[59]

Sambhaji did not have cordial relations with the Portuguese. The Marathas on every possible action seized the Portuguese vessels. A bitter conflict took place in 1735 between the Marathas and the Portuguese, but it ended after a short period. In 1738, a Portuguese ship surrendered to the Maratha navy without any engagement belonging to the port of Diu. In the same year, Marathas seized another ship belonging to the Portuguese East India Company, which was carrying valuable goods belonging to the merchants of Goa. Sambhaji also seized one Portuguese ship carrying cash worth Rupees 40,000. Not only Portuguese ships but the Dutch ships were also captured by Sambhaji's navy. To avenge the attack, the Dutch formed an alliance with the Portuguese and attacked Gheria, the naval base of the Marathas. This joint attack did not last long and was a complete failure, the then forces retreated.[60]

In 1739, a bitter fight took place between the navy of the Marathas which comprised ten pals and seven galbats led by the Angrias and the Portuguese fleet, which comprised "*Da Victoria*," "*Senhora*" and "*Nossa*." This naval engagement took place near Mangalore and lasted for a day; because of superior naval force, the Maratha navy had to retreat. Next year Marathas dealt a severe blow to the Portuguese naval prestige by seizing their grain ships. Maratha navy fought with the Portuguese navy at Gheria and controlled the port of Honavar. The port of Honavar was equipped with two galbats, grain ships, two galleys, etc. After a small conflict all these were captured by Sambhaji and taken over by them to the Maratha territory.[61]

Sambhaji was equal to his father as far as his leadership over the sea is concerned, but he hardly had wisdom and sagacity as far as political affairs is concerned. He firmly believed that a divided house would benefit the Europeans. The other problem was that the house of the Angrias which was incorporated firmly with the Marathas was facing family dissensions. On the other hand, the Peshwas never got the required support from Sambhaji which were facing a bitter fight for the liberation of north Konkan against the Portuguese during 1737–1739. Marathas lacked unity among its leading noblemen.

The relation between the English and Manaji, Sambhaji's successor was cordial in the beginning but it declined in the years to come. Like Sambhaji, Manaji too attacked the European vessels, i.e. the Portuguese and the English vessels. By 1739, he captured the island of Gharapuri or Elephanta.[62] The control over the island of Elephanta posed a serious threat to the English who were controlling Butcher's island nearby. The next important territory, which was annexed by Manaji, was Rewari, which was a great concern for the English in Bombay. Control over Rewari was crucial for Marathas because it was from here that they could keep an eye on ships anchoring at Bombay harbour.

Control over Coasts and Conflict: Rising Maratha Naval Strength and the Dutch Response

Kanhoji Angre was no better than a common pirate, who seized every ship and caused disasters for most of the Europeans. For this reason, his conduct was often termed piracy by these trading nations. His activities, however, did not vary from that of the Portuguese, the English and the Dutch. All of them invariably denied permitting any vessel, except their own, to sail without their passport, unless a treaty or a convention had been secured. "No self-respecting nation would concede to another the right of controlling or regulating the movement of their merchant-men across the high road of the sea, and the result was constant friction."[63] Kanhoji was determined to defend his rights against all his neighbours jointly or individually, and at different times he fought the English, the Portuguese, and the Dutch. The struggle did not come to an end with Kanhoji's death in June 1729 but continued with varying success by his sons, and the Angrian fleet was a terror that the seafarers of the 18th century were glad to avoid.

After the death of Sambhaji, Kanhoji Angre, an admiral of outstanding ability took over the Maratha fleet in 1699 to revive Maratha sea power. He came into conflict with the Dutch East India Company very early in his career. In the early months of 1703, Kanhoji captured a Dutch man-of-war, known as John Burniston, Deputy Governor of Bombay, informed Sir John Gayer. In a letter, dated 11 March 1702–1703, Burniston wrote:

> we have a report of Cannajee Angria's trapping a Dutch ship of 30 guns who put in near their port for wood and water, which their boats went. The villain took his opportunity of seizing them and sending his people in galvets on board, who being baled by the ship, answered that they had provision for them, and on such a pretense surprised and mastered her.[64]

Throughout his reign, peace and amity could not be established between them and Kanhoji, who repeatedly made prizes of a sloop and a galley in 1710.[65] The Dutch firmly complained to him and requested him to restore the vessels with all their belongings, but Kanhoji quietly replied that

> he is not aware of any existing friendship between them nor of any correspondence on the matter. He does not molest such merchants ... as for example the Portuguese, English, and Moors. Lastly, he does not hold himself responsible for the return of prizes.[66]

Throughout the period, any European power was not adequate for any serious political intervention in the region. The prior experiences of the Portuguese, the Dutch and the British had shown that the European nations were not yet in a situation to enforce their claims even against minor rulers. The attempt of the British to expand their authority to the region in the vicinity of Madras led to their coercive eviction by the local powers at the beginning of the century. Even on the sea, as far as in 1722, Kanhoji Angre had defeated and put to flight a combined attack of the British and the Portuguese. During these years, the Dutch themselves had been more careful and cautiously avoided the Maratha fleet. In 1738, the British naval superiors on the west coast noted that "Our strength is not sufficient to withstanding him (Sambhaji Angria) for I assure Your Honour that he is a stronger enemy than you and a great many other think." In fact, nearly for the last quarter of the century after Plassey, British military power was not so serious a factor as later historians have been inclined to think.[67]

Sambhaji also attacked the Dutch ships and seized two of their vessels in 1738. The Dutch, in reprisal, sent their fleet to Gheria (Valandra), but it failed to make any impact against the strong walls of the fort. In order to avenge this, the Dutch, joined by the Portuguese, appeared before Gheria. The joint plan of attack ended in failure, and the fleet retired.[68] From a letter of Lauren Kerkhoven and some other prisoners, dated 19 June 1738, we get to learn of the casualty of war, as well as the strength of the Maratha navy from the following:

> On our side 26 were killed, many injured, both our Captains were alive with 38 European soldiers and sailors, 20 Moors and Bailnese .... Their

> naval force consists of 11 large goeraps, eacel with 16 or 18 guns (six and nine pounders) manned with 300 men each and 29 galliots, wach with 2 or 3 guns. At our arrival we found 6 Europeans in service of the pirates. Viz., two Englishmen, one as gunner-major and secret councilor of the head of the nation.

Further, Van Gollanese, Commander of Malabar, started making negotiations with Sambhaji for releasing the captive crew as well as two shallops to the residents of the company. Sambhaji then replied to the letter sent to him on 13 June 1738, saying:

> Perhaps you know that all over the world peace is made by a contract signed by both the parties. Therefore, if you intend to make peace, please send some intelligent and able men to make up the treaty, and if you send ships with merchants, we will live with them in perfect understanding and friendship. As regards the shallops, if you had made peace earlier, we would never have taken these, but now we met them in times of war. As to punishment which you purpose, you have felt our power once or twice and in future you will know it again.[69]

From the correspondence above, we get to know how evidently Sambhaji had complete confidence in his fleet; otherwise, he would not show this bold defiance against the Dutch. However, this fitting reply of Sambhaji did not go well with the Dutch, and they prepared a formidable fleet under Reinicus Siersma, who subsequently succeeded Van Gollanese as Commander of Malabar to avenge the insult and injury they had suffered at the hands of Angria. In 1739, the Dutch fleet appeared near the bar of Agoda; however, it was a lost cause. In 1743 Van Gollanese wrote that "these Pirates were growing stronger every day to the great chagrin of all European and native traders."

Another correspondence from the English Report of Bombay Castle mentions the instruction given to Mr. Rigby for having full authority to negotiate with Sambhaji Angria. He also wanted to know the reasons why Sambhaji was eager to enter into a treaty. The fifth point of the letter was:

> to try to find out whether he was threatened by the Dutch and hence wanted to enter into a treaty. As such treaty would be entered into only with a view to lessen one enemy, such a treaty without real and substantial security being given, cannot be had the least dependence upon, when that motive or dread subsist no longer.[70]

After Tulaji succeeded Sambhaji, some negotiation for peace was offered by the Dutch, but nothing much came out of that. Later in 1747, a letter from Cochin referred to aggression on Tulaji's part which resulted in the loss of two Dutch ships, *Zwijndregt* and the *Coilan*. In 1754 the Dutch chiefs of

Batavia issued special instructions to all their vessels sailing from Surat "in order to avoid an encounter with the pirates of Cangria Angria."[71] Hence, we see how afraid the Dutch were with the Angrias attack as they continued to seize their vessels constantly. As far as calling Angrias as pirates by the Europeans is concerned, this was their perspective of the vilification of the opposition to European monopolistic claims on the sea.

Another naval confrontation took place in 1754 between Dutch ships, namely *Wimmenum*, *Vrede* and *Jaccatra* and Angria fleet, which was 36 in number near Vijaydurg on the Malabar Coast. The battle took place for two days, at the end of which the Angre navy prevailed, and the three Dutch ships were either destroyed or captured and repaired. Most of the men were taken captive, and probably one Dutchman survived and reached the VOC settlement of Nagapattinam. The news was then conveyed to Batavia and to the Netherlands and the rest of Europe.

The loss of the three ships was immensely felt by the authorities at Batavia, which resulted in a quick issuing of orders to the ships departing for Surat from Batavia to drastically change the shipping routes. They conveyed this to the outgoing ships as well as the Heren XVII in Holland as follows:[72]

> With sadness, Batavia is mentioning that the ships *Wimmenum* and *Vrede* exploded in the air and the *Bark Jakatra* was plundered by the pirates of Angria. Heren XVII must note it down. This misfortune is caused by the superiority of the Angria, which can be seen from these encounters as to how extremely strong they are at present. They can also prevent us from sailing the silence of the sea ... And the brave captain Philippi and other people have done everything that can be expected from them in this heavy attack. He (Philippi), having killed 1600 men of the enemy before his death and beaten up the whole fleet of the enemy, such that the ships which are not burnt or shot in the ground, won't be seaworthy again. In the sixty of our men taken prisoners by Angria, the aforementioned Corporal was also present; he deserted it and came here (Batavia) via the Coromandel Coast. To prevent such disasters, Batavia has decided ... That the ships departing from Batavia at the beginning of August should go west of the Maldives, though those departing in September and October may go to Malabar and from there, immediately take a westerly course through North Maldives and not be near the shore as well as the "Caab St. Jan".[73]

Further, it has been reported that the

> ships coming from Surat to here (Batavia), should keep to open sea immediately after leaving Surat if their destination is not Ceylon. If, however, the ships from Surat are destined to Ceylon, then and only then are they permitted to go to Malabar coast South of Cochin. But even then, they are not to stay close to shore, because Angria never goes in the open sea.

> But then one is forced to stay close to the shore because one needs fresh water as there is little space of the same due to a large number of men on the vessel, so one should sail as silently as possible. We know this from the long experience with the pirate and most of the ships used by him in this manner, and he never ventured in the coldness of the sea.[74]

Thus, we see from the above naval conflicts, Angrias proved to be the biggest threat for the European naval authority. They fought on the sea both with tactics and strategies that resulted in their victory. The Angrias-planned tactics continued to destroy their big ships and killed most of the crew. It was also a strategic victory for them because Batavia authorities changed their shipping routes, leaving the entire Malabar coast free. The internal family feuds and the alliance of Anglo-Maratha against the Angrias in 1756 played a significant role in destroying the Angria Supremacy forever, although this was far from being the destruction of the Maratha Navy.

The French Attempts at Finding a Foothold: French Territorial Ambitions and the Maratha Power

Since the 1520s Frenchmen had competed for trading rights with the Portuguese in India. They were the first to challenge Portuguese claims, and success was obtained outside India. de Gonville is believed to have rounded the Cape in 1503 and reached Madagascar, and Jean Parmentier of Dieppe landed at Sumatra in 1529. These were however isolated enterprises unexploited by their compatriots who left to the Dutch and the English the task of breaking the Portuguese hold.[75] It was only in the 1660s that a company by the name of Compagnie des Indes Orientales was founded by Colbert with the King as the largest investor. It is well known that early trading companies were formed primarily to trade and not conquer. Colbert writes to the Presidents and tresories generaux de France at the finance office of Bourges, Paris, on 20 November 1664, where he says,

> The King, the Queens, the Princes of the blood and all the persons of quality in the kingdom, together with innumerable members of all kinds of professions, have acquired an interest in the East India Company, in the certain knowledge that they have each gained a hold on the great rewards that will result; His Majesty does not doubt but that you would profit from this wonderful opportunity which is offered to you for earning merit in the eyes of God (the principle motive of this most impressive undertaking being carrying the light of the Gospel to these distant lands); of the King, who has contributed so strongly by advancing a million crowns.[76]

Thus, the appearance of the French on the Indian coast was primarily for religious purposes, and it is only with the intrigues made by the other

European powers and the native powers that the French got involved in a territorial dispute. Between 1500 and 1800 the process of European naval warfare on open seas was marked by two important developments. First a change in naval tactics became possible with the mounting of guns in the centre of ships. Second with the help of naval superiority European powers successfully dominated international waters.[77]

The French established their first factory at Surat, and within two years of their arrival, they had persuaded the Sultan of Golconda, Abdullah Qutub Shah, to issue a *farman* on 9 December 1669 and established themselves at Masulipatnam.[78] In the 1720s a new company was formed, and by 1725 they had tried their luck to establish themselves on the western coast. A fleet of ships sailed under the command of Commodore M. de Pardaillan from Pondicherry to the coast of Malabar. Between Cannonore and Calicut, Captain Bertrand Francois Mahe la Bourdonnais negotiated a narrow creek, landed his troops and captured a small town and named it "*Mahe*" after the captain.[79] Simultaneously they expanded their settlements on the east coast and acquired Karaikal.

The acquisition of Karaikal from the Tanjore Marathas gave a major fillip to their territorial ambitions in the region. Ever since the days of Francois Martin the French had been trying to secure a territory in the kingdom of Tanjore, which was rich in the production of rice.[80] The French set their eyes on Karaikal; firstly, its importance lay in the fact that the whole port was intersected by rivers and therefore the place was fertile for rice production. Secondly, Karaikal being very close to the sea and situated on a river could manage big vessels, and this offered great commercial activities. Thirdly, Karaikal provided political advantages as well since the Raja of Tanjore and the English were not always on friendly terms, the French accurately calculated that an establishment of a fort there would provide for defensive tactics and the Raja would perceptibly look towards the French for help. Thus, Karaikal would not only serve as a granary but also operate as a warehouse for provisions and equipment.[81]

A simple chance event brought their objective within sight. Shahaji or Kattu Raja (pretender to the throne of Tanjore), a victim of court intrigues, offered to cede to the French the port of Karaikal, the fort of Kirkangadhi and five villages in the adjacent territory, in return for aid to recover his lost kingdom. Duma the present Governor General of Pondicherry did not hesitate to accept the offer. The quick and easy acceptance of the offer was due to the fact that the French had been facing hostilities from the Dutch at Nagapattinam which was a few miles from Karaikal. Perhaps Dumas thought that by gaining possession over Karaikal, he would easily drive away competition from the Dutch and the cost of helping Kattu Raja was diminutive in terms of military aid.[82] But as ill luck would have it, the ruler who had other means of achieving his end intimated them that their help was not required.

The French were thus compelled to await a more favourable opportunity to gain their end. It was only in 1730s that the French could finally establish their authority over Karaikal. They found a friend in Chanda Sahib (Nawab of Trichinopoly) who had great admiration for them and who always wanted their support.[83] He got support from a Muslim chief by the name of Syed; this Muslim chief gave his daughter in marriage to Chanda Sahib and invited the latter to attack Tanjore. However, Raja Pratap Singh soon found out the plot which was disclosed by Syed's brother, Kasim. He therefore executed Syed.[84] G.B Malleson's justification of siding with Chanda Sahib seems to amplify French interest in India. M. Dumas did not simply help Chanda Sahib to make the Raja of Tanjore subordinate him. It seems as though the French were not interested in acquiring territorial possession, but the reality was Dumas had been laying down the groundwork for the French to grasp power in the South. By allying themselves with Chanda Sahib, Dumas thought that Chanda Sahib was a powerful potentate, and thus, in the coming years with the help of Chanda itself, the French would be able to expel the other European competitors. Chanda Sahib on the other hand wanted to capture Tanjore and establish his authority, he offered the French help to capture Karaikal.[85]

As soon as Chanda Sahib got the news from the French, he dispatched 4000 horses to aid the French, the Tanjore forces fell back at their approach, and the commander of Chanda Sahib's infantry landed on the fort of Kirkangarhi on the river Karaikal and found many Tanjoreans there. He immediately attacked the fort and hurried towards Pondicherry to announce the news of his success. M. Dumas then sent a vessel with a 150 ton goods to proceed to Karaikal.

On 14 February 1730, the French got possession of the port of Karaikal, the fort of Kirkangadhi and the adjacent territory, as previously promised by Kattu Raja. Chanda Sahib could now safely rely on the French to help him achieve his goals. But the war in the Coromandel which ensued between the English and the French proved detrimental to the fate of Chanda Sahib. The war at Trichinopoly will be discussed in detail. I would also look into the critical position of Tanjore who had to choose sides in order to protect her kingdom.

The year 1739 was a critical period for Raja Pratap Singh, since the English stepped up their political hold in the Coromandel, and Tanjore was caught in the middle of the political chess game. This drained the Raja of his treasury; so in 1739, the Raja decided to grant the French Karaikal along with 60 villages in and around the area under a mortgage deed for getting a loan from them.[86]

According to S.P. Sen, the French possessions at Karaikal in the kingdom of Tanjore were more extensive than anywhere else, including Pondicherry. S.P. Sen argues that throughout the conflicts of the 18th century Karaikal remained outside the theatre of military and political activities. However, the events of 1749 prove him wrong. Karaikal was the main area of contest between the English and the French; in March 1749, the English with the help of Kattu Raja (pretender to the Tanjore throne) attacked Karaikal.

The pretext for such an attack was to replace Raja Pratap Singh with Kattu Raja. The most authentic source of information regarding this expedition is Orme; he said that "an unfortunate Prince by the name of Kattu Raja came to Fort St. David and implored the assistance of the English to reinstate him and in return for their assistance would give the Company the fort and territory of Devikottah and pay all the expenses of war."[87] The force appointed for the conquest amounted to 430 Europeans and 1000 sepoys with four small mortars; this army accompanied by Kattu Raja left fort St David at the end of March and encamped on the banks of river Valaru on the 13th of April. The army then proceeded towards Coleroon; it was Captain Cope who commanded the army. On reaching the river they were intercepted by the troops belonging to the Tanjore Raja, they were moving up and down on the opposite side and seemed determined to dispute the passage of the river. Captain Cope was not expecting to be intercepted by the large Tanjore army, and hence he decided to halt till reinforcements arrived.

Reinforcements soon arrived, and he decided to cross the river; difficulties soon arose as they advanced because of the thick forest and the enemy from behind the bushes began to irritate the English. Thus, this was the first expedition.

Kattu Raja in turn would help end the French by laying siege to the French settlement at Karaikal. Raja Pratap Singh on the other hand called upon the French for assistance. The *French Correspondence* says, "The King of Tanjore in the Course of this war was incessantly, by Letters to Mr. Le Riche, Commander at Carical and myself, summoning Us to give him the Assistance we were engaged to do, by the Treaties which my Predecessor and the superior Council had concluded with him."[88] The Treaty signed between the two states that, "And in case your Enemy attempts to disturb me, you are to assist me with People and Warlike Necessary's to destroy them, and we promise to act in the "same manner by You."

The French operations from Mahe offer another illustrative example of how they were attempting to balance their commercial and territorial ambitions while negotiating with other powers in the region. Mahe is situated at the mouth of river Mayyazhi which provided safe harbour for vessels up to 80 tonnes. This river has a total course of about 34 miles from its origin in the forests of the Wayanad Ghats to its merger with the Arabian sea. It was navigable in all four seasons for country boats (*dhonis*) for a distance of about 12 miles from Mahe to Parakkadavu.[89] Cardamom, sandalwood, turmeric and other commodities collected from further hinterlands and the Wayanad Ghats were brought along land routes as far as Parakkadavu in order to transport them to Mahe by country boats. The convenient location of Mahe which provided easier access to the hinterland had attracted the French as early as the 18th century.

The establishment of the French at Mahe fulfilled the grand scheme of French colonialism. In 1721 the French received permission from the ruler of Kadathanad for the right to pepper trade on the condition that the French would pay a tax of 13 *fanoms* of Calicut per candi cardamom to Vazhunnavar. The other agreement was that the two powers would support each other against their enemies.[90] It was after this that a series of Anglo-French conflicts started at the coast. The English at Tellicherry were now cautious and wanted to expel the French from the coast. They convinced the Vazhunnavar to oust the French; he too was dissatisfied with the French for not purchasing pepper produced in his country and for not maintaining the monopoly contract. He therefore welcomed the English and expelled the French, but in 1725 the French recaptured Mahe. This event shows the anxiety felt by the English and only strengthens the French hold on the Malabar coast.[91]

In 1728, the officials of Mahe and Tellicherry signed a peace treaty whereby both parties agreed on safe conduct of trade operations. The French factory at Mahe was meant for establishing good relations with the local rulers such as the Marathas and Mysore. By having good ties with these powers, the French thought that they could easily control the Malabar coast since the English were their common enemy. The officials at Mahe always respected the friendship of Haider Ali; they saw in him a strong ally against the English. The English anxiety was strongly felt when the officials at Tellicherry wrote to Madras and St David. The letter says,

> the French have two ships arrived at Pondicherry a third expected and one to touch on the Malabar coast in her way to Mocha this may keep the French longer in the country don't question getting them out of Bombay don't starve the cause are now treating with Boyanore[92] if can't get them out this year fear shall not hereafter if they build will be too strong to be removed without Europe's help."[93]

With regard to the Marathas, King Louis XVI wrote to Ramraja in 1776: "I have no intention to acquire territories in Hindustan ... All that I desire is the establishment of reciprocal trade between your subjects and mine."[94] In 1771, when the Marathas were planning an expedition to the Coromandel Coast via Malabar, the Commander of Mahe Picot de la Motte wrote to the Governor of Pondicherry Law de Lauriston to give him advice. The French were afraid of the Marathas and did not want to do anything that would offend them. The council at Pondicherry advised the commander to maintain neutrality, the council further explained to him, "this power, Sir, the most formidable and most solidly established in the whole of India, requires most tactful handling." It added that despite the policy of neutrality, the Marathas were able to force Picot de la Motte to adopt a course of action. Therefore, if the Marathas asked for any assistance, he was instructed to obey them without reluctance.[95]Jean Law de Lauriston stressed the need of having naval superiority in Indian waters and admitted that the French could wage a purely maritime war.[96]

However, French naval power never materialized; firstly, they were very much engaged in the internal politics of the Indian Princes, and hence their prime focus was for sovereignty on land; they were not wholly able to dislodge the English from the coast, and secondly, most of the French officials did not agree on having a naval base in India; it was only Jean Law de Lauriston who stressed on naval superiority on Indian waters. The attitude of the other French officials may be due to the fact that maintaining a naval base would be a huge burden on the French government. Most early modern European states were economically incapable of exercising an overwhelming naval supremacy on the high seas.[97]

Behind the Quest for Sovereignty over Seas: Strategy, Tactics and Organizational Principles of the Maratha Navy

Elements like the coast of Konkan, qualities of seafaring communities, coastal forts and weapons comprising guns and warships contributed to the naval warfare of the Marathas. Though the strategies involved in naval warfare changed from time to time with the progress of technology, certain traditions remained the same which had universal applications and thus could be elevated to general principles. To use the sea decisively infers some form of strategy. The main purpose of the Maratha navy was to fight naval battles and also to keep the enemy at bay.[98] The *Sabhasad* gives information regarding the raids and plundering activities by the Marathas in the enemy's (Mughals, Europeans, etc.) territories. *Sabhasad* writes,

> The Raje's (Shivaji) ships began to plunder the cities and forts at various places belonging to the Mughals, the Firangs, the Dutch, the English and the *Kilatav*, and twenty-seven such sea powers, as well as various sea coast towns as Bednur, Sunda and Srirangapattan and subsist. They fought at various places and used to bring the Raje grains and other provisions, after providing for their own needs.[99]

During the 17th century, naval battles were limited only to imposing damage or destruction of the enemy. The acts of destruction and damage and capture of the enemy's ships constituted to be the basic principles on which the Maratha naval strategy was based. The Marathas projected their force and terror into the heart of their competitors by seizing enemy's ships and crew as war booty. This strategy constituted another important element of the naval battles which were also adopted by the European Companies against each other. According to a Portuguese document, Shivaji's fleet detained as many as 121 trading ships from the Karnataka ports of Honavar, Mangalore, Barcelore and Gangoli (Cambolim).[100] It has often been noted that both the Portuguese and the Marathas were in the habit of capturing and detaining each other's ships. In a Portuguese letter of March 1665, there is a reference to a battleship of the Portuguese *(navio)* having been captured by Shivaji's fleet. One more Portuguese warship *(Pataxo)* was taken captive by Shivaji's fleet in November 1670 while it was sailing from Surat to Daman. In retaliation, the Portuguese captured 11 unarmed Maratha cargo ships and took them to Bassein.[101]

Another strategy adopted by the Marathas was to allow the Europeans to establish suitable trading sessions, harbours and support facilities from which they could progress and expand their position as a naval power.[102] For example, the Dutch and the French had a commercial relationship with Shivaji. The former made an offer to assist him in capturing Janjira in return for his armed assistance in attacking Bombay. This proposal was rejected by Shivaji. While the French tried to secure his goodwill by providing him with ammunition, for which the French were allowed to open a factory at Rajapur and were granted certain concessions.

In earlier times, naval warriors did not require any special expertise as far as fighting skills were concerned. The naval fights basically involved ramming each other's vessels (in order to sink them) or boarding the enemy vessel and having a close-quarter battle (physical duel) with the enemy's soldiers. The majority of the fighting crew consisted of people from the Bhandari and Koli caste and also Muslims. In addition to managing the ship and constituting as the fighting crew, the services of these people could also have been utilized for the purpose of boat-building. A study of the *Son Kolis*, a fishing community scattered along the present Raigad district, reveals that they have preserved the tradition of boat-building with their community.[103] They had, therefore, the absolute knowledge of the nature of sea in the surroundings with the precise location of the submerged rocks, reefs and sand bars.[104]

The *Sabhasad Bakhar* gives details regarding the different types and categories of ships and vessels of the Maratha fleet. These ships were built by Shivaji keeping in mind the naval strategy and varied requirements of the state. For instance, flat-bottomed boats were suited for specific purposes which were being used in the shallow and rocky waters of the various creeks, while small rowing boats were used for towing the heavy vessel (particularly from the coastal forts and bases) which could attain speed once its sail is used after reaching out in the open waters and to deliver an offensive on the enemy. *Sabhasad* writes, "Ships of various types, such as *Gurabs* and *Tarandes*, *Tarus*, *Galvats*, *Sibads* and *Pagar* were fitted and organized under two Subedars ... A Suba consisting of two hundred ships."[105] These ships were specifically designed for gaining speed in war and were equipped with few guns for the purpose of self-protection.

During the Angria period, we see a change in the construction of these ships. For instance, a number of fighting ships were constructed on the English model. These ships were sea-worthy and could even meet their European rival on more or less equal terms.[106] The *gurabs* carried broadsides of six and nine pounder guns. On their main deck were mounted two, nine or 12 pounder, pointing forward through the port-holes cut in the bulkhead in such a manner that they could be fired over the bows,[107] while another ship, *galbat*, carried light guns fixed on swivels, and some of them had six or eight pieces of cannons from two four pounders.[108] With the coming of the Europeans we see there was a change in the structure of the ships. The original round sterns of the Konkan ships were replaced by the square sterns of the ships.

The weapons used by the Marathas in their naval fight consisted of swords, bows and arrows, spears and guns. The Marathas cast heavy artillery and shots with the aid of the local iron smiths. But they were of inferior calibre. They often broke when fired. As a result European guns were highly prized in this country. Every ship that came from Europe brought guns heavy and light for which there was a ready market. Adventurous Europeans well-trained in the technique of artillery found lucrative appointments in the armies of the native prince.[109] Marathas had to depend upon the Europeans for superior guns and artillery.

Ship-building industry was one of the aspects which went through changes from the time of Shivaji to the Angrias. Places like Kalyan, Ratnagiri, Jaytapur, Malwan and Vengurla were some of the chief ship-building towns in the 17th century. As these regions were rich in fine quality of teak wood, Shivaji selected these places as his docks. The art of building the ships reached its maturity in the period of Kanhoji Angre. Like Kolaba, the coast of east, Suvarnadurg and Vijaydurg were very popular. The design of these ships, besides their durability, was of high quality in comparison with the other ships in the world. Later we see how Bombay became a famous centre for shipping industry of the region. Timber which grew on the side of north Bombay was brought into use for the construction of ships. Also, in order to encourage the industry a lot of measures were taken by the state.

During the Peshwa period a number of amenities were provided for ship owners. His ships were exempted from *octroi* and other goods when they loaded goods for household use and brought them from other ports to the villages.[110] During Shivaji's period, the construction of the ships was done by the Hindu artisans known as "*Sutars*" or carpenters who belonged to the Konkan region. Later we see a rise of family of Wadias who have been referred to as the master builders of the Mercantile Marine and navy warships.[111] Kanhoji had to depend on the western shipwrights for technical skills as the local shipwrights were mostly illiterate. Several Dutchmen were appointed by him who provided technical skills for improving the designs and weapons of the Maratha ships.[112] Foreign technicians were employed as gunners, shipbuilders, etc. by him. There was a shortage of skilled gunners, and it was believed that these gunners were mere mercenaries who shifted their services from one master to the other.

The art of Maratha naval warfare could not be complete without a reference to the organization of forts. Forts played a very crucial role in Maratha's political sovereignty as they not only acted as a symbol of resistance on land but also a medium of projection of the state's authority over the Arabian

Sea. Shivaji not only utilized the land and the hills in his territory for the construction of forts but also did not spare the sea when he understood the importance of navy.[113] When Shivaji came to power, he paid special attention to the defence of the coastal region in view of the challenges he perceived on the oceanic front of his "*Swarajya.*" He was accurate in his judgement as the western coast very soon witnessed a keen struggle for mastery in which the coastal forts played a major role. According to Amatya, "the essence of the whole kingdom is forts. If there are no forts and a foreign invasion comes, the open country becomes supportless and the surrounding country becomes desolated and the people get routed and broken up. After the desolation of the country what would be left to be called a kingdom."[114] Just like several hill forts of the *Swarajya*, the position of natural advantage and strategic value dominated the condition for selection of the site for the marine forts too. The Konkan coast is known to have many such fortified locations which had military as well as strategic value. Most of these locations are found to be surrounding the important ports or sheltering dockyards.[115]

Shivaji seems to be fully aware of the fact that for a navy to operate and function properly, naval bases were the prime requisites. He realized that during the time of naval fights, the naval bases act as the most immediate source of supply of war materials and also the place of safe refuge for the fleet in case of adversity. The bases, if properly fortified, and with ample store of water, ammunition and garrison, would successfully stand against the attack of any enemy. At the same time, the artillery and guns of the coastal forts would keep the creek or bay safe for navigation. Forts such as Bankot, Anjanvel, Jaygad, Vijaydurg and Sindhugarh formed excellent naval bases. Vijaydurg was the main base of the Maratha navy, particularly under the Angrias who fitted out and repaired Maratha war vessels in the Vijaydurg dockyard.

Even the Europeans built a number of naval forts on the western coast. The forts supplied war requirements and were a place of refuge for the navy. They erected a web of forts at choke points of sea routes on the western coast that were used simultaneously as commercial factories and naval bases.

Therefore, to conclude, while the other indigenous powers failed to realize the importance of navy, it was Shivaji who understood the significance of controlling the waters of Konkan coast and established his own navy during the time when various European powers like the Portuguese and Dutch were establishing their sovereignty over the sea. By establishing their own indigenous navy, the Marathas posed a strong threat to these European companies. With the rise of the Angrias, we see that there was continuous change in the power struggle at the sea between the Marathas naval power and the Europeans. Besides the use of various naval warfare strategies, the Marathas under Shivaji and later Angrias constructed many warfare ships and coastal forts which enabled them to emerge as one of the chief naval power of its times.

Notes

1 https://worldhistoryconnected.press.uillinois.edu/12.1/forum_delagarza.html, accessed on 04 January 2020, 6:30.
2 B.K. Apte, *History of the Maratha Navy and Merchantships*, Bombay, State Board of Literature and Culture, 1973, p. 1.
3 B.G. Paranjape, ed., *English Records on Shivaji*, Pune, Shiva Charitra Karyalana, 1931, Part 1, p. 307.
4 Baldeo Sahai, *Indian Shipping: A Historical Survey*, New Delhi, Publications Division Ministry of Information and Broadcasting, Government of India, 1996, p. 144.
5 A.C. Roy, *A History of Mughal Navy and Naval Warfare*, Calcutta, The World Press, 1972, p. 17.
6 Shireen Moosvi, "The Mughal Empire and the Deccan-Economic Factors and Consequences", *Proceedings of the Indian History Congress,* Vol. 43 (1982), p. 366.
7 Syed Hasan Askari, "Mughal Naval Weakness and Aurangzeb's Attitude Towards the Traders and Pirates on the Western Coast", *The Journal of Bihar Research Society*, Vol. XLVI (January–December 1960), p. 4.
8 Abul Fazl, *Ain-i-Akbari*, translated by H. Blochmann, Calcutta, Low Price Publications, 1989, p. 1001.
9 Ashin Das Gupta and M.N. Pearson, eds., *India and the Indian Ocean*, Calcutta, Oxford University, 1987, pp. 71–93.
10 Niccolo Manucci, *Memoirs of the Mogul Court*, translated by Michael Edwards, London, Published by The Folio Society, 1957, p. 47.
11 Jadunath Sarkar, *Shivaji and His Times*, Calcutta, S.C Sarkar & Sons, 4th ed., 1948, p. 244.
12 Baldeo Sahai, *Indian Shipping*, p. 176.
13 P.L. Saswadkar, "The Siddis' Tyranny over the Hindus in 18th Century Konkan", *Proceedings of Indian History Congress,* Vol. 37 (1976), p. 224.
14 https://worldhistoryconnected.press.uillinois.edu/12.1/forum_delagarza.html, accessed on 27 March 2020, 6:30.
15 S.R. Sharma, *Mughal Empire in India*, part II, Bombay, Karnatak Printing Press, 1934, p. 543.
16 Joshi,Shankar Narayan ed., *Krishnaji Anant Sabhasad Virachita Chhatrapati Shri Shivajiraje Yanchi Bakhar, 2020,* pp. 84–85.
17 Deccan College Post-graduate Research Bulletin, Vol. II, Nos. 2 and 3, pp. 404–05.
18 Joshi, *Krishnaji Anant Sabhasad Virachita Chhatrapati Shri Shivajiraje Yanchi Bakhar,* p. 238.
19 A.R. Kulkarni says that Shivaji attacked and plundered Basrur in 1665 with his armada of 85 Shibars and three big Galbats. A.R. Kulkarni, *Explorations in the Deccan History*, Delhi, Paragati Publications and ICHR, 2006, p. 52.
20 Ibid., p. 7.
21 James Douglas, *Bombay and the Western India*, London, Marston & Co., 1893, p. 110.
22 Joshi, *Krishnaji Anant Sabhasad Virachita Chhatrapati Shri Shivajiraje Yanchi Bakhar*, p. 265.
23 Ibid., pp. 262–72.
24 *Deccan College Post- Graduate Research Bulletin*, Vol. IV, No. I (1942), pp. 81–90.
25 Charles Rathone Low, *History of the Indian Navy*, London, Richard Bentley and Son, 1877, Vol. I, pp. 70–71.
26 Y.N. Kelkar, *Vasaichi Mohim*, Diamond Publications, Poona, p. 26.

27 Apte, *A History of the Maratha Navy and Merchantships*, p. 117.
28 D.G. Dhabu, *Kulabkar Angre Sarkhel*, Government Central Press, Bombay, 1939, p. 5.
29 Ibid., p. 5.
30 Ibid., pp. 13, 7.
31 Ibid., pp. 16, 74.
32 Ibid., pp. 5, 22.
33 Ibid., pp. 64, 66.
34 Apte, *A History of the Maratha Navy and Merchantships*, p. 124.
35 Dhabu, *Kulabakar Angre Sarkhel*, p. 137.
36 G.S. Sardesai, *Selections from the Peshwa Daftar*, Vol. 34, Bombay, Government Central Press, 1933, Letter 179.
37 Dhabu, *Kulabakar Angre Sarkhel*, p. 85.
38 Ibid., p. 160.
39 Joshi, *Krishnaji Anant Savhashad Virachita Chhatrapati Shri Shivajiraje Yanchi Bakhar*, p. 42.
40 Ibid., p. 344.
41 Ibid., pp. 349–50.
42 Ibid., pp. 362–65.
43 Kelkar, *Vasaichi Mohim*, p. 27.
44 G.M. Moraes, *Maratha Portuguese War of 1683-84* (Reprinted from the *Journal of University of Bombay*, 11–4, January, 43), pp. 31–33.
45 Kelkar, *Vasaichi Mohim*, p. 31.
46 D.R. Banaji, *Bombay and the Siddis*, University of Bomaby, Bombay, 1982, p. 55.
47 Surendranath Sen, *Military System of the Marathas*, Calcutta, The Book Company Ltd., 1928, pp. 197–98.
48 Ibid., pp. 200–02.
49 Dhabu, *Kulabkar Angre Sarkhel*, p. 10.
50 Sen, *Military System of the Marathas*, pp. 206–08.
51 Apte, *The Maratha Navy and Merchantships*, p. 78.
52 Sen, *Military System of the Marathas*, p. 173.
53 Moraes, *Maratha Portuguese War of 1683-84*, pp. 37–42.
54 Ibid., pp. 42–45.
55 Dhabu, *Kulabkar Angre Sarkhel*, pp. 64–66.
56 Sen, *Military System of the Marathas*, p. 215.
57 Dhabu, *Kulabkar Angre Sarkhel*, pp. 82–83.
58 Low, *History of Indian Navy*, Vol. I, p. 115.
59 Ibid., p. 119.
60 Sen, *Military System of the Marathas*, pp. 218–19.
61 Ibid., p. 229.
62 Dhabu, *Kulabkar Angre Sarkhel*, p. 84.
63 S.N. Sen, "The Angrias and the Dutch", in *Early Career of Kanhoji Angria and Other Papers*, Calcutta Review, February 1938, p. 26.
64 Ibid., p. 27.
65 Ibid.
66 A.J.M. Heyligers, Press List of Ancient Dutch Records from 1675 to 1825, in Supplementary Catalogue of Dutch Records Madras Record Office, Madras, 1952, pp. 7–8.
67 K.M. Pannikar, *Asia and the Western Dominance, A Survey of the Vasco Da Gama Epoch of Asian History 1498-1945*, London, George Allen & Unwin, 1953, p. 94.
68 Apte, *A History of the Maratha Navy and Merchantships*, p. 125.

69 Letters from Malabar to Holland, 1739, 4th Vol., p. 2225. 5-1328 B, cited in Sen, "Angrias and the Dutch", p. 33.
70 Bombay Castle, Wednesday 10 October 1739. pp. 636–42, Cited in B.K. Shrivastavya, *The Angreys of Kolaba in British Records (1719 AD to 1884 AD),* Poona, Prashant Printery, 1950, p. 56.
71 Sen, *The Angrias and the Dutch,* p. 34.
72 Generale missiven van gouverneurs-generaal en raden aan heren XVII der Verenigde Oostindische Compagnie, Deel 12, pp. 475–76.
73 This translation has been done by Nikhil Bellarykar in "Dutch-Maratha (i.e. VOC-Angre) Naval Battle of 1754: Multiple aspects of a little-discussed but important incident", *Prag Samiksha,* February 2018, pp. 49–66.
74 Ibid.
75 Virginia Mclean Thompson, "Frenchmen prior to Dupliex", in *Dupliex and His Letters, 1742–1754,* Ph.D Thesis, Columbia University, 1933, p. 13.
76 Umesh Ashok Kadam, *History of the Marathas (French-Maratha Relations),* (1668-1818), New Delhi, Sundeep Prakashan, 2008, p. 7.
77 Anirudh Deshpande, "Limitations of Military Technology: Naval Warfare on the West Coast, 1650-1800", *Economic and Political Weekly,* Vol. 27 (1992), p. 901.
78 Aniruddha Ray, "French-Golconda Relation Between 1671 and 1681: Problems of Attitudes and Resources over St. Thome and Masulipatnam", in *Studies in History of the Deccan: Medieval and Modern,* M.A. Nayeem, Aniruddha Ray, K.S. Matthew New Delhi, Pragati Publications, 2000, p. 47.
79 Rear Admiral Sridharan, *A Maritime History of India,* Delhi, Publications Division Ministry of Information and Broadcasting, 1982, p. 83.
80 V.G. Hatalkar, *Relation between the French and Marathas,* 1668-1815, Bombay, T.V Chidambaram, 1958, p. 62.
81 H. Dodwell, ed., *The Private Diary of Ananda Ranga Pillai,* Vol. IV, Madras, Government Press, 1916, p. 53.
82 G.B. Malesson, *History of the French in India,* London, W.H Allen & Co., 1893, p. 76.
83 Ibid., p. 78.
84 S. Gopalan, *Bhonsle Vamsa Charitra,* Tanjore, Vetrivel Press, 2009, p. xiii.
85 G.B. Malleson, *History of the French in India,* London, W.H. Allen & Co. Ltd., 1893, p. 79.
86 V. Gopal, *Modi Documents in the T.M.S.S.M Library,* Vol. I, Thanjavur, 1999, p. viii.
87 Robert Orme, *History of the Military transaction of the British Nation in Indoostan,* Vol. I, Madras, Luke Hansard Printer, 1861, p. 112.
88 *Records of Fort St. George,* French Correspondence of 1752, Madras, printed by the Superintendent, Govt. Press, p. 2.
89 Joy Varkey, "The Significance of Mahe in Eighteenth-Century French India", *Proceedings of the Indian History Congress,* Vol. 58 (1997), p. 297.
90 Alfred Martineau, *Origins de Mahe des Malabar,* Paris, Paris E Champion, 1917, p. 29.
91 Varkey, "The Significance of Mahe in Eighteenth-Century French India", p. 296.
92 He was a vassal under the rule of Kolathiri Raja (Cannanore in British records and Kolathunadu in indigenous records). He had declared himself Raja of Kadattanad.
93 India Office Records, The French in India, Vol. 1, 1664–1810 (Unpublished).
94 V.G. Hatalkar, trans. and ed., *French Records relating to the History of the Marathas,* Vol. 2, Bombay, 1983, p. 34.

95 Ibid., Vol. 3, pp. 97–98.
96 Kadam, *History of the Marathas*, p. 213.
97 Deshpande, "Limitations of Military Technology", p. 900.
98 Apte, *History of the Maratha Navy and Merchantships*, p. 87.
99 *Sabhasad Bakhar,* p. 94.
100 Portuguese letter dated 28 November 1657, quoted by P.S. Pissurlencar, Portuguese Mahratta Relations, Maharashtra State Board for Literature and Culture, Bombay, 1983, *op. cit.,* p. 44.
101 Ibid., p. 46.
102 Philip MacDougall, *Naval Resistance to Britain's Growing Power in India, 1600-1800: The Saffron Banner and the Tiger of Mysore*, London, Boydell and Brewer Ltd., 2014, Preface.
103 Jain Kirti, "Boat Building and the Son Kolis of the Raigad District, Maharashhtra", in *Marine Archaeology,* Vol. 4 (1993), pp. 89–91.
104 *The Gazetteer of the Bombay City and Island*, Vol. 1, Bombay, Printed at the Time Press, 1909, pp. 227–31.
105 *Sabhasad Bakhar,* pp. 93–94.
106 Apte, *History of the Maratha Navy and Merchantships*, p. 122.
107 Ibid., p. 121.
108 Gazetteer of the Bombay Presidency, *Kolaba and Janjira*, Vol. XI, Bombay, Government of Bombay, 1880, p. 147.
109 B.K. Apte, "The Maratha Weapons of War", *Bulletin of the Deccan College Post-Graduate and Research Institute*, Vol. 19, No. 1/2 (1958), pp. 113.
110 T.T. Mahajan, *Industry, Trade and Commerce during the Peshwa Period,* Jaipur, Pointer Publishers, 1989, p. 33.
111 M.S. Agaskar, *Early History of the Bombay Docks and Shipbuilding,* Potdar Commemoration, Prof. D.V. Potdar Commemoration Volume, p. 329.
112 Kaushik Roy, *War, Culture and Society in Early Modern South Asia, 1740-1849*, New York, Taylor & Francis, 30 March 2011, p. 17.
113 A.R. Kulkarni, *Medieval Maratha Country*, Pune, Diamond Publications, 01 July 2008.
114 S.V. Puntambekar, "A Royal Edict on the Principles of State Policy and Organization", *Journal of Indian History,* Vol. VIII, Parts I and II, 1929, pp. 81-106..
115 M.S. Narwane, *Forts of Maharastra,* New Delhi, APH Publication Corporation, 1995, p. 270.

3 Prospects and Perspectives of Symbiosis

Osmosis of Deccan Society and Culture

The medieval period of Deccan represents a striking feature of a mixture of cultures comprising varieties of religions, cults, folks and castes which countered each other with a certain amount of opposition but at the same time gradually submitted the ongoing unconscious idea of assimilation of ideas and knowledge. This chapter examines the nature and intensity of acculturation in Deccan with some references to the Maratha country. It therefore explores the nature of the caste system and the response of the Europeans towards Deccan culture. This chapter is an illustration of what Deccan symbolizes, A Melting Pot of Cultures of cultural assimilation, and consequently, it studies the relation between various social and cultural entities.

The "Melting Pot": Ethnicities, Migrations and Cultural Fusion in the Deccan

The diversity in the Deccan represented a mosaic of mixed cultures; first, there was the Persianite tradition that emerged from Northern India or from Central Asia and that was absorbed by the Deccani courts. The Deccan-born Muslims were rooted in the plateau's indigenous tradition and over time became assertive of their cultural identity. They came to be known as Deccanis, and they developed their own form of Urdu language known as "*Dakhni*."[1] *Dakhni* became quite commonly used in the courts of Bijapur and Golconda. The Qutub Shahi rulers also supported the use of Telugu as a literary language. As early as 1535, Bijapur had switched the language of its revenue and judicial records from Persian to Marathi, and by 1600 Golconda followed suit.[2]

Second, the demand for military labour brought to the forefront a community of East Africans known as *Habshis*. They were recruited as military slaves by the Bahamani and later by the Sultanates, especially Bijapur and Ahmednagar. For example, Malik Ambar (1548–1626) fell into the hands of slave dealers operating between the Ethiopian highlands and the coast of Eastern Africa and later re-exported to the Deccan plateau to meet the demand for military labour. He was raised by a prominent merchant in

DOI: 10.4324/9781003377511-3

Baghdad and sold to Chengiz Khan in the Deccan who was holding the office of Peshwa or chief minister in the Nizam Shahi sultanate of Ahmednagar. Malik Ambar's presence shows how slaves got assimilated into society over time and evolved from slaves to clients to patrons and in some cases became slave holders.[3]

The third military group which was of immense importance to Deccan was the Marathas, the indigenous warrior clans of the western plateau. Adil Shahi dynasty hired 30,000 Maratha cavalries. The Maratha *deshmukhs* not only collected revenue and adjudicated disputes but also raised troops and made them available to the Sultans. Ahmednagar in 1624 enlisted 40,000 Marathas into its service. This is the first instance of the Deccani Sultanates integrating with the local indigenous groups.[4] The second class of military warriors was the *nayaks* who were Telugu warriors of Kakatiya descent. They lent their services to the sultanates in exchange for land grants for maintaining their troops. Thus, these two warrior groups dominated the military division of the Sultans.

The fourth group to enter Deccan was the Europeans. Although their presence was based on the coast at first, these Europeans sent commercial agents, mercenaries and missionaries to fulfil their objectives of proselytization, commercialization and territorial conquest. European companies from Portugal, the Netherlands and France came to the shores of Deccan and changed the scenario. The policies adopted by these European companies towards the indigenous people are discussed in this chapter.

Syncretic Movements and Cultural Exchange

A. Politics, Society, Culture and Sufi Influence in the Deccan

Sufism in India and broadly in the Islamic world may be seen as an alternative to the orthodoxy that had rendered business to the Ulema for a good time. Originating originally in Central Asia, mainly in the newly conquered lands of Persia, Sufism or *Tasawwuf* spread far and wide, and when Islam entered, Sufism ushered in as well as a distinct perception of Islam. The trajectory of Sufism in Islam can be looked at, through different vantages at different levels as well. Sufism, in India, was like Islam, an alien, different thought process while Islam had limited interaction with the surroundings. In Sufism, many historians argue, lay more open to interaction, cross-fertilizations and assimilation. What can be concluded, thereby, is that Sufism and the role that it played in medieval India was determined to a large degree by the conditions in which it was placed, and the institutions, people and ideologies that it encountered.

Sufism emerged not as a coherent doctrine but as loose strands by men of a mystical bend, men and women who explored beyond the pedantic injunctions of the *sharia'h* and Ulema and looked for a deeper meaning. Essentially, these mystics were looking at a deeper; less mediated relationship with god.

Delving into the world of the intangible, the illogical and the irrational, most of them were ready to give away their all, for the sake of uniting with god and understanding the real truth. Simplistic as it may seem, Sufism had acquired structures and a spiritual role in the lives of the common people. This multi-layered Sufism thought entered India through many channels and in many forms. The Ghaznavids rule of the 11th to 12th centuries saw the infiltration of the first phase of Sufi saints and centres, which was expanded in the times of the Delhi sultanates when the Chistiya, Suhrawarddiya and Firdawssiya orders made a mark till the era of the great Mughals, by which time of course, most of the orders had indigenized and found unequivocal, independent support in India vicinities.[5]

The most famous of the Chishti saints included the founder Shaikh Muinuddin Chishti (1235) his khalifa, Shaikh Qutubuddin Bakhitiyar Kaki (1235), Shaikh Fariduddin Ganj-i-Shakar (1265), Shaikh Nizam-ud-din Auliya (1325), Shaikh Nasiruddin Chiragh of Delhi (1356) and Sayyid Muhammad Gesudaraz. (1422). Of the Suharwaddiya, sheikh Bahauddin Zakarriya (d. 1262) and Shaikh Jalaluddin Tabrizi were prominent. Shaikh Ruknuddin (1334–35) of the Firdawssiya, and Shaikh Sarafuddin Ahmad Yahya Munyari's khanqahs became a famous Sufi hall during the reigns of Muhammad Bin Tughluq and Firuz Tughluq. He is said to have disciples in excess of 10,000.[6] In the Deccan Sufi Sarmast and Pir Mabari Khandayat who belonged to the Qadirriya and Shattari orders were prominent.[7]

The above account bears testimony to the vast, quantitative and qualitative, presence of Sufism in medieval India. Sufism may have entered India as a religious institution, but its impact reverberated into the wider socio-cultural lives of the people. It cannot be denied either that Sufism weaved itself into the fabric of medieval Indian society, making Sufism and its saints their very own.

When a Muslim ruling class moved to India, so did a class of learned men (Ulema). In the new environs the two sections had stuck close together and the Ulema and the ruling class shared an essentially love–hate relationship. The orthodox stand of the Ulema and their constant nagging could have been a great source of trouble for the rulers. Again, the hardened stand that the Ulema promoted could not have gone down well with the sultan and his ministers who were trying to establish a political base in a country where the majority population was identified as *kufr*. Thus, for example the Qazis of the Delhi Sultanate applied relentless pressure on the sultan to subdue the Hindus and give them the option of Islam or death. For a newly established state, this was similar to a case of political suicide. But what could the Sultan do? Flanked on all sides by these conditional supporters, he could only negotiate.[8]

In this context they emerged as an alternative that the sultan could befriend. It was, in some cases, a less demanding and more integrative vision and understanding of power and its subjects. This is not to suggest that the Ulema as a class was replaced or sought to be replaced by the Sufis. Nor is it our contention that the Sufis were generally unorthodox, less stringent and easier to deal with but in comparison to the Ulema as a class they were so. But in hindsight we can see that the monopoly of the Ulema on religious matters was questioned from time to time by the Sufis, from within the Islamic realm, thus reducing their moral authority.

While there was ample diversity even within the Ulema, in reference to the relations with the sultan, they stood as a class accusing actions of the sultan and considering it to be deviation and innovation. Any support for the Sultan was seen as an attempt to erase the Islamic fabric of the state. But now this support could come from within the Islamic realm. There is of course also the question of who needed whom? Was it the Sufis or the sultans? For Muzaffar Alam, the Sufis intervened deliberately so as to be able to define a political direction and to drive home their belief that *sharia'h* was only a small portion of the whole of Islam and its laws and values. This was a move that benefited the sultan who till now had to try and achieve legitimacy, howsoever from the *sharia'h* and the Ulema. Also, the Sufi saints, whether in life or after death, enjoyed popularity from the masses, which was not so much the case with the Ulema leaders (though Iqtidar Hussain Siddiqui would argue on the basis of Ibn Battuta's accounts that orthodox scholars' *dargahs* were venerated as well).[9] Anyhow this association would help promote the image of the sultan as a king of all those residing in Hindustan, but this is only a much-generalized view.

This association reached highs and lows depending on the saints, their attitudes and beliefs as well as those of the sultans. K.A. Nizami argues that the early Chishti chose to stay away from the state and its institutions. He talks about this aloofness that the shaikhs maintained. He elaborated on the comment that Nizam-ud-din Auliya made regarding non-involvement in politics and government services. For Nizami not only were the Shaikhs so oriented but conditions in medieval India during the 13th and 14th centuries had maintained the supremacy of the Ulema. He seems to be arguing therefore that the shaikhs did not and could not enjoy a healthy friendship with the sultanate after Iltutmish, because neither did they have such ambitions and nor were the conditions ripe for such an alliance, which may have very well ended in a failure. This isolation or aloofness is for other scholars an erroneous reading. Muzaffar Alam suggests that the connection ran deep if one looks at the state as a Muslim or rather, Islamic state. For him the Sufis concerned themselves with the "dissemination and consolidation of Islamic power." It seems then that support was dependent on whether the Sultan was an Islamic ruler, furthering the cause of Islam or not. Sufi interface with political power and authority is also the subject of an article by Simon Digby.[10] This interface, Digby shows in his article, happened at various levels. Some of these were symbolic encroachments over the king's authority and others were dangerously real. In this context he raises the question of *wilayat* (delineated territories of spiritual jurisdiction). It's the territorial space where the shaikhs reigned supreme, where his *pir*, his *murid* came to meet him and which housed the *Khanqah*. The presence of such a *khanqah* was supposed to bring good fortune for the sultan, yet these *wilayats* also had a nuisance value, as they were an alternative, although, miniscule centres of power. In a similar manner he tries to decipher the logic behind such pompous titles as the "sultan of all shaikhs" used for Nizam-ud-din Auliya, in which the political terminology put to use only confirms the worldliness of these saints.

It is important to record a caveat here: the competition, the encroachments that the Sufis provided were not an actual threat to the sultan or his material possessions, in any considerable degree. They were, after all, not political competitors, but legitimizers, and by withdrawing legitimacy, they confirmed their role and niche in the political arena. There are innumerable instances of antagonism and affection as well as more mild relations between the shaikhs and the sultans. Many shaikhs accepted monetary gifts from the sultan and recommended persons for services. While Nizam-ud-din Auliya did nothing to hide his disdain for kings, there were others who prayed for their victory and blessed the sultans and his successors. Carl Ernst would argue that "they enjoyed a privileged political position."

Their roles in shaping the political arena cannot be underestimated. The presence was liberating as well as binding for the sultans. They were an additional and sometimes alternate source of legitimacy. They could come in handy in verbal battles and polemics against the Ulema. Through them a large section of the population, Muslim and non-Muslim, could have reposed their faith in the sultan. Yet the same saints could also act as rebels when they would refuse to comply with the sultan's orders, not visit the royal courts and follow its norms and even refuse meetings with the sultan at his own *khanqah*.[11]

It is clear from the above discussion that the Sufi intervention in politics was at various levels and determined by an array of variables. Indeed, the attitude might have been based on whims, predilections and idiosyncrasies but also on political outlook because these Sufi sheikhs were religious men who were anything but politically naive. The sultan's attitude was also determined by political expediencies and emergencies. The breadth of the political roles that they performed would become clearer if one looks at the Deccan. Deccan in an important region in this respect because the Qadarriya, Shattariya and the Chishti saints that came to Deccan differed from the general image of the saints in north India as popular, unorthodox, etc. Indeed, in the case of the Deccan it becomes quite difficult to differentiate between the Ulema and the Sufi saints, owing to the mutuality of the roles that they performed.

The popularity of Sufism in different parts of India led to the spread of Muslim culture among the masses in India. The Sufis became popular among the masses because they preached monotheism, equality, universal brotherhood and social justice. Sufism concept of love and equality of men attracted many people from lower strata of the society. There was no differentiation between high and low in the *khanqahs* of Sufi saints. These saints showed a spirit of tolerance towards all religions and creeds. They believed in unity and similarity and not in differences among various religions. These *khanqahs* were open to all the communities irrespective of caste, creed or religion and played an important role in bringing both the Muslim and Hindu communities together on the same platform. Thus, the Sufi attitude towards other religions especially the Hindus was one of understanding and adjustment. They believed that all religions are as different roads leading to the same destination. They had free social intercourse with the Hindus and tried to understand their approach towards the basic problems of religion and morality.

The Sufis' relationship with the local population and their method of preaching to them at their hospices led to the development of a new language. The formation and development of a dialect came to be termed as *Dakhni*. It was in the Deccan that the first Sufi prose work in *Dakhni* language was written during the reign of Sultan Firoz Bahamani, known as *Mi'raj al-Ashiqin*. The tradition attributes this to the renowned Chishti Saint of Gulbarga, Khwaja Banda Nawaz Gesu Daraz. Gesu Daraz was a well-known academician and scholar and had composed a number of works in Delhi. After settling in Gulbarga, he is known to have compiled several books and also established a *madrasa* at his *khanqah*.[12] Gesu Daraz was a learned scholar and was also well versed in Quranic studies, Prophetic traditions, theology and Sufism.[13] He is said to have known an extensive understanding of different languages like Arabic, Persian, Hindawi and Sanskrit. This helped him to converse with all classes of people. He also wrote a commentary on Quran and another on *Mashariq-ul-anwar*, which is a well-known collection of Prophetic traditions.[14] The *Dakhani* or Hindawi dialects were not the only regional languages that were developing as literary languages during the medieval period. For instance, Chishti Sufi Shaikh Farid al-din Ganj-i-Shakar was the first to use Punjabi as a literary language. These saints also produced literature in the Marathi language. These saints studied Sanskrit and old Marathi texts and wrote in Marathi or *Dakhani* explaining the mystic philosophy of the Hindus. For instance, Husain Ambarkhan wrote a commentary on Bhagvatgita in Marathi.[15] While the Chishti practice of *Sama* provided the foundation for a syncretic musical tradition. The collection of religious songs known as *qawwali* is said to have begun with Amir Khusrau.

Richard Eaton talks about the dualism inherent in the roles performed by the Sufi Saints and his followers (in the present context Sufi Sarmast). He argues that they came to the Deccan not only with the imperial armies, thus attributing a degree of legitimacy to them but also functioned as a ghazi or religious soldier, while maintaining their identity as a Sufi. They prayed incessantly for the success of such belligerent campaigns which were styled as jihad or religious war. The pertinence of this argument becomes clear when one considers the Islamic tradition which is replete with the ideas of inner and outer jihads. Historians have argued that the distinction between the two is an unnecessary construct of later times and that the two are really rolled into the term jihad. If that be the case, then it does seem plausible that they supported the political ambitions of the rulers and gave religious legitimacy and furthered the cause of Islam by Proselytization as well. Eaton states that unlike the common notions of peaceful conversion, there was also the spread of Islam by the sword. Eaton clearly traces the trajectory of these warrior Sufis and argues that they came into an area considered the *Dar- al-Harb* and remained there only as long as there was a Muslim military presence. They came along with the aim of providing legitimacy and furthering the cause of Islam. Eaton then lays stress on the collaboration of the Muslim rulers and *shaikhs* and how the two stuck together when standing against a non-Muslim state and population. When the state of Bijapur had a Muslim power at the centre, the role of the Sufi was diversified. The Sultans were not looking for religious legitimacy and the Sufis were no longer wandering mendicants but rather people with a stake in the state of Bijapur. Here the Sufis assumed an anti-shia stance and involved themselves in the working of the day-to-day court procedures and tried to change the heterodox ways of the sultan.[16] Such an attempt is redolent of the task that was assumed by Shaikh Ahmad Sir Hindi, who tried to control the heterodox elements that had entered the court during the times of Akbar. These two Sufis acted as the Ulema and tried to end the loose unity of all religions that certain kings had about. For them there were clear distinctions between the Hindus and the Muslims and the Shia's and the Sunnis, and these divisions were to be respected by an Islamic ruler. In this manner they were divisive as well.[17] Indeed, in the case of the Deccan barring a Sufi saint or two, not many tried to build close contact with the common people. The non-elite Kannidiga and Maharashtrian non-Muslims were not the people with whom Sufis worked at all, and they were merely rejected as infidels.[18]

In regards to conversion, of non-Muslims in the Deccan, Thomas. W. Arnold has argued that peaceful Muslim saints were the most important agents in the spread of Islam. Eaton would argue that the conversions attributed to them in oral folklore are highly exaggerated and need to be brought down considerably. For him, this task was also not as peaceful as made out to be and we have already discussed the role of the warrior Sufi.

B. Spirituality, Culture and Politics in Deccan's Bhakti Legacy

The Bhakti movement is treated mainly as a literary movement and can be regarded as an "ideological phenomenon" which had religion as the basis of its inspiration. It cannot be denied that every religious reform movement has a certain purpose. It rises out of certain socio-economic conditions and aims at the upliftment of the unprivileged and oppressed sections of the society. Bhakti has been a sustaining strand of Indian thought. But a close look at the medieval variation of it would immediately reveal that far from being unidirectional, it flourished in multi-stream currents. While Bhakti celebrated the revival of the essentials of Indian scriptures, simultaneously, it was a dissent movement that went against the Brahminic authority and dependence on Kshatriya royalty; on the other hand, it succeeded in winning the confidence and mass support of the people at large. While they went forward to purge Hinduism of its accumulated ills, they were also prepared to combat the ruthless oppressions of the new religionists enjoying royal patronage. These dimensions of social protest and independence of position lent Bhakti movement a unique character. The tradition began with the Tamil Saiva saints, the Nayanars.[19]

It should also be considered that around this period, of the three major kingdoms of South India, the Cholas were Saiva in faith. The Pallavas and the Pandyas were converted from Jainism to Saivism by these two poets Appar and Sambandhar. After gaining royal support, when Saivism was penetrating the masses as well, the Jain-Buddhist monasteries were transformed into Saiva shrines. Bhakti poets, nevertheless, had forsaken their roles as crusaders soon.[20] Rather than being involved in external struggles, they concentrated more on attaining self-control and pacification of desires.

Although the earlier Bhakti literature was more concerned with sin-penance-redemption, the later phase was more society oriented and hence could penetrate deep into the chasms of discriminatory social orders. The advent of the Islamic powers precipitated this change extraneously. Attracted by the spell of congregational chanting of the name, people like tailor Namdeva, potter Gora, gardener Samvata, goldsmith Narhari, untouchable Chokha, barber Sena, maid Janabai or dancer Kanhapatra assembled at the altar of Pandharpur.

The movement was a significant milestone in the cultural history of medieval India as it was the silent revolution in society brought about by various socio-religious reformers. This movement was responsible for many rites and rituals associated with the worship of God by Hindus, Muslims and Sikhs of the Indian subcontinent. For example, Kirtan at a Hindu Temple, Qawwali at a Dargah (by Muslims) and singing of Gurbani at a Gurdwara are all derived from the Bhakti movement of medieval India (800–1700). The leader of this Hindu revivalist movement was Shankaracharya, and this movement was propounded by Chaitanya Mahaprabhu, Namdeva, Tukaram and Jayadeva. The movement's major achievement was its abolition of idol worship.

In Deccan and medieval Maharashtra Bhakti cult is essentially known as "devotional theism, differed in its orientation and teachings from other contemporary religious movements both orthodox and reformative, it became a dominant phenomenon which influenced the socio-political and religious life."[21]The Maharashtra Dharma was a part of the Bhakti movement. It emerged as a reform movement from the fold of Hinduism, for socio-religious readjustment in order to achieve a better social position for the lower class of people. It was the cult of *Vitthal* or *Vithoba* which evolved at Pandharpur in the late 13th century and subsequently became popular in all of Maharashtra, Andhra Pradesh and Tamil Nadu. The cult was greatly under the influence of the Nathpanthis, since its founder, Gyandev or Gyaneshwar. The cult was led by Saint poets, who generally belonged to the lower strata of society, such as Kunbis, tailors, carpenters, potters, gardeners, barbers and even outcaste Mahars.

Umesh Ashok Kadam says that "it was not a revolt against caste like-Buddhism and to remove or end it but to reform and revitalize it. The elevated teachings of the saints challenged caste exclusiveness." The Saints raised the downtrodden class to a spiritual position and social importance by understanding and accepting their skills for the building of *Swaraj*. The Bhakti saints expressed against self-mortification, meaningless fasts and penances, and endless pilgrimages, and their attitude towards God was entirely personal, and they even practised intense devotion. They rejected Sanskrit as a language and preferred to interpret the ethos and essence of the teachings in vernacular languages, which attracted the masses.[22]

Both the idea of Bhakti and the temple as the focus of the devotional cult get crystallized and promoted in the bhakti hymns. In the Deccan and Andhra, the transition from a predominantly commercial/trading economy to a new agrarian order based on land grants also marks the decline of Buddhism and the transition towards the emergence of the Brahmanical or Puranic tradition as the dominant one. It can be seen in the contemporary Saiva and Vaishnava temples of these regions from 4th to 6th centuries A.D. ushering in a new socio-political order, that is monarchial polities (some 40 of them), which crystallized from about the 6th century. R. Champakalakshmi says that under the new socio-political order of the not yet polarized in the form of sectarian organizations Saivism continuously had an edge over Vaishnavism due to its "greater assimilative and incorporative capacity."[23] Many of the Buddhist centres were taken over by the Brahmanical centres of worship. The Bhakti movement of Tamilakam had no direct influence over the early medieval religious developments in the Deccan and the Andhra until the 12th century, when the Vira Saiva movement emerged as a more radical challenge to the Brahmanical socio-religious hierarchy in Karnataka. The socio-political function of bhakti varied according to the chronological and spatial appearance of the concept in different contexts, and despite the protest against caste hierarchy, it did not succeed in overthrowing the caste system.

The Tamil Bhakti concept inspired a socio-religious movement. It was developed systematically by the Alvar hymns and further promoted by the Nayanar hymns for popularizing the sectarian Saiva and Vaishnava religions. Developing into an ethical and moral principle, capable of evolving new value systems, the bhakti concept succeeded in providing the basis for a dominant ideology, consciously promoted by the ruling families like the Cholas who founded the most enduring regional state in south India. It proved to have immense capabilities to sustain and revitalize itself during a situation of crisis. The political role of Bhakti in Tamilakam as said by R. Champakalakshmi appears to have overshadowed its socio-religious purposes.

The later Hagiographical literature shows that the protest was against the Vedic Brahmans or Chaturvedis, along with temple administration of the Brahmadeya sabha, in the social and religious spheres, their orthodoxy, that is, claims to purity and proximity to the divine and expressing a strong criticism of Varna hierarchy, denouncing the followers of the law books, their *kula* and *gotra*.

The socio-economic context in which this opposition was the change from a predominantly trading (urban) and commercial (money) economy to a new agrarian system based on land grants to Brahmans or Chaturvedis along with the special privileges, economic and administrative/political. The movement became popular because of the hagiographical writings marking a societal crisis caused by the sectarian rivalry between the Saivas and Vaishnavas and also due to a diversified economy and urbanization, with non-agricultural groups becoming increasingly influenced and even high caste *velalas* (agriculturists) competing for a greater share in the authority structure, which was dominated by the Brahmans. Some of the major sacred centres of Shiva and Vishnu later came to be linked to a larger pan-Indian pilgrimage network, when attempts were made to bring all the strands of the mainstream Brahmanical and the lesser non-Brahmanical folk traditions within the ambit of the "Hindu" framework in the Vijayanagara period. The creation of temples in various centres by the early medieval royal and chiefly patrons meant, apart from new shrines, also the conversion of local cult centres into shrines of Shiva and also of Vishnu, in some cases through the process of acculturation.

The movement of Vira-Saivism began at a time of a major economic diversification, with agriculture and trading occupations gaining importance, first in the 12th century and more intensively in 15th and 16th centuries. The propagators of this anti-Brahmanical religion tradition came from all sections of society, especially from the lower caste. Work was considered as worship. Working tools and work were considered a media through which worship and devotion could be expressed. Importance was given to achievement and doing well in this life. It also includes the significant contribution done by the women saints in the propagation and creation of awareness on various issues related to freedom, spirituality and self-expressions of the feminine gender at large through the bhakti movement.

The bhakti movement or the devotional movements in medieval India witnessed the emergence of downtrodden saints who have been revered as intellectuals and organized a reformation movement along with their contemporaries like the rising of the anti-caste leaders and women saints. Given a patriarchal social setup that denied freedom to women, spirituality provided the only means of self-expression. Women saints ranged from the conformists who were wives, daughters or sisters of male saints and the rebels who broke every social norm, including the discarding of clothes. It is interesting that not only the conformists but also the rebels were accepted in the Hindu pantheon. Spirituality provided Indian women with the freedom which orthodox Hindu society had denied them. The emergence of women saints took place in the context of bhakti or devotional movements which characterized the medieval age in India. The bhakti movement was marked by the large rejection of the existing ritual hierarchy and Brahmanical superiority, the use of the vernacular in preference to Sanskrit. There was emergence of the low caste, non-literate persons as great spiritual leaders. There was also the large-scale participation of the peasantry, artisans and other lower classes as well ritually inferior but economically powerful groups such as skilled craftsmen in these devotional movements.

All movements were a part of the social structure, geophysical landscape, economic environment, etc. The notion of devotional movement keeps changing. Every structure could produce its own variation of devotion. By and large what seems to be running as a thread was patriarchy as something that characterizes all these structures. But patriarchy had different forms in different structures. Women were not invisible in the historical movements. Sometimes society valorized one figure, leading to the submission of other figures.

Imaging of a devotional movement can be of two types: self-imaging and superimposed representation. These include self-imaging of women such as Vaishnavai's autobiography written in 14th-century Maharashtra. Women were using familial metaphors to subvert the family. Gender dissent had various ways of expressing itself and one's sexual sublimation which does not reject the idea of wifehood. The concept of the bride of the lord can be emphasized upon. A woman could project herself as the bride of the lord. Just like Mirabai who represented a bridal mysticism. The language of patriarchy would be used to subvert patriarchy. Defiance would be the third mode of dissent.

However, the extreme forms of defiance were often not well accepted by the sects themselves, because there are many writings about naked male saints but not about women. Viraivites hagiography never opened up about Akkamahadevi and Lalleivari's nudity. Paintings did not depict her first and later depicted Akkamahadevi with very long hair covering her private parts. Lalleivari wrote that no garment could be fairer than her garment of air and sky. Janabai though in a milder way than Akkamahadevi speaks of throwing away the cover from the head, holding the head high and walking on the street taking herself as a prostitute of God.

However, in ordered patriarchal society an ideal woman is considered passive, submissive and silent. Her spirituality was to be defined by her sacrifice for the service to her male owner/husband. Thus, widows, prostitutes and ascetics were often considered dangerous because they had no owner. However, both prostitutes and the female ascetic conceiving herself often as the bride of the lord were granted an auspicious status. The married spiritual women in most cases faced opposition from their household. Their reactions were different and diverse, like leaving the family, leaving a householder's life but not consummating the marriage and doing service to their family.

The duality in dealing with strong and creative women seems to be a characteristic of our culture that persists even today. The entrance of women into the monastic order was never easy and she should be ready to risk everything, by openly defying family, community and social opinion and by flouting all norms. If she survives it all and still is creative, she will get recognition, but a very special kind of honour is reserved. And they are worshipped for being a category apart. These types of women by definition are considered to be in a different category from other women. So, the freedom allowed to her will not be extended to other ordinary women. These women saints become an object of adoration rather than a model or a guide for other women.[24]

The Vira-Saivism doctrine of Sakti vishishtadvaita assigns a special place to women according to Siddharama. The Vira Saiva rejection and criticism of the idea of pollution which applied to women illogically in several contexts, especially in the menstrual period, directly questions the patriarchal, gender subordination of women in various ways. In Vira-Saivism women could touch the *linga* even during the menstrual cycle. Women could participate in or perform any ritual. Overturning the traditional societal (patriarchy, Brahmanical) values of caste pollution and gender inequalities, even creation was said to be taken from *maya* (parama sakti) who herself emanates from Shiva.

The women saints in medieval south India emerged in the atmosphere of discrimination and suppression but blossomed forth into thinkers, scholars and realized souls. Their life and works constitute the supreme form of the self-expression of women. The life and work of the women saints is shrouded in mystery unlike that of the men saint.[25] This was partly due to the fact that none of them established a *guruparampara* or the monastic tradition with disciples who would have preserved the composition of the saints. Very few of the North Indian women saints gained any recognition of their spiritual greatness during their lifetime. They were usually scorned off by calling them mad and shameless. But this is not true for the South where the Women saints like that of Akka Mahadevi and Karaikal Ammaiyar were held in great reverence by their followers. Vijaya Ramaswamy says that it is possible to explain the differential impact of women saints in north and south in terms of perception of real or imaginary threats to the social fabric in the north leading to the greater rigidity and restrictions on women in contrast to the south.

The most important thing is to look at the social background of these women saints. They came from all classes. But most of them came from the priestly class or from the Shudra professional group. The reason for this may be because of the higher awareness levels of both groups. While the Brahmin women had some access to education, both sacred and secular, for example Lalleswari of Kasmir, Muktabai and many more, the awareness of the Shudra women arose, and economically they were almost coequal to men. It can also be seen that number of women saints related to Vaishnavites was less in comparison to the women saints related to Saivite cult. This may be because that Saivism was an anti-Brahmanical cult. Many of the lower caste saints were associated with Saivism. Many of the traders and craft groups like weavers, tanners, the *panchala* or group of five smiths and untouchable craftsmen had joined the Vira-Saivism movement in anticipation of the greater protection of their craft against oppressive taxation and enslavement by priestly intermediaries and the state.[26] Although lower caste women do figure in the work of Ramanujan's Srivaisnavism, this was still essentially orthodox in its essence. Even in the north there was no difference in the Vaishnavism trend; there too excessive liberation was not allowed.

The women saints can be classified into two broad categories on the basis of the spiritual path which they had chosen. One spectrum was the rebel, the other was being the conformists. The rebels gave up the conventional lifestyle when they were left with no option like that of Akka Mahadevi. It is said that she went to the palace of king Kausika but never married him. She walked out of the palace naked with her long hair covering her. Even in North India Mirabai and Lalla had walked out of marriage due to ill-treatment. The conformist category of women had accepted the yoke of marriage.

Thus, we can find three different trajectories about the role of women in the devotional movement. The first is the canonical exclusion where women could not enter. They could not become *sanyasi*. The order prescribed for women salvation lay in the notion of *pativratya*, not in the questioning of the order. Women were not to be part of the monasteries. One of the most powerful modes of dissent came from women questioning the canonical exclusion. The second trajectory was reluctant exclusion. The presence of women was accepted after a bitter contestation. So, women were admitted up to a certain level. Another way of entering the path of femininity was by denying femininity. The third way was the way of radical entry through dissent. Such was the way how a large number of women were included in Viraivite movement or the Varkari movement.

The Bhakti Movement also had strong political implications. It was a counter-culture to the existing atrocious culture. Bhakti stood for the propagation of dynamism in society; it threw away the prevailing orthodoxy in society. It practised a spirituality development in society which paved the way for a scientific temperament to re-question and review the existing religious orders which were encapsulated in the Sanskrit versus and trying to interpret them their ethics and essence with a vernacular base. This paved way to a different level of energy to understand the "*Maharashtra Dharma*" shedding off the social norms, taboo rituals for the betterment of the society as a whole, with an inclusive character which now gave way to understand the plight of the downtrodden, understanding and accepting the various skills of these downtrodden for the building of the "*swaraj*."

These reformation and protestant movements shaped Shivaji's idea of *Hindawi Swarajya* (a state of the sons of the soil)[27] an upsurge intended for the propagation of spiritual quest, he stood forth as the champion of Hindu religion. M.G. Ranade gave an explanation on the concept of *swarajya*, he says "the ground was prepared partly by nature, partly by the ancient history of the country, partly by the religious revival ... under Mahomedan rule for three hundred years."[28] It was to protect his religion that he started his campaign against Muslim aggressions. G.S. Sardesai argues that ever since the advent of Muslim rule, the people of Maharashtra lived in depressing times and their religion was treated with open disregard.[29] Ramdas was a big influence on Shivaji, the contemporary saints spoke of Deccan being under Mohammedan rule, and they inspired Shivaji for the regeneration of Hinduism in the South.[30] Therefore, Shivaji's struggle for independence was for the re-establishment of the traditional order of society. As J.V. Naik points out, "It was not directed against Islam, nor was it intended for the propagation of the Hindu religion. Its basic aim was to carry forward the ancient religion and culture of all the people residing in Maharashtra."[31] The ideal of *Swarajya* came into being in response to the pressing need of the times. According to V.V. Joshi, Maratha nationalism was a compound of geographical integration and linguistic and cultural affinity, cemented by a common religious faith and stimulated by galling Muslim domination.[32]

However, it would not be right to consider that this political idea was for the establishment of a communal empire. *Swaraj* was ideal for the state established by Shivaji and *Maharashtra Dharma* was its ideology. Almost all saints were pacifists except for Ramdas who advocated the spread of *Maharashtra Dharma*; the Maharashtra Dharma did not differ from Hindu Dharma.[33] None of these saints ever directly attacked the caste system. But the democratic atmosphere created by Bhakti was properly used by Shivaji. He provided equal opportunity to men of merit from all castes and grades of society, including the Muslims.[34] Shivaji revived the Hindu customs and Hindu administrative system and compiled a glossary of administrative terms in Sanskrit, the *Raj-Vyavahara-Kosha*.[35]

He then followed the policy of Deccan for the Deccanis to accomplish his concept of *Hindawi Swarajya*. The integration of the Deccan was twofold: firstly, there was the task of unifying the Maratha chiefs under one umbrella; and secondly, an alliance with the Deccan kingdoms-Bijapur and Golconda was essential.[36] He then visualized the need to unite together the scattered forces of the Maratha chiefs to form a sovereign alliance. By doing so, he hoped that it would destroy the Shahi dynasty and enable him to form the Maratha state. He began to gather a band of young faithful comrades; he started holding secret meetings, planning to capture forts, and secure funds by attacking private and public treasures. With his persuasive tongue he moved his fellow comrades on two fronts: political and religious. The religious aspect had the moral fervour of "Maharashtra Dharma," to animate the people for a common purpose and sanctified by a common devotion to the country. He eventually succeeded in creating a feeling of new spirit among the people of common interest and common patriotism born of liberal religious fervour.

A Closer Look into Marathi Culture

Assimilation of the northern culture into medieval Deccan and specifically into Maharashtra was an outcome of the political development that can be seen much before the Maratha period. Deccan first witnessed the political campaign from the north, when Alauddin Khilji, the Sultan of Delhi attacked the Yadava ruler Ramchandradeva of Devagiri in the last decade of the 13th century A.D. Malik Kafur, the commandant of Allauddin, annexed Devagiri in the second decade of the 14th century. Malik Kafur's other conquest of the south included the ones over Kaktiyas of Warrangal, Hoysalas of Dwarasamudra and Pandyas of Madura. Such political campaigns brought with them the trends of Islamic culture that were alien to the people of the Deccan. The establishment of the Bahamani Empire in the Deccan was the most visible form of Islamic culture. Such political developments triggered anti-theatrical reactions in the minds of the Hindu population in the Deccan; the infusion of new cultural trends was unavoidable.[37] It was impossible to ignore these trends, the manifestations of which were language and the performing arts. The literary and artistic evidence suggests that both religious ties and the long-standing commercial links between Persia and the Deccan provided important channels for cultural traditions during the reign of Bahamani rulers. By 15th century, the Deccanis created their own vernacular language known as *Dakhani,* an early form of Urdu. The development of this new language in the Deccan contributed towards the fusion of Hindu-Muslim cultures. Literary *Dakhani* had attained such respectability that not only the Sufis but the rulers like Golconda's Sultan Muhammad Quli Qutb Shah and Bijapur's sultan Ibrahim Adil Shah composed poetry in this language.

The great saint poet Dnyaneshwar and others also used some *Dakhani* words in their Marathi compositions. These saints composed verses in Hindi or *Dakhani* for their non-Marathi audiences and pointed out the common features between the two religions of the Hindus and the Muslims. For instance, Eknath, another well-known Marathi poet used *Dakhani* Urdu words like *phakir*, *maula*, *sab*, etc. in his Marathi compositions. In fact his famous work *Hindu-Turk Samvad* is composed in Marathi and *Dakhani*. Saints like Tukaram and Ramdas also composed many devotional songs in *Dakhani*. Not only did the Hindu saints write in *Dakhani*, but the Muslim saints also reciprocated by producing literature in the Marathi language. These saints studied Sanskrit and old Marathi texts and wrote in Marathi or *Dakhani* explaining the mystic philosophy of the Hindus. For instance, Husain Ambarkhan wrote a commentary on Bhagvatgita in Marathi.[38]

V.K. Rajwade and Y.M. Pathan[39] have given an account of Persian influence on Marathi literature. For instance, the administrative documents in which Persian language was used are mainly *ajnapatras* (orders), *sanads* (grants), *kaulnamas* (agreement), *parwanas* (permission letter), *dastaks* (permits), etc. Persian influence can also be seen in the personal histories or chronicles of the rulers known as *tawarikh* in Persian and its Marathi adaptation known as *bakhars*. Besides administrative usage, Persian words were used in various other types of Marathi documents like dress material, war and military equipment, format of official letters, etc.[40] Later an attempt was made by Shivaji to expel the Persian terms from administrative usage and even replaced them with Marathi or Sanskrit terms. After his coronation, he not only promoted Marathi as *raj bhasha* (court language) but also put Raghunath Pant Hanumante in charge of compiling an administrative glossary, *Rajvyavahar Kosh*.[41] Shivaji continued to promote Sanskrit language by naming the *ashta pradhan* (council of ministers) as per Sanskrit nomenclature with terms such as Nyayadhish and Senapati.[42]

The coming of the Europeans and catholic missionaries to Deccan not only changed the social structure but also had an impact on the culture of the region. These missionaries not only learnt the local language of the region but also translated quite a few Hindu texts with the help of Indian scholars. They even translated Christian catechisms, prayers and New Testament gospels into local languages and even composed original texts about Christianity in these languages.[43] One of the early compositions was the Christian *Purana* written in Konkani-Marathi by the English Jesuit Thomas Stephens. The need for studying Hindu religions, customs and traditions was obvious; for the missionaries it was a tool used to convert the locals. A fuller understanding of Hindu beliefs often led to the study of Sanskrit; however, European missionaries often concentrated on vernacular literature.

Music

The Maratha rulers of Tanjore according to K.R. Subramanyam "made Tanjore their home and continued the traditional policy of protection of the subjects and patronage of religions, art and letters."[44]Tanjore was a city of erotic delights in which the king encouraged recreational activities in many ways despite instability in the political scenario and developed it as a seat of art and Music. From the time of the Nayaka period, Achyutappa Nayak, a lover of fine arts gave away free gifts of lands and villages to the Telugu families of scholars, composers and musicians. One such village Melatur was consequently renamed Achyutarayapuram and came to be a centre of dance drama.[45] Thragier or Thyagaraja a Telugu Brahmin was mainly responsible for spreading the fame of Tanjore as the seat of music in the 19th century. He was a poet, saint and philosopher combined in one. He was under the tutelage of Sonthi Venkataramanayya, a great musician at Rajah Tuljaji's court.[46] Direct Maratha influence on Carnatic music is attested by the presence of instruments like the *gottu vadya* and the *jaltarang*. Many Maratha musicians who migrated to Tanjore also made a strong contribution to south Indian music. The most important contribution of the Marathas to Deccan was the *kirtan*.[47] The Maratha court was almost singularly instrumental in defining an official standard for the tradition by virtue of its location at the crossroads of cultural and religious influences; it helped foster a new imagination and musical conception.[48] Rajas like Shahaji, Tukkoji, Pratap and Amar Singh were well versed in music. Shahaji composed many songs (*kirtis*) on Lord Tyagesa. He also composed *Tarus*, *Gitas*, dance dramas and *padams*.[49] Another Maratha ruler Tukoji was himself a musician and wrote a treatise entitled *Sangita Saramrita*.[50]

Caste, Status and Social Hierarchy in the Deccan

Each caste in Deccan, as elsewhere, had its own socio-economic and cultural traditions. Each caste looked after its members by providing them with educational and other facilities such as dwellings, wells, etc. Assistance was given to the handicapped, destitute, widowed, orphans. It also served as an agency for social action against those who violated caste regulations and declared them unfit for social intercourse, until they had undergone prescribed penances.

A body of caste members gathered to look after the preservation of the castes was called *Jati Gotra* or *Daiva*.[51] Each caste had its own economic aspect and members of different castes served the village community by following their traditional occupations. Another important social body that helped to preserve the social structure of the Marathas was the *Brahmasabha* (a bench of learned Brahmins). It was composed of the local learned Brahmins and the *Dharmadhikari* or a public censor of morals as the head. It was his duty to administer justice; their advice was also sought after by the government officials. As H. Fukazawa argues that the role of the state in preserving the caste system was very much prominent in protecting the social order.[52] The *Gotasabha* or *Hajir Majlis* looked after personal matters such as social, religious and judicial spheres.

The village community consisted of cultivators (*Mirasdars* and *Uparis*) and artisans (*Balutas*). *Baluta* system was the relationships between *Balutedars*, village communities, village officials and the state. All of them acquired rights and socio-economic positions according to their land tenures. Therefore, it is necessary to discuss the land tenures, which were held in the villages, because the hub for socio-economic and administrative activities was the village.[53] Village land was divided into two categories: land for production and land for habitation (*Kali* and *Pandhari*)[54] that was possessed by the three kinds of land tenures—*Miras*, *Upri* and Inam *Watan*. Agriculture was the backbone of the people and the standard of living was very poor, the barter system was in practice. The office bearers and the servants of the village community received their remuneration in kind. Dadaji Khondev, Shahji's regent was the first to bring land under cultivation, under these circumstances the rulers found it necessary to recognize the hereditary rights of an individual so as to bring many cultivators to the land. The Muslim rulers approved these lands in the form of *Mirasi* tenure, while those in offices (*Deshmukh, Deshpande* of a pargana and *Patil, Kulkarni* of a village and occupations (such as *Shete*, *Mahajans* and *Khooms* of a *Peth* or a Mart and 12 *Balutas* of a village) in the form of a watan tenure. Thus, politically self-sufficient economic units in the form of village and administrative divisions of parganas evolved over time.[55]

The Muslim state was perpetually at war with the non-Muslims. *Jazya* was collected from the *zimmis* as a religious as well as a political duty. The comparatively less fanatical rulers of Deccan were no exceptions by any means. These acts done in the name of religion did pave a way for resentment among the sentiments of the Marathas.[56] We see such concerns raised by Chhatrapati Shivaji in his correspondence to Aurangzeb on the issue of the implementation of *jazya*, as a reaction against the Muslim rule.

The political structure of the Marathas created a complex social structure which necessitated establishment of cordial social relations, peaceful co-existence and integration.[57] Shivaji succeeded in making his subjects realize certain moral principles coupled with material interests. Jadunath Sarkar has called this unifying spirit as "community of life and thought without readiness on the part of the people to dine and marry freely together."[58] Shivaji was inspired by Swami Ramdas, he says "By love and cordiality make all the different classes in the kingdom your supporters. Unite multitudes of men together, fill them with one spirit and hurl them upon the enemies. In this way establish Maharashtra Dharma everywhere."[59] It was the upheaval of the population strongly bound together by the "common affinities of language, race, religion and literature, seeking further solidarity by a common independent political existence."[60]

During the Peshwa period the dominant groups among the Brahmins, the *Konkannasthas/ Chitpavans* and the *Deshasthas* became very influential.[61] Brahmins engaged in religious duties, studied the Shastras, acted as temple worshippers and preached the traditional religion by citing the Puranas to the masses. Besides spiritual work, they were also engaged in clerical work. Important administrative posts at all levels such as village accountants, district accounts and ministerial posts all belonged to the Brahmins. These duties gradually got hereditary confirmation.[62]

The Maratha caste engaged in military, agricultural and mercantile activities. They claimed to be the Kshatriya caste due to military activities and engaged in protecting the frontiers, foreign aggression and in maintaining law and order in their respective areas.[63] They were divided into two groups. The first group included the *Patil*, *Deshmukh*, the village and Pargana Officers or the chief landholders (*Watandars*). The second group consisted of the cultivator caste known as the *Kunbis* and is referred to as *Mirasdars*, *Thalkaris* and *Uparis* in Marathi records. The *Mahar* caste formed part of the lowest societal hierarchy. They were engaged in low works such as scavenging and clearing dead animals, keeping watch at night and acting as messengers and guides to the officials.

The Gram Sanstha a village community organization played an important role in the social and economic life of the people of Maharashtra. Every village was a close-knit and an isolated self-contained unit.[64] The active inhabitants of the village were known as *Desaks*, i.e. cultivators (Mirasdars and Uparis), village officials (Patil, Chaugula, Kulkarni) and the *Balutedars*. These inhabitants formed the village community which always existed as the socio-economic unit in the Maratha territory. The system of *Balutedari* can be traced from the 13th century onwards, and by the 17th and 18th centuries, this system became an important part of Maratha society and economy. The village servants who served village communities through their craft, services and articles and in exchange for their services and articles were given "*Baluta*" at the time of harvest; certain rights and privileges by the village communities were recognized as *Balutedars*.[65] The system was a "servant-cum-caste system" therefore the socio-economic positions of *Balutedars* remained backward in the social hierarchy of the village. This system either degraded their social status because the services of the *Balutedars* were caste based and were considered very low by the villagers. Therefore, the social rank of *Balutedars* was hardly uplifted in the social hierarchy of the village as it was based upon the caste status. Their social status (caste status) was unchangeable.

This being said, castes themselves were not uniform or monolithic, as is shown by the conflicts among the Brahmins in the region. Social life is a continuous process and keeps evolving with the course of time, but it does not change in its essentials. Likewise, the social fabric of Maharashtra from 1645 to 1818 could be viewed as a single stream with varying strands and shades. The caste system also established a system of hierarchy. In the reign of Shivaji, a balance of power was maintained among the different castes at the court and in the administration. The key to the vigour of Maharashtra lay in the secular and spiritual values which inspired the people of the region. These values stemmed from a religious upsurge which coincided with the advent of Islam in the Deccan, and which affiliated the elite castes, like the Brahmans, and the lower and middle castes, like the *Kunbis* and *Mahars*, to a common corpus of religious ideas. Later we see conflicts between these castes and sub-castes. The Brahmins placed themselves at the top of the caste hierarchy on the basis of ritual purity.[66] They were not, however, content with the recognition of their caste superiority; they wanted to establish their social superiority as well. To achieve this, they declared certain civil and religious rights as the exclusive privileges of the Brahmins and at the same time imposed certain disabilities on others. Brahmins of the region were the *Desastha* from Central Maharashtra and

Konkanastha or *Chitpavan* from Konkan. In the early days of the Maratha state, *Desastha* Brahmins were in greater prominence in administration, but with the rise of Balaji Vishvanath Peshwa they lost their pre-eminent position to the *Chitpavanas*, where we see this balance of power was disturbed. Within a few years, the Peshwas usurped all political power and used it for caste aggrandizement. The practice of *Danadharma* (charity) was accorded a high place and the Brahmins were taken as the most eligible people to receive the charity. The revenue on land owned by Brahmins and the customs duties on goods they imported were reduced. The Brahmins, particularly under the Peshwas, were given preference in its services, they were exempted from payment of ferry charges, octroi duties on transport of goods, house tax, etc.[67] They were further permitted to pay land assessments in cash at low rates. They were exempted from forced labour, death punishment, mutilation of limbs and other harsh punishments for any serious crime. Justice Ranade has remarked that "Brahmans at this time came to regard themselves as a governing caste with special privileges and exemptions, which were unknown under the system founded by Shivaji." This concentration of religious, political and economic power in the hands of one small caste was bound to arouse the jealously and resentment of other castes which often gave rise to sub-caste disputes among themselves.

For example, there was a conflict between *Kokanastha* Brahmins and *Kramavant* Brahmins from Konkan and Goa areas.[68] The same kind of dispute took place between the South Maharashtra and Konkan area. In this case also the Peshwa declared that they should continue to practise common dining with each other. The bitter controversy between the Brahmins and the *Prabhus*[69] from Puna, Pen and Konkan areas, over the eligibility of the latter to practise *vedoktakarma*, i.e. performing thread ceremonies and such rites prescribed for higher castes, is the best example.[70] The bitter controversy between the *Prabhus* and the *Kokanasthas* or the *"Vedokta Karmas"* reflects the growth of rigidity of castes under the Peshwa rule.

The *Deshastha* and *Saraswat* Brahmins and *Kayastha Prabhus* migrated to these kingdoms which offered them opportunities for employment and promotion. The suspicion and antagonism bred by this narrow sectarian policy led to conflict between Brahmins and non-Brahmins in Maharashtra.

There was severe discrimination among the sub-castes in the society. The practice of untouchability had its own peculiarities as they were treated as a distinct social stratum (*varna*) by some but not by others. This distinction was also made in relation to the degree of pollution caused by the untouchables, and thus certain castes stood on the lowest rung of the caste hierarchy, and they had to experience extremely humiliating and unkind treatment at the hands of society under the cover of religion. For example, members of the Shudra castes were not permitted to enter the Brahminical shrines. As such, clearly prescribed by the rule and regulations framed by Peshwa Balaji Bajirao concerning the management of Tryambakesvar temple at Nasik, they should not enter the holy shrine; they may have a *darshana* of the deity from the outer entrance.[71]

Hence, we see a transition in the society, in the form of caste distinctions and rigidity from the Chhatrapati to the Peshwa period. During the Peshwa period caste became the most dominant social institution. Prior to this period, the caste divisions were not so rigid. It was only the Peshwa's contribution to the making of a more orthodox and ritualistic society. As Sudha Desai remarks that

> the religious orthodoxy in the form of Brahmanism and casteism gained ascendency during the Peshwa period and worked against the unity in the society and state. It may be remembered that under condition of religious operation and insecurity during the preceding Shivaji's times, the Marathas as a whole had closed their ranks and had come together as co-religionists.[72]

Examining how the Bhakti saints observed the caste system gives us a valuable insight into contemporary critical appraisal of the social setup. The Bhakti movement was a product of a transitional society as a number of changes were taking place in the society on the political, economic and social front. The society was dominated by the Brahmans who in order to maintain their status quo, practised complex rites and rituals. The Brahmans believed that people who did not fit into the traditional four castes were termed outcastes or *chandalas*.[73] The Bhakti movement, characterized by protest of lower classes against the higher classes, witnessed the rise of a number of saints from the lower castes. Many bhakti saints, poets and philosophers sprang from the lower levels of Maratha society like Namdev (*Nhavi*), Gora (*Kumbhar*), Sena (*Nhavi*), Narahari (*Sonar*), Chokhamela (*Mahar*) and Savtia (*Mali*). All of these saints belonged to the lower strata of society and believed in a monistic view of the world and the supremacy of bhakti. The circumstances of their own birth and education naturally predisposed some of these preachers to take up such a position.[74] These bhakti saints not only elevated spiritual and ethical standards of the people but also gave the foundation for edifying thoughts.[75]

These saints believed that all humans are equal in status and also expressed their views on caste-based practice. For instance, they expressed their views on the practice of dinning that was limited to people of equal social status. According to Dnyanadev

> there was none high or low with God. All were alike to him. Never entertain the thought that I am high born, and my neighbor is low of birth. The Ganges is not polluted, nor is the wind tainted, nor the earth rendered untouchable, because the low born and high born bathe in the one, or breathe the other, or move on the back of the third.

Similarly, Eknath fed a *Mahar* at his house and believed that "the merit of feeding a hungry *Mahar* was proved to be far greater than that of feeding many hundred Brahmins."[76]

Another saint, Chokhamela protested against the caste-based entry to the temple. He even challenged the priests of temple at Pandharpur when they did not let him enter the temple and said,

> On this sacred earth all men and women walk alike and enjoy its fruits. Similarly, in the holy Ganga, all men and women have their dip to wash away their sins. The earth and the Ganga are common to all, irrespective of caste creed and religion. Likewise, the temple and the Lord the abode of love-are common to all. Hence my entry into the temple and worship, are not defilement.[77]

Not only the ideas but also the egalitarian practices by these saints caused betterment in social positions of the women. For instance, saint Mahopant married a *Mahar* woman and the status of his wife was associated with Mahopant, and both Mahopant and his *Mahar* wife were considered holy by the people. When she died, he performed her death rites according to Veda. Like Saint Mahopant, Krishnadas master of Jayaram Swami married a *Nhavi* woman. The social status of his *Nhavi* wife was associated with Krishnadas and his marriage was accepted and recognized by the people and person like Shankaracharya raised no objection. The idea of inter-caste marriage by saints uplifts the social positions of those women who married them and somehow it must have influenced their followers for practising inter-caste marriage.[78]

Not only the saints belonging to the lower castes but also saints from the higher castes condemned discrimination on grounds of caste, creed and sex. According to Vipranarayan, an Alvar saint belonging, to the Brahmin caste, there should be no discrimination among the devotees whether they belong to Brahmin caste or Shudra. He even praises a Shudra if he is a true saint than a mere Brahmin. In his work named Tiru-Maiai he says: "Is it not better to be born in the lowest caste with service to Thee, then those who have practiced Vedas without remembering that service to Thee is the sole goal?"[79] He hence gives importance to merit than to caste and believed that it is better to be born in a low caste and become a devotee than to be born in the Brahmin caste and remain ignorant.

However, somehow the elevated ideas, teachings and practices of these saints reduced the limitations of social relations, reduced the buffer spaces and caste-based behaviours and caused improvement in the social positions of lower castes. It also caused social improvement in those communities of *Balutedars* who belonged to the community of these Saints. Besides, these egalitarian ideas caused the assemblage of heterogeneous communities in one spiritual and probably in one social space. "It modified the strictness of the old spirit of caste exclusiveness. It raised the Shudra classes to a position of spiritual power and social importance, almost equal to that of the Brahmins."[80]Thus, these Bhakti saints illuminated the period they lived in, tried to educate and uplift the people through their teachings and also succeeded in creating a space for the lower castes.[81]

Christianity in the Region: Ecclesiastical Discourses in Deccan

By 1775 a substantial number of Roman Catholic missionaries had been active in South Asia, particularly in the Deccan, for 275 years. Almost all the missionaries were fully literate and many had learnt the local languages. Most had understood the importance of undertaking a serious study of Hindu religious beliefs and practices, and quite a few embarked on a translation of the Hindu texts with the help of Indian scholars. Some missionaries compiled dictionaries or wrote grammars of Sanskrit and vernacular languages.

A. Christianity Grows Local Roots: The Portuguese Mission in Deccan

The pressure on the missionaries for quick conversions was also a result of their dependency on the crown under the patronage system. The appearance of new Christian communities was a part of the king's overseas policy because it was expected that converted groups would become allies of the Portuguese Empire and its trading systems. As Frykenberg pointed out in his work that one has to understand the profound implications of religious activity for the inner workings of economic, social and political institutions.[82] So the Jesuits were trying to use every possible measure to convert people. Wherever the Jesuit missionaries went, they faced similar issues and challenges. The ways and methods by which they were adopting were also quite similar to each other.

Propagation of any religion and its acceptance in the society has to be seen in relation with its ability to culturally assimilate into the society. Adaptation to one's environment is very necessary. Rajamanickam says that "a teacher has to adopt himself to the nature of the student, otherwise what is taught becomes useless."[83] Same is the case with the scriptures; Nobili and even other priests in different places of Asia had to adapt themselves to their environment and to their social customs. The Jesuits were adapting themselves so that the new religious faith would be relevant to the Asian culture. The work of the Jesuits was carried out according to the commandments, but this fact cannot be denied that the temperamental, cultural and eclectic factors had an important role to play in the functioning of the Jesuits in many other exotic places.[84]

Andrew F. Walls says in his work that throughout Christian history two forces are distinguished in contrast tension. One is an indigenizing principle, a homing instinct, which creates in diverse communities a sense that the church belongs there, that it is "us." Another trend is to localize the vision of the church and also to universalize it.[85]

John W. O'Malley in his work has pointed out how the Jesuit missionaries could not overcome the racial prejudice in one go and they had to cope with it. Like Francis Xavier who had come to Goa and he was trying to catechize poor pearl fishers on the eastern coast of the cape of Comorin with basic prayers which he had translated into Tamil for them. So here we can see that Francis Xavier had to adopt the local language in order to teach the local people. This is how he had accommodated himself with the indigenous culture.[86]

In India we see the coming of Robert de Nobili; he was working in Cochin. He learnt a new language and was also looking into causes of why conversion was being prohibited.[87] He found that the people there held their holy religion in very low esteem. So, he was thought to be among them. So, Nobili claimed to be a *sanyasi*, a *sanyasi* to the local people meant one who leads his life in penance and chastity. He portrayed himself as a teacher of new spiritual law (religion). He even adopted the new lifestyle of the common people where he ate only rice and vegetables, touched or dealt with the people who were considered low by them and even took a Brahmin cook with him. He also adopted the dress of this place.

Another method that he adopted was that he did not meet any important dignitaries. No one was allowed to meet him and speak to him. Whenever somebody came to his house hoping to meet, he would send a word saying that he busies reading the holy laws that he is teaching. This act was very important to acquire and preserve the good opinion and esteem of these people. One day it was enquired at the court as to why this father never paid a visit to the court, it was then said that such was the chastity of the father that his eyes should not fall on a woman. And this virtue was held in high esteem there.

The trend of *Guru Shishya parampara* which was quite prevalent in India was also taken up by father G. Fernandes. He was running a school there for the children of that place, and he had already gained the title of Guru. Father Fernandes gave a book to a school teacher to translate into Tamil, and after reading this book he wanted to know more about this religion. So, he was sent to Nobili for further discussion on this topic. An auspicious date was quite important in India in the same way Nobili too fixed a day of a solar eclipse when the discussion would start. Nobili showed that man had some errors in his faith and some of them were a multitude of Gods present in his faith. Nobili said that there is only one God. There were rigorous discussions for 20 days; he finally said he wanted to be baptized and his wish was fulfilled and he was given the name Albert.[88] But there was some fear which had crept in after the conversion and that Albert's Guru had returned back from a journey and he was very angry with him, and the father feared that his Guru would go and complain to the Nayak and he would be expelled out of Madurai instead he was well regarded. The Guru came to meet the father, and to his surprise after a long discussion about the Christian religion, he had concluded that the ashes which they put on the forehead and the Lingam which they adore as God was all non-sense.

Later the converts were taught many things like they should help the father in propagating this religion further and they had already told him that all these idols and ceremonies were just tissues of lie.[89] The dress code which Father Robert started to wear was a long robe pale yellow in colour. He wore a cord which was made from five threads, three of Gold and two of white linen with a cross. He did not wear boots, he took a stick in his hand and a round vessel called *camandola* in one hand. He took up the dress of a *sanyasi*; he adored his forehead with ash. He adopted the dressing style of a *sanyasi* to look like one among the local people.[90]This was a sign of austerity. Father only talks to the high caste people to obtain greater credit and he was very difficult to access. Visitors had to come twice or thrice to be able to meet him. He was doing this to enhance his reputation according to the custom of the country. He learnt Tamil very fluently, and he could pronounce words as clearly as a Brahmin could. When visitors came to him he would sit on a raised platform covered with red cloth and a red cloth would be spread around on straw for the visitors to sit down. All had to bow down and join their hands. In short, the Jesuits were accommodating themselves within the framework of the existing culture in India. Nobili had byhearted many laws of his religion in order to impress his visitors, and he had written a book which showcased his deep knowledge of the Tamil classics.

Father Laerzio became his companion. He too had to follow the norms like eating on a plantain leaf and eating with hands which were very difficult for him. It is told in one of the accounts by Rajamanickam that Father Robert was very happy by seeing this new companion's complexion similar to the local people there. So here we can see how much the Jesuits wanted to adopt the local culture of the place in order to spread their religion in a way the local people could understand and feel a part of this new religion. Father Nobili would take only one meal a day which was not sufficient for Father Laerzio so he would dine separately. The account in detail mentions how Fr. Nobili had built the church keeping in mind the architectural style of the country. They even wanted to adopt the architectural style of the place. They had a separate space for women in the church behind the curtains so that the men could not see them. Nobili was called by a local name "*Aiyar*" which meant master.

But unfortunately, he had a lot of opposition around him. The Brahmins were very angry at him because he was converting so many Hindus to Christianity. People who were with him at the beginning left him alone and ran away. People believed in many superstitions. Like in an incident where a meeting was called by all Brahmins to find out the reason for the scarcity of rain that year, everybody concluded that Nobili was converting people so God was angry at him and that Nobili should be expelled from Madurai.

But later when things settled down he took up the title of Brahmin because he knew that a Brahmin would not accept a Guru until he was also from the same caste. He would tell stories that he belonged to a noble family in Rome and it was very similar to the ruling class in India. So, by birth Nobili was a Raja, by profession he was a Brahmin *Sanyasi*, this sounded so much like the Indian culture and tradition. But later when he was attacked by Fr. Buccerio for using Brahmin as a title which indicated race, and this was not appropriate for them as priests. Nobili argued by saying that Brahmin actually meant Doctor and anyone who was a doctor of Latin could use this title.

The two schools which were prevalent were the progressive and the conservative. Nobili and Ricci were people who belonged to the category who believed in adaptation to the environment and making the words of the Gospel acceptable to the people.

Ines G. Zupanov says that the Western notion of epistemological progress merged at a certain point with the indigenous. As the Brahman teacher Nobili had learnt of the fragmentary nature of the most sacred and secret text: the Vedas or *marai*. This gave him a scope to fulfil two of his objectives; one was to implant Christianity in the new-found region in assimilation with the pre-existing notions and to give a proof through its texts that Christianity as a religion was in progression with other indigenous religions.[91]

Portuguese were not familiar with the caste system; for them it was a very strange practice. It was very difficult for the Christian minority to fight against the caste system which was so universally prevalent in India. So, we can say that it was a great achievement for Nobili to at least bring all the lower caste people together in the same church, but according to their status. If he would have tried to outdo this system, then Nobili would have been harassed and the teaching of the Gospel would not have been possible. He had to adhere to the law of the land. Nobili, as said by Rajamanickam, condoned the caste system in order to destroy it.[92]

In India if Christianity could be shown as the religion which crowned the Vedas, it would have a claim on every orthodox Hindu. With such plans in mind, Nobili began to extract from approved commentaries of the Vedas a collection of the texts and allusions best suited to serve as a basis of demonstration of the truth of Christianity.[93] Translation is a matter of seeing the vernacular as a gift from God it takes the form of a ritual aspect as this took place during conversions. It was based on the promise of salvation.[94]

To make their practice relevant to India the Jesuits started to use music in religious services most frequently and elaborately. Masses were sung, along with it musical instruments were played. The musical instruments were shawms, kettledrums, trumpets, flutes and violins. A procession would be taken out on the street along with the musical instruments.

Nobili had adapted *Ponkal* festival because it had the traits of eating and cooking which is culturally universal.[95] He adopted a new model of *Pantaracami*; it was a new kind of "nativized" missionary model. This institution of *Pantaramacami* existed side by side with the Brahman *sanyasi* model. This model was introduced to reach out to the lower section of society. As Ines Zupanov points out that Martin hinted at this caste stratification and social mobility to higher status was a sign of "Sanskritization" a concept introduced by M.N. Srinivas.

Nobili proposed the view of Hindu custom as divided roughly into two spheres: political (social, civil) and religious. While the religious sphere consisting of superstitions had of course to be eliminated, the social was not seen as simply "neutral" or "indifferent," but as necessary for the grafting of Christianity.

The expansion of any large religious system was usually a slow process and Asia was no exception. The successful propagation of religion by the Portuguese missionaries was the result of Syncretism—the compromise between alien and indigenous concepts. The Jesuits adopted to combat the issues, which they were facing in a new land and which had different cultural diversities. They really had to understand the customs and traditions of the place and more importantly become one among them to propagate their religion. They had to have deep knowledge of the classics which were prevalent so that they could make their new religion relevant to the Deccani culture.

B. Commercial Interests, Cultural Observation and Conversion: The Dutch Mission in Deccan

The Dutch East India Company hired Protestant priests in the Deccan in the mid-17th century to create an amicable moral climate in the trade posts. There were some inquisitive Company Employees in the 17th and 18th centuries who contributed to the public welfare on Coromandel Coast through their writings. These employees were quite impressed by the learning of the brahmans and their views on life and death. Clergymen Abraham Rogerious, who lived at Pulicat for 17 years (1630–47) on the Coromandel Coast, wrote a book on the life, customs, faith and religious practice of Tamil Brahmans. He was the first to mention the four Vedas, but their description, according to J. Gonda, was more in harmony with the Tamil Vaishnava than Sanskrit sources.[96]

The next was Phillipus Baldaeus[97] (1632–1672), a cartographer and writer; the Company appointed him as a priest, and he was responsible for converting the Tamil communities of the region to the Dutch Reformed religion. He moved among the people and learnt the Tamil language so that he could preach and converse. He opined, "it is more befitting and seemlier that a teacher or minister masters the language of their minister." Baldaeus compiled several manuscripts to be used by native proponents of Protestantism and schoolmasters and prepared a Tamil Psalter. It was published in book form in 1755, the earliest vernacular book of music.[98]

Baldaeus' personal observation of the life and mores of Hindus constituted a monumental work in Dutch, which was printed in Amsterdam in 1672. Around this year it was also translated into German, and in 1703 abridged in English. An account of the daily habits and the manner of living of the Dutch in Coromandel was given by Baldaeus, who was the minister on the coast during the "Sixties." They had accepted many of the local customs, like washing the mouth after every meal and chewing betel leaves. The Dutch also commonly took a siesta. The major meal was taken between three and four in the afternoon. Overall, their diet was the same as in Holland and a large share of the meat and bacon for the Coromandel factors was supplied from back home as hopes of procuring victuals cheaply on the coast had was false. A bend of water, beer, and sugar boiled together and prepared, as it was a common drink at midday and in the afternoon was. On occasions, some Spanish wine or rum was added too. Spanish, French, and Rhenish wines were sent from Holland in limited quantities. Indian arak and Shiraz wine from Persia were very popular. Tea-drinking was new in fashion, and Chinese tea was considered the best. According to Baldaeus, some Dutch women drank too much tea; he also disapproved of the habit of mixing sugar-candy with it. Green tea-leaves were also used as a salad in those days on board the Dutch ships.[99]

Daniel Havart in his well-known work defended the Dutch employees on the coast against charges of drunkenness and debauchery and attributed their bad reputation to slanders spread by the English and the French. The records of the Dutch factories are, however, full of accounts of their inequities. As early as 1616, the Heeren XVII complained of the dissolute life of the employees on the coast, and matters did not improve in this respect with the passage of time. Coromandel, according to a Dutch governor, "was more prey to Bacchus and Venus than any other place in India," and many of the coast factors believed that "men must follow the ways of the land." Their zeal in this respect often involved the Dutch in serious difficulties with the local people and the other European companies. In 1633, it was decided to pay the Coromandel factors only the amount considered necessary for keeping house, the balance of their salary being paid when they returned to Batavia, so that they should have no surplus money in their hands during their stay on the coast. The measure was directed against both illegal private trade and habitual drunkenness and debauchery.[100]

A clergyman, with his headquarters at Pulicat, looked after the moral and spiritual welfare of the Company's employees in Coromandel and other Christians living under the protection of fort Geldria. In the subordinate factories, sacristans attended the necessary religious functions. As Portuguese was widely understood by the Indian Christians in Coromandel, the Dutch ministers were required to preach both in Dutch and Portuguese. Some clergymen like Baldaeus worked hard to spread the Protestant faith. Attempts were made from very early times to convert the Indian Catholic fugitives from San Thome to Protestantism, and the Dutch minister at Pulicat baptized 40 of their children in 1615–16. The idea of developing a Christian colony at Pulicat under the protection of fort Geldria was approved by Coen, and later accounts suggest that it was implemented to a certain extent. Not all the clergymen sent out to the coast were men of impeccable character. Nathaniel de Pape was sent to Coromandel in 1672, after Baldeaus, he made considerable progress in the Portuguese and Tamil languages, and by the encouragement, and under the protection of Cornelius Speelman, the Governor, spread the Gospel in the neighbouring villages. Thus, the Dutch had the honour of being the first Protestants who made any efforts for the evangelization of Indi.[101] But according to Raychaudhuri, he was recalled eight years later for his scandalous way of life. Another minister, Johannes Ruterus, fell out with the Coromandel Council and was sent back to Batavia. Some of the clergymen were also suspected of participating in illegal private trade.[102]

The attitude of the Coromandel factors towards Catholicism was far from tolerant. After the Portuguese church at Negapatam was handed over to the Company by the Nayak, the Negapatam Council was in favour of destroying it. Batavia, however, took a kindlier view of the matter and also enjoined that the Catholics should be allowed to take possession of the church and practise their religion without hindrance. When a Portuguese priest, in accordance with the policy of Batavia, was allowed to perform religious service in the church, he was seriously maltreated by the local Dutch residents, and his altar and cross were destroyed.[103]

The interest of at least some Dutch employees was not restricted to commercial matters. Several of them, particularly among the clergy, took an interest in the language and religion of the country. Abraham Rogerius, who served as a minister on the coast from 1631 to 1641, wrote a standard work on the Hindu religion, *De open deure tot het verborgen heydendom*. The famous linguist Herbert de Jaeger was posted in Coromandel during the 1670s, and he developed such a great interest in the languages of the region that in 1676 he appealed against an order of transfer so that he might continue his studies.[104]

The VOC appealed to personnel with certain expertise in native speech, local culture and political intrigue, which could prove handy in trade transactions. Others produced a detailed account of the local conditions, climate and plants, and everyday life of various Hindu castes. Wouter Schouten, a surgeon, attached to the Dutch fleet, wrote the book *The East Indian Voyages*. Hendrik Adriaan van Rheede tot Drakenstein, Malabar Governor in 1671–77 and Vice-Admiral, prepared the voluminous botanical treaties Hortus Indicus Malabaricus; while Daniel Havart, the Company's senior official and a keen observer, published in 1693 a book with the title *The Rise and Fall of Coromandel*. The administration organization of the Company's settlements in Coromandel and the social life of the Dutch community had barely any impact on the socio-economic life of the region. They were significant only in so far as they provided the immediate social and administrative framework for a unit of commercial expansion in an alien setting.[105]

C. Religious Conversion, Contest and Conciliation in Pondicherry: The French Mission in Deccan

The French Crown and its agents were engaged in two central efforts in India; firstly, building the town of Pondicherry into a prosperous trading hub and converting local men and women to Catholicism. The role of missionaries is not very difficult to recognize, reconfigure local spirits and beliefs and substitute them with Christianity. This section examines the phenomenon that was prevalent during the time of such conversions and the response from both sides. It also examines the relationship that existed between the company officials and the missionaries. The French were very much involved in commercial and spiritual gains and were engaged in an effort to transform the spiritual, cultural and political landscape.

The French Crown and the Company of the Indies had since the early 1630s commissioned Catholic missionaries to convert natives and to catechize and "civilize" French colonists. Beginning in 1639, French Ursuline nuns joined Jesuit capuchins and Dominican missions in ministering to Amerindian women and establishing schools for the daughters of French inhabitants. Their role in colonial project put them right at the centre of colonial jurisdictional squabbles, and their story reveals the level to which power struggles among church, state and commercial entities (and between central and peripheral authorities) threatened the very success of early modern French colonies.[106] Thus, one can say the influence of missionaries on the political level cannot be ignored.

Pondicherry significantly showed progress in the first decade of the 18th century both in urbanization and demographics; this period transformed Pondicherry into an important regional centre with several thousand Frenchmen and tens of thousands of Tamil-speaking inhabitants. In 1769, the French population was estimated to have been 1000, they consisted of traders, clerks, soldiers, doctors, engineers, etc. The non-French population consisted of 120,000 roughly, and they consisted of weavers and merchants mostly. They practised the local religion Hindu and were from different castes. The judicial records also show the presence of a much smaller population of local converts to Christianity, small community of Muslims and a handful of Armenian merchants as well as new arrivals from other parts of India beyond the Coromandel Coast. They consisted of immigrants from various castes, races and religions from the north. According to a report by Bedier in 1824, these groups were divided into Right Hand and Left Hand. Abbe Dubois records that disputes between the two groups happened, he says,

perhaps the sole cost of the contest is the right to wear slippers or to ride through the streets in a palanquin or on horseback during marriage festivals ... perhaps it is simply the particular kind of musical instrument suitable for such occasions, that is in dispute.[107]

The town's spatial segregation speaks tons about their policy and attitude towards the local inhabitants, separated into so-called White Town and Black Town. The white town was adjacent to the water, encompassing the port and fort, and the larger black town lay mostly to the west, in the area of higher elevation.[108] The Proclamation of 1708 by the French officials showed that merchants from different nations, regions and castes could pursue their activities without disturbance; the town's segregation expresses something else. The three groups of French Missionaries were the Jesuits, Capuchins and the Missions Etrangeres et Paris (MEP).

Francois Martin in 1701 issued an order prohibiting Hindus and Muslims from conducting ceremonies during Easter and on Sundays. This was done on the orders given by the Jesuits who wanted to control Hindu practices. This resulted in a mass exodus of the natives thereby crippling the commercial activities of the French.[109] In 1713, orders were given by Louis XIV at the instance of the Jesuits that the French Governors of Pondicherry should appoint only a Christian native as Mudalier or Courtier, to close down the Hindu temples and to go hand in hand with the Jesuits in any decision. The Governors, however, found it very difficult to follow these orders.[110] Dupleix, however, appointed Ananda Ranga Pillai as his Courtier, and this caused outraged among the Jesuits; he therefore looked at trustworthiness, merit and sincerity. The priests of St. Paul directed him to appoint a Christian Courtier his response to them was,

> In what way does it concern them (Priests)? Their words are exactly like cackling of ducks in a pond ... these are not the days of yore.[111]

When Lenior was Governor (1721–1735), the Vedapuri Isvaran temple had to be demolished by order from home. There was a big agitation among the local people and the government then directed, "All should be allowed to follow their own respective religions."[112] Thus Lenoir allowed temples to be built and protected them as well. He even allowed the local people to follow their traditions and convictions. However, in 1748 when Dupleix was the Governor he caused the destruction of Vedapuri Isvaran temple during the siege of Pondicherry by Admiral Boscawen. This temple was very close to St. Pauls church and was a source of anxiety for him because the Christian priests irritated the temple priests quite often. There was one instance on 31 January 1746 when an earthen jar filled with filth was thrown into the temple from the church. With the defeat in 1748 by the English, he did whatever he could to gain the support of the Jesuits and Capuchin priests and destroying the temple became necessary.[113] Sixteen or seventeen persons rushed to Ananda Ranga Pillai for help, but he replied and said that he could not disobey his Governors wishes.[114] Thus Dupleix used religion to fulfil his personal and political ends. Scholars have attributed Dupleix's action mostly because of the influence of his wife and the Jesuits.

When Godehu became Governor in 1754, the *mahanattars* presented a petition requesting him to build the Vedapuri Isvaran temple, Godehu replied by saying that he needed to obtain permission from the Company. On 3 April 1767 permission was given to rebuild the temple but on a different site. However, neither the site nor the money was ever granted for building the new temple.[115] Thus, Jeyaseela Stephen argues that the locals therefore preferred to migrate than stay in Pondicherry which was equivalent to adopting non-cooperation principles with the French. These events show the attitude of the locals towards the Company and the Jesuits. Thus, each Governor followed his own decision according to the need of the hour. They did not totally submit to the dictate of the Jesuits but followed a liberal policy towards the natives.

There is no evidence of mass conversions taking place in Pondicherry; however, most of the local converts to Catholicism have been from depressed classes, but there is evidence of converts from high class who were migrants from Tamil Nadu.[116] The French Governors wanted to follow a policy of religious harmony in order to attract the local people to settle in Pondicherry; the Missionaries, especially the Capuchins, wanted to follow an aggressive policy. They wanted to prevent them from taking out religious processions and ceremonies. The Jesuit missionaries on the other hand wanted to follow a policy of religious tolerance. They felt that they should not interfere in the traditions and customs of the native Christians. For example, Robert de Nobili said to Laerzio: "I will become a Hindu to save the Hindus." He left home, family and country for the Indian mission; he was ready to give up the language and the habits of the Europeans and submit to the manifold of the caste system. He dressed as a Brahmin, a yellow robe with a cape of the same colour and a turban around his head. He claimed to be a Roman Rajah.[117] Therefore, Christianity succumbed to the caste orthodoxy of the society. The permanence of caste was also seen in the Notre Dame de la Conception church; the scheduled caste Christians were segregated by a small wall erected as a barrier inside the church. Under the instigation of a foreign missionary, the scheduled caste Christians represented the matter to the Superior Council which ordered the demolition of the wall.[118]

In matters of conversion the role of the French Governor (Dupleix) should be considered. He adopted favourable measures in which funds were allotted for the catechists who worked on the mission. Madame Dupleix was also interested in missionary work; she made frequent liberal donations like the two villages of Marakaam and Cheyyur to the Jesuits in 1751. She had given these villages for the purpose of promotion of the Catholic faith.[119] The Reformation Movement that took place in Europe in the 16th century changed the attitude of the Jesuits. The Movement which challenged the doctrines of the Roman Catholic Church and papal authority radicalized missionary activity outside Europe. Their methods of conversion changed. They baptized only after complete instruction and imparting of proper knowledge of the principles of Catholicism.[120]

During the famines of 1737, 1743 and 1744 conversion rates were high. The missionaries came to the aid of those affected; several Hindus found comfort and assurance through baptism. Thus, by providing stability during times of difficulty it aided in high conversions. The work of the missionaries and the French Governors helped in the smooth process of such conversions.

Here, it would be worthwhile to consider in some detail the case of Abbe Dubois. Abbe Dubois was one of the greatest missionaries of the society of the Foreign Missionaries of Paris (MEP). As a missionary and native of Ardeche in France, his proselytizing mission in India was motivated by the outbreak of revolution in France in 1789. The order of the Second Republic insisted on equality among the subjects. Dubois arrived in India in 1792 and spent 31 years in south India, mostly in the Deccan and Madras Presidency both as a missionary and as an observer. His famous book *Description of the Character, Manners and Customs of the People of India: And of Their Institutions, Religious and Civil* shows that he actively wanted to learn about the culture of the people. His missionary activity differed from the British missionaries; firstly, the French saw India as a land of past glory, and secondly, the underlying principles of social and religious organization were praiseworthy, and hence the system merely needed to be cleansed of its impurities which had crept over time. The French Indologists focused more on Sanskrit studies and Hindu institutions.

He was convinced that only a missionary who knew and loved the manners, customs and habits of the people can be an effective messenger of the Gospel. He became the forerunner of inter-religious concord and amity in India. His book helped his fellow missionaries love the culture of the people among whom they worked.[121] The most important achievement was the conversion of a Brahmin followed by the renunciation of Hindu customs and traditions. He was aiming for spiritual achievement rather than conversion in numbers. The preoccupation with Brahmanical India was peculiarly a French image of India.[122]

Individual "Transformation" or Collective Developments? Re-examining the Phenomenon of Conversion with reference to Mass Conversions

It's unfortunate that conversions are understood in a communal background moved by the present political scenario. Attached with religious connotations, conversions are generally regarded as "disruptive" and "dramatic" covered under themes like colonization, partition, conquest and crusades. When seen through worldly spectacles, conversions are seen as destructive events bringing "civilizational loss" using Zupanov's words.[123] However, it's often "rationalized" in terms of enlightenment, raising better understanding of self, ending the heresies and all the wrong practices by bringing cultural gains. Though there has been so much work done on conversions, many of these lack the correct approach. Scholars have not independently looked at conceptualization of the conversion process, which is important before we place it in the context it takes place.

Traditionally regarded as an inner, individual transformation, now scholars have started exploring the deeper meanings which come out of collective or mass conversions. They now raise issues like what is meant by conversion? And who is a convert? Where can we draw a line between alternation, regeneration, consolidation and a dramatic often called conversion? Also, how far can it be understood as a change of inner self? Does it take place at individual level or is moved by the socio-political and economic shifts of the paradigm resulting in collective conversions. Is it justified to see conversions only as a change from one religion or belief to another or it involves larger questions of self-identification? Is it possible to build clear-cut ideas of self-identification in a pluralized society? These are various issues which now scholars of various disciplines like History, Anthropology and Sociology have started to raise. This section discusses a few of these issues and questions the traditional Christian view of conversion being an individual, self-centred, inner transformation for heavenly gains. Conversions are mainly studied in the Asian context from the time period of the 16th–18th centuries under the Portuguese and later the British colonial attempts. With reference to the conversions that happened in India from the 16th century onwards, it becomes difficult to accept the traditional Christian view as conversions now come out as a gradual process which is shaped by the politico-socio and economic realities of the place and the time period.

The work done by the scholars does not stand in the same line with the traditional Christian view. The early scholarly work has focused on the conversions of individual rulers, scholars, ordinary men and women, completely discounting the presence and possibility of collective or mass conversions. They have also ignored the impact Reformation had on a large population who had to adopt the Protestant faith following their ruler. Even if we do not call this mass conversion shaped by political scenario, then also we need to study the impact these religious movements have on questions of identity. For the time we can say that the decision to convert or not is indeed one's own, but it rarely happens because of the internal thirst for enlightenment as it's majorly shaped by the social-political and economic realities of life.

For the Portuguese Estado it was a tool for colonization. Prof Malacanthid suggests that the religious idioms and languages used by the Portuguese were fabricated within the frames of their larger mercantile interests and were used to create an atmosphere that would in turn help them to expand their political and commercial frontiers.[124] Thus, conversions are important state-building tools as they bring about "spiritual conquests" in the minds. Thus, many conversions in Estado especially Goa were forced conversions which were brought about using state and military apparatus. Some happened due to material inducements or with the promise of government jobs. However, conversions are not easy and simple as the people whom the colonial powers wish to convert already have their own religiosity through which they exercise enough agency in the conversion process. Thus, to supplant them with another requires complex, continuous and influential efforts. The Portuguese were successful in converting the native population only in areas under Estado da India due to their political and military control of the area. However, even in these areas many local people constantly and strongly resisted the conversions sometimes by fleeing away and sometimes by taking up violent measures. Attacks on the Jesuits who were very active in the conversion process were very common. There are many pieces of evidences on counter attacks by many Hindus and Muslims who oppressed the new Christian converts to create difficult conditions for them to survive. There were provisions laid for re-conversion to Hinduism by performance of purification rites. Such counter attacks discouraged many conversions so much so that the missionaries and state officials had to intervene and form laws to safeguard the new converts. This continued till the 20th century when Munro (a British officer) had to pass a law that a Christian judge should be present in each Zillah court to impart justice to the Christians.[125] Thus, violence, coercion and bloodshed are also common features associated with conversions. Hence the converts display ample agency and dynamics in the process. It is this agency of the natives which made the missionaries to resort to the notions of accommodation and incorporation of local traditions.

Agriculture was an important part of the economy. The prevailing caste system gave the dominance to the highest caste. Land was owned by the lineage of *guancar*, who are the male descendants in the patrilineal of the original inhabitants of a village.[126] Most of them were from the Brahmin and other higher Maratha castes. These higher castes would employ lower castes to work in their lands whose payment was made in terms of shares in the harvests and some were also given small lands which were less fertile. Mostly it was for self-consumption. The *guancars* paid taxes to the ruling class and distributed the surplus among themselves. The caste system was a water-tight compartment. The *guancars* also the *mahajan* class were the leading members of the village temple. The best land was set aside for the maintenance of the temple cult and for those who rendered services to the temple. This agricultural society was based on the patrilineal kinship; it provided legitimacy to the hierarchical social structure. When conversions began, if the *guancars* refused to get converted a series of laws were imposed on them and prohibited them from accessing the temple and the land attached to the land.[127] So, here is an alternative perspective that there was no bloodshed during conversions always. It is accepted that, in order to keep their position intact and keep their hold over the land the *guancars* too got converted to Christianity. One can also argue that Catholicism which was propagated by the Portuguese did not do away with the hierarchical order of the society, but in turn it led to the *dessais* to only strengthen their position by aligning themselves with those in power.

It's important to note that the spread of any idea, belief, etc. requires a popular mode of propagation. Thus, local language, vocabulary, rituals, etc. become important to understand the psychology of the people. Thus, many of the Christian missionaries learnt the vernacular language, many times drawing parallels between Christ and the Virgin Mary and various indigenous Gods and Goddesses and common notions of salvation. Many texts were translated into local languages, as translation was important to reach out to the locals and teach them the Gospel.[128] Roberto Nobili depicts the classic example of adaptation and accommodation. On his Madurai mission he learnt local languages like Tamil and Sanskrit, dressed like the Brahman *sanyasi*, and adopted the same dietary habits to be one with the locals and represent Christianity not as an alien but as a new faith with common beliefs. The missionaries understood the caste system of the subcontinent very well. Though Christianity does not believe in this caste differentiation, in the subcontinent instead of erasing the caste boundaries, they preached their message within them. Thus, on the one hand missionaries like Roberto Nobili were active among the high caste people (as he declared himself as a Brahmin from Rome he could not interact with the Shudras), on the other hand Fr Balthasar da Costa was active in converting low caste people (being a *pandar* he was a wise religious man but not a Brahmin and could interact even with the Shudras).[129] The Jesuits had internalized the caste system well and divided their mission into two: *Brahmin sanyasis* and *pandaraswamis* dealing with high and lower caste people respectively.[130] Thus, conversion is a dynamic process which involves accommodation on both sides. The traditional understanding of conversion discounts all these factors and provides a simplistic view of conversion.

The mass conversion of *Paravas* shows that conversions are not only individual phenomena. Secondly, they are not always about internal change but shaped by the realities of surroundings. As for the Portuguese, the *Paravas* were an important group with expertise who were important for controlling the coastal activities. Also, it helped them maintain their social caste structure and also make space in the dominant Hindu high caste society, by formulating their local versions of Christian festival celebrations, vocabulary, etc. Thirdly, it shows that conversions do not mark clear-cut end of past practices instead they brought about an amalgamation of Hindu and Christian practices. Thus, one should see conversion as a process and not a final event.

As, suggested earlier conversions have different motives and is "multi causal." For the low caste people, conversion comes with the hope of a better future even if they are not able to benefit or rise up the social ladder, conversion provides a parallel support base. The Portuguese were moved by religious zeal and thus understood conversions as the way to make allies. Thus, religion and economy were inseparable for them. This also appeared to be true for the people who converted to Christianity in the subcontinent as the missionaries provided various incentives like schools, hospitals, orphanages, etc. to the people. Not to say that these moral initiatives were always politically laid, but many times this was the case. Often when the political control became strong, conversions took the face of forced and oppressive measures. Often Hindus chose to convert to Christianity as compared to Islam. Some of the wealthy Hindus converted to protect their property. S. Clarke suggests that the conversion of Dalit communities in the 19th century was a "conscious and collective" act to cut through the Brahmanical caste structure of oppression in the "vision of a new and better world." The missionaries indeed provided a scope of better social and economic conditions for them, but the initiative to convert was deliberately taken by the Dalits. Thus, in some way conversions depict a critique of prevailing oppressive caste-ridden Hindu society. However, it did not have a liberating impact all over. It did uplift many low caste groups, but in the case of women, it's difficult to give a clear verdict. Women were still tied to the notions of purity and one cannot see them as liberating out of the old order.[131]Thus, neither the motive nor the impact or the cause is monolithic; the conversion process shows enough variety.

Hefner correctly suggests that when a society comes in contact with another large socio-political order, the older forms of identities come under stress. At times they are questioned and sometimes subverted while sometimes they are reinforced. In such dynamic and flexible periods, religion, values or beliefs that provide a larger degree of dignity and rewards in society are readily accepted. In such cases the world religions (like Christianity and Islam) enjoy an edge over the others they come in contact as they promise a new life based on transcendental truth and divinity. By this, they open up new religious roles for the long secluded groups. Thus, it provides a new "locus of self-identification."[132] It comes out clear from this, that conversions are not just internal, individual change but evolve in the dynamic matrix of accommodation, reinvention and adaptations fervent socio-political and economic settings with different causes, impacts and motives.

Mixed Marriages, Cultural exchange and the Creation of *Topasses*: Europeans and Socio-Cultural Fusion in the Deccan

The coming of the Europeans to India saw the permanent settlement of these Europeans as soldiers, clerks and merchants. As a part of the culture of permanent settlement, these Europeans especially the Portuguese, formed relationships out of marriage or even married local women.

Historians like M.N. Pearson and Sanjay Subramanyam have emphasized that marriages between Portuguese settlers and Indian women were actively promoted as a tool of colonization from the earliest days of the viceroyalty of Goa. Marriages between Portuguese men and Indian women were regulated by the Catholic Church within the moral and political frameworks of early modern colonization.[133] There was an absolute hierarchy within the composition of the Portuguese society; for example the "*fidalgos*" formed the highest rank in the social composition of the society. "*Fidalgos*" were the noblemen who were the highest in the hierarchy. The Portuguese soldiers who were "*solteiro*" who were also known as "*soldados*" were encouraged to become *casados* by marrying local women and various inducements were offered to them to become permanent residents of the new settlements.[134] For instance, men who married and settled in Goa were relieved from military duties and were given freedom to devout their time to family life. While this policy produced generations of Portuguese citizens with mixed blood and a hierarchy of status defined by colour, it also signified a will towards an assimilation of cultures and the diffusion of the Portuguese language as a means of communication and learning. By the second half of the 16th century, there were people of Portuguese origin in the Indian Ocean who had never visited Europe. The women who entered into unions with these Portuguese men usually belonged to the marginal such as widows, *bailhadeiras* or Nautch girls.

In contrast, respectability belonged to the *casados*, who operated under the jurisdiction and patronage of the Estado. These civilians were long-term residents of Estado settlements. *Casadosmoradores* or married settlers were the most important group in the Asian trade of the Portuguese. Although a small segment of the *casado* community in Portuguese Asia had a landed character, the bulk of this group made its money by engaging in maritime trade, some amassing huge fortunes. Their trade extended up to Japan in the 16th and 17th centuries.[135] The group consisted of both "white" and "black" *casados*, the latter being native Christians. The former was subdivided into *reinois*, born of white parents in Portugal, the *castico*, born of white Portuguese parents in Asia, and the mestizos, born in Asia usually of a Portuguese father and an Asian or Eurasian mother.[136] *Casado* traders constituted a powerful pressure group, even lending money to the Portuguese state in Goa.

The Portuguese communities living in various towns and cities of the Indian Ocean did not directly pay political allegiance to the Lusitanian crown and worked alongside local merchants at the western coast. But this kind of process of integration was lacking in other European companies, in spite of being well aware about the lack of European ladies, which posed difficulties for their personnel. Later the girls of Portuguese descent were considered for marriage by these European company's personnel, who were called the "Black Portuguese," but they were Roman Catholic Christians.[137] Under the direction of Portuguese colonial governor, Alfonso de Albuquerque, marriages between Portuguese men and Indian women were encouraged. The reason for this was to actively increase the number of catholic subjects to strengthen the political constituency of the Portuguese presence in an era of intense European competition for the East India trade.[138]

In the 18th century, there was a large settlement of Portuguese private traders. Some Portuguese settlers led licentious lives, keeping several women as concubines. At Sao Tome, the Franciscans and Jesuits tried to improve the anarchic conditions and lawlessness, and the visit of St Francis Xavier in 1545 gave the place some respectability. Portuguese settlements were around the churches, with service to God and to Mammon as the leitmotif. Powerful clan-based factions, such as the *Raposos* and *Pereiras*, derived support from the *Palaiyakkara*, in return for military service. When Aravidu Venkatapati Raya moved his court to Chandragiri in 1592, the political climate became suitable for the Portuguese. In 1600 Sao Tome had two distinct quarters, one with approximately 600 private Portuguese settlers, some *mestiços* and Armenians. The art of intermingling the Portuguese with indigenous communities gave them a better understanding about the prevailing local conditions better than their other European counterparts. In this region the Portuguese were grouped together in communities which can be considered true and spontaneous colonies. This allowed interesting situations of dialogue and cultural exchange to occur. This new form of encounter was open and without borders, barriers and the constraints of forced acculturation. The Portuguese struck deeper roots in the East than the Dutch and became more acceptable to the western coast.[139]

Coming to the Dutch, in the early decades of the 17th century, the Company did not allow any Dutch to settle on the Coromandel Coast, although small Dutch colonies had settled in some places in the coromandel surrounding the Company's factories. However, Batavian authorities permitted the Dutch employees to settle only in the territories where the Company had sovereign authority. It was promulgated as late as 1665, and all evidence seems to indicate that frequent exceptions to this rule were permitted at Coromandel. The widows and children of deceased employees were allowed to stay on. At Pulicat, the Dutch colony was fairly sizeable, and one entire quarter of the town was inhabited exclusively by the Dutch.[140] These Dutch Colonies were permitted to marry Indian women adopted as early as 1614 on the condition that the prospective brides must first accept Christianity. For the first time, many Dutch soldiers married Indian women in 1614. Again, in 1622, when the usual practice of keeping concubines was prohibited by orders from Batavia, in one day, 38 persons got married to their Indian women at Pulicat, and the governor of the factories arranged a wedding feast to celebrate the wedding. The practice of mixed marriages was highly applauded by Wemmer van Berchem, as "this is the only means," further he wrote, "whereby we must hold and maintain our power in India, as the Portuguese have done before us." The married soldiers were treated with special favour and allowed to live in the fort, at least during the rainy season.

In the latter decades of the century, a large proportion of the population at Pulicat consisted of *mestizos*, i.e. children of mixed Dutch-Indian marriages, and castizos, or quadroons. Nieuhof mentions one particular caste called "*Thiola*" which frequently intermarried with the Dutch. Nieuhof mentions marriages between "*Thiola*" men and Dutch women, but he failed to trace any instance of such marriages in the records. English factors wrote a letter at Pulicat, in 1622, it sums up the manner of living of Dutchmen who were married to Indians.

> All those that soe marry heere to blackes are bound and tyde to everlastinge service in India and cannot returne to there cuntrye ... and to speake truly most parte of thi base nacion desyer not to see moore there owne cuntrye; yea, there carryadge and manners of lyving is more

> heathenlicke then thee people of the cuntrye themselves, whoe take much notice thereof; to which brutishness we leave them.[141]

Marriages among Dutch men and women on the coast were common. In 1625, six Dutch girls stayed at Pulicat on their way to Batavia and five of them got engaged to local Dutch employees within a few days.[142] Married employees were given an additional allowance, and many of them got married just to be able to claim this allowance and then got rid of their wives. In order to check this practice, Hans de Haze recommended in 1619 that few persons should be permitted to get married.[143]

Later the economic measures of 1678 came as a severe blow to the Dutch servants. Some lost their jobs while many others left on their own due to the reduced salaries which were no longer attractive. After a few years, Superintendent Adriaan van Rheede ordered a further reduction in the number of officers, and all widows of Dutch officers as well as retired married men, with the exception of the chief factors, were sent to Batavia. The speed with which this measure was carried out caused great hardship to many, as they failed to sell the houses in which they had invested much of their capital. The policy henceforward was not to appoint any married men in the Coromandel factories. After 1690, there were only a minimum number of officials in the different factories, while a large and expensive garrison was posted at the castle at Negapatam.[144] The Dutch community in the more significant part of Coromandel was now reduced to a small body of bachelor employees who came to reside there for short periods of service.[145]

Regarding the French, linguistic and cultural policies adopted by the French in India led to an assimilation of French culture with the native culture. This was the difference between the English and the French Orientalism. The French integrated themselves with the society by learning the indigenous language, they promoted themselves as good administrators and looked after the welfare of the people. They provided good quality education and improved the transportation system.

The first French-Tamil dictionary was compiled by Fr. Dominique De Valence who was the superior of the Capuchin fathers at Pondicherry in the 1730s and 1740s. The dictionary contains 12,450 entries arranged alphabetically, from A to Z with their Tamil equivalents. This was useful for the French administrators and the Missionaries who wanted to learn the Tamil language. It also gave a desire for the locals to learn French and it served as a bridge between the locals and the French.[146]

French language had a continuous influence on the Tamil dialect of Pondicherry. For example, S. Arokianathan cites the diary of Verra Naickar II; it was written between 1778 and 1792, the diarist's grandfather previously worked in the French Government as the second Commander for the canon squad.

The diary of Veer Naickar II was written in the spoken variety of Pondicherry Tamil dialect, S. Arokianathan argues that the influence of

French was at the phonological and lexical levels. Thus, the Pondicherry Tamil dialect has two social varieties, one with the interference of the French Language among French-Tamil bilinguals and another with the interference of the English language alone at all linguistics levels.[147]

In the field of education, the French opened schools to all, earlier the *thinnai*[148] school system was followed in which a small number of students who belonged to the same caste attended. The traditional method of learning consisted of the teacher teaching the student to write on sand or on the student's slate. The French in 1761 introduced printing technology by establishing a printing press at the Governor's house. The need for spreading education was due to the fact that the French needed help in the administration. The missionaries on the other hand wanted to train the preachers in the local language and culture. Thus, schools were started in Pondicherry in 1882. The missionaries gave special attention towards educating girls because they knew the stigma attached towards women's education. The congregation of St. Louis De Gonzague with Fr. Ansaldo started opening orphanages and schools for girls. Fr. Savinien Dupuis was in favour of nuns running the congregation for providing primary education to women through schools.[149]

Fr. Louis Savinien Dupuis was outstanding in his literary pursuit; an old unused press was lying in the Government House of Pondicherry. He along with the then Bishop Bonnard requested the Governor to sell the unused press. The Government donated it to the mission. Fr. Dupuis then repaired it and started printing books which then gave a boost for others to set up printing presses so that books could be circulated in Pondicherry.[150]In the 1800s printing developed not only for official purposes but for printing newspapers as well. On 17 May 1827 the then French Governor, Des Bassiyon Richmond established a *Bibliotheque* mainly for storing instructions coming regularly from France, and there were others who wanted to read during their leisure time.[151] Around the same time the French established in Karaikal a library for the benefit of the French officers.

Thus, the French wanted to build a good relationship with the locals because there was much distrust among them because of their political ambitions. Hence, a better way to pacify the people was by engaging in a benevolent policy and integrating with them through assimilation in culture, architecture and education. Unlike the British, the French stood for an Orientalism which was compassionate towards the locals and which contributed towards the development of their colonial territories.

Therefore, to conclude, although this chapter is dedicated to society and culture in Deccan, we have found that the sources available both in foreign and indigenous/vernacular have no direct connections or references as related to Europeans in relation to Marathas. However, one can read the influences and confluences taking shape as a multi-cultural and diverse society due to the presence of the Europeans and the exchanges taking place on behalf of the Europeans on various frontiers.

The aim of this chapter is to understand transition happening at all levels in the society. When we talk about Deccan undergoing transition in the social context, we see a complex web of societal change. Right from the time of carving out an identity for a region to the assimilation of all religious beliefs and customs, the period under study has been marked by social mobility which paved a way for the formation of a new social order. The presence of various European countries and their commercial interests gives birth to a new kind of population and settlements in Deccan. The presence of a new or mixed population is a very significant aspect of Deccan during this period because this in turn helps us to study transitions through various parameters such as culture, dress, food, customs, rituals, art and architecture. Thus, tracing the transition in Deccan is not complete without studying the society which was undergoing a sea change.

Notes

1 S.R. Faruqi, *Early Urdu Literary Culture and History*, Oxford, Oxford University Press, 2001, pp. 95–104.
2 Muhammad Qasim Firishta, *Tarikh-i-Firishta,* Vol. 2, Lucknow, Published by Munshi Nawal Kishore, 1864–65, p. 27.
3 Richard Eaton, *A Social History of the Deccan, 1300–1761: Eight Indian Lives (The New Cambridge History of India)*, Cambridge, Cambridge University Press, 2008, pp. 106–07.
4 Richard Eaton, "A History of the Deccan, 1500–1700", *Sultans of Deccan India 1500–1700: Opulence and Fantasy*, ed. by Navina Najat Haider and Marika Sardar, New York, Yale University Press, 2015, p. 11.
5 S.A.A. Rizvi, *A History of Sufism in India*, Vol. 1, New Delhi, Munshiram Manoharlal Publishers Pvt Ltd, 1978, p. 83.
6 Iqtidar Hussain Siddiqui, "The Early Chishti Dargahs", in *Muslim Shrines in India: Their Character, History and Significance*, ed. Christian W. Troll, New Delhi, Oxford University Press, 1989, p. 11.
7 Eaton M. Richard, *Sufis of Bijapur, 1300–1700: Social Roles of Sufis in Medieval India*, New Delhi, Munshiram Manoharlal Publishers Pvt Ltd, 1996, p. 55.
8 Muzaffar Alam, *The Languages of Political Islam in India*, Chicago, University of Chicago Press, 2004, p. 95.
9 Iqtidar Hussain Siddiqui, "The Early Chishti Dargahs", in *Muslim Shrines in India*, ed Christian W. Troll, Marc Gaborieau, Oxford Publication, New Delhi, 2003, p. 170.
10 Digby Simon, "The Sufi Sheikh and The Sultan: A Conflict of Claims to Authority in Medieval India", *Iran*, Vol. 28 (1990), pp. 71–81.
11 Rizvi, *A History of Sufism in India*, p. 192.
12 Muhammad Suleman Siddiqi, *Bahmani Sufis,* New Delhi, South Asia Books, 1990, p. 76.
13 Ghulam Ali Musavi, *Mishkat-un-Nubuwwah* (Urdu Trans), vol. 5, Hyderabad, Sayyid Abul Hasan Qadiri, Oriental Manuscript Library, 1982–85, p. 43.
14 K.A. Nizami, "Sufi Movement in the Deccan", in *History of Medieval Deccan*, ed. by H. K. Sherwani and P. M. Joshi, Vol. 2, Hyderabad, Andhra Pradesh Govt Textbook Press, 1973, p. 186.
15 A.R. Kulkarni, *Explorations in the Deccan History*, New Delhi, Pragati Publications, ICHR, 2006, p. 100.
16 Richard, *Sufis of Bijapur, 1300–1700*, p. 150.

17 Alam, *The Languages of Political Islam in India*, p. 120.
18 Richard, *Sufis of Bijapur, 1300–1700*, p. 210.
19 Swapan Majumdar, "The Dense Desolate Pathway: Routes of Bhakti in Medieval Indian Literature" *Sahitya Akademi*, Vol. 35, No. 3 (149), (May–June 1992), p. 103.
20 Ibid.
21 Umesh Kadam, "The Whole Universe is my Home': Bhakti in Medieval Maharashtra: Essays in Memory of Nandita Prasad Sahai", in *Looking within Looking Without: Exploring Households in the Subcontinent through Time*, ed. by Kumkum Roy, Delhi, Primus Books, 2015, p. 220.
22 Ibid., p. 220.
23 R. Champalakshmi, *Religion, Tradition and Ideology –Pre-colonial South India*, India, Oxford University Press, 2011, p. 18.
24 Madhu Kishwar and Ruth Vanita, "Poison to Nectar", *Manushi*, Number 50–51, New Delhi, 1989, p. 92.
25 Vijaya Ramaswamy, "Rebels-Conformist? Women Saint in Medieval South India", *Anthropos*, 1992, p. 134.
26 Vijaya Ramaswamy, *Walking Naked-Women, Society, Spirituality in South India*, Shimla, Indian Institute of Advanced Study, 2007, p. 148.
27 Setumadhavarao S. Pagadi, *Shivaji,* Delhi, National Book Trust, 1983, Introduction.
28 M.G. Ranade, *Rise of the Maratha Power*, Delhi, Ministry of Information and Broadcasting, 1961, p. 17.
29 G.S. Sardesai, *The Main Currents of Maratha History*, Calcutta, M.C Sarkar & Sons, 1926, p. 3.
30 Ibid., p. 65.
31 J.V. Naik, "The Foundation of Swarajya", in *Shivaji and Swarajya*, ed. by Indian Institute of Public Administration, Delhi, Orient Longman, 1975, p. 44.
32 V.V. Joshi, *Clash of Three Empires (The Rise of the Maratha Nation)*, Allahabad, Kitabistan, 1941, pp. 49–70.
33 B.K. Apte, "The Contents of Maratha Nationalism", *Proceedings of Indian History Congress*, Vol. 16 (1953), p. 285.
34 S.R. Sharma, *The Founding of Maratha Freedom*, Bombay, Oriental Longman, 1964, p. 2.
35 Apte, "The Contents of Maratha Nationalism", p. 286.
36 M.A. Nayeem, "Shivaji—The Integrationist of the Deccan", *National Seminar on "Chhatrapati Shivaji as a Nation Builder,* 8th–10th January1975, p. 1.
37 Varsha S. Shirgaonkar, *Eighteenth Century Deccan, Cultural History of the Peshwa*, New Delhi, Aryan Books International, 2010, p. 22.
38 Kulkarni, *Explorations in the Deccan History*, p. 100.
39 Y.M. Pathan, *Marathi Bhakriti Parsiche Swarup*, Aurangabad, Marathawada University, 1973, pp. 14–17.
40 Kulkarni, *Explorations in the Deccan History*, p. 101.
41 Ibid., p. 98.
42 Jeneet Sorokhaibam, *Chhatrapati Shivaji: The Maratha Warrior and His Campaign*, New Delhi, Vij Books India Pvt. Ltd., 01 January 2013, p. 225.
43 David N. Lorenzen and Marco Della, "Tomba and the Brahmin from Banaras: Missionaries, Orientalists and Indian Scholars", *The Journal of Asian Studies*, Vol. 65 (February 2006), p. 118.
44 K.R. Subramanyam, *Maratha Rajas of Tanjore*, Madras, Asian Educational Services, 1928, p. 77.
45 V. Seethalakshmi, "Marathas of Thanjavur and Land Grants", *IOSR-JHSS,* Vol. 20 (2015), p. 36.

46 T.K. Venkatasubramanian, *Music as History in Tamil Nadu*, Primus Books, 2010, p. 65.
47 Ashok Gopal, "Shivaji's Forgotten Cousins", *Poona Digest*, August 1986, p. 15.
48 Lakshmi, Subramanian, "Court to Academy: Karnatik Music", *India International Centre Quarterly*, Vol. 33, No. 2 (2006), p. 126.
49 Venkatasubramanian, *Music as History in Tamil Nadu*, p. 83.
50 Jaya Appasamy, *Tanjavur Painting of the Maratha Period*, Vol. 1, New Delhi, Abhinav Publications, 1980, p. 12.
51 V.T. Gune, *The Judicial System of The Marathas,* Poona, Deccan College Postgraduate and Research Institute, 1953, p. 3.
52 Hiroshi Fukazawa, "State and Caste System (Jati) in the eighteenth century Maratha Kingdom", *Hitosubashi Journal of Economics*, Vol. 9 (1968), p. 33.
53 Anuradha K. Ranade, *Socio-Economic Life of Maharashtra (1100–1600 A.D.)*, New Delhi, Serials Publications, 2009, pp. 66–69.
54 T.N. Atre, *Gavgada*, Pune, Rajhans Prakashan, New Addition, 2015, p. 129.
55 Gune, *The Judicial System of The Marathas*, 1953, p. 5.
56 Apte, "The Contents of Maratha Nationalism", p. 286.
57 A.R. Kulkarni, "Social Relations in the Maratha Country in the Medieval Period", *Proceedings of the Indian History Congress*, Vol. 1 (1970), p. 233.
58 M.R. Kantak, "The Political Role of different Hindu Castes and Communities in Maharashtra in the Foundation of Shivaji's Swarajya", *Bulletin of the Deccan College Research Institute*, Vol. 38 (1978–79), p. 40.
59 Ibid.
60 M.J. Ranade, *Rise of the Maratha Power*, Delhi, Ministry of Information and Broadcasting, 2012, p. 3.
61 Grant Duff, *A History of the Marathas*, Vol. I, Oxford, Oxford University Press, 1921, p. 6.
62 S.N. Joshi, ed., *Sabhasad Bakhar*, Poona, 1960, pp. 81–82.
63 *Shiva Bharat*, ed. byS.M. Divekar and D.V. Apte, Poona, BISM, 1927, p. 6.
64 S.N. Sen, *Administrative System of the Marathas*, Calcutta, Ananda Press and Publication Pvt. Ltd., 1925, p. 139.
65 Ranade, *Socio-Economic Life of Maharashtra*, pp. 66–69.
66 G.B. Joshi, "Caste Conflicts of the Brahmins in 18th and 19th Centuries Maharashtra", *Proceedings of the Indian History Congress*, Vol. 43 (1982), p. 418.
67 G.S. Ghure, "Features of the Caste System", in *Social Stratification*, ed. Dipankar Gupta, Delhi, Oxford University Press, 1991, pp. 43–44.
68 Ibid., pp. 418–23.
69 Chandraseniya Kayastha Prabhu (CKP caste of today).
70 Sudha Desai, *Social Life in Maharashtra Under The Peshwas*, Bombay, Popular Prakashan, 1983, p. 40.
71 Ibid., p. 39.
72 Ibid., p. 198.
73 Rekha Pande, "The Bhakti Movement—An Interpretation", *Proceedings of the Indian History Congress*, Vol. 48 (1987), p. 217.
74 M.G. Ranade, *Rise of the Maratha Power*, Publications Divisions, New Delhi, First Published in 1961, Second in 1966 and Third impression in 1974, p. 65–67.
75 K. Ayyappa Paniker, *Medieval Indian Literature: Surveys and Selections*, New Delhi, Sahitya Akademi, 1997, p. 351.
76 Ibid., pp. 67–68.

77 Eleanor Zelliot, "Chokhamela Anand Eknath: Two Bhakti Modes of Legitimacy for Modern Changes", in *Tradition and Modernity in Bhakti Movement*, ed. by Jayant Lele, Leiden, E.J. Brill, pp. 138–39.
78 Ranade, *Rise of the Maratha Power*, pp. 67–68.
79 K.C. Vardachari, *Aivars of South India*, Bombay, Bhartiya Vidya Bhavvan, 1966, p. 97.
80 Ibid., p. 76.
81 Meenakshi Jha, "Locating The Space For Sudras In Medieval Bhakti (A.D. 600–1400)", *Proceedings of the Indian History Congress*, Vol. 66 (2005–2006), p. 393.
82 R. Eric Frykenberg, "On the Study of Conversion Movements: A Review Article and a Theoretical Note", *IESHR*, Vol. 17 (1980), p. 122.
83 S. Rajamanickam, *The First Oriental Scholar,* Thirunelveli, De Nobili Research Institute, 1972, p. 54.
84 John W. O'Malley, *The First Jesuits*, Cambridge, Harvard University Press, 1993, p. 53.
85 Andrew F. Walls, *The Missionary Movement in Christian History*, New York, Orbis Books Publications, 1996, pp. 61–78.
86 O'Malley, *The First Jesuits*, p. 76.
87 Rajamanickam, *The First Oriental Scholar*, p. 19.
88 Ibid., p. 21.
89 Ibid., p. 23.
90 Ibid.
91 Ines Zupanov, *Disputed Mission: Jesuit Experiments and Brahmanical Knowledge in Seventeenth-Century India,* New York, Oxford University Press, 1999, p. 168.
92 Rajamanickam, *The First Oriental Scholar*, p. 66.
93 Vincent Cronin, *A Pearl to India, the Life of Robert de Nobili*, London, E.P Dutton & Co., 1959, p. 91.
94 Vicente L. Rafael, *Contracting Colonialism: Translation and Christian Conversion in Tagalog Society Under Early Spanish Rule*, Durham and London, Duke University Press, 1993, p. 34.
95 Zupanov, *Disputed Mission*, p. 168.
96 Luba Zubkova, "Dravidian Studies in the Netherlands Part I (1605–1690s) Pioneers of Orientalism at the VOC", *International Institute for Asian Studies*, News Letter, 35 (2004), p. 14.
97 Philippus Baldeus, *A True and Exact Description of the Most Celebrated East-India Coasts of Malabar and Coromandel,* Amsterdam, Asnalso of the Isle of Ceylon, Vol. 3, 1672.
98 Zubkova, "Dravidian Studies in the Netherlands Part I (1605–1690s) Pioneers of Orientalism at the VOC", p. 14.
99 *Philip Baldaeus* on the *Malabar* and *Coromandel Coast* (1672), Ch. XXV.
100 Tapan Raychaudhuri, *Jan Company in Coromandel, 1605–1690: A Study in the Interrelation of European Commerce and Traditional Economies*, The Hague, Antiqbook, 1962, p. 205.
101 William Brown, *The History of Christian Missions of the Sixteenth, Seventeenth, Eighteenth, and Nineteenth Centuries*, London, 1863, p. 30.
102 Raychaudhuri, *Jan Company*, p. 207.
103 Ibid.
104 Ibid., p. 208.
105 Ibid., p. 207.
106 Heidi Keller-Lapp, "Who is the Real Sovereign of the Ursulines of Pondicherry?", *French Colonial History,* Vol. 13 (2012), p. 112.

107 Abbe Dubois, *Hindu, Manners, Customs and Ceremonies*, Rupa, Third Edition/Ninth Impression edition (10 January 1992), 1978, p. 26.
108 Keller-Lapp, "Who is the Real Sovereign of the Ursulines of Pondicherry?", p. 13.
109 K.S. Mathew, ed., *Indian Ocean and the Cultural Interactions, A.D 1400–1800*, Pondicherry, Pondicherry University, 1996, p. 120.
110 K. Isreal Mark, "Governor Joseph Francois Dupleix-His Religious Policy", *Proceedings of the Indian History Congress*, Vol. 38, 1977, p. 534.
111 J.F. Price, ed, *The Private Dairy of Ananda Ranga Pillai*, Vol. II, Madras, Asian Educational Service, 1914, p. 256.
112 C.S. Srinivasachari, *Ananda Ranga Pillai, The "Pepys" of French India*, Madras, Varadachary & Co., 1940, pp. 276–77.
113 Mark, "Governor Joseph Francois Dupleix-His Religious Policy", p. 535.
114 S. Jeyaseela Stephen, *Pondicherry under the French, Illuminating the Urban Landscape, 1674–1793*, Delhi, Primus Books, 2018, p. 50.
115 Ibid., p. 504.
116 Mathew, ed., *Indian Ocean and Cultural Interactions, A.D 1400–1800*, p. 113.
117 Robert de'Nobili published by an Irish Jesuit, *The Irish Monthly*, Vol. 9, No. 102 (December 1881), p. 650.
118 R. Velmuragan, "The Upper Caste and Lower Caste Christians in Pondicherry during the Eighteenth Century", *Proceedings of the Indian History Congress*, Vol. 60 (1999), p. 457.
119 Stephen, *Pondicherry under the French*, p. 513.
120 Ibid., p. 514.
121 K.S. Mathew, ed., *French in India and Indian Nationalism (1700–1963 A.D)*, Vol. 1, New Delhi, B.R Publishing Corporation, 1999, p. 308.
122 Jyoti Mohan, "British and French Ethnographies of India: Dubois and His English Commentators", *French Colonial History*, Vol. 5 (2004), p. 233.
123 Ines G. Zupanov, "Conversion Historiography in South Asia; Alternate Indian Christian Counter-Histories in Eighteenth century Goa", *The Medieval History Journal*, Vol. XII (2009), p. 304.
124 Pius Malekandethil, *Religious Rhetoric, Mercantile Strategies, and a Revolting Community*, New Delhi, Jamia Millia, 2011.
125 Penelope Carson, "Christianity, Colonialism and Hinduism in Kerala; Integration, Adaptation or Confrontation?", in *Christians and Missionaries in India*, ed. R.E. Frykenberg, Cambridge, Cambridge University Press, 2003, p. 143.
126 T.R. De Souza, *Medieval Goa: A Socio-Economic History*, Delhi, Concept Publishers, 1990, p. 94.
127 Rowena Robinson, "Some Neglected Aspects of the Conversion of Goa: A Socio-Historical Perspective", *Sociological Bulletin*, Vol. 42, No. 1/2 (March–September 1993), p. 75.
128 Rafael, *Contracting Colonialism*, p. 21.
129 S. Jeyaseela Stephen, *Portuguese in the Tamil Coast 1507–1749*, Pondicherry, Navajyothi Publishing House, 1998, p. 290.
130 Walter Fernandes, "Jesuit Contribution to Social Change in India (16th–20th centuries)", in *Jesuits in India, A Historical Perspective*, ed. Teotonio R. De Souza, Charles Borges, Goa, XCHR, 1992, pp. 174–75.
131 Elisa F. Kent, *Converting Women*, New York, Oxford University Press, 2004, p. 33.
132 Robert W. Hefner, "Introduction: World Building and the Rationality of Conversion", in *Conversion to Christianity*, England, University of California Press, 1993.

133 Adrian Carton, *Mixed-Race and Modernity in Colonial India: Changing Concepts of Hybridity Across Empires*, London, Routledge, 2012, p. 13.
134 Kirti N. Chaudhuri, "The Portuguese Maritime Empire, Trade and Society in the Indian Ocean during the sixteenth Century", *Portuguese Studies*, Vol. 8, Special Issue supported by the Comissão Nacional para as Comemorações dos Descobrimentos Portugueses (1992), p. 68.
135 C.R. Boxer, *The Great Ship of Amacon, Annals of Macao and the Old Japan Trade, 1555–1640*, Lisbon, Centro de Estudos Historicos Ultramarinos, 1959, p. 131.
136 Om Prakash, *The New Cambridge History of India*, Vol. II. 5, European Commercial Enterprise in Pre-Colonial India, 1988, p. 56.
137 Chaudhuri, "The Portuguese Maritime Empire, Trade and Society in the Indian Ocean during the sixteenth Century", p. 69.
138 Carton, *Mixed-Race and Modernity in Colonial India*, p. 14.
139 Raychaudhuri, *Jan Company*, pp. 100–01.
140 Daniel Havart, *Op- en ondergang van Coromandel,* Rise and Fall of Coromandel, in Jan Company Coromandel, p. 203.
141 Gijs Kruitzer, *Xenophobia in Seventeenth Century*, Leiden, Leiden University Press, 2009, p. 63. Also see in Raychaudhuri, *Jan Company*, p. 204.
142 Raychaudhuri, *Jan Company*, p. 204.
143 Ibid.
144 Erik Odegard, "A Company of State. The Dutch East India Company and the Debates on the Company-State in Asia, 1660s–1690s", *Mechanisms of Global Empire Building*, ed. By Amélia Polónia Cátia Antunes, Brill, Leiden, 2011, pp. 127–44, p. 76.
145 Raychaudhuri, *Jan Company*, p. 208. For an example of such a family network at work, p. 120. The example given, as case from 1671, implicated governor general Maetseuijcker himself.
146 P.P. Xavier, "French Missionaries and Social Changes in Pondicherry", in *French in India and Indian Nationalism, (1700 A.D–1963 A.D)*, Vol. 2, ed by KS Mathew, Delhi, BR Publishing Corporation, 1999, pp. 305–06.
147 S. Arolianathan, "Influence of French in 18th Century Pondicherry Tamil Dialect", in *French in India and Indian Nationalism, (1700 A.D–1963 A.D)*, Vol. 2, ed by KS Mathew, Delhi, BR Publishing Corporation, 1999, pp. 358–63.
148 Calaichelvy Ezhilan, "Library Movement in French India", in *French in India and Indian Nationalism, (1700 A.D–1963 A.D)*. Vol. 2, ed by KS Mathew, Delhi, BR Publishing Corporation, 1999, p. 366.
149 Xavier, "French Missionaries and Social Changes in Pondicherry", p. 31.
150 Ibid., p. 309.
151 Ezhilan, "Library Movement in French India", p. 369.

4 Efflorescence and Manifestations
Art and Architecture in Deccan

Architecture originates from culture and it affects and reflects the culture of that society. Culture is something that originates from human interaction, and it is the main element of social and individuals' identity. Culture is not constant. It keeps changing and also accommodates changes. This cultural assimilation represents a new type of civilization, whose singularity is given by the unique symbiosis of European culture and the cultures of the people of Deccan.

Early Indo–European Experimentations: Portuguese Architecture in the Deccan

Indo–Portuguese architecture, which is a fusion of both Indian and Portuguese architecture, is a good example, in which a fusion of both the cultures could be seen.

Indo–Portuguese design is a consequence of the amalgamation between the conventional Portuguese design and local Indian engineering. Portuguese settlements in India fall under three primary classifications: the factory, the fort and the city.[1] Based on the type of settlements the settlement pattern also differed. For example, a factory type of settlement is usually situated at the mouth of a river or near the sea shores consisting of numerous warehouses and markets, to boost commerce. Houses are present in the highland and a single main road connects the residential spaces with the commercial spaces. While a fort settlement will have a fort in the centre and will be surrounded by numerous houses. Indo–Portuguese architecture adapted well to the Indian climate having high wooden ceilings with sloped roofs, large openings, *balcoes*, etc. It is a perfect example of a cross-cultural architecture. Indian people are usually introverted in their lifestyle which is contrary to the Portuguese people. This nature has been well adapted in Indo–Portuguese houses by having lots of openings facing the street but being covered partially using wooden screens. Such a nature of adapting and blending both cultures has led to the creation of a very unique and distinct architecture.

But Factories were trading stations that are sometimes a little more than a house surrounded by a *palisad*. They were located in privileged trading

DOI: 10.4324/9781003377511-4

places, often near the mouth of a river, facilitating communication within the hinterland.[2] The forts were always fortified with trading stations that accommodated a number of settlers. Forts were built in locations where food and water supply were easy. Most cities had evolved from factories or forts, particularly where commercial activities were intense. The settlements were founded by the state, and they became the foundation stone for new Portuguese cities.

The urban structures under the Portuguese depended upon the time of the construction, for example, the construction evolved from the previous settlements or completely new territory, points like the political attitude and strategies which governed construction.[3] In Deccan the Portuguese had to proceed with their construction work at a faster level to mark an effective military and political presence to protect the commerce in spices. They had to defend themselves against the Muslim traders and make a show of diplomatic activity and allegiance towards the local rulers.

Goa, the political, commercial and religious capital of the Portuguese in Asia, is probably the clearest example of the structure and spatial characteristic of a Portuguese colonial city. By the end of the 16th century it had a population of nearly 300,000 people, and it had been dubbed the Lisbon of the Orient because of its close resemblance to that city. In a location strangely similar to Lisbon's on the left margin of a river, Goa presented an irregular semi-circular plan.[4]

Trade, Military Conquests and Reinventing Cityscapes: Dutch Architecture in the Deccan

Dutch architecture can be seen in the form of castles, forts, churches, mansions and cemeteries. They preferred to take over existing structures and modify them. On the Coromandel, the forts were fortified by erecting a thick wall around their property, which was usually surrounded by a ditch, the earth from the ditch being used to construct the wall. The garrison consisted of men taken off their ships, one or two of which would remain anchored in the harbour. In Pulicat, Dutch first constructed Fort Geldria, which some criticized as being one "maintained at great expense, but too little profit." The new grant of 12 December 1612, which gave the Dutch the right to maintain a fort at Pulicat, was to be constructed by Venkata's chief queen Bayama at her expense.[5] The Governors, chief factors and important employees were accommodated within the fort. The first fortress that they built in South Coromandel Coast was Castle Geldria[6] at Pulicat, 535 meters in circumference, with walls seven meters high. On its ramparts and bastions were 36 cannons. It was named after Geldria, the native province of Wemmer van Berchem, the General Director of the Company, and it was estimated that 200 men would be required to defend it.[7] All the high administrations, officials and miscellaneous employees like surgeons, a priest and a school teacher, who needed high security, were all accommodated within the fort. A garrison of Dutch and Indian soldiers was also maintained under a captain within Fort Geldria. Private Dutch housing colonies, despite constraints, came up in the Pulicat town. Nearly one-fourth of the town was inhabited by the Dutch, perhaps the present Big Street, across the main road, in front (south) of the Dutch fort.

The Dutch lived in grand style in some of their settlements on the coast. At Golconda, before the economy measures were introduced in 1678, the *opperhoofd* of the factory kept an open house for all Christians in the city. Many of the Indian palanquin-bearers, horn-blowers, trumpeters, etc. were employed at that factory so that the local and the royal court would be impressed with the opulence and power of the Dutch Company. The factory was situated in the best part of the town, not far from the royal palace. When Thevenot visited Golconda in 1666, he found that the Dutch chief factor was escorted by standard hearers and trumpeters whenever he went out. The Dutch quarter of the town, at Pulicat had houses built in the Dutch style with avenues with parallel rows of trees. The fort was situated at the centre of the town and surrounded by a wide moat and had four stone bastions and a stone wall. The houses of the head officers were inside the fort wall and well furnished. Construction of a church within the fort was also done where the Dutch minister used to preach regularly every day. Other subordinates and soldiers, for the most part, had their lodgings outside the fort.[8]

Similarly, on the Konkan Coast, a factory was built at Vengurla, with permission from Adil Shah in 1639, to build a fort-like structure at the cost of 3000 guilders. The construction of the fort began in 1639 and was fully completed in the 1650s. It was built as a secure retreat during conflicts and emergencies, while also serving as the residence-cum-office of the Dutch factor. The ruins reveal a fort-like structure with extensive walls, strong bastions and gates that would've been well protected in its time by guards with heavy canons.[9] The building, made of stone and wood, has a rampart fence around. The factory building has an impact of Portuguese Architecture. Thus, we can see that the Dutch occupied many strongholds, which once belonged to Portuguese. They remodelled them and established new forts and cities. The other example of this reconstruction is Fort Cochin at Malabar Coast.

A Blending of Influences: French Architecture in the Deccan

The urbanization and town planning of Pondicherry reflected the French Imperial efforts. A cross-cultural examination of the town shows their attitude towards the natives. The French who were merchants, administrators and leaders in religious and political ideologies had a direct influence in the architectural interactions of the towns they built. The segregation of the town is a testimony of French policy towards the locals. However, their efforts at separation only led to architectural interactions, and this is seen in the various buildings present today. The locals imitated the architectural designs of the French in building their houses and the French followed suit.

The French had colonized a fishing village in Tamil Nadu and turned it into a blooming port. Francois Martin set up a factory and built a fort to attract craftsmen. The old town of an oval shape was planned in a grid pattern and is surrounded by boulevards. A large canal separates the "White Town" from the "Black Town."[10] The Muslims were the first to settle on the grand canal. Local tradition has it that this was at the time when the body of the saint Maula Sahib was transferred to its *dargah* at Muhammadia Pillai. After the Muslims, the craftsmen came and built their houses in between the big garden of the Company and the canal. In these areas the Governor imposed brick and tile construction in place of straw and clay. There was a growing class of elite Indians who prospered with the pepper trade. A small bazaar was located in the white town and a Grand bazaar was located in the back town.[11] Dumas turned his attention to the outskirts of the city, rebuilding the streets and planting 12,000 trees near Ariyankuppam.

The town had the Governor's house *Gouvernement* which was an office as well as a residence. From the Governor's house one street ran east towards the beach and the other west towards the fort. Dupleix's biggest achievement was completing the Palais du Gouvernement. It was completed in 1752. Dupleix and his wife supervised the construction. The south façade had 24 iconic columns, repeated on the first floor and grouped symmetrically to support a triangular fronton in the centre and a rounded fronton on either side. On the ground floor was a central hall with four beautiful statues and two large rooms-one for the Conseil and one for state functions.

In 1699 when Francois Martin took back Pondicherry from the Dutch he started building Fort Louis. Engineer de Nyon took inspiration from Fort Tournai (now in Belgium). The fort was the major landmark of the town, Fort Louis lay surrounded by the city. A narrow moat separated the fort from the town. Dumas improved sanitation by digging up land from the moat for better waste circulation.

The fort was built on a polygonal plan with low fortifications.[12] A clock tower was above it, and inside the fort was a chapel and cloth store.[13] On the East of the fort, a wall ran along the beach, with a gate opening to the sea. The fort had two gates, one on the seaside and the other on the town side. The Eastern Gate was called Porte Royal,[14] but Ananda Ranga Pillai does not tell us the name of the other gate. The royal gate symbolized the grandeur of the sovereign. The gates of the city and fort were adorned with the coat of arms of the King and the Compagnie. Dupleix's first construction was a rampart on the coast, for reasons of security as well as for embellishment. Dupleix also built a magnificent colonnade from Porte Marine to Porte Royale with 168 carved pillars probably brought from Gingee.[15] He also reused materials which were brought from Madras after the French under La Bourdonnais captured it in 1746.

The first court for Indians (*chauderie*) was built in 1729 on the plans of Father Louis. Skilled labour from France was hired to build these buildings.

During the Governorship of Lenoir, he invested in a grand project to develop the port of Lorient, this was an example of architectural activity between 1733 and 1740. He was assisted by Dupleix, Indians and Frenchmen for the construction of the ramparts.[16]

Ananda Ranga Pillai also mentions the churches in Pondicherry, the Fort church located within the walls of Fort Louis and the Capuchins' Church popularly known as Kappus Koil. He also refers to two popular churches on the outskirts of the town, the St. Paul's at Ariyankuppam and the St Andrew's at Reddiarpalayam.

An example of fusion between Indo–French architecture is the 18th-century Tamil building: Ananda Ranga Pillai Mansion. This mansion has two storeys: on the ground floor, it was typically Indian in which it has a courtyard surrounded by exquisitely carved wooden pillars, and on the first floor the terrace is supported by elegant masonry columns of European influence. The ceilings are adorned with heavy wooden beams and wooden joints supporting terrace roofing made of brick-on-edge masonry in lime mortar called *argamasse* in French. Their purpose was mainly for protection from the heat.[17] The French architectural features on the other hand followed the usual Greco–Roman orders of columns and pilasters and the presence of decorative motifs, flat roofs were crowned by a parapet of terracotta balusters, and they borrowed the lean-to in front of the Tamil tinnai-veranda.[18]

Interaction, Continuity and Change: The Architecture of the Marathas

The Maratha architecture, though preserving its affinities with earlier Hindu traditions, particularly in its religious and civil verities, was influenced to a certain extent by the architecture of other parts of Deccan. The Marathas were the patrons of art and architecture and had promoted fine arts such as painting, dance and music, during their rule.[19] Later the political contacts established with Mughal and Rajput courts influenced the artistic splendour and cultural ethics of the Marathas. Many prosperous and aristocratic classes of Maharashtra undertook the construction of temples and mansions and embellished them with wall paintings and other styles of decoration. The architecture in Maharashtra is world renowned, especially the one created by the Buddhists. They are known as the pioneers of architecture in and around Maharashtra. The architecture of Ajanta and Ellora are classic examples, while the temple architecture in Maharashtra took its shape under the Chalukyas. The architecture of the Marwar region under the Parmars known as the *Nagar* or *Hindustani* is of the Bhumij kind. During the Shilahar-Yadava times, a completely new architectural style known as *Hemadpanti* became the face of Maharashtrian architecture. In the Satara–Solapur region we see the Karnatak architecture, while in the Varad region we see the Varkandi architecture. All these architectural forms are quite different from Bahamani and Shahi architecture and have been endorsed in the vernacular spirit. But we do not find such kinds of architecture taking form in public spaces, and they remain confined to temple architecture at least for the period between 1500 and 1600.

Apparently, one cannot claim that there was any specific kind of architecture that can be categorized under Maratha architecture. As such after the establishment of *swaraj* by Chhatrapati new urban spaces were developed which paved the way for the Marathi people to create new patterns of architecture. Most of the time researching and studying the architecture of the Marathas during the medieval has been denied by historians. Architecture developed in the form of bastions and *vadas* throughout the 17th and 18th centuries, but most of these *vadas* have not survived to date nor proper care has been taken to keep them intact. Only some of these palaces and *vadas* in Satara, Nasik and Kopargaon have survived while most of them in Pune are in ruins. One of the most important buildings that Shahu commissioned is his *Vada* (Marathi term for big residence) known as *Adalatvada*. During the Peshwa rule, patrons and craftsmen were also influenced by the architecture in their immediate surroundings, the religious architecture of the Yadava temples and the more proximate architecture of the Deccan Sultanates. Among the building projects of Peshwa Baji Rao are the fortified residence of *Shanivarvada* and the temple of *Omkareshwar* in Pune.[20] Shanivarvada is said to be modelled on the architecture of *Purandarevada* at Sasvad. The reason behind it could be that the two families were on good terms with each other throughout the 18th century. In fact the family of Purandare patronized architecture, and the temples they had built in Sasvad are fine examples. Not only Peshwa Bajirao but also his family members are known to have constructed several buildings. For instance, his wife Kashibai built a Ghat (a flight of steps and terraces alongside the river bank which provided utilitarian and ritualistic access to the river) and a temple at the village of Chas which was her paternal home. These Ghats are an early example of such construction in the 18th century. While Bajirao's sister Bhiubai built a temple in Pune, the second sister Anubai was responsible for suggesting a designer-builder for Shanivarvada.

The erection of a temple or palace must have been the occasion as much for the discovery of fresh talent as for the empowerment of known skills, and judging from the monuments that have survived, we may as well say that there was a dearth of artisans who were also great artists. At least temples have been maintained and architecture can be studied only through temple forms. A rough historical analysis of the architecture can be done from the private collections and correspondences from the planning designs and the expenditure information as well as the materials procured. The *bakhars* and the *powadas* also give details on the magnificence of the *vadas* and temples built in contemporary times. The *powadas* of Ram Joshi are an excellent piece of ballad source to understand the pattern of development of Pune as a city; also the travelogues of European travellers give information on the various aspects of architecture in the Deccan region. Throughout the 17th and 18th centuries the architecture which took its form and shape has been endorsed as *Dakhini* architecture. No doubt it had influence of Malwa and Rajasthan, while most of the court culture was an imitation of Hindustani Mughal. The Marathas gave huge donations to the construction of ghats in Benaras. So, an enormous amount of Deccani cultural influence is also seen in the north of India. Most of the works have solid black rock lime and lead constructions of various kinds of chowks, wells and *deewankhanas*, and using teak wood with carve patterns is also seen throughout this region. The villages seem to have a distinctive pattern, although small were maintained well. Most of the roads were constructed to be wide while the river banks were maintained well with the proper construction of ghats and small temples. The commercial markets and residential areas were divided and were at a safe distance from the agricultural area. In the Ahmednagar and Bijapur areas there are many constructions of underground irrigation facilities as well as drinking water facilities with a connecting network throughout the city. Construction of underground tunnels to bring in was taken as a prime activity. Beautification of these lakes and waterbodies was also done while planting of trees along the roads was also taken care of. Various forts and palaces were built throughout the 17th and 18th centuries; the capital forts like Raigad and Rajgarh depict the architectural heights of the 17th century. While the various *vadas* and palaces in Pune Shaniwarvada, Vishrambagh, Nasik Sarkar vada, Kopargaon, Raghunath Rao peshwa vada, Chhatrapatis new and old Peshwavada were the height of architectural development in the 18th century.

Throughout the architecture the importance of religion is depicted as it was customary and tradition. Most of the houses were built by using brunt brick and those in the urban spaces were built of solid rock, the width of most of the walls was never less than three feet. The use of *vastu* was also eminent in the construction of houses, and the houses had paintings depicting the various puranic stories. Every room was used for different purposes. The central places of the house were never covered, always remained to be open while the other rooms were named as majghara, swayampakghara, Jevanaghara, Sajaghara, i.e. living room, kitchen, dining, bedroom, etc. The houses also used to have a small office space, and the houses of the rich people used to have various items made out of ivory. They were a mix of Rajasthani, Gujarati and Hindustani forms. One of the things which can be strikingly noted is that temples lacked symmetry. It developed from the Nagar to the Bhumij in the 18th century. The temples have three main portions one is Mukhyamandapam, i.e. porch; cornice, i.e. sajja; and the garbhagriha, i.e. sanctum, sanctorum. The other architecture form of Maratha temple is that of Hindustani also known as the Nagar. The Ram Mandir at Nashik, the Shiva Mandir, Mohiniraj Mandir, etc. are some of the examples of such architecture. They have an influence of Rajasthani and Mughal architecture and also have a resemblance to the symmetry patterns.

We see a lot of stucco art on the outer portions of the temples, i.e. idols made of lime pasted on the outer walls of the temples, while the "shikhra" has the influence of Karnataka Dravidian architectural style and also the use of Meghadambri. In all they are a mix of Rajasthani, Mughal, Shahi and Dravidian architectural forms. In the 18th century we see expertise was also borrowed from European artists to develop certain architectural techniques. The beauty and accuracy of the engraving of most temples, forts or living *Chatarams* attest to the high degree of literary achievement. The Marathas had their own distinct art and architectural traditions and that reflected in their establishments in India and mainly in South India. But when they invaded Tamil Nadu, they took up the Tamil culture and their architectural styles. Thus, the buildings made by them were a fusion of both the traditions. The pursuits of these rulers are reflected in the monuments such as the Great Anaicut, Big Temple and Saraswathi Mahal Library.[21]

The art of building forts in the form of citadels and city fortification has been known since early times. The maximum number of fort-building activity in the Deccan took place during the early years of the Maratha period. Forts were regarded as the manifestation of kingly authority. If there is any architectural monument to the genius of Shivaji, it is the many forts up and down the Ghats of Maharashtra.[22] These forts present us with a rich diversity of site, history, architectural style and cultural heritage, each with a wide range. At one end of the broad spectrum is the mighty mountain fort of Salher, one of the highest in the entire Deccan. Another fort is the hill fort of Daulatabad, both in design and construction, which was one of the most powerful (as it is one of the best preserved) fortresses of the Middle Ages in existence.[23] Further the territories comprised within the boundaries of Maharashtra are crowded with forts like Purandhar, Harishchandragarh, Ankai, Shiveneri, Panhala, Sholapur, Pratapgarh, Kalyan, Janjira and Torna. These forts were designed and constructed to serve as a defence in warfare, military bases and some for residential purposes. Several new features in fort architecture were introduced by the Marathas. For instance, the underground approach to the fort is one of the striking features. During Shivaji's time, the excavated tunnels on wall walks were used for fortification purposes. Other features like Merlons (Ardhadal), Embrasures (Falika) and Machicolations (Zaroka)[24] were also introduced. The merlons gave protection to the soldiers standing behind it and firing through the loopholes. While the embrasures[25] were the openings which could be used for observation or for hurling missiles on the enemy below. The importance of these features declined sharply with the advent of improved artillery. Machicolations were openings on the top of the gateways and entrances. They were used to fire upon the enemy who may have reached the gate. If the enemy tried to burn the gate, then water could be poured from here to extinguish the fire.

Influences, Traditions and Developing a Unique Style: Evolution of the Maratha Painting

Maratha painting saw a gradual change as a cultural development in the form of renaissance in painting. It brought out a unique Maratha style of painting and also manifested through various proportions. There was a steady development in the form and shape of practising painting with a varied amount of technical know-how and skill by various artists side by side giving enough scope for the development of a class which could appreciate the various aspects of painting. Maratha painting developed on the basis of the subject of the art and the tradition of the technique. The earliest example of painting in Maharashtra is the famous mural painting in the caves of Ajanta. Other than Ajanta, fragmented remains of paintings have been noticed in the caves of Bhaja, Karla, Bedsa, Junnar, Pitalkhora, etc.[26] Frequent references to an earliest literary work dated 2nd century B.C., the *Gathasaptashati* by the Satavahana King Hala, in Maharashtra, show how the art of painting was part of the cultural life of contemporary society. While another work by western Chalukya King Someshwara in Sanskrit dated 12th century A.D. contains important technical information about painting.[27]

In the early period wall painting was widely popular.[28] The Marathi poet Chobha of the 16th century in his work *Usha-haran* gives the technique of wall painting and makes it clear that this technique (application of cloth below the plaster) was in practice since the early period.[29] The Bhakti movement in Maharashtra not only influenced the socio-religious life of the people but also influenced various branches of Fine Arts. Many art forms like dance, drama, poetry, music, literature, painting, etc. represent the manifestation of God, and images of God in painting was considered one of the most direct and effective method to reach God. It became customary to paint the Puranic scenes and images of God on the walls of temples and residential buildings. Later with the contact and influence of the Islamic courts of the Deccan in Maratha society, painting no longer remained restricted to mural painting depicting religious themes alone. Painting like miniature painting which depicted religious as well as secular themes became popular with the Maratha patrons. The range of themes in Maratha painting became diverse like portrait, scenes depicting court-life, Ragamala, etc. Painting was now treated by them as a thing of aesthetics and entertainment and not just a religious custom. Maratha rulers constructed a large number of buildings which became the symbols of Maratha power and affluence. The rulers erected numerous temples and renovated ruined ones. While the religious themes dominated the subject matter of the murals, several secular themes depicting contemporary court-life can also be seen like procession of the king, meeting of royal persons, court scenes, war scenes, horse-riding portraits of kings or princes, dance and music performance in the court, Ragamala, portraits of dignitaries. The art of painting was employed extensively for the decoration of these buildings.[30] Even the rulers of Tanjavur extended full patronage to the art of painting. At Tanjavur some of the important places with mural work are Tanjavur palace, Brihadishwara temple.

Most of the paintings which one witnessed in the *diwan khanas* or on the walls of the temples have a traditional and religious connotation. While practising art as a leisure for entertainment in the sense of personal connection was seen as a part of a luxurious life and status in the society, owning such art pieces was also a symbol of class citizenship. It was in this manner that painting developed in the Medieval Maratha country. Information related to the paintings and painters during the medieval Maratha period is available in various Maratha documents and these sources orient scholars even before seeing the paintings. Most of the recorded sources belong to the reign of Chhatrapati Shahu. The information related to paintings preceding the reign of Shahu is very scanty.

Peshwa Bajirao got many paintings painted on the walls of his residence Shaniwarvada. The caretaker of this residence Jivaji Ganesh Khasgivale in his letter writes "RaghoTanaji, Anuprao were very good painters." Before the coming of Peshwai "Shivram" was a very famous painter. Madhavrao I had in his service a painter named Bankoji who was paid a salary of rupees 30 for 45 days. He had kept him in his services during his visit to Raghobaanandavali in the year 1765. He was introduced to him through Nana Fadnavis. In 1764, Peshwa Madhavrao ordered 36 paintings of the Ragmala series to decorate his Diwan-i-Khas. He had spent an amount of 195 rupees. All the above references do give an idea of the amount of patronage which was guaranteed by the rulers of Medieval Maratha country for the development of paintings which ultimately paved way for its development and progress.

The Peshwas also brought various types of paintings from Jaipur. Nana Fadnavis had procured a copy of Bhagvat Gita which had paintings in it. Apart from these various artisans were also been invited from Delhi and Agra, of which information is recorded in various correspondences. The Peshwa also received various kinds of gifts from the English government which had a collection of 24 different paintings related to the theme ocean. When Charles Mallet visited Pune, he asked two of his painters James Whales and Daniel at the court of the Peshwa Madhavrao. Local painters were trained by these western painters of which Gangaram Tambar became very famous. The Peshwa sardars also imitated the Peshwa and they too patronaged painting by having various painters at their services and getting vadas painted.

Sardar Khasgewale got painted the paintings of the Munji ceremony (sacred thread ceremony) from Dhanajay and Bapu Chitari. He paid Rs 8 for these paintings. The whole of Tulsi Bagh was painted under a contract with Ramji Chitari in the year March 1826. Due recognition must be given to the Peshwa for promotion and motivation of this art. The period brought out a wide range of paintings and ceiling paintings all through Maharashtra. One can say that there was no single village in Maharashtra which did not have such art pieces during these times. The Marathi people were so fascinated that they got their walls painted during every festival and the main subject line always remained to be religious depicting various mythical stories. This fascination can be traced without any discontinuity at least for a span of five decades. Apart from this one can see various idols and statues being placed on vadas and temples all through Pune, Satara via Nasik, Chandawar, Nepani, Pandeswar, Morgao, Ghandopachipal, Benwari, Pashan, etc. We also find wooden pillars with carvings and paintings being done on them. Paintings done in the form of tracing also in 2D and 3D dimensions can be traced.

The palace of the Rastes in Vai has the depiction of the *dasartars* in the form of painting. Such kinds of other paintings can also be identified in the new palace of Satara with them. We also find the painting of Ganpati, Ridhi and Sidhi while one can figure out the painting of Shiva in an isolated form. Apart from the themes of the gods and goddesses painters also tried to depict paintings of Shiva-Parvati and Vishnu-Lakshmi. In Vidharba especially Jamore, one finds paintings related to Jain religion and culture in the Jain Mandirs. In a similar fashion at Bazargao, the Jain mandir paintings figure out the fine details of the subject but along with religion the subject of the paintings also focuses on the traditions and Puranic stories which talk about the emotions of the medieval society.

One finds many paintings depicting the epics like Mahabharat and Ramayan and the various episodes like Swayamvar of Draupadi and various leelas of Krishna like gopivastraharan, rangapanchimi, rasyanritya, etc. We find many fine paintings at the Patwarthanvada at Vai, the Gokhale Vada and Holkar Rangmahal at Chandwar. We also find different kinds of paintings as still paintings in the form of a Rajput drinking water near a well or a painting of Laila Majnu, a hunter hunting or a rider riding a horse. We find paintings especially related to personification at Talegao Dabhade at Chandawar.

All through the medieval paintings the religious traditions were taken forward and the society depicted close resemblance to the practice of religion. One can make out the status gender through the use of colour combinations. The backgrounds of the painting are mostly done with the use of colours like white, red, green, blue, saffron and yellow. Most of the times the buildings are white and the mountains are grey and black. Maratha paintings come very close to the Rajasthani paintings yet they have a very significant and unique texture of separating them from any imitation.

Reviving an Antique Tradition: Development of Maratha Sculpture

The most ancient sculptures of Maharashtra are the Buddhist sculptures at the Karle Bhaje caves in the district of Pune. One can date these sculptures to be from the 2nd century B.C. on the basis of their features. There are fine arts of the ancient Satavahana period. The Shunga art also can be seen significantly in them. All other sculptures in western Maharashtra are more related to the Buddhist caves scattered all around. One can figure out changes during the 4th and 5th centuries for the Vakataka rule. The Vakatakas had established inter-marriage and inter-dining relations with the Guptas of the north due to which we can also trace the Gupta influence on the sculptures in Maharashtra. The Mahayan caves at Ajanta belong to the 5th century that is of the Vakataka king Harishen. The numerous paintings on the walls also have the presence of many different sculptures all around. It was ruled by the Rashtrakutas during the 8th century. The Rashtrakuta king Krishna the II initiated the carvings at Bellur in the year 753 B.C. It was popularly known as the world-famous Kailash temple. We find many other sculptures around Ellora, and one can trace the development of sculptures till the 10th century. After which during the Silaharas and Yadavas we don't find any references to cave sculptures rather we find the creation of many temples all throughout Maharashtra. These temples are known for their hemadpanthi style. The temples have many sculptures carved all through the outer walls as well as the Shikhar. Maharashtra has a rich tradition of such kinds of sculptures, but due to the Islamic invasions during the medieval times one can see a gradual discontinuity. It was during the Yadava times that there was a severe setback in this field, especially from the 13th century onwards it became very crucial. The Islamic invasions were more of iconoclastic behaviour. The people of the book (Ehle Kitab) had zero tolerance for the worship of idols, and most of the masterpieces created during the classical times were ruined during these invasions. What we find today are ruins of these magnificent structures. All the Hemadpanthi temples constructed during the 13th and 14th centuries have no sculpture on the outer walls. It was a reaction to these invasions.

In the 15th and 16th centuries during the rule of the Muslim rulers we find very less patronage given for the construction of temples, but during the times of the Peshwa period one can find a new vigour taking shape in this field of sculpting and Maharashtra again witnessed many more new temples all around. In the Indian orientation architecture and sculpture go hand in hand. Hence, they are completely indifferent to the Greek patterns of free sculptures. We find such sculptures only during the time of Ashoka in the form of pillar capitals or in the form of yaksa-yashika of Shunga times. Although we don't find many sculptures on the wall of temples constructed during the Peshwa times. The art of sculpture could not progress all throughout the 17th and 18th centuries as the Chhatrapati and the Peshwas could devout very less time from their continuous expeditions against Mughals, Nizams and the English for the development of the art of sculpture. We also find most of the influential Maratha Sardars facing huge debts and at times becoming bankrupt. This kind of environment was completely adverse for the development of art, architecture and sculpture. One can also figure out that all through the Indian continent during medieval times there were very less states which were controlled by the Hindus. There are some sculptures of Shivaji, his horse and his dog being carved in the 18th century. These sculptures tried to depict a story of certain important events which took place in the local areas. Some also depict the Karnataka expedition of Shivaji and his conversions with the local leaders and their resistance to Shivaji. The development of this art can be periodized in three parts:

First 1646–1720, i.e. the period from Chhatrapati Shivaji to Peshwa Balaji during which there was less patronage, second from 1720 to 1740 the period of Peshwa Bajirao I and third 1740–1761 the period of Balaji Bajirao, i.e. the Maratha expansion of the north. Due to the Maratha expansion policy in the north and the day-to-day interaction with the culture of the north, the Marathas brought new patterns of making sculptures into the Deccan. After the Battle of Panipat in 1761, especially during the times of Madhavrao I, Narayan Rao, Sawai Madhavrao, Nana Fadnavis, we see a huge development in the construction of temples and palaces. With an equal influence of the Rajput and Gujarati style most of the cultures depict the costumes in the North Indian style. Another development which is a signature to this art is that of the Veergarhs (hero stones). The Veergarhs are a tribute to the local warriors who fought the battles courageously and tried to save their localities. In their remembrance the local communities have erected hero stones. The hero stone is approximately 3–4 feet in height. The upper portion is a semi-circle and the event is divided into three parts. The first part, i.e. from below, depicts how the warrior is sent off to the battle with pomp and show and the courage and valour shown by these warriors in the mid portion. We see various apsaras carrying the martyrs on their soldiers to the heavens where they are carried in palanquins. On the uppermost third part it is depicted that the warriors are offering their prayers to the god Shiva. Such hero stones are found throughout Maharashtra, but they are not a very fine piece of artefact; most of them are crude and have certain chronology and names carved on them in a very irregular unsymmetrical manner. Another important development was sculptures made of metals. We see the use of metal and metallurgy for manufacturing sculptures throughout the 17th and 18th centuries. Fine artefacts of metal works can be seen during the Peshwa period. Metals like silver, bronze and gold have been used to make different kinds of sculptures of gods and goddesses. We also find wood carvings on a large scale throughout the medieval Maharashtra region. This art was exclusively borrowed from the Rajasthani and Gujarati artists but were of less durability in comparison manufactured by the Rajasthani and Gujarati artisans. Many of these artefacts were burnt down; the only pieces which can be traced are those found in palaces, vadas of noblemen or Sardars.

Politics, Spirituality and Poetic Aesthetics: Marathi Literature in the 18th century

If we have to trace the development of literature and the motivation and nature behind its development, then it would not be justifiable to understand its trajectories strictly in the chronological sense or its development through the centuries. It can be only understood as a historical process cutting across the barrier's region, regionalism, rationality, time and space. Though we can figure out a number of significant years which actually changed the course of Maratha history in particular and Deccan in general like 1680 the demise of Shivaji, 1682 the demise of Ramdas, 1707 the demise of Aurangzeb in Deccan or the assassination of Shamabji in 1689 and the demise of Rajaram in 1700. The Maratha state saw a loss of three Chhatrapatis just in a span of two decades, while these two decades have been the most occupied decades in terms of expeditions and diplomacy. It ignited the Marathi war of independence which actually influenced the whole of the Indian continent and reviewed the political equations throughout the continent. While 1761 saw the peak of development with the decline of the Marathas for a temporary period due to the third Battle of Panipat. The development of Marathi literature during the 18th century was never separate from this crux of historical trajectories, but to understand the ethos and essence behind its progress one should always know the prior developments during the early medieval and late ancient. The late ancient and early medieval literature had its scope categorically confined to religion and religiosity. Popular cults like Mahanubhav, Nath Sampradaya, Varkari, Dutt Sampradaya and the cult of Ramdas highly influenced the spiritual and religious life of the Marathi speaking masses as well as the non-Marathi speaking masses of Deccan which lay in close proximity of the peripheries of these cults and Sampradayas. Most of the literature which took its shape and form through the important saints who themselves belong to various castes and stratums of the society brought in an enormous amount of dynamism, renaissance and reformation with the values of humanism. The works of Shri Chakradhar, Shri Namdev and Shri Janeshwar right from the 12th to 18th centuries did a critical analysis of all the interpretations of the known religious texts. They revolutionized the value of literature by rewriting and analyzing the Sanskrit texts into Prakrit (vernacular). It brought tremendous upheaval in the society by paving way for establishing the values of humanism. The literature which developed through these ages till the 18th century was the prime factor to challenge the social norms, taboos ideas and institutions which existed in the Sanatani form and was an eye opener to the masses to rethink on the logic of interpretation which not only changed the personality of the individual but churned a very ethos and essence of the established credibility of the structural forms of society. Literature in a sense was a wheel of revolution to broaden the vistas of understanding knowledge in the sequence to humanism. It challenged the stigmas of social hierarchies, gender inequalities and the application of reason to conscience. But there was a radical change in the form of literature produced during the 17th century in the wake of the 18th century. In the 18th century under the Peshwas and the rise of the new aristocracy the court culture got more and more influenced by the Persian language, its customs and traditions, attire and food habits and became more and more elite which created a distance between the high-class and the low-class citizens. Not only this, but the Peshwa period also witnessed the rise of Brahmani culture which had its foundations laid on the Varnashrama system. Sanskrit as a language regained its importance. Events like the coronation of Shivaji, creation of the council of eight ministers and the preparation of Rajyavyaharkosh, all are very fine examples of a return to the Sanatan tradition. The theatre was again replaced by Sanskrit plays, and the elite class turned to the value of vernacular languages by distancing themselves by symbolic behavioural patterns. They were more interested in the Panchamahakavyas. Due to rapid urbanization the standard of living also changed. This attributed to the change in existing learning and expressions. People became more interested in epic literature and accordingly plays like Shakuntala, Ramcharitmanas and Kavya Prakash which were classical but very technical became more important. Marathi literature witnessed a new era, but its connotation power was not as strong as compared to the one that preceded it. The Varkari sampradaya gave more importance to kirtans and bhajans. It showed an inclination towards recitation in Sanskrit, Shlokas in Sanskrit poetry and Sanskrit compositions which did influence the masses to a certain level. The literature created by Shridhar and Mahipati almost lost their essence on the scale of popularity. Poets and Kirtankars engaged themselves in performance not for the cause of knowledge but for the cause of making a livelihood. In all the academic pursuit and the value of humanism deteriorated slightly. From the face of erudition Marathi literature entered the domain of philosophical interpretation. Philosophical depth to literature was for the first time given by Vaman Pandit. He died in the year 1695. Though his demise happened in the 17th century, his works had a great bearing on Marathi literature in the 17th century. His style created a new tradition in the realm of philosophy of literature. His works like Yatharthadipika, Brahmanamsudha, Nigamsara, Karmatatva, etc. are masterpieces of philosophical depth. They cover a varied analysis of the Vedantic and Upanishadic discourse. It was Vaman Pandit who first brought out a critical analysis of the work of Janeshwar in which he says that Janeshwar was able to give the emotional understanding of Bhagvat Gita. He was trying to give the contemporary relevance of the Gita. He took pride in propagating his works and criticized his contemporaries. He was more interested in the contemporary relevance of each and every aspect of literature than in its fictional value. He had a deep inclination for the logical interpretation. Another scholar of the contemporary times Shivram produced important works like Gita Chandrika, Madhavswami and

Mahadji Shinde. He also wrote a critique on the ekadaskand of Bhagvat Gita. Poet Madhavswami of Tanjavur was another important personality who brought out his works in 1736. Another important personality was Gangadhar who wrote a critique on Das skanda. One of the finest critiques on the philosophy of literature was Krushnadayarnab. He was able to write 42,000 powies (stanzas) of the Bhagvat. His famous work is known as Harivarada. Apart from Sanskrit many works were also written in Prakrit. As Prakrit was the language of the masses, scholars produced epics in vernaculars for they gained popularity like the stories of the life of Ram and Krishna as well as the various episodes on Ramayana and Mahabharata. Harivansh Bhagvatare wrote some works which were appreciated by the masses. Literature also witnessed in forms of stories represented through paintings. The first comprehensive work on Marathi language which came out as a prose entitled Leelacharita. Others like Govindaprabhucharita Tirthavari are excellent examples of this kind. By 1700, a female poet named Bahinabai brought out her autobiography in the form of abhangas. Under this genre we see many autobiographies and biographies of various saints of Maharashtra were produced like Sant charitre of Udhavchidhar, Samarthpratap by Gridhar, Dasvishrammadham by Atmaram Swami, etc. This period also witnessed the literature produced by the Jain and Lingayat of the Avedic genre. Marathi literature also witnessed a genre in the form of sonnet. Some of the famous works of this kind which became very popular are Kay karuke may by Keshav swami, Nana Parimal Druva by Gosawi Nandan, Jaijainarayan by Udhavchidam, etc. One of the most important genres in Marathi literature was the powadas. There were many powadas produced during the 17th and 18th centuries, and this genre of literature came to be recognized as a historical source. The form of recitation of this literature has been very exciting as it talks about the valour and courage of the heroes who created the Swaraj. Powadas also gave birth to a new form of folk songs named lavani. Literature has played a dominant and effective role in the making of the culture and pursuit and the mentality of the medieval Deccan in general and the Marathi mind in particular.

Influence and confluence can be seen in European architectural style in Deccan and as well as Maratha architecture and various art forms. As we have discussed that amalgamation of culture influenced every aspect that we have dealt with in this chapter that is Maratha painting, architecture, sculpture and literature. We see a co-existence of culture in Deccan. Deccan has everything on its platter which we see in form of a rich cultural heritage. Art and architecture, sculpture, painting and temple art say a lot about our period under study. The raw material used, the portrayal of various sculptures on the temple walls and vadas tell a lot about the rituals, traditions and beliefs of the people of Deccan, especially the Maratha country. Thus, the study of art, architecture and paintings becomes very important when we attempt to study Deccan in transition in a holistic manner.

Notes

1 Tony Marcel Nisha and P. Jayasudha, "Portuguese Architecture in India—The Architectural Scenario of Mandap, an Indian Coastal Village", *Indian Journal of Scientific Research* Vol. 14, No. 1 (2017), pp. 138–42, p. 2.
2 Mauel C. Teixeira, "Portuguese Traditional Settlements, a Result of Cultural Miscegenation", *Traditional Dwellings and Settlements Review*, Vol. 1, No. 2 (Spring 1990), p. 24.
3 Ibid., p. 27.
4 Ibid., p. 26.
5 Robert Sewell, *A Forgotten Empire (Vijayanagar) A Contribution to the History of India*, London, Swan Sonnenschein & Co. Ltd., 1924, p. 223.
6 Om Prakash, ed., *The Dutch Factories in India,* 1617–1623, Delhi, Munshiram Manoharlal, 1984, pp. 6–7.
7 Owen C. Kail, *The Dutch in India*, New Delhi, Mac Millan India Ltd., 1981, p. 104.
8 Tapan Raychaudhuri, *Jan Company in Coromandel, 1605–1690: A Study in the Interrelation of European Commerce and Traditional Economies*, Brill, The Hague, 1962, p. 204.
9 Sachin Pendse, "The Dutch Factory at Vengurla", *IJMH, Sage*, Vol. 30, No. 4 (2018), p. 726.
10 J.F. Price, ed., *The Private Diary of Ananda Ranga Pillai (1736–1746)*, Vol. I, New Delhi, Asian Education Services, 1904, p. 272.
11 S. Jeyaseela Stephen, "Urban Growth of Pondicherry and the French: A Study of the Town Plans 1702–1798", in *French in India and Indian Nationalism (1700 A.D. - 1963 A.D.)*, ed. K.S. Mathew, 2 Vols., New Delhi, B.R. Publishing Corporation, 1999, p. 420.
12 Jean Marie Lafont, "Reminiscences (The French in India)", in *INTAC (Indian National Trust for Art and Cultural Heritage),* New Delhi, Munishiram Manoharlal, 1997, pp. 26–27.
13 Arvind Sinha, *The Politics of Trade: Anglo-French Commerce on the Coromandel Coast* (1763–1793), New Delhi, Manohar, p. 103.
14 Price, ed., *The Private Diary of Ananda Ranga Pillai*, Vol. V, p. 440.
15 Lafont, *Reminiscences (The French in India),* p. 30.
16 Ibid., p. 28.
17 Francoise L'Hernault, "Pondicherry in the Eighteenth Century: Town Planning, Streetscapes and Housescapes", in *French in India and Indian Nationalism, (1700 A.D–1963 A.D)*, ed. K.S. Mathew, Vol. 2, New Delhi, B.R. Publishing Corporation, 1999, p. 376.
18 Ibid., p. 377.
19 Satish Deshmukh,"Maratha Paintings" unpublished thesis, Marathwada University, 1986, p. 14.
20 George Michell and Mark Zebrowski, *Architecture and Art of the Deccan Sultanates*, Vol. 1, Cambridge, Cambridge University Press, 1999, p. 21.
21 A.R. Kulkarni and G.H. Khare, *MarathyanchaItihas*, Vol. 2, Pune, Continental Prakashan, First Print, 1994, pp. 370–89.
22 Stewart Gordon, *The New Cambridge History of India*, Vol. II-4, [*The Marathas 1600–1800*], New Delhi, Cambridge University Press, 2000, p. 82.
23 Sidney Toy, *The Strongholds of India*, Heinemann Educational Publishers, 1 December 1957, p. 33.
24 Ibid.
25 Ibid., p. 432.
26 S. Nagraju, *Buddhist Architecture of Western India*, Delhi, Agam Kala Prakashan, 1981, p. 283.

27 Kamal Chavan, "Maratha Painting", *Bulletin of the Deccan College Post-Graduate and Research Institute*, Vol. 58/59 (1998–1999), pp. 181–96.
28 B.K. Apte, *Maratha Wall Paintings*, Bombay, Secretary, Maharashtra Board for Literature and Culture, 1988, p. 23.
29 V.K. Rajwade, *ChobhakritUshaharan*, Bharat ItihasSamshodhakMandai Annual Report (Ahwal) Shake, 1833, p. 13.
30 Kamal Chavan, *Maratha Murals*, New Delhi, B.R. Publishing Corporation, p. 56.

5 Trajectories of Entrepreneurship

Trade and Commerce in Deccan

Deccan was that part of land whereby travellers from diverse lands descended upon the plains. Drawn to its heartland, the Deccan plateau, they encountered a world where other cultures, those of the Middle East and Africa, had already met and been absorbed into India's powerful embrace. Receptive to outside influences, Deccan became home to foreign immigrants, Sufi mystics, Shi'a Muslims and global traders. The policies of the Deccan Sultanates were to transform Deccan into a seat of international cosmopolitanism. The Deccan's past so far was defined by its Hindu lords and by their great temples—then it was part of a web that stretched not only from Cairo to Delhi but deep into the heart of India, turning Deccan into an important node on the global map.

Deccan came to be perceived as a land of fortune; the diamond-rich mines fostered an opulent court culture, one which is represented in textiles, rare treasures and refined objects. In the 15th and 16th centuries, a steady stream of so-called Westerners (*gharbian*), settlers from the Arab and the Persian world, flowed to the Deccan having been attracted by offers of favoured status. Since these newcomers arrived "to seek their fortune ..., they proved more hard working and industrious than their counterparts, i.e., the old nobility from Delhi."[1]

Peninsular India occupies the middle of the Indian Ocean, with ports on both coasts that made the region a commercial hub. On the Western side, Chaul, Dabhol and Goa connected Deccan to the Middle East via Maritime routes, while on the Eastern side Masulipatnam connected it to Southeast Asia. Deccani rulers desired overseas trading partners to buy locally produced textiles. In turn they needed to purchase warhorses from outside. In fact, it was Bidar's insatiable demand for warhorses that attracted foreign merchants such as the famous horse merchant Nikitin, who described one market near Bidar where 20,000 horses were sold.[2] Cotton of Deccan had long ago earned a reputation abroad, and from the Bahamani period, the silk industry became thoroughly globalized. Silk procured in cocoon stage from China was brought to Konkan, where it was reeled, dyed and woven before being exported to Middle Eastern markets. Goods from Deccan travelled across the world, thus what followed was the pouring in of the various

DOI: 10.4324/9781003377511-5

East India Companies in the 16th and 17th centuries who encroached on the territories of the Deccan states to carry the vast riches of the region. This provided for an aura of dynamism, diversity and cosmopolitanism that was perhaps unique in the early modern period. This chapter unfolds the economic diversity that had occurred due to the region's wealth and the interplay of the European Companies in the region's exports.

Commerce across Seas: Ports, Hinterlands and Maritime Trade

The commercial activity in the numerous ports along the entire east and west coast of the Deccan was generated by the economy of the hinterland, varying in depth and in the intensity of its productivity and consumption. Like the ports and the coastline, the hinterland also shows a volatile and changeful character in respect of its political and administrative organization. The main ports on the Konkan coast of Deccan were Chaul, Dabhol, Kalyan, Bhivandi, Vengurla, Pen, Dahanu, Tarapur, Kelve, Mahim, Agashi, Vasai, Bandre, Nogothane, Shrivardhan, Jaitapur, Rajapur and Kharepatan. In the Coromandel region, a number of ports emerged as places of outlet for the textiles and other commodities produced within that region. The important ports along the coast are Madras, San Thome, Cuddalore, Nagore, Masulipatnam, Pulicat, Negapatam and Porto Novo.

During the time of Shivaji, Chaul, Danda-Rajpur, Dabhol, Ratnagiri, Vijayadurg, Sindudhurg and Vingurla were the important seaports. Of these Chaul, Danda-Rajpur, Dabhol and Valandra had an early history of maritime trade. Commodities like pepper, stick lack, seed lack, *dungarees* and *percollas* were sold from Dabhol to the East India Company in Bombay. Dabhol came under control of Shivaji in 1662 and also traded with Malabar and Cambay.[3] Chaul was chiefly known for its silk fabrics, opium and indigo. This port was taken under control by Shivaji in the 1670s. Rajapur had a brisk trade in saltpetre, pepper, cardamom and calicoes. Both the English and French had their factories here. The French traded in iron and lead. Rajapur had trade contacts with the Red Sea and with Basra in Persia.[4] Vengurla, where the Dutch had set up their factory, was visited by ships sailing from Batavia, Japan, Ceylon, Persia and Arabia. The seaports in the Ratnagiri district exported calicoes, silks, grain, coarse lac and, above all, pepper which was their main export. This pepper was brought here from Kanara and then shipped to Surat, Persia and Europe.[5]

Chaul, Dabhol, Rajapur, etc. were big harbours on the Konkan coast whereas Nagothana, Mahad, Chiplun, Ratnagiri, Vengurla, Malwan, Keliya, Belapur, Jambusar, Balsar, Panwel, Kolambe, etc. were small ports. Kalyan-Bhiwandi had a harbour which was visited by merchant ships. The goods were unloaded at these ports and carried inland to various markets over long distances by huge caravans of Lamanis, who sometimes numbered as many as 10,000.[6] In the 18th century, after conquering Bassein and Salsette from the Portuguese, the Peshwas tried to develop these harbours by granting houses and house sites to the merchants who had come there to settle and by affording help to those who volunteered to build ships. For example, the Peshwa Government issued orders for giving three Khandis of iron to Krishnaji Vishwanath, an officer of Taluka Anjanwel, for building a new ship.[7]

Some of the imported articles came through the European factories set up in India. For example, gun-powder and lead came through Goa. Textiles were brought by the Armenians, the Dutch, the French and other Europeans. In 1735 the Arabs were allowed to reopen trade with India in response to a request made by their chief at Muscat. Malik Muhammad was treated with respect by the Peshwa and, on completion of his work, was provided with a ship for his return journey to Muscat. From Shivaji to other Chhatrapatis, the Maratha rulers were controlling the maritime trade along the western coast between Daman in the north and Goa in the south. Any vessel plying in the Konkan waters had to secure a permit from the Peshwa Government. Otherwise it was in danger of being confiscated by the powerful Angre. The Peshwa Government endeavoured to develop its harbours. In 1744 two Shevni merchants, Vithoji Krishna Kamat and Pundalik Krishna Kamat, offered to settle in Bassein with five of their ships. The Officer of Prant Bassien was ordered by the Peshwa to remit part of the octroi on the goods carried in these ships for trade, to honour Pundalik Krishna Kamat with a palanquin and robes, and to decide for his accommodation and warehouses besides giving him a *khoti* village. Three merchants who settled at Bassein and Salsette opening their shops were given houses to live in, and the custom duty on their goods was reduced to half. Some land also was ordered to be granted to them. Similarly, the customs duties were to be reduced for the commodities of a Bombay merchant named Dayaldas Jiwa, who intended to carry on trade at Bassein and other ports (probably Salsette and Jambusar).[8]

The Commercial Exchanges Within: Deccan's Internal Trade

The two types of internal trade were the riverine trade and the land trade. The commodities in which the merchants traded in the region were food-stuffs, fruits, spices, metals, textiles, animals, luxury goods and articles of daily use. The foodstuffs consisted of various kinds of grain such as rice, wheat, millet, paddy, pulses, etc. Metals comprised tin, copper and lead. The textiles were of various types and included silk fabrics, cotton stuffs such as *pasodis* and *dhotees*, coarse cloth, *taftas*, shawls, muslins, sarees, *kinkhaps*, velvets and *kads*. *Pasodis* were purchased in Khandesh, and shawls and rose-attar were brought from Delhi. Cotton fabric came from Sihor Duraha, *dhotees* from Maheshwar and silk from Paithan.[9]

The internal trade was carried on by three types of routes: waterways, Ghatways and landways. The Ghatways in Maharashtra were as important as, if not more important than, the landways on the plateau. The Ghatways ran through passes, down the valleys, over the hills and along the villages.

For regulating traffic on these tracks, for affording protection to the caravans and for levying transit dues on the travellers, custom houses were set up at several places on these Ghatways, each in charge of an officer called *ghatpande* assisted by a staff consisting of the *Modhawi*, the *Pansare*, the *Pathakdar*, the *Bidwai*, the *Gujar* and the *Gumasta*. The *Modhawi* maintained the Ghatways in good condition. The duty of the *Pathkdar* or *Pathaki* was to afford protection to the travellers on the Ghatways from one *chauki* to another. In this work, the *Patakis* were assisted by a band of guards called *Gujars*. The *Bidwai* was originally an officer of the market place, who maintained a list of the merchant families coming to the market. His duty was to afford protection to the roving merchants camping at the market place and to keep a watch over the stand where their vehicles were parked till their trade transactions were over. As the roving merchants moved along the Ghatways, the *Bidwais* had to do their work here also and were required to submit the lists of the merchant families which they maintained, to the *Ghatpandes*. The *Bidwai* probably worked under the supervision of a *Sarbidwai*. The *Gumasta* or *Mutalik* was directly under the *Ghatpande* working as his secretary. The *chaukis* had to perform the double function of protecting the travellers and of collecting transit dues from them. These dues were charged according to the type of vehicles and the volume of merchandise.

The Engines of Production and Trade: Deccan's Indigenous Industries

During the 17th and 18th centuries, several industries were extensively developed in cities and towns in the Deccan. As agriculture was the main occupation of the people of Deccan, a number of crafts and industries based on agriculture produce were carried on in every village. Konkan was economically a prosperous region, and places like Chaul, Dabhol, Kalyan, Bhivandi, Pen and Vengurla have been frequently referred to in the Factory Records as flourishing commercial and industrial centres.[10] Salt industry was an important and one of the oldest industries of Konkan, as manufacture of salt on the seashores was moderately inexpensive, and salt was exported in large quantity. It was Shivaji who realized the significance of the salt trade and decided to give protection to the industry. Places like Nagothana, Mauje Kelwe, Rajapur, Thana, Pen, Panvel, etc. were major centres of salt manufacturing on the western coast of Maharashtra.[11] This industry was next to agriculture in importance and provided employment to the agriculturists when they were not engaged in the cultivation of land.[12] During the Peshwa period, the policy of low tax and the concession given to manufacturers of salt in the form of exemption from taxes not only gave an impetus to the salt industry but also helped the industry to flourish.[13]

Other important urban industries were cotton and silk weaving. The cities of the Qutbshahi kingdom produced a large quantity of printed cloth, which was considered to be the best in India. Peshwa also encouraged this industry in their region by inviting artisans from other territories. For instance, they invited artisans to Solapur from Nizam's territories. Silk weaving was associated with regions like Thana and Chaul. Bombay was also famous for its cotton and silk weaving industry from ancient time.[14] Silk was imported from China, and the reeling, dyeing and weaving operations were carried out locally.[15] The foundation of the European trading factories on the coast led to the expansion of the textile industry in the sea ports of the Coromandel Coast. For instance, Masulipatnam developed as a large manufacturing centre and was mainly a city of weavers and dyers. In the first half of the 18th century urban industries in the western Deccan seem to have further developed, and brass works of Kalyan, ornamental paper and silk works of Aurangabad, and ordinary paper of Newasa were some of the most reputed. Among the handicrafts industry, woodwork, pottery and rope making were in flourishing stage during the Peshwa times.[16]

Economically the most important and organizationally and technologically the most developed industry was shipbuilding. The largest shipyard was at Narasapur. Lesser ones were at Masulipatnam and Pulicat. On the western coast, ships were built and repaired in Cranganore and Cochin. In Maharashtra, places like Kalyan, Ratnagiri, Jaytapur, Malwan and Vengurla were some of the chief shipbuilding towns in the 17th century. Later Bombay became a famous centre for the shipping industry of the region. In order to encourage the industry a lot of measures were taken by the state. For instance, Peshwa provided a number of amenities for a ship-owner. His ships were exempted from octroi and other goods when they loaded goods for household use and brought them from other ports to the villages.[17]

The most important industry in medieval Deccan was the **diamond industry**. During the late Medieval and Sultanate periods, the diamond mines were under the control of various local powers in three main areas: Berar and Ahmednagar in the north, Vijayanagar in the South and Golconda in between the Krishna and Godavari rivers. These areas produced some of the world's famous gems such as the Kohinoor and "Idol's-eye" diamonds, which became the fascination of European royalty. The "Idol's-eye" is a rare blue diamond, and at 70.2 carats, it is the largest cut blue diamond from India. Although little is known about the diamond, the history of the "Idol's-eye" has its past in the Deccan according to 19th-century literature. Its name is related to the romantic idea that a diamond had formed the eye of a temple statue in India.

Jean-Baptiste Tavernier gives an account of diamond mining, cutting and trading in the Deccan.[18] The want of other metals, except for copper, iron and lead in the Mughal Empire, notes Careri, was "abundantly made amends for by the rich mines of diamonds and other precious stones."[19] Diamonds are alluded to in a variety of Indian classical texts and had powerful royal and symbolic associations. The role of diamonds in India was doubtlessly one of the important factors in the European reception. An appreciation of diamonds had likely been fostered in the medieval courts of south India preceding the establishment of the Deccani Sultanates. In 1669, a French diamond dealer and traveller sold to King Louis XIV of France (1643–1715) a selection of diamonds he had purchased in India. One of these was the famous French blue diamond, now known as the Hope diamond. Jean Pitau, the court jeweller, cut this stone in 1673 into a brilliant cut, and it is one of the earliest examples of this style. The fashion for the brilliant cut quickly spread and reached London, where, according to later reports, it was perfected.[20]

With the expansion of trade routes from the late medieval period, European treasuries came to be filled with diamonds. Over the centuries, diamond cutting developed in European centres such as Bruges, Paris, London and Antwerp and also to some extent in India, and styles influenced by European taste. European gem cutters probably introduced the faceting of diamonds in India, although it is believed that Indians possessed the skill of shaping diamonds since ancient times.[21]

European Companies and Their Engagement in Deccan's Economy

A. The Portuguese in the Deccan

With the discovery of the new route to India round the Cape of Good Hope culminating in Vasco da Gama reaching Calicut on 20 May 1498; a new chapter in the history of the trade of Indian Ocean came to be writ large marking the beginning of what K.M. Panikkar termed as "the Vasco da Gama epoch of Asian History." As their spice trade in India began to flourish, the Portuguese under the camouflage of a sacred motive actually delved deep into commercialism and etched out the areas under their control as Estado da India (State of India). The Portuguese primarily "used the word 'India' to denote sometimes the Indian subcontinent and sometimes the narrow strip of land between the Western Ghats and the sea."[22] Nevertheless, if we take for granted the big-time clash between their religious and commercial interests, we need to inspect what actually helped the Portuguese go so far as to be able to establish a number of fortified factories in western India, gain the right to issue *cartazes* and have a virtual monopoly in the Indian Oceanic trade; so much so that even the ruler of Quilon in the Malabar Coast invited Pedro Alvares Cabral in 1501 to take cargo from there, and the great Mughal Emperor Akbar agreed to buy *cartazes* for conducting *hajj* safely from the Portuguese. This writing ventures to trace the changes that came along in the trade and polity of western India and their causes, with special emphasis on Gujarat and Malabar, that accounted for even the shift in power equations in 16th century both within India like that of the King of Cochin and the Zamorin of Calicut and outside India between the Muslim world mainly Egypt and the Christian powers backed by the Pope, not to forget the subtle trade rivalry between Lisbon and Venice as well which enabled King Dom Manuel to acquire the title of "Lord of the conquest, navigation and commerce of Ethiopia, India, Arabia and Persia."[23]

Before analyzing the changes that were introduced by the Portuguese, it is necessary to understand that western coast prior to their arrival had been inhabited largely by Muslim merchants most of whom lived out of overseas trading, but there was no paramount authority as such to regulate these trading activities at a centralized level. The Mughals at most could have been concerned about the inland trade, but at the port cities, there was hardly any serious check apart from the local power bases. Hindu, Christian or Jain merchants were testified by the presence of the Hindu *vanias* or *Chettis*, but then Muslim competition far outnumbered their participation. Often ships owned by Hindus were manned by Muslims. Also, there were large groups of foreign Muslim merchants from the Middle East as well as a number of Chinese, Genoese and Venetian merchants who flocked at these ports for trade in spices, and when the Portuguese came, they too used the pretext of seeking "Christians and Spices."[24] This entire process for carrying goods to Europe followed two routes: "one through the Persian Gulf and the other through the Red Sea."[25] While the Gujarati merchants engaged in overseas commerce in abundance, the Zamorin in Calicut commanded the status of the most powerful ruler of Malabar. Calicut as the greatest spice market in the Indian Ocean turned out to be the haven of all merchants from several corners of the world.

With the arrival of the Portuguese, the question that loomed large was whether to follow the policy of peaceful competition or of sheer force. But instant suspicion from different quarters of the trading community made them zero in on the option of viewing the discovery of the Cape route less as a "technical innovation enabling them to compete with their rivals"[26] and more as "a monopoly leased upon brute force."[27] True that the Portuguese demand of eliminating all Muslim traders from Calicut was not feasible on the part of the Zamorin which actually accounted for much of the Muslim hostility drawing in Malik Ayaz and the Mamluk Egyptians, but the initial resistance after facing a slapping defeat at Diu in 1509 gave way to compliance. The Portuguese, sensing the merchants' will to co-operate, tactfully resorted to the system of retaining monopoly and simultaneously devising a vital source of income by introducing the system of issuing *cartazes*[28] and organizing *cafilas*,[29] thus shunning unprovoked violence.

Consequently under Almeida and partially under Albuquerque's governorship, roughly covering the first 20 years of the 16th century, the major strands of the Portuguese imperial policy in Asia came to be shaped as—claim to an exclusive sovereignty in the Indian Ocean expressed through efforts to eliminate Muslim trade to Red Sea and East Africa and to compel Indian merchants to buy *cartazes* from Portuguese officials; diversion of pepper and spice trade from Alexandria and Venice to Lisbon and Antwerp and eventually the growth of a Portuguese inter-port or emporia trading in Asia made possible by their control over the former free maritime commercial cities. It was only after Albuquerque's death that the pressing task to control, if not altogether eliminate, the Gujarati merchants based on the northern ports of Diu and Cambay assumed significance and the capture of these ports began to be pursued vigorously so that the Red Sea trade could have been effectively stopped.

Given the differences in the structure of trade and polity of Malabar and Gujarat, one needs to deal with them separately. The political arrangement of Malabar represented some kind of a feudal setup, which was characterized by shifting loyalties amongst the rulers of various principalities with certain vested interests in sea trade.

The Malabar was comprised of around 17 principalities which included Kolatunad or Cannanore, Kottayam, Kozhikode or Calicut, Tanur, Kodungalloor or Cranganore, Cochin, Edappally, Vadakkenkur, Parur, Venad or Travancore, Kollam or Quilon and others. Amongst these the kingdom of Calicut was the most eminent with the powerful Zamorin as its king, and it traded with Chinese, Gujaratis, local merchants, foreign Muslim merchants, *Al-karimi*[30] merchants and Italians. Among the local merchants the Muslims were predominant, and though there were few Hindus like the *Cetis* from Tamil Nadu, Hindus, in general, on account of religious prejudices didn't enter trans-oceanic trade thus giving way to the Arabs and other Muslims. Cochin, on the contrary, remained much less vibrant, more so because of the King of Cochin and the Zamorin being at loggerheads. All foreign merchants had warehouses on the coast—factories, *fondachi* and *funduqs*. The pre-Portuguese period in Malabar was thus marked by a state of free trade where every merchant could at his sweet will frequent the port of his choice on the Malabar and conduct trade, where no inter-state treaty was concluded among the rulers on the coast, where certain concessions were also granted for foreign merchants[31] and where there was the existence of factories but not fortified ones.

In the post-Portuguese period, a number of changes in trade and polity were discernable. At the political level, as Cabral and Vasco da Gama kept negotiating with a defiant Zamorin, which at times terminated in violent attacks on the Portuguese fort at Calicut and the bombardment of the city in turn by the Portuguese, relations with the King of Cochin remained amicable and with the *peso* (weighing area) being set up at Cochin, the importance of Cochin as a trade port increased manifold vis-à-vis Calicut. Cannanore too had a Portuguese fort, but perhaps it was the ruler of Quilon who had been way too eager to develop trade relations with the Portuguese and eventually had the St. Thomas fortress built there. The Portuguese also managed to bring all the petty lords like the rulers of Purakkad, Diamper, Vadakkenkur, Tekkenkur, Parur, Mangatt and Carta of Alwaye under their friendship through the ingenious distribution of annuities (*tencas*), whereby the recipients were obliged to see that pepper and other spices were not carried to any other places than the Portuguese factories.

At the commercial level the Portuguese repeatedly proved that they were invincible at sea. Though initially, the merchants "regarded them with suspicion and jealousy,"[32] with time, they came to effectively occupy the commercial vacuum that the disappearance of the Chinese and *Karimi* merchants had created and brought within their folds the confidence of the local merchants as well. With the enforcement of *cartazes*, the once flourishing coastal trade in the Indian Ocean declined.[33] Nevertheless, the local merchants became indispensable as intermediaries.[34] The Portuguese, at any rate, had two viable options—(a) to go around from cultivator to cultivator offering them rice, cloth and other necessary commodities in exchange for pepper[35] or (b) to have enough money so as to be able to purchase the spices in a short time at the disposal of the ships. Both of these, however, weren't feasible because of cash and time constraints.[36] Thus inevitably one had to rely on the brokers[37] who mostly happened to be Muslims. It is a paradox that those Portuguese who wanted all Muslims to be flushed out of Calicut and who actually came with a mission to help in the triumph of Christianity against the infidels cared so less about these aims amidst the turmoil of their commercial ambitions. The King had particularly instructed the officials on the Malabar Coast to favour Hindu and Christian merchants in preference to Muslims, but on account of lack of funds and superstitions neither the Christian nor the Hindu merchants were able to come up to the expectations of the Portuguese. Consequently, they relied on "the Muslim merchants who had better funds and were well favoured by the local rulers themselves."[38] Also, many of the locals were employed in the shipbuilding industry that was coming up vigorously.

Goa, for instance, was a port that was contested for by the Bahamanis and the Vijayanagar rulers because of the horses that came through this port from Arabia. With increased use of cavalry in the Deccan, the horse became an important commodity as its use determined success in times of war. According to Albuquerque, the famous commander of the Portuguese fleets who conquered Goa,

> Through this harbour of Goa was always the principal passage to the kingdom of Narsinga (Vijayanagar) and of Daquem (Deccan); and for this reason, it contained much merchandise, and large caravans of merchants came from the interior country in quest for it, and brought other commodities in exchange. And from this commerce which they had one with another the inhabitants of Goa grew so prosperous that it was said that Goa in those days alone had revenue of two hundred thousand *pardaos*.[39]

In the transactions at the ports, there was no marked change in the commodity structure, though there could have been an increase in volume and kind right up to the period of the rise of Bombay as an important port. Incense, textiles and semi-precious stones, horses, areca nuts, betel leaves, food provisions and lacquered furniture were the main commodities exchanged during the medieval period through the Konkan ports.[40]

Meera Kosambi adds to this understanding by saying that the direction of these ports differed when one considers "the indigenous phase" and the "European phase." In the former period, the ports of the Konkan

> were dependent on direct connections with their inland and coastal land-based powers whose support and patronage were usually crucial-for their sustenance. The European ports, on the other hand were peripheral to the Maharashtra region in both the geographical and commercial sense, serving primarily as naval bases of maritime powers.[41]

The Transition at Sea and the Age of the Portuguese Private Traders: A Note

When we look at transition, we should explore transition that was happening at all levels. Transition in geology, climate and technology cannot be ignored because these parameters have a great influence on social life. It is reflected through language exchange, migration and social mobility. Transition also happens on land, occurring in relation with land-based systems and economic systems. Steinberg[42] talks about the transition which was happening in the 16th century. We notice a shift from a land-based to a sea-based social and economic system because we see the advent of mercantilism. A second shift can be seen in the 18th century with the advent of capitalism. It is important to note the transition at sea and the shifting of networks.

The Portuguese maritime empire also had a private side, the small and large merchants and pedlars of Portuguese origin or descent, who merged into the trading world of Asia. Some gained from their affiliation with the official Estado, while some traded independently, side by side with their Asian counterparts. As private entrepreneurs, the Portuguese were another addition to the number of ethnic groups trading in the Indian Ocean. These modified contours created a porous frontier between the Portuguese empire and Asian political structures.

During 1510–1520, Portuguese private brokers reached the Coromandel Coast. Mostly they were trouble-makers either from the Melaka army or from the western Indian littoral. Since the compensations of administration for the Crown were insufficient for the normal warrior, or in any event, for the lower respectability, the point was to make private fortunes from independent trade.

Within the Estado da India, specific families dominated dispensation of patronage. Frustrated with this system, many Portuguese fled to Pulicat, and also to Satgaon and Chittagong in the Bay of Bengal. It was logical to adjust to the already existing cosmopolitan centre at Pulicat and form a resident foreign community, with its own structure and leadership.[43] Gradually, two groups of Portuguese private traders' settlements emerged.

Pulicat or Palaverkadu was the dominant port of early 16th-century Coromandel, linked via Tirupati and Penukonda to the imperial city of Vijayanagar. Portuguese merchants took advantage of the regular trade links with Cochin. It was the centre of the jewel trade, especially related to south Indian diamonds. Italians like Piero Strozzi, mentioned in Portuguese records as "Pero Estroco," traded in gems.[44] The annual trade with Pegu brought back rubies. Coloured and painted textiles were manufactured at Pulicat. The Portuguese on the Coromandel went into the surrounding villages of the coastal plain to purchase textiles. Pepper and spices were directly imported from South-East Asia to Pulicat.

The period of 16th and 17th centuries witnessed the dominance of official company trade with a smaller number of private traders, whereas the 18th century saw the induction of private trading system at a large scale. The old mercantilist was broken, and a new model was set up, which promoted private trade. Various collaborations such as Anglo-Portuguese and Danish-Portuguese grew stronger during this time period.[45] Tempest Miller was employed by the Portuguese private traders from Lisbon, and his association with the Dupleix private trading network is also known.[46] This gave impetus to the local *sarafs* and dealers who were getting familiarized with new currencies.

But the expertise and capital of private Portuguese traders enabled them to survive in Asia. The absence of a single centre of maritime power also enabled individual private merchants like Manuel Teixeira Pinto to carve out their own commercial empire. Portuguese private traders continued to flourish even in the late 18th century. Unencumbered by an overly statist ideology, their ideology was that of a stateless and adaptable commercial group. The decline of the Portuguese empire was not the decline of their trade. Trade and empire were not related in a linear way.

The Portuguese had adapted themselves to the Asian method of doing business and conducting diplomatic relations. The English and the Dutch learnt this skill from them.[47] There was a clear sense of awareness among Portuguese settlers of the need for local partners.[48] The Portuguese learnt from the Kling merchants of Melaka and did not completely displace them. The latter, along with Chetti and Muslim merchants, transitioned from independent merchants to merchant middlemen. At Nagapattinam, many of the Chetti merchants worked in partnership with the Portuguese and even colluded with them against the Dutch. The art of amalgamation into the society had given them an upper edge in comparison to their other European counterparts.

B. The Dutch Trade and the Deccan's Economy

Even before the arrival of the Europeans the growth of commerce both by land and sea led to the emergence of commercial centres in the Deccan. Yet, like the ports and the trading activity around them, this vast hinterland of eastern and western peninsular India presented uniformity in the patterns of its economic activity and the broad directions of its relationships with the coastal town and ports. The economy of the hinterland was a cardinal feature of the active commercial life of the ports. The first Dutch factory in India was established at Masulipatnam in 1605, followed by Pulicat (1610), Surat (1616), Bimilipatam (1641), Karikal (1645), Chinusura (1653), Kasimbazar, Barangore, Patna, Balasore, Nagapatnam (all in 1658) and Cochin (1663).

On the Coromandel Coast, VOC established a factory in 1605 at Masulipatnam. Their main interest was South Indian textiles, which they initially used in their spice trade in South East Asia and later brought back in some quantities to Europe as well. Masulipatnam had the advantage of access to a very productive hinterland of surplus rice cultivation, iron and steel production, indigo cultivation, diamond mines, saltpetre, salt, etc. but its major advantage came from its capacity to draw from the weaving and dyeing industry both north and south.

Iron, steel and saltpetre constituted the chief mineral wealth of Coromandel. Diamonds from the Gingi district and the Kollur mines in Golconda reached the coastal markets and eventually became, for some time, one of the chief exports of the Dutch. Bezoar stones, a supposed antidote for poison extracted from goats and some other animals, were also of some value as an export.[49]

Pulicat had shipping links with the other Dutch settlements in Asia, such as Malacca, Batavia and Colombo. From Ceylon areca nuts, elephants, Cinnamon and ivory were imported to Pulicat, and in turn, Ceylon received rice, white sandalwood, seed pearls, cloth and other merchandise from the port of Pulicat.[50]

The Dutch, at least as much as the English, were held responsible for introducing some significant innovations in the organization of production and commerce, though not on a very large scale. Dutch relations with the "chief merchants" had introduced innovations in the "putting out system" which was extended considerably under their auspices. In the putting out system, the merchants provided the craftsmen not only capital but also raw materials and essential tools for craft production. The Indian craftsmen enjoyed the full freedom of using the working capital provided to them and purchased the raw materials on their own. They also owned the tools they enjoyed in the process of production. In several places, they set up establishments for processing cloth, bleaching and dyeing in particular, and manufacturing gun-powder[51] and ironware, whereas as many as 50 to 100 artisans worked as wage labourers under the direction of the Dutch factors and experts.

The demand for Coromandel cloth in Asian countries was highly specialized in nature. A particular market would only consume certain specific varieties of cloth, which were often manufactured exclusively in some specialized centres of production in Coromandel. Besides cloth, the Red Sea port of Mokha received supplies of rice, tobacco, rattan, iron, steel, indigo, benzoin and lac, which eventually reached various parts of Arabia. Indigo, sent overland to the west coast, was shipped thence to Persia. Among the countries to the east, Arakan imported tobacco, iron and steel from Coromandel while quantities of cotton yarn were exported to Pegu and Tenasserim. From Tenasserim, Coromandel textiles and yams were carried overland to the interior of Siam. Iron, steel and rice were exported to Achin.

In 1675, Ekoji of Tanjore kingdom withdrew the concessions given by Nayak Vijayaraghava to the Dutch. However, the Dutch got them back by force. Ekoji succeeded in recovering the ports of Thirumalairayanpattanam and Karaikal, but the success was short-lived. He granted a *cowle* on 30 December 1676, and thus, restored all the concessions given earlier by the Nayak and also restored to their possession the ports of Thirumalairayanpattanam and Karaikal. The local Governor of Sirkali gave the Dutch a piece of land to build a factory at Thirumullaivasal. Thus, within the Tanjore–Maratha Kingdom, the VOC had many places under its control. From the southern extremity of Nagapatnam, it had the important port cities of Karaikal, Trimelavas or Trimelapatnam, and others. The VOC also succeeded in getting permission to build lodges at new places like Arani, Sadraspatnam, Karaikal, Darasurpette and Trimelepatnam.[52] In addition, the company also had warehouses at various other places, e.g. Munanpette and Mannarcoil. In 1690, Nagapatnam became the new headquarters of the Coromandel directorate of VOC.

The successors of Ekoji were weak pressed by financial problems. They often approached the Dutch for advance payment of the tribute. In 1691, Sahaji Raja invaded Nagapatnam and was defeated by the Dutch, and he sued for peace.

On the Konkan Coast, VOC established its factory at Vengurla, just 50 kilometres north of Goa, a Portuguese territory. Vengurla lies at the heart of South Konkan and had been a harbour and a trading centre since ancient times. The Dutch base was initially established in Konkan for strategic reasons, but over time these became less significant, and the commercial advantages of the place were exploited as much as possible.

i. VOC and the Indigenous Merchant: Some Observations

As VOC had a vast commercial network of Coromandel Textiles during the 17th century and to centrally organize the supply with Coromandel textiles, the VOC was reliant on the assistance of local merchants such as Chetti Achyutappa, who, due to his political and economic influence, subsequently became Chief Merchant of the Dutch at Pulicat. The evidence suggests that Achyutappa[53] first came into contact with the Dutch East India Company in 1608 as an interpreter of Jacob de Bitter in the Sinji area, who was negotiating with the local *Nayaka* on behalf of the company about the right to erect a factory at Devanampattinam. Early records of Achyutappa's commercial activities indicate that he maintained business relations with both the English and Dutch until he left his base at Devanampattinam to enter into permanent service of the VOC at Pulicat. He therefore quickly ascended to one of the most important brokers of the Dutch East India Company, supporting the company in commercial as well as political affairs. In a letter written by Pieter Gilles, the Dutch agent at Masulipatnam, to his company, listed all the prominent Hindu and Muslim merchants in that region.

Raghav Chetty a merchant in Pulicat region in 1627 was put into prison by them because he refused to discharge his debts to the Company. He retaliated by escaping to Armagaon and placing himself under English protection. The Hindu merchants operating in the Porto Novo, Cuddalore region, are named Tendatie Chetti, Ariecaltsie Chetti and Kommaty Chetti. Kesara Chetti was another leading merchant in south Coromandel, who eventually became a middle man for the Dutch East India Company. Another merchant Mirza Mohammad operating in Pulicat, as the Dutch records state, was very influential and close to Haqueekat Khan, the governor.[54]

The first figures revealing the extent of Malaya's participation in Pulicat's textile trade, available for the year 1632, show that Malaya received a Dutch contract to supply 23,565 pagodas in textiles while seven other merchants were to supply a total of 9,000 pagodas. In 1633 Malaya succeeded in persuading the ruler of Chandragiri, whose area of authority encompassed Pulicat, to grant him Pulicat's revenue farm on payment of 33,000 pagodas, considerably more than twice the investment he had made in Dutch Trade a year before.[55] He had persuaded Dutch to give him some cannon, which he intended to put to use at his fortified house in Devanampattinam, and in prosecuting the career of his brother Chinanna as field-general in the *palaiyakkar* wars in the surrounding.[56]

Chinanna succeeded as a chief broker at Coromandel, after the death of Malaya in 1634. Already holding a position of authority in Tegenepatnam in the early 1620s, Chinanna in the 1630s participated in the struggle for the throne of Chandragiri, leading an armed force in support of the contender favoured by the Nayaka of Jinji.[57] When Malaya died in 1634, Chinanna chose to remain in Tegenepatnam and in proximity to the court of Jinji. In 1636–37 he continued to extend his influence by acting as the Nayaka's emissary to a peace conference with the Nayakas of Tanjore and Madura. At about this time, another relation, Chinanna's brother Sesadra, was a member of the Nayaka of Jinji's council of advisors. A third brother was located in a port a few miles north of Tegenepatnam, Pondicherry. Entrenched on the coast and influential at court, Chinanna's family in the 1630s was a major factor in Jinji's politics. But Chinanna's strength was not all that it appeared. His family was far from unified behind his leadership.[58] From the 1630s till the end of the 1640s, Dutch Trade was dominated by Chinnanna. Later Chinanna decided to shift to Tanjore and to take on lease Thirumullaivasal and another port to advance Dutch Trade. In 1642 he ran into problems with Nayaka of Tanjore as well. With active support from the Dutch, Chinanna then gained the favour of the Vijayanagar king in 1643. During all these political adventures, he was carrying on an extended trade from Pulicat and other ports, both on his account and an intermediary.

More importantly, he lacked the military power to support his exposed political position. The seriousness of this last weakness became apparent in 1638, shortly after Chinanna returned to Tegenepatnam from the peace conference of the three Nayakas. At this time, Chinanna's nephew, Konara Chitti, a resident of Jinji, quarrelled with the powerful Jinji noble, Tupaki Krishnappa Naik. Konara fled to Tegenepatnam and his uncle's protection with Krishnappa Naik in pursuit. Although he possessed a sturdy house, Chinanna could not withstand a siege. The briefness of his resistance suggests that he was unable to organize a defence. Krishnappa's terms were costly. He demanded not only Konara Chitti's person but also an indemnity of 40,000 pagodas, three elephants and the lands which Chinanna held in the vicinity of Tegenepatnam. With this loss and the promise of considerable insecurity in the future, Tegenepatnam and Jinji were much less attractive to Chinanna, therefore he made plans to leave. He first sent 200,000 pagodas, his "principal report," to Pulicat for safe-keeping; then, after a Tegenepatnam, he took his immediate family assuming his late elder brother's position as the leading broker.[59]

Initially, the Dutch had supported Chinanna's political ambitions as a means to threaten the English in Madras. However, in late 1644 they began to fear losing control over their broker, for they took the extreme measure of imprisoning members of Chinanna's family still in Pulicat in order to ensure Chinanna's payment of his outstanding debts.

The Dutch did not have a chief merchant to succeed Chinanna for a while, and especially because their textile exports to Asia and Europe grew, they also discovered the problems of dealing with smaller merchants. The total resources of these merchants could not match the resources of the merchant capitalists, and therefore they ended up quite hopelessly behind on their contracts and in debt to the Dutch.

During the first half of the century, the Dutch traded through members of the Malaya family without giving more than passing consideration to the consequences of permitting one merchant to gain a near-monopoly over their respective investments. But following the decline of the Malaya family, the authorities in Pulicat and Madras had an opportunity. Without Chinanna acting as "Chief Merchant," the Dutch experienced difficulties in their relations with various petty merchants who now served as their brokers.

ii. The Private Trade of VOC's Employees: Some Observations

The Company's factors were also involved in large-scale private trade carried throughout Asia. On the excuse of getting paid extremely meagre salaries to the employees by the company, they were involved in a quick fortune making through Private Trade in Intra-Asian Trade. However, the Company never allowed to engage in private Trade, but that did not stop the servants from doing so. Over time, the Bengal-Batavia branch became probably the most notorious for private Trade. The main reason behind this was opium, a high value, low bulk and therefore ideal item for contraband trade. Governor Comans (1700–1705) was charged with forging the alloy of pagodas in the Nagapatnam mint. His wife was alleged to be engaged in private trade, and he was accused of having allowed the extortion of money from merchants and others.[60] Pieter van Dam has proposed that, at one phase, the volume of the clandestine private Trade from Bengal was as extensive as that of the Company's own. Undoubtedly, for example, in 1676, the volume of opium pirated into Batavia could be a few times the sum imported on the record of the Company.[61]

A major milestone in the Dutch Company strategy towards private Dutch interest in intra-Asian Trade was the incomplete opening up of this Trade in the mid-1740s. In this regard, an initiative had been taken by Gustaf Willem Baron van Imhoff, the Governor-General designate of the Dutch East Indies. Van Imhoff has argued in a memorandum submitted in 1741 that the Company's Trade in the factories west of Malacca had been on the decrease for quite a while and now compared very unfavourably with that carried on by its rivals such as the English and the French. He, therefore, recommended that it would be in the considerable advantage of the Company to declare trade with that region, except in strategic items such as spices and Japanese copper, open to all. Additional customs duties charged from the private traders who, Van Imhoff believed, would mainly be the burghers from Batavia, would compensate in part for the loss of profit that the partial abandonment of its own trade in the region would entail. Jacob Mossel (1750–61) withdrew some of the concessions granted by Van Imhoff.

In addition to this official Dutch support for political reasons, the Marava ruler also received unauthorized aid from Company sources for reasons of private gain. The Company Merchant and Chief of Tuticorin Joan Nieuhoff later ignominiously discharged and fined after having been found guilty of private trade, opportunistically dispatched a Parava sampan with *kachchai* textiles, rice and other commodities to Rameswaram during the initial stage of the Tevar *aranmanai* conflict when grain prices in the area were skyrocketing. This supply of rice to its opponent was taken very seriously by the *aranmanai*, which at one point even threatened to burn all Parava vessels on the Madurai Coast.[62]

C. *Exploring the Presence of the French Company in Deccan*

Though European contacts with the Deccan initially concentrated on the Western part, by the 16th century European presence was felt in the Eastern part, particularly with the Golconda region. By the 17th century, there was a complex presence of official and unofficial Europeans in the Deccan, largely on the coast and even in a variety of interior centres and garrison towns. This is what the French Compagnie des Indes Orientales (East India Company) found when it entered the region for the first time in the 1660s. The French could count for support on physicians, such as Antoine Destremau, long stationed at Golconda; well-informed jewel traders like Jean-Baptiste Tavernier and a host of others to help them in their dealings.

Against the backdrop of the various political developments and the French rivalry with the English and native powers, it is necessary to look at trade and commerce conducted by the French East India Company which had a great impact on the urban growth, monetization and commercialization of the economy. Apart from the role played by the Company the merchant seemed to have played a dominant role in the process. The development of the merchant capital had widespread implications in the various fields of economic activity such as agricultural and non-agricultural sectors. With political developments taking their course, as mentioned earlier a large number of migrations took place. Merchants, weavers and artisans made their way to the port town of Pondicherry. The families of Mudaliars, Chettis and Pillais were some of the most important merchants who associated themselves with the French. K.S. Mathew describes the relationship between the French and the Indian merchants as one of partnership.[63]

Founded by Francois Martin in 1674, he tried to bring with him an eminent merchant named Tanappa Mudaliar from Poonamalle to Pondicherry; he became the chief broker of the Company. Within a year, 40 houses were built for a small number of weavers. Francois Martin received from Sher Khan Lodi 300 men whose services were utilized not only as soldiers but also as colonists. Thus, he engaged them to develop the economy to produce a large quantity of textiles for export.[64]

But in 1677, when Shivaji captured Jinji he threatened to attack Pondicherry as well. Francois Martin managed to obtain a *firman* from Shivaji to ensure the protection of Pondicherry by sending an envoy to Shivaji's camp. At the same time, he was granted permission to collect land revenue from the districts of Pondicherry from Sher Khan Lodi. Hence, Francois continued to construct houses and warehouses to store textiles for shipment to France. Nearly two years after the establishment of the factory, internal and external trade began to flourish.[65] Cotton textiles constituted the major component of trade. Thus, the commercial growth of Pondicherry sped up after the arrival of Governors such as Lenior, Dumas and Dupleix. Hence, politics and the economy cannot be alienated from each other. By 1736, French got the right to mint money from the Nawab of Arcot.[66] But Ananda Ranga Pillai observed that it was Governor Lenior (1721–23) who laid the foundation for the right to mint rupees and Dumas who obtained a *firman* from the Emperor reaped the fruits of Lenior's labour. Cloth was the major item of trade of the Company, and naturally, the cloth market was a prominent place in Pondicherry. Blue piece-goods were sold at 50%

profit; coarse cloths, striped and ordinary, at 20%; and Bandar cloth at 80%; Chandernagore cloth at 80%; and flowered cloth and fine Chennai chintz at 20–25%. The principle branches of trade constituted the importation of goods, not for sale in Pondicherry, but for exports to the islands of Malay Archipelago, Macao, Manilla, China, French islands, Persian Gulf and Red sea.

The Company's cloth warehouse at Parangippettai was placed under the charge of Ananda Ranga Pillai. He often went to that town to get the cloth made and to obtain bales, which were to be loaded onto the ships which were sent to various destinations such as Mocha and Achin. Orders were placed with weavers in nearby villages like Kanchipuram, Tiruvottiyur and neighbouring villages for the weaving and supply of different kinds of cloths for the Company. Salem, Udayarpalayam, Arni, Kanchipuram, Kunnathur and Saidapettai were famous weaving centres.[67] The French Company's merchants procured cloth from them, when the cloth was delivered by them, it was sent to the washer men for bleaching and pressing.[68]

Before the arrival of the French, the weavers had their settlements around temple complexes. But later, we find considerable movement of weavers towards the French territories under the patronage of the Company. This was a new trend which encouraged the development of textile manufacture. With favourable conditions prevailing in Pondicherry, various groups of weavers like the *Kaikkolars*, *Devangas*, *Saliyars* and *Seniyars* from Kanchipuram, Arani and Arcot entered into the Company's service to pursue their specialized occupations and necessary facilities were provided by the French.[69]

In order to procure the goods for export and overseas markets, the French had to depend on the local merchants, brokers and *gumashtas* (agents). This was known as the *dadni* system.[70] A contract for supply of cloth was also entered with the native merchant every year. Government merchants were also appointed who were also in charge of money lending.[71] For instance, a contract was signed with Sunguvar Seshachala Chetti for the supply of 1,471 bales of piece-goods valued at 1,20,491 pagodas to the Company. Such contracts were regularly signed.[72] The first annual contract after Dupleix took over was made in April 1742 under which old merchants received a share and the prominent merchants a much larger share in the revenue. Ananda Ranga Pillai too signed an agreement to supply the Company with cloth.[73]

In terms of company trade, the coastal trade of Pondicherry developed considerably under the patronage of the French. The means of transports were ships of small tonnage, vessels, boats, *catarams*, *dhonies* and frigates[74] which were engaged in carrying commercial goods in bulk from one port to the other. The coastal ships took four to five months to sail between coasts, for example between Coromandel and the Malabar. However, a large part of this trade was carried out by the French trading Company.

The diarist has also given evidence of Indian merchants who owned ships and transported cargo. The *Sakaraparik* was owned by an Indian merchant;

it took cargo at Pondicherry and sailed to Mylapore to load more goods to sail to Pondicherry. Ananda Ranga Pillai owned a ship named *Anandapuravi* which sailed between Pondicherry and Colombo. Other small Indian merchants too had vessels and were engaged with other Europeans as well.[75] The Company's ships plied between Pondicherry and Chandernagore in Bengal touching the ports of Kunimedu, Alambarai, Marakkam, Kovalam, Santhome, Madras, Pulicat, Masulipatnam and Yanam on the one hand and on the other hand it reached Surat through Cuddalore, Porto Novo, Tranquebar, Karaikal, Nagapattinam, Tondi round Cape Comorin, Mahe and Goa. Chandernagore in Bengal was one of the most important places where the Company had regular ships from Pondicherry. A variety of goods such as muslin, kerchiefs, silk, food grains, saltpetre, threads, candles and wooden oil were shipped to Pondicherry. Imported silver money and coins and other merchandise from Europe were sent to Chandernagore.

From the time of Francois Martin, the French had longing eyes for the port town of San Thome. Martin has given an account of the events which had been undertaken by de la Hayne (Commander) for its capture from the Dutch.[76] The French were attracted to this port because of its excellent cotton textile, plain cloth, calico bleached, dyed, *chintz* and striped cotton cloth. There were great demand for these products in Malacca, Siamese, Cambodian and Burmese markets. The Company's merchants who had been trading at San Thome transported cotton fabrics of various sorts to Pondicherry for overseas markets.

Kaveripattinam was a small port town which the French had trade relations with. In July 1688, Francois Martin obtained this port from the Nayak of Tanjore. From this port, rice was shipped to Pondicherry for local consumption. Trade in this port was affected from 1744 to 1748 on account of wars with the Raja of Tanjore, who wanted a large sum from the French. In 1747, when he received 2,000 pagodas from the French, the ban was lifted. Textiles such as *salempores*, *tarnatanes*, *guinea*, *guingham*, table cloth, towels and scarfs (handkerchief) supplied by the local merchants were shipped to Pondicherry.[77] When Pondicherry was faced with famine in 1750, six *grases* of paddy were transported to Pondicherry through vessels for local consumption.[78]

In spite of the ongoing rivalry between the French and the English, the diarist records that trade between the two took place. Arvind Sinha is of the opinion that the Anglo-French commercial relationship pertaining to trade was not always based on competition and rivalry. In fact, a close relationship developed between the English and the French trading houses after the abolition of the *Compagnie des Indes* to finance the Indian trade. Seven chests of silver were landed by a ship from Tarangambadi (near Karaikal) and sent to the silver mint to be coined into rupees, which, when ready, will be sent to Bengal.[79] The French Company, from the time of its establishment, tried to have a relationship with the Portuguese on the basis of religion as well as geographical reasons.[80] The Portuguese often conducted trade for the French; they carried the Company's goods, rice and silk thread from Chandernagore and Bengal. Thus, we can see that the internal trade of Pondicherry was enhanced due to the presence of the French to a large extent. They brought a number of centres and ports in direct contact with Pondicherry, which contributed to the development of local merchants. A number of centres of production, especially textile-producing areas of the hinterland, were closely connected with Pondicherry through land routes.

In terms of overland and private trade, it may be seen that even before the rise of the European settlements along the Coromandel Coast, Indians had developed well-marked pattern of oceanic trade. French participation in this trade began in 1719 when they started to search for partners both among the European merchants and the local trading communities having sufficient capital and expertise. Chanda Sahib and his son Imam Sahib were prominent notable Mughal officials who invested large sums in the French trade. A *memoir* of 1738 mentions and refers to Pondicherry's trade with China, Manilla, Mocha, Persia, Merguy, Pegu and Achem.[81] Besides the Company, we find that the private merchants and employees of the Company also participated in this trade for their private dealings. The various Governors such as Lenior, Dumas and Dupleix found considerable profit to add to their income. It was usual for the French to form "societies" or "associations" which undertook one or more voyages. Each participant in the venture could be an independent merchant or an organization, and a certain amount of money could be put up.[82] Dupleix had established a "society" for trade, and his associates ranged from direct participants to providers of loan. His French associates included Costanier, one of the directors of the French Company, and Lenoir and Dumas, two successive governors of Pondicherry. Mahe de la Bourdannais is believed to have left Asia with more than three million livres.[83]

Ships from Manilla brought camphor, frankincense, Benjamin, Brazilwood, resin and horses; some of these were meant for Chandernagore.[84] Tobacco was exported to Manilla. In 1740, the piece-goods were sold at a low rate due to the arrival of goods by two or three ships from Surat. Both Hindu and Muslim (*Chulia*) merchants and Armenian and French privateers also participated in this trade. Several boxes of silver were imported from Manilla, and these were converted to coins in the mint at Pondicherry.[85] Ships sailed to Achin in Sumatra, too, via Pondicherry, Tarangambadi and Parangippettai, taking goods belonging to the French Company and other traders. The French conducted trade with the Dutch in spite of hostilities that existed. As Ananda Ranga Pillai records, oranges were brought from Achin by the Dutch, and Dupleix sent for baskets of them to be purchased.[86] The *Phenix* sailing for France carried a cargo of piece-goods, redwood and pepper. Sugar, sugar candy and Chinese goods were brought from Mocao.

The Company's ships frequently sailed to Mocha with various sorts of textiles, and these were sold there to purchase coffee, as Ananda Pillai tells us that coffee drinking was popular among Europeans.[87] This trade brought considerable profits to the Superior Council. It is worthwhile to note that in 1740 the Superior Council freighted the ship *le Maurepas* to the merchants and made up to 600,000 pounds of coffee for the Company on the basis of 5% commission.

All ships of the Company left port Lo'rient in France and touched the port of Cadiz where they took quantities of silver and wines. From there, these ships reached the islands of Bourbon and Mauritius round the Cape of Good Hope through Mozambique with frequent stops at Anjouane and set sail to Pondicherry. The main articles of import from Europe were gold and silver *marcs*, copper bar, coral, woolen bed sheets, broadcloths, iron and wine. Rarity goods included glass items, watches, scissors, nails and war materials. The goods exported from Pondicherry were mainly cotton textiles of the Coromandel Coast, pepper of Malabar, saltpetre, coffee of Mocha, redwood, sappanwood and leather. Among the imported articles, bullions such as gold and silver *marcs* occupy the first place.[88]

Thus, we can see that Pondicherry had a well-knit connection with Asia and Europe. It served as a centre of assembling goods for export to France. Because of this trade, Pondicherry developed into a lively and flourishing centre. But one major problem for such financial loss in the overseas trade was the French Company's organization. It was not a strictly private organization like the English but consisted mainly of amateurs who depended on the support of the government. The government as we know is always slow in its functions and many times refused to fund investments.

The Lifeline of Trade and Commerce in the Region: Banking Institutions in the Deccan

Though the system of banking in India was very different from that which was practised in Europe, there is plenty of evidence to show that even prior to the advent of Europeans, the people of India were much aware of the concept of banking. From the 5th century B.C. onwards, we get evidence regarding the details of money lending and payments of money in cash or by credit instalments. In Arthashastra, Kautilya gives details regarding the banking system during Mauryan Empire. According to him, the early bankers were traders and often combined trade with banking and exerted great influence on society.[89] The historical evidence shows that there was an emergence of indigenous bankers during the Mughal period who performed three important functions: lending money, lending for internal and foreign trade with cash or bills and giving financial assistance to rulers. The production of various kinds of metallic money in different parts of the country gave these indigenous bankers great opportunities for developing profitable businesses of money-changing, and the most important among them were appointed as mint officers, revenue collectors, bankers and money changers to the Government in various parts of the empire. One of the important financial instruments that were widely used during the Mughal period was *hundi* (letter of credit), which helped merchants in transactions meant for long distance trade. These hundis were issued by reputed merchant banking firms, and their acceptability among merchants depended on the reputation of the issuing banking firms.[90]

A great change in the political and economic conditions in Deccan came about in the 18th century. The establishment of Maratha political power and its subsequent expansion offered an excellent condition to Marathi people for development in different occupations and business activities. This provided congenial grounds for the emergence of banking, and a new class of indigenous Sahukars (mainly Brahmans and among them the Chitpavans seem to be predominant in this field) emerged under the patronage of Peshwas. Earlier, these banking jobs were done by the *Mahajans*, *Deshmukh* and *Deshpande*. As far as the banking system under the Marathas is concerned, *sahukars* deserved special mention. The job of *sahukars* or *savkars* in the financial and political life of the 17th- and 18th-century Maharashtra merits some exceptional thought. The term *sahukar* is utilized in Marathi reports in the prior period as vendor industrialist, yet later on, it indicated, the moneylender, financier and in a constrained sense merchant or business visionary. For example, *Ajnapatra* (Royal Edict), a contemporary treatise on the strategy of Shivaji's occasions, says, Sahukars (traders) are the trimmings of the kingdom and the magnificence of the lord. They are the reason for the thriving of the kingdom. A wide range of merchandise which are not accessible come into the kingdom. That kingdom ends up rich. In the midst of challenges, whatever obligation is essential is accessible.[91] The writer of this Ajnapatra, Ramachandrapant Amatya, while composing on the "business approach" of Shivaji has mentioned this objective fact especially with reference to remote vendors like the Portuguese, the Dutch, the Danes, the French and the English and as opposed to the *sahukars* under the Maratha rule, who were basically moneylenders or investors. In the 17th century, there were no sorted out financial foundations doing the customary financial business, for example tolerating stores and propelling advances, and these employments were mostly done by the indigenous brokers, in particular the *Shete*, the *Mahajan* (officers of the market), the *Deshmukh* and the *Deshpande* (officers of the town networks) and by certain Brahmans.[92]

Anyway, in the 18th century, maybe because of the developing political exercises of the Marathas, another class of *sahukars* fundamentally of brahmans rose under the support of the Peshwas, which overwhelmed the political and monetary existence of the Maratha nation for a very long while. Among the significant financial houses, notice might be made of *Tulshibagwale*, *Chiplunkar*, *Khasgiwale* of Pune; *Biwalkar* of Kalyan; *Dixit Patwardhan* of Nasik; and *Vaidya* of Wai (Satara). Bramhendra Swami Dhavadshikar (Satara District), a principled individual, and some *Gosavis* responsible for monastries likewise propelled extensive aggregates to the individuals from groups of the Maratha lords, rulers, Peshwas and various *sardars*. The records or record books of these *sahukars* are accessible, and if appropriately examined, one would show signs of improvement and true image of the financial and political history of the 18th-century Maharashtra.

Other than their customary business of cash loaning to private people, they propelled cash on a huge scale to the Peshwas and different dignitaries for their own use for different religious, social and family works. They provided cash to the Maratha Chiefs, including the Peshwa and others, for conveying undertakings in different pieces of the nation.[93] Therefore, one may say that the investors in Maharashtra of the 18th century were mostly in charge of cash exchanges like loaning and obtaining and so forth.

The advances progressed by the brokers to the merchants demonstrate that the matter of cash loaning in the 18th century encouraged the exchange and trade of the Maratha nation. The capacities performed by the investors of the period under audit can be extensively ordered under the accompanying heads: Accepting deposits, advancing loans to the state traders, army commanders, individuals, buying and selling the currency & bullion, exchanging the currency, as saying the rupees or coins and bills of exchange, etc.

From the record books of *Dixit* and *Patvardhan*, it gives the idea that ordinary citizens used to store their sums with the brokers for safe authority, on a specific measure of intrigue. At the end of the day, the brokers by tolerating stores acquired capital required for their business at a specific rate of intrigue. The investor must return the sum on interest at the appropriate time. A fascinating store account found in Dixit-Patvardhan books is as per the following:[94] A man (Amritrao Vishwanath Peale) had kept 7000 rupees with the investor. Be that as it may, the contributor got the advantage of keeping the sum with the financier just when the investor's money kept with the broker was utilized in the exchange. In any case, these were uncommon. The rate important to be charged on the store kept with the broker changed from one rupee and six annas to one rupee and a half.[95]

The genuine centrality of the investors lay in loaning cash to borrowers. For loaning, cash was something imperative for the exchange and trade of the state. The Maratha state under the Peshwas dependably acquired advances from the brokers. There are various records referencing a lot of cash obtained by the Peshwas from the financiers. References found in our archives that the Peshwas were vigorously in debt are satisfactory to demonstrate that the investors gave credits to the condition within recent memory. The Maratha state brought credits up in request to meet its own responsibilities. The investors charged an ordinary enthusiasm at the rate of 1 per cent for each month. It gives the idea that the government provided request drafts on the broker, and guidelines were passed with respect to its instalment. It is obvious from the record that the state got material too from the broker in lieu of a money advance. In such cases, the state gave no other surety yet securities bearing a 12 per cent rate of intrigue every year. A record uncovers that credits adding up to Rs. 16,22,292 had been gotten by the Peshwa from the investors in real money and in the material.

It demonstrates that the investors propelled credits to the legislature in real money as well as in-kind by giving the required need of the state. Another component of the financial business of the period under investigation was to give credits to the military administrators.

The advance in that capacity was unbound. In such cases, brokers offered advances to military commandants who gave just credit bonds and individual security to them. Such credits were, for the most part, transient advances. Numerous records uncover that the administration officers got transitory advances from the financiers. Numerous occasions demonstrate that *Subedars* and *Kamaysdars* additionally got advances from the brokers, at whatever point request drafts were gotten from the state. In some cases, the receipts of the incomes appointed to different Kamavisdars were gathered by the investors. There are different occurrences of the instalments made to military officers for preparing warriors or his company for a battle. Commonly the financiers propelled credits for the instalment of the month to month compensations of the administration representatives. Advances were given for the most part for gathering the administration contribution in regard of the *Sardeshmukhi* or *Mamlat* of a specific town or the portions of the *Kamavisdars*. The investors propelled advances to the officers of the administration just on the desire that they would get back the cash credited from the treasury with a regular rate of premium.

The dealers required cash for their business. Giving momentary advances to dealers and the business network was regular back then. Advances were progressed at a specific rate of intrigue. A letter in the Vaidya Daftar[96] dated 30 January 1755 demonstrates that an indebted person, Kanhoji Sirake, acquired rupees 100 at the loan fee of two rupees for each month for exchange purposes. It recommends that the rate of intrigue singed on a little momentary credit was twofold. The records demonstrate that credits progressed to different individuals from the general public; for example, stone cutters, potters, sweepers, cooks, oilmen, goldsmiths, tailors, coolies and so on were for the most part close to home advances progressed by the investors against specific securities like gold decorations, land structures, farming produce and so forth and the rate of premium charged changed from 1/2 to 2 per cent for each month.

The exchange in the day-book for the year 1787–88 of the record book of *Dixit-Patvardhan* gives important data about the advances progressed to dealers by the financiers. A silversmith got an advance from the investor by selling articles made of the gold-like *bangles*, *laurels* and *putalis*, weighing from 10 to 20 Tolas. The rate of intrigue charged on such a sum was eight annas for every hundred every month.[97]

Another merchant, for instance, a confectioner got a transient advance for a month from the broker by selling a rose-water holder made of silver.[98] It gives the idea that for a momentary advance of a little sum the rate of intrigue was higher than for a long haul advance of a major sum. Another exchange referenced in the record of that year demonstrates that the financiers additionally used to propel credits to the merchants who managed in jaggery and gems.[99] There is an intriguing case of propelling a momentary advance to a borrower. The credit was progressed against individual surety for the time of a year at the rate of eight annas for every hundred every month. In any case, as the advanced sum was not returned inside the stipulated time, the investor gathered it with enthusiasm from the surety.[100] Here and there, the broker propelled advances to merchants like oilmen depending on the prerequisite that they would pitch oil to him at the fixed value rate as referenced in the credit security or *Karjat-khat* for the stipulated period advance reimbursing. Be that as it may, if the cost rate of oil descended, an oilman needed to pitch it to the broker at the diminished rate; despite what might be expected, the oil was to be sold at the fixed rate when its cost expanded. There are references that cash moneylenders acquired such offices and concessions from the expert indebted individuals.

The bankers additionally acknowledged ardent property like a shop or house as security against credits taken by the traders.[101] From the records of Tulshibagwale[102] dated A.D. 1762, it creates the impression that gold, swords and garments were sold by the borrowers to the investors when credits were to be progressed from the last to the previous. In some cases, a borrower could likewise get a credit from the investor on the security of his very own town Watan. A record dated A.D. 1777–78. demonstrates that the town of Singwe in Pargana Nasik having a place with the symbol admirer had been sold for accepting credit. Advances were additionally cutting-edge by the brokers on the home loan of the *Watans* of *Kulkarni* and *Deshpande.*[103] The records of Tulshibagwale allude to Malhar Mauje Dobole, which was sold for obtaining a credit.[104]

Presently given is a chance to think about the strategy of giving advances. The advances were given for the most part against composed bonds. There were three kinds of securities: (1) loan security *(Karjarokha)*, (2) forward credit security (*Wadarokha*) and (3) partnership advance security (*Sharkatrokha*). In an advance security the borrower gave an endeavour about the reimbursement of the sum and the rate of intrigue was additionally settled. If there should be a rise of an occurrence of default, certain punishments were forced. The bond was required to be countersigned by a free observer. This security was the most widely recognized type of propelling cash to a borrower.[105] The record of Tulshibagwale uncovers that occasionally it was referenced in the understanding that the essential ought to be returned in a similar coin wherein it was given as advance. A similar record of Tulshibagwale alludes to the credit taken in stamped Mohars and to be reimbursed in similar coins. The borrower was expected to pay the fine mentioned in the bond, in case he failed to repay the commitment in the stipulated time. Accounts show that if the premium along with the loaned amount is not returned to the bank, then the sold property was to be appended by the cash bank.

A record dated A.D. 1747 states that it was set down in the bond that if the credit was not reimbursed in the stipulated time, the *Kulkarni Watan* of Mauje Shivane was to be connected.[106] Another record dated A.D.1750–51 states that the *Kulkarnis* of Kasba Mahalunge owed an obligation to Moro Ballal, but did not return it. For the default, their *Watan* of *Kulkarni* was set under connection.[107]

Another kind of bond was a forward credit bond. "In this bond a credit was taken by the borrower depending on the prerequisite that he would restore the equivalent in specific portions in future." "In organization advance bond advances were progressed generally to the ranchers for developing area." Buying and selling cash and bullion was one of the elements of the investors. It was a typical practice with the investors in the 18th-century Maharashtra to purchase and sell gold coins, for example *Mohars* and *Hons*, which were in vogue back then. The rates to be charged on the buy and clearance of the money differed from 1 rupee to 14 rupees and relied on the need of the client and the sort of currency.[108] Next, the financiers were to play out another significant capacity—that of testing rupees or coins. The exchange of the day-book for the year 1787–88 of the record book of *Dixit-Patvardhan* demonstrates that the investor tested rupees 150 against which he got six annas at the rate of four annas for every hundred.[109] To convert one sort of cash for another was one of the valuable and significant administrations of the indigenous brokers of Maharashtra in the 18th century. They generally gave the correct kind of money to each client consistently. It is uncovered from the record books that the commission at various rates was gotten by the brokers for trading one kind of cash for another.[110]

As it has been explained, this chapter deals with trade and commerce, commodities of trade, trade routes and markets in late medieval Deccan. It can be inferred from the evidence of various indigenous and European sources that Deccan was very rich in resources as it attracted various foreign traders and brought the Deccan economy into the global market. The various European Companies, viz. the Portuguese, the Dutch, the English and the French, established and consolidated their factories along the East and West Coast. In these settlements, they had evolved their own commercial and administrative organization for the management of their trade. By the coming of the 18th century, the introduction of private trading systems at a large scale was a common occurrence. The old mercantilist was broken, and a new model was set up, which promoted private trade. The medieval Deccan's commercial world was influenced and facilitated by multiple trading castes/communities, and their changing nature of role from conflict to collaboration with the indigenous rulers as well as with the European Companies is visible throughout the region.

With the rise of Maratha rule in the mid-17th century, besides the other Deccan Sultanates, Chhatrapati Shivaji was reported to be keen on promoting and encouraging trade and business activities in his region. He gave concessions to traders, levied tariffs and built permanent markets on the capital forts of Raigad. Several industries were extensively developed in cities and towns in the Deccan. As agriculture was the main occupation of the people of Deccan, many crafts and industries based on agricultural produce were carried on in every village.

We see a transition in the economic condition in Maharashtra during the 18th century with the establishment of Maratha political power, and its subsequent expansion offered excellent conditions to Marathi people for development in different occupations and business activities. A banking system and a new class of indigenous *sahukars* (mainly Brahmans and among them the *Chitpavans* seem to be predominant in this field) emerged under the patronage of Peshwas. Hence, we can say from our study of the period that Deccan in the 17th and 18th centuries was experiencing a transition in all spheres, but the transition in economy was characterized by the change in the structure of power which initiated necessary social and economic reconfigurations.

Epilogue

This project under consideration has aimed at highlighting all related issues whether political, economic, social or religious to research the macro and micro historical ingredients to underline the specificities of transition evolving in the 17th- and 18th-century Deccan. The research is grouped into five distinct chapters, each dealing with politics and diplomacy, navy, society, art and architecture and economy of Deccan. The expansive nature of the European powers on the Indian coast was bound to have a cohesion or incoherence with the Marathas; due emphasis is also placed on the people of this region, their society, economy and fusion of cultures.

In the 17th and 18th centuries the Maratha idea of diplomacy is depicted from the Ajnapatra. *Ajnapatra* is a volume of about 7000 words, compiled in A.D. 1715 at the instance of Shambhu or Sambhaji, the King of Karveer (Kolhapur) State, by Ramchandra Pant Amatya a veteran statesman-cum-administrator of Shivaji's times. This is the only work related to Maratha State Policy. The second part of the *Ajnapatra* deals with seven chapters. The fifth of them relates to "*Shukar*" meaning financiers, indigenous and foreign merchants like the Portuguese, the French, the English, the Dutch, the Danes, etc. It reveals the attitude of Shivaji towards the foreign merchants and the importance of the existence of "*Shukars*" for the economic prosperity of the State. The commercial policy discusses the character, political ambition and the policy to be followed towards them during peace and at war. It clearly states that the Marathas gave importance to administration in comparison to the economic policy. The "*Ajnapatra*" also makes it clear that the Marathas differentiated between the European and understood their administrative and economic interests in India.

Throughout the period from 1668 to 1818 the Portuguese, Dutch and French came into contact with the Marathas and developed relations.

Broadly these relations can be categorized into five time brackets, as the nature of the relations between them varied accordingly, i.e.

i) 1630–1680—Period of establishment of Swaraj and Sovereign authority
ii) 1681–1689—Period of resistance and turmoil
iii) 16901707—Period of Maratha Independence
iv) 1707–1761—Maratha expansion and consolidation in Deccan and North India
v) 1761–1818—Post Panipat: Power Politics-Consolidation through Confederacy

The relations between these powers have been studied with their interaction with other major and minor contemporary powers, viz., Indian powers like the Mughal, the Nizam, Haider Ali, Tipu Sultan, the Siddi of Janjira, etc. The Maratha State which gradually got transformed into a Confederacy was a geographically centrally located power and right from its very inception as a state it came into contact with nearly all the major and minor powers in the Hindustan, the Deccan and the Karnatak.

The first chapter gives a detailed analysis of the art of diplomacy followed by the Marathas towards the Deccan Powers and the European Powers in Deccan. Their combat strategies and methods of deploying the art of warfare were effective in the 17th century, and they manoeuvred their enemies on the battlefields. Their style of warfare, popularly known as *ganimi kava* or guerrilla warfare, was tacitly deployed against their enemies. Their military strength was dependent upon its infantry and light cavalry, and matchlocks, flintlocks as well as the range of artillery were important parts of the Maratha warfare. However, by the 18th century the Marathas adapted to new techniques of warfare major; thrust was invested into cavalry with the introduction of various martial groups/communities, especially who were not Marathas which also led to an organizational change and at times left chances of compromise and conspiracy against the Swaraj. The deployment of the French mercenaries by various Maratha Sardars brought the European traditions of disciplined warfare to be deployed on open battlefields in the north of India. Forts lost their importance and prominence with the changing scenario of the 18th century as they proved ineffective against the use of cannons and huge artillery. The 18th century was a period of Maratha ascendency, the transformation of the state itself from the State to Confederacy and then to Barbhai Council (Karbharis) is a testimony of its resilient nature to the needs of the time. Their relation with the Europeans was based on alliances which were pertinent to upkeep the cause of the establishment of *swarajya*. In the 18th century the Marathas remained to be the only formidable power which checked and resisted the English throughout, and they were able to retain cordial relations with the European powers other than the English thus filling the power vacuum and creating a balance of power not only in Deccan but in the Indian subcontinent.

The Portuguese who have been underestimated by historians seem to have displayed excellent diplomatic skills in all their concordat with their contemporaries, safeguarding their interest and political cum economic ambitions in trying to exploit the situation in Deccan for their personal gains. They adopted the "*policy of Subordination*" with the other states. The period under our study has seen various changes in diplomatic relationships between the Marathas and the Portuguese.

The period of 1630–1680 marked the period of establishment of swaraj; it was the period when Shivaji was establishing sovereign authority over Deccan. Initially, Shivaji did not consider the Portuguese as a threat because of his engagements with the Deccani states. The Portuguese were supporting his ambitions with a motive especially when Shivaji was in direct conflict with Bijapur thus helping Shivaji to eliminate their strong rival. They display a remarkable diplomatic capability during this period by not engaging themselves in direct conflict with their neighbours and rivals rather utilizing their good terms with the Marathas for their own benefit.

The period of 1681–1689 saw the period of Maratha resistance and turmoil. During the time of Shambhaji the relationship between the Marathas and the Portuguese remained vacillated most of the time due to the existing political chaos and uncertainties. The Portuguese favoured alliance with Aurangzeb as they tried to defend their interests in the Deccan by not offending the Mughals.

The period of 1689–1707 records a hostile relationship between the Portuguese and the Marathas. Rajaram's period witnessed the long ensuing Mughal-Maratha War during which it was difficult for all European powers to take sides as they all were uncertain of the outcome of this war.

The period of 1707–1761 witnessed the Mughal-Maratha war, and the Portuguese took full advantage of this situation by regaining most of their lost territories; the war came to their advantage as they switched on their loyalties as time demanded very tactfully whenever they found the sides of the Mughals and Marathas to be weak thus maintaining the balance of power. The Portuguese true to their nature never wanted to directly engage in war with the rival, they instead explored and exploited the situation to fulfil their egotistical interests. The Mughals were never welcome in Deccan by the Portuguese or by the Marathas. The Portuguese only under the duress of the situation tried a policy of appeasement towards the Mughals to reap diplomatic concessions for the economic advantage. The Marathas policy under Bajirao rather maintained the checks and balances against the Portuguese keeping in view their past records with the swaraj, it now gave up the policy of neutrality, thus capturing Vasai which led to the fall of Bacaim. The Marathas with the help of the English defeated the Portuguese at Bacaim in 1739.

The period 1761–1800 is marked by the coadunation of the confederacy in Deccan. The existing powers were trying their best to militate by becoming allies and by entering into different diplomatic relationships with each other. All the states were trying to recover their lost political ground. Khem Sawant had lost militarily with the Portuguese, and he used various modus operandi to prepare grounds to re-ignite Maratha-Portuguese diplomatic relations. Mahadaji Shinde was Khem Sawants's brother-in-law and controlled the state of Gwalior. After the death of Mahadaji Shinde there was no diplomatic relationship between the Marathas and the Portuguese. The relationship between the Portuguese and the Marathas was de-escalating and was in its last phase.

The period of 1800–1818 marked the Period of "*subsidiary Alliance.*" "*Pedne*" which was strategically located remained the bone of contention between the Portuguese and Khem. After the death of Nana Phadnis on 13 February, the Portuguese attacked *Pedne*. Later the Bhonsles capitulated *Pedne* to the Portuguese. Portuguese entered into a permanent peace treaty with Khem Sawant till his death in 1803. The period is marked as a crucial period in the history of modern India as almost all the powerful Maratha confederates like the Peshwas, the Shinde and the Bhonsles of Nagpur had entered into a subsidiary alliance with the British. Khem's territory was taken by the British in 1818 under the subsidiary alliance system.

Dutch factory at Vengurla was in close proximity to the territory of Maratha Swaraj, it brought them into contact, conflict and collaboration on numerous occasions between 1630 and 1680. The Dutch got involved with the Marathas and shared an extensive relationship throughout the period. Shivaji's diplomatic relations with the Dutch were relatively cordial and commercially motivated during the initial phase. The Portuguese and Dutch were arch-rivals, Shivaji took advantage of this situation by opening negotiations with the Dutch and in several correspondences with his tactical expertise gained the loyalty of the Dutch against the Portuguese. At times, we find that the Dutch also took advantage of the rift between Shivaji and the English (in the 1670s), promising assistance of navy against the English. As a diplomatic move Shivaji maintained neutral relations with the Dutch factory at Vengurla during his expeditions in the area, thus striking to secure a balance of power between the Portuguese and the English.

The year 1677 saw the southward expansion of Shivaji to the Karnatak expedition. Dutch had secured several *Kauls* (charters) from Shivaji and Ekoji. The most prominent was the one given to Jacques Caulier, the Governor of the Coromandel division of the VOC in 1677. At Porto Novo too, a *Kaul* was granted to Dutch with the help of an able diplomat of Shivaji, Raghunath Pant which allowed Dutch lodge at Porto Novo, on the condition that it was not fortified. Thus, inviting the Europeans and granting them concessions were his economic policies for promoting trade and commerce in the region. Still, at the same time, they also ensured that these foreigners did not establish any territorial control, which could be a threat to them in the long run.

1680–1689: This phase brought the most turbulent times in the Deccan as the Mughals annexed the states of Golconda and Bijapur bringing a setback to the diplomatic dominance of the Marathas. There are not many significant records that discuss the Dutch contacts with Sambhaji. It is recorded that the Dutch tried to maintain cordial relations with the Mughals during their Deccan intrusion, and they also sent an embassy to congratulate Aurangzeb on his victory. In 1689, to safeguard their commercial interest, Joannes Bacherus sought confirmation of Dutch privileges in the Deccan from the Mughal Emperor.

During the period of 1690–1707, an active relationship between Rajaram and the Dutch has been traced. As the Marathas were at continuous war with Mughals, the state's revenues faced acute shortage of money for funding the army. The soldiers were deserting due to the lack of pay. Rajaram tackled this complicated situation in a very diplomatic way by announcing the allotment of jahagirs to his sardars likewise succeeded in his negotiations with the Dutch and the French through his officers. Rajaram had initially supported the French, but later on, he chose Dutch, who paid a better price over the French for Pondicherry. This behaviour of Marathas is best characterized as being motivated by the sheer need for money and the urgency of immediate survival. At the same time, the Dutch generally had amicable relations with the Maratha rulers of Thanjavur and were successful to secure privileges in Nagapattinam.

1707–1761: However, with the changing political scenario in the 18th century, which resulted in the change of Tanjore–Maratha's attitude towards the Dutch. Serfoji took offence over several issues. He was dissatisfied with the Dutch presents given to him at his accession. In 1712 he repudiated the tax concessions given to them and imposed full tolls on goods brought into Negapatnam. Later in the next few decades, the Dutch relations with the Maratha were lesser found as their factories became increasingly squeezed by the ongoing political conflicts in the interior, involving the states of Hyderabad, Arcot and the Marathas, and also by the increasing pressure from the British and the French.

The period of 1761–1818 was one when the situation got worse for the Dutch as well as for the Tanjore state with the Nawab's attacks on Tanjore in the 1770s and the expanding English authority over the coastal and hinterlands areas of the Coast. Despite several attempts by the Raja of Tanjore to shore up his finance by leasing out land to the Dutch, it came to nothing. During the 18th century, unlike the other European powers, the Dutch contacts with the Marathas almost eclipsed, as the Dutch stayed neutral and preferred not to interfere in the local politics of the region. The Dutch activities in the Deccan began to decline by this time, and the war with England proved disastrous to the finances of the Dutch Republic. Finally, in 1800, the Company was dissolved and four years after the States-General was replaced by the French-supported Batavian Republic. Later all the settlements and factories were reverted to the English.

The French-Maratha relations in 1630–1680 were initially a commercial one, with the French gunning for trading rights in Rajapur on the Western

Coast. Shivaji, however, during this period concentrated on consolidation and expansion in the South. Thus, by allowing the French to settle at Rajapur, he astutely assumed an alliance with them; since he was at war with many Deccan Powers, he needed their help in terms of ammunition. When the Marathas descended on the Karnatak, the French by 1674 had firmly established themselves at Pondicherry; in that way, we notice a shift from their commercial activities from the West to the East. They, therefore, could rely on the Marathas for protection during their expedition.

The demise of Shivaji brought French-Maratha relations to a standstill for the period between 1685 and 1707. However, we can trace an indirect contact which is highlighted from the regular correspondence between the French and the Portuguese on the west coast and the French on the Coromandel Coast.

The period of 1707–1761 was one of great importance to the Marathas. They became the most formidable power with expansion plans towards the north. Their bond with the French was desired even more. The period also witnessed a shift in the internal politics of the Marathas, whereby power was transformed from the Chhatrapati to the Confederacy. During the same time the French under Dupleix altered their relationship with the regional powers while they became involved in the internal politics due to the political vacuum created in the Deccan Vice-royalty. The period also saw the short-lived success of the French which eventually paved way for its downfall in 1761 after the capture of Pondicherry by the English. The Battle of Panipat in 1761 did shatter the Maratha dreams in the north of India for a while, but it also paved way to the rise of the State of Mysore of Woodeyars under Haider Ali in Deccan which secured wide recognition in a very short span.

The post-Panipat period of 1761–1818 marks the resurgence of the Martha State in Deccan. The Maratha wars against Mysore saw the French allying with both Marathas and Mysore, but the French also tried to form a triple alliance between the Marathas, Nizam and the Mysore to deal with the common enemy the English. The English on the other hand subjugated one state after the other. While the French and the Marathas worked together to check the growing menace of the English. This period also witnessed the transformation of power from the Maratha Confederacy to the Barbhai Council. The Barbhai Council were strong enemies of the English. They therefore sent their agents to the French court for diplomatic alliances. The second reappearance of Bussy in Deccan created a hopeful atmosphere for the Marathas and the French; however, the untimely death of Bussy only deteriorated their relationship. The Marathas could not even think of having an alliance with Mysore, thus the proposals made by the French could not materialize, and this only pushed them further into the hands of the English. The fall of Pondicherry for the second time in 1793 served a severe blow to the French-Maratha relation.

Diplomacy was not the only factor responsible for the rise of the Marathas; together with their naval exploits and diplomatic skills the

Marathas became the most challenging power of the 17th and 18th centuries. They demonstrated to the other powers what they were missing, for example the Mughals never concentrated on the sea, they were mostly confined to riverine battles. Thus, by not investing on the seas they lost an important aspect of monopoly on customs trade and taxation. Navy forms an important aspect of Maratha naval politics and administration. The Maratha navy played an important role in the maritime history of Indian in general and Deccan in particular and also proved a blunt instrument for offensive warfare against the Europeans who by the 16th century had developed more advanced instruments of sea power. While the other indigenous powers failed to appreciate the significance of navy, it was Shivaji who understood the importance of controlling the waters of western coast and established his own navy at the time when various European powers like the Portuguese and the Dutch were establishing their sovereignty over the sea. By establishing their own indigenous navy, the Marathas possessed a strong threat to these European powers. With the rise of the Angres, we see that there was continuous change in the power struggle at the sea between the Maratha naval power, the Europeans and the neighbouring kingdoms.

The Marathas later during the Angria rule achieved technological improvements in the domains of naval construction, shipbuilding and other sea-related skills. They built warships like Gurabs and Gallivats, which were more sea-worthy and could even meet their European rival on more or less equal terms, thus giving Marathas a clear supremacy in ocean-going warships. They even constructed a web of fortresses at choke-points of sea routes on the western coast that were used not only as commercial factories but also for naval bases. Besides the use of various warfare ships and coastal forts, the Marathas used many naval warfare strategies, which enabled them to emerge as one of the chief naval power of their times. By establishing a strong navy the Maratha state challenged the European powers over their right of "Sovereignty over the Sea." The period witnessed a series of naval battles between the Marathas and the European powers especially the Portuguese and the Dutch.

The Europeans, especially the Portuguese, claimed exclusive sovereignty over the sea and compelled all trading in Indian seas to purchase their licences (cartaz and cafila) which were used to implement monopoly and supremacy over maritime trade in Indian Ocean regions. They were of the opinion that the sea belonged to them and they had every right to exercise control over the sea and curb all competitors. The Portuguese were not the only ones to claim this sovereignty; the Dutch and the English too issued passes and denied the right of free navigation. It was for the first time that an indigenous power like the Marathas tried to challenge these European powers at sea, who have purposefully constructed a historiographical narrative about the Marathas as "the pirates," but it is a recorded fact that the Europeans were actually exploiting the resources of the Indian subcontinent while the Marathas were resisting it. Such Colonial misconceptions and influences were handed down in the historiography by many colonial historians who termed Kanhoji Angre and his successors as pirates. It was Shivaji and later Kanhoji Angre who became a defender of indigenous sovereignty and possessed resistance to these European incursions. Kanhoji Angre and his successors wrongly depicted as pirates were trying to defend the Maratha sovereignty at sea and exercise their maritime rights on their own waters. They refused to accept European sovereignty at sea and instead made the European powers buy their licences.

With the rise of the Maratha Navy, the European powers were checked at sea. The rise of the Maratha flotilla under Shivaji had become a potential threat to the Portuguese, who earlier had the monopoly over the sea. The naval relationship between the Portuguese and the Marathas was a combination of conflict, rivalry and cooperation.

The Portuguese by the 17th century had recognized the Maratha naval supremacy and their presence on the entire Konkan Coast (west coast). The naval engagements between the Marathas, the Portuguese and the English are proofs that the Maratha navy under Shivaji had become an arduous power and threat at the sea to the European powers.

"Sarkhel" Kanohji Angre drove the Maratha naval force higher than ever during his tenure and battled intrepidly with his European partners. Kolaba was made the home office or office of the chief naval officer's central station, and this strategic location made the English miserable. The English authorities got anxious with the loss of the island of Khanderi under Maratha's order. The cruising time between Bombay to Khanderi and Kolaba was couple of hours during ideal wind. The control over Khanderi implied that it was difficult to keep an eye over European vessels moving towards Bombay. The command over these locales by Kanhoji Angre was a consistent danger for English exchange and trade taking place from Bombay.

The English got to know the adversaries of Kanhoji Angre to counter the developing risk of the Marathas in the area since it was difficult to counter the threat. One significant part of this stratagem was that they allied with the Siddis and gave them every single imaginable assistance to utilize them to counter to Angrias. The English specialists permitted their allies to sail their ships with English banners even without pass; however, this was not adequate for Kanhoji Angre. Kanhoji made it clear to the expert that beyond a point he would haggle with the vessels as indicated by his own will. In this situation, memorandum or settlement will fail even at the smallest imbalance of power. The naval relationship between the Portuguese and the Marathas underwent changes at various levels in different phases.

Although Europeans possessed strong artillery, this advantage was, more than often, neutralized by the tactical superiority of the Maratha navy. Rather showing in their accounts that Marathas were also participating in maritime trade, they had achieved a considerable success in trading vessels, which were sent out yearly to Persia, Basra, Mocha, Muscat, etc. they often reported in their accounts that their vessels had been seized by Shivaji and the Maratha fleet which resulted in huge loss to them. Scholars working on these aspects have traced the records along the lines of the narratives constructed by the Europeans in their accounts and have completely ignored the engagement of the Maratha ships in the maritime activities and trade, it was all about reaping profits by securing more trading rights and establishing sovereignty in the Indian waters, especially the west coast through permits; hence we find the Marathas to be frequently targeted as "pirates" by the Europeans in their records. Kanhoji Angre was determined to defend his rights on the sea against all his neighbours jointly or individually. At several times he fought with the Europeans and proved to be a disaster for their trade. He came in conflict with the Dutch East India Company very early in his career. Throughout Kanhoji's reign, peace and amity could not be established between them. Kanhoji repeatedly captured many of their vessels, of which the Dutch firmly complained to him to restore the vessels with all their belongings, which actually we never returned due to which the struggle went on even after Kanhoji's death and continued with varying successes by his sons, and the Angrian fleet was a terror that the seafarers of the 18th century were glad to avoid. The naval conflicts of the Angres proved to be the biggest threat to the Europeans on west coast of the Indian Ocean. They fought on the sea both with tactics and strategies with complete valour, courage and statesmanship for the upkeepment of the ideal of swaraj.

All the European East India Companies had their own interests and goals to be fulfilled. The companies had laid their objectives to be achieved. The French took a completely different stand when it came to gain sovereignty at sea. Maratha-French relations over the high seas could not materialize because the French were interested in sovereignty over land. The French were successful to establish themselves on both the eastern and western coasts. They gained Karaikal from the Marathas of Tanjore State as the Raja was in debt; he leased out villages in Karaikal to the French. Mahe on the other hand attracted the attention of the French because it provided easier accessibility to the hinterlands. Mahe provided large proportions of pepper for trade, and Mahe also provided an entry point to the Marathas for their expeditions to the South. It's strategic and manufacturing cum trading capacity as a centre became a core cause for Anglo-French conflicts; as a result Karaikal and Mahe could not be developed into any kind of naval base the French restricting it only for their activities related to trading operations.

The French naval power couldn't enhance itself in India due to their engagements in the internal politics of Deccan and its indigenous powers. The sole purpose behind establishing factories at Mahe and Karaikal remained the trade, the other was to use this as a base to dislodge the English. The failure of its naval enterprise on the west coast was due to the French policy and that most of the French officials have a strong disagreement on having a naval base in India; it was only Jean Law de Lauriston who stressed to maintain a naval superiority on Indian waters.

In order to have a holistic approach while studying Deccan, the examination of diverse cultures, social formations, diverse religions, etc. becomes mandatory. The study of society gives us a clear picture about people, beliefs and their practices. As we have studied this section through the lens of different orientalist approaches, it becomes more interesting to see that each European company has its own colonial goals and mechanism to implement them. An attempt has been made to discard the British orientalist approach and bring to light a nuanced understanding of different apparatuses used by these European powers to make their presence felt in Asiatic societies.

This chapter is a comprehensive study of amalgamations of various cultures, religious patterns and people in Deccan. Deccan experienced a transition in the social context, right from the time of carving out an identity for a region to the assimilations of all religious beliefs and customs. The region became home to many foreign immigrants, Sufi mystics and European traders. The period under study has been marked with social mobility which paved a way for the formation of a new social order. The presence of various European countries and their commercial interests gave birth to a new kind of population as well as settlements in Deccan. The presence of a new or mixed population is a very significant aspect of Deccan during this period because this in turn helped us to study transitions through various parameters such as culture, dress, food, customs, rituals, art and architecture. Religious ties as well as the long-standing commercial links between central Asia and the Deccan provided important channels for cultural and literary traditions. For instance, *Dakhani*, which was an early form of Urdu, contributed towards the fusion of different cultures.

Sufism had brought about an alternative to the existing orthodox Islamic religion. The Sufi Mystics were posing a serious threat to the legitimacy of the emperor. Khanqahs of the Sufi saints were the centre of pilgrimage for people of all religions and cultures. The suzerainty of the Sufi saints was accepted from the Emperor to the common man. There were certain sections of the Sufi saints who held high posts in the courts. Like the Chistiya order of Sufism, who believed in indulging in luxuries of life and holding powerful positions at the court. Whereas the Surawardiya order of the Sufi saint believed in leading a life of complete austerity. The coming of Sufism had influence and impact on all levels like most importantly polity, to be followed by society and the economy.

Bhakti also tried to give an alternative to the people belonging to all strata of society. It provided mobility in the existing rigid framework of the traditional Hindu practices. Many bhakti saints composed verses in Dakhani for their non-Marathi audiences and also pointed out the common features between the two religions of the Hindus and the Muslims. Not only did these bhakti saints write in Dakhani, but the Sufi saints also reciprocated by producing literature in vernacular languages like Marathi.

These reformation and protestant movements shaped Shivaji's idea of *Hindawi Swarajya*. An upsurge intended for the propagation of spiritual quest, *Swaraj* was ideal for the state established by Shivaji and Maharashtra Dharma was its ideology. The democratic atmosphere created by Bhakti was properly used by Shivaji. He provided equal opportunity to men of merit from all castes and grades of society, including the Muslims. Shivaji revived the Hindu customs and Hindu administrative system and compiled a glossary of administrative terms in Sanskrit, the *Raj-Vyavahara-Kosha*.

The Bhakti movement in Maharashtra also witnessed the rise of a number of saints from the lower strata of the society. These bhakti saints, poets and philosophers like Namdev, Gora, Sena, Narahari and Chokhamela sprang from the lower levels of Maratha society and believed in a monistic view of the world and the supremacy of bhakti. These bhakti saints not only raised spiritual and moral values of the people but also gave the basis for enlightening thoughts. These saints believed that all humans are equal in status and also expressed their views on caste-based practice. The ideas, teachings and practices of these saints reduced the limitations of social relations and caused improvement in the social positions of lower castes as well as the position of women in the society. The women through Bhakti have carved out a niche for themselves. It gave them an equal opportunity to attain salvation and refute the prescribed domestic obligations of household. They have composed hymns and poetry in different languages which have earned them a status of sainthood.

When we study the establishment of European companies, the religion which came along with them also needs to be analyzed. It is interesting to notice the mechanism which was employed by each of the missionaries to make their religion relevant to the people of Deccan. The chapter incorporates such ideas of implanting a new religion and propagation of the same. The argument of various authors regarding conversions and acceptance has been taken into consideration, and I have tried to put up a counter argument for it.

The Portuguese missionaries came with a mindset that they would convert the people and they would become allies of the Portuguese Empire and its trading centres. Propagation of any religion and its acknowledgement in the general public must be found in connection with its capacity to socially absorb in the general public. Adjustment to one's condition is fundamental. According to Rajamanickam, an educator needs to embrace himself with the idea of the understudy; in any case what is instructed gets pointless. Same is the situation with sacred texts so Nobili and significantly different clerics in different places of Asia needed to adjust to their condition and to social traditions. The Jesuits were adjusting, so the new strict confidence would be important to the Asian culture. Crafted by the Jesuits were done by the edicts yet this reality can't be denied that the variables like sensitive, social and ecclesial had a significant task to carry out in the working of the Jesuits in numerous other exotic places.

Portuguese were unfamiliar with the existing caste system and its exceptionally peculiar practice. It was hard for the Christian minority to battle against the rank framework which was so generally pervasive in India. So, we can say that it was an extraordinary accomplishment for Nobili to at any rate bring all the lower position individuals together in a similar church yet as per their status. It was difficult to work within the given framework of the caste system, and the inclusion of the caste system was equally important, otherwise the preaching of Gospel would be in vain. He needed to follow the law of the land. Nobili as said by Rajamanickam rejected the caste system.

Conversions were forceful or was it voluntary is a contentious topic. The logic behind this deliberation is that there is no one factor responsible for conversions. Evidences supporting both the sides exist. Conversions had various reasons and are "multi causal." For the lower caste people, this was the opportunity to have upward social mobility in the society, conversion arouses the desire for a better future. Portuguese were moved by religious zeal and, thus, understood conversions as a way to make allies. Christianity in the subcontinent gave different motivations like schools, clinics, halfway houses and so forth to the individuals.

The amalgamation of different cultures leads to the making of a new type of population, also known as *Topasses*. The marriages happening across different ethnicity leads to the formation of new ethnic groups. So, we can see that social transformation trickling down through various levels.

Dutch oriental perspective was quite different in its approach. Their understanding and goals were different from their predecessors and successors. Though Dutch were completely mercantilist in their approach, we do find interesting references of their missionary activities in Deccan. Although the Dutch never indulged in religious persecution, which was in contrast with the Portuguese who placed conversion before commerce. The circumstances in which the Dutch missionaries had to work were entirely different from those of the Portuguese. Their liberal religious policy was more noticeable on the Coromandel coast. Phillipus Baldaeus was appointed by the Company as a predicant responsible for converting the Tamils on the Coast to the Dutch Reformed religion. He moved among the people, mastering the Tamil language in which he could preach and converse. Baldeus compiled several manuscripts to be used by native proponents of Protestantism and schoolmasters and prepared a Tamil Psalter. Abraham Rogerius has the distinction of having been the first Westerner who gave a systematic account of South India.

The Dutch were mainly Calvinists, and they built several churches in Pulicat, Nagapattinam and Tuticorin, mainly for their nationals. They showed very little missionary zeal and made almost no impression on the Coromandel coast. One of the main difficulties under which these predictands laboured was the short duration of their stay in their parishes. On the contrary, if they succeeded in learning the language, a transfer meant that such knowledge was useless. Realizing that Calvinism could make no headway, they were more tolerant and moderate in their treatment of people, thus adjusting themselves to the people of various religions around them. The VOC lacked cultural support systems, unlike the Portuguese, with the Jesuit order and church. Moreover, the resilience of the traditional cultural systems of this region acted as a barrier against Dutch incursion into the religion and society.

French orientalists had their own understanding about the Asian society. While colonizing in Deccan they were particular about their missionary activities. They had devised various apparatus to propagate their missionary activities.

The French Missionary activities encircled two aspects: one was to civilize and the other was for spiritual gains. Time and again the activities of the French Governors were dictated by the Missionaries; the three groups of Missionaries were the Jesuits, Capuchins and the Missions Etrangeres et Paris (MEP).

Conflicts arose between these groups. They often interfered in the politics of the French Governors which led to a conflict between the Church and the State. The defiance of the French Governors towards temple destruction also led to religious contests with the natives. Thus, with pressure from the various missionary orders the Governors in some instances acted harshly. The Earlier Missionaries were orthodox in their approach and wanted conversions to happen through harsh measures. The later missionaries such as the Abbe Dubios (MEP) took effective efforts to know the customs and traditions of the people and hence resorted to having an amalgamation with the natives. The French attitude towards the Orient was different from that of the British, they integrated themselves with the society by learning the indigenous language, they promoted themselves as good administrators and looked after the welfare of the people. They provided good quality education, and improved the transportation system. Linguistic and cultural policies adopted by the French in India led to an assimilation of French culture with the native culture.

The discussion on the different faiths and their tools through which they were trying to blend into the social arena of Deccan makes it imperative to explore their influence and confluence on art, architecture and literature. Chapter four delves into the various efflorescence and manifestations of art and architecture in the Deccan.

The impact of indigenous as well as Europeans on art and architecture of the Deccan region has been immense; the architecture of the Marathas preserved its affinities with earlier traditions and has registered enduring influences to a certain extent by the architecture of other parts of Deccan as well. The Marathas were patrons of art and architecture and promoted fine arts such as painting, dance and music, during their rule. Later the political relations with Mughal and Rajput courts influenced the artistic grandeur and cultural ethics of Marathas. Many affluent classes of Maharashtra undertook the construction of temples and mansions and embellished them with wall paintings and other styles of decoration. Several hill and sea forts were also constructed by the Marathas which can be viewed as the expression of royalty and grandeur.

Along with the forts, paintings and sculpture-making also played a major role in diversifying the Maratha architecture and cultural heritage. Several painting works including murals, miniatures, manuscript illustrations and glass paintings were executed under the patronage of Marathas. A distinct style of Maratha painting evolved in Maharashtra with the rise of the Bhakti movement. The movement not only influenced the social and religious life of the people but also had an impact on the various branches of Fine Arts. It became customary to paint the Puranic scenes and images of God on the walls of temples and residential buildings. Later with the contact and influence of the Islamic courts the Deccan miniature painting demonstrating religious as well as secular themes became widespread. Thus, painting was seen as a thing of aesthetics and entertainment and not just a religious custom.

The chapter also discusses the influence of European building traditions and culture in the region. Like all other aspects of culture, the coming of the Europeans also had a great impact on the art and architecture of the Deccan region. Portuguese architecture can be seen in the amalgamation of both traditional Portuguese and local Indian design. The Portuguese settlements constructed several churches, fortresses and cities like Goa which exhibit a mixture of Indian, Islamic and Portuguese styles of architecture. Goa which was the political capital of the Portuguese in Asia is most likely a clear case of the structure and spatial quality of a Portuguese pilgrim city. Before the end of the 16th century the city had a population of almost 300,000 individuals and had been named the "Lisbon of the Orient" in light of its close similarity to Lisbon city.

Not only the Portuguese but other Europeans like the Dutch also left an imprint of their legacy and culture through their unique architectural styles like castles, forts, mansions, churches, and cemeteries, which are regarded as paragons of Dutch architecture in Deccan. They preferred to modernize the existing structures and modify them in their style. In some of their settlements, they lived in grand style like, at Golconda, the "*opperhoofd*" (the chief or supreme head) of the factory kept open house for all Christians in the city. Many of the Indian palanquin-bearers, horn-blowers, trumpeters, etc. were employed at that factory so that the local and the royal court would be impressed with the opulence and power of the Dutch Company. These factories were situated in the best part of the town, not far from the royal palace. At Pulicat, the Dutch houses of the town were built in the Dutch style with avenues with parallel rows of trees, which gave a uniform appearance along the avenues. The factory building has an impact of Portuguese Architecture. One can say that Dutch inherited the forts from the Portuguese and modified and fortified them with their design. Dutch cemeteries and memorials reflect hybrid architecture made from a combination of Indo-Dutch models.

While the urbanization and town planning of Pondicherry reflects the French Imperial efforts. A cross-cultural examination of the town shows their attitude towards the natives. The French who were merchants, administrators and leaders in religious and political ideologies had a direct influence in the architectural interactions of the towns they built. The segregation of the town is a testimony of French policy towards the locals. However, their efforts at separation only led to architectural interactions, and this is seen from the various buildings present today. The locals imitated the architectural designs of the French in building their houses and the French followed suit.

While relations on art and architectural forms blossomed, last but not least, this chapter discusses the trajectories of entrepreneurship and explores trade, commerce and mercantile practices that led to entrepreneurship among Indian and foreign participants in Deccan. The region came to be perceived as a land of fortune, as both indigenous and foreign merchants kept the economy vibrant. Deccan is flanked with excellent (natural and artificial) harbours and coastal regions on both sides, which experienced extensive trade links that made the region a commercial hub in the world economy. On the western side, Chaul, Dabhol and Goa connected Deccan to the Middle East via maritime routes, while on the eastern side Masulipatnam connected it to Southeast Asia. The activity in the numerous ports along the entire east and west coasts of the Deccan was generated by the economy of the hinterland, varying in depth and in the intensity of its productivity and consumption. Like the ports and the coastline, the hinterland also showed a volatile and changeful character in respect of its political and administrative organization.

The period also saw the emergence of several indigenous industries in cities and towns of Deccan. No doubt agriculture remained to be the main occupation of the people all over the Deccan; as a result a number of crafts and industries based on agriculture produce emerged in every village. "Salt" industry was recognized as a state-sponsored industry and was one of the oldest industries of the Konkan coast; throughout the Maratha rule it generated a huge volume of revenue, and it also remained to be an industry which became a bone of contention among the Marathas and the English as well as the Portuguese. In a similar manner the "Ship" building industry was also a state-sponsored industry of the Maratha state, and its craftsmanship and skill were known far and wide across the globe, nearly all the European companies were interested in employing these Maratha craftsmen who had achieved mastery of the art. The flanking of the vessels was done so well and appropriately that it not only increased the durability of the vessel but kept a very low cost on the maintenance part. The other important urban industries of Deccan were the cotton and silk weaving cottage industry which was encouraged and patronaged not only by the Qutub Shahi of Golkonda but also by the Maratha state. Among the handicrafts industry, woodwork, pottery and rope making were in flourishing stage during the Maratha rule.

The period of 16th and 17th centuries witnessed the dominance of official company trade with a smaller number of private traders, whereas 18th century saw the inclusion of a private trading system at a large scale.

The old mercantilist was broken and another model was set up which advanced private exchange. Different coordinated efforts, for example, Anglo-Portuguese and Danish-Portuguese, became more grounded during this timeframe. Storm Miller' knowledge and his relationship with Dupleix was utilized by the Portuguese private dealers from Lisbon in the private exchange system. This offered obstructs to the nearby *sarafs* and vendors who were getting acclimated with new monetary forms.

The Portuguese had adjusted to the Asian strategy of working together and directing political relations. The English and the Dutch took this skill from them. There was a clear sense of consciousness among Portuguese settlers of the need for local partners. The specialty of amalgamation into the general public had given them an upper edge in contrast with their other European partners.

Deccan in the 17th century witnessed an interaction between the traditional Indian Economy and European merchant capital. The Dutch were most knowledgeable in Indian trading methods, very proficient with the Indian market. They still had some influence on native Indian rulers and their officials. With their control over the trade of East Indies, they enjoyed an advantage denied to their rivals. Some of the Dutch main interest was South Indian textiles, which they initially used in their spice trade in South East Asia and later brought back in some quantities to Europe as well.

In the 17th century, the Dutch participation in intra-Asian trade increased sharply. They were exempted from transit duties from the native rulers of the Deccan. Within the Thanjavur Maratha Kingdom, the VOC had many places under its control. From the southern extremity of Nagapatnam, it had the important port cities of Karikal, Trimelavas or Trimelapatnam, and others. In the internal economy of the Coromandel coast, the activities of the Dutch provided a great impetus to production in the region.

The Dutch were further responsible for establishing some significant innovations in the organization of production and commerce, by developing a relation with the "chief merchants" and introducing the "putting out system." In several places, they established a setup for processing cloth, bleaching and dyeing, and manufacturing gun-powder and ironware, whereas as many as 50 to 100 artisans worked as wage labourers under the direction of the Dutch factors and experts. The Dutch Company's shipbuilding technology was beneficial to the Coromandel Coast Merchants and workers.

The Company's factors were also involved in large-scale private trade carried throughout Asia. On the excuse of getting paid extremely meagre salaries to the employees by the Company, it was only the possibility of making a quick fortune through private trade in Intra-Asian Trade. However, the Company never allowed to engage in private trade, but that did not stop the servants from doing so.

The last Company examined in this research is the commercialization and trade conducted by the French East India Company which led to economic developments in Deccan. When the French established themselves at Pondicherry, migrations took place because of the stability provided by them. Pondicherry became a commercial hub for textile exports to the islands of Malay Archipelago, Macao, Manilla, China, French islands, the Persian Gulf and the Red sea. The French were shrewd to employ well-connected families as their Courtiers and Interpreters. Thus, a partnership arose with the Indian merchants, and the French had to depend on the local merchants, brokers and *gumashtas* (agents). The coastal trade of Pondicherry developed considerably, and they brought a number of centres and ports in direct contact with Pondicherry which contributed to the development of local merchants. A number of centres of production, especially textile-producing areas of the hinterland, were closely connected with Pondicherry through land routes.

The Governors resorted to private trade because of the low income from the Company. Governors such as Lenoir, Dumas, Dupleix and Mahe de la Bourdannais are believed to have left Asia with more than three million livres. A *memoir* of 1738 mentions and refers to Pondicherry's trade with China, Manilla, Mocha, Persia, Merguy, Pegu and Achem. Besides the Company, we find that the private merchants and employees of the Company also participated in this trade for their private dealings.

By bringing to light the various aspects of Deccan history, I hope that I have covered a totalistic view of Deccan in the 17th and 18th centuries. The transitional approach method which has been adopted gives a holistic overview of the important developments and changes taking place at all levels of the society, economy and cultural structures. I have tried to pick up every strand of Deccan history for a critical analysis to give a new insight into the already existing theories and tried to open up new avenues of research in the "History of Medieval Deccan."

Notes

1 Manu S. Pillai, *Rebel Sultans, The Deccan from Khilji to Shivaji*, New Delhi, Juggernaut Books, 2018, p. 56.
2 Richard M. Eaton, "A History of the Deccan, 1500-1700", in *Sultans of Deccan India 1500-1700: Opulence and Fantasy*, Yale University Press, New York, 2005, p. 12.
3 B.G. Paranjape and D.V. Kale, eds., *English Records on Shivaji*, Shiva Charitra Karyalaya, Poona, 1931, p. 277.
4 Abbe Carre, *The Travels of Abbe Carre in India and the Near East, 1672 to 1674*, trans. and ed. by Charles Fawcett, Vol. I, Routledge, New Delhi, 1992, p. 201.
5 K.N. Chitnis, *Socio-Economic History of Medieval India*, New Delhi, Atlantic Publishers and Distributors, 1990, p. 352.
6 Ibid.
7 Ibid., p. 353.
8 Ibid., p. 354.
9 Ibid., p. 355.

10 N.C. Kelkara and D.V. Apte, *English Records on Shivaji, 1659 – 1682*, Part I, Shiva Charitra Karyalaya, Poona, Shivaji Tercentenary Memorial Series, 1931, p. 51.
11 T.T. Mahajan, *Industry, Trade and Commerce during the Peshwa Period*, Jaipur, Pointer Publishers, 1989, p. 30.
12 A.R. Kulkarni, "Protection to Salt Industry by Shivaji", *Proceedings of the Indian History Congress*, Vol. 24 (1961), pp. 188–90.
13 Mahajan, *Industry, Trade and Commerce during the Peshwa Period*, p. 30.
14 *The Gazetteer of Bombay City and Island*, Vol. I, Compiled under the Government of India orders, Times Press, Bombay, 1909, p. 462.
15 Lotika Varadarajan, "Konkan Ports and Medieval Trade", *Indica*, Vol. XXII, No. I, Heras Institute of Indian History and Culture, St. Xavier Institute, Bombay, 1985, p. 14.
16 Mahajan, *Industry, Trade and Commerce during the Peshwa Period*, p. 32.
17 Ibid., p. 33.
18 Jean-Baptiste Travernier, *Travels in India*, Vol. II, ed. by V. Ball, London, 1889.
19 S.N. Sen, *Indian Travels of Thevenot and Careiri*, New Delhi, National Archives of India, 1949, p. 251.
20 Navina Najat Haider, "Diamonds of the Deccan", *Sultans of Deccan India 1500-1700: Opulence and Fantasy,* ed. by Navina Najat Haider and Marika Sardar, Yale University Press, 2015, p. 329.
21 Ibid., p. 326.
22 C.R. Boxer, *The Portuguese Seaborne Empire, 1415-1825*, London, Hutchinson & Co., 1969, p. 39.
23 Ibid., p. 48.
24 M.N. Pearson, *The Portuguese in India*, Munshiram Manoharlal Publishers, Cambridge University Press, 1987, p. 5.
25 K.S. Matthew, *Portuguese Trade With India In The Sixteenth Century*, New Delhi, Manohar Publications, 1983, p. 25. There was apart from this another land route from India which took the direction of the areas of Persian Gulf, Bassorah, Baghdad, Aleppo and then through the regions of the gulf of Alexandretta, Ankara, Constantinople and from there to other parts of Europe.
26 Neils Steensgaard, *The Asian Trade Revolution of the Seventeenth Century: The Decline of Caravan Trade*, Chicago, The University of Chicago Press, 1974, p. 82.
27 Ibid.
28 Matthew, *Portuguese Trade*, p. 61. These were actually naval passes. Merchants and rulers interested in sending commodities to Ormuz, Gujarat and other places were expected to take permit from the Portuguese officials and similarly those who would come to the Malabar Coast also had to have the same sort of permit failing which the ships could be captured by the Portuguese. This practice remained in force for a long time. This sort of permit given by the competent authorities to ship commodities from one port to another was called *cartaz*. Its legal justification was derived out of Portugal's responsibility towards certain international tasks, *viz.*, combating of piracy and the spreading of Christianity according to the papal mandate. See Matthew, *Portuguese Trade*, p. 61.
29 Convoys offering protection to fleet of ships sailing from one port to another that have sought Portuguese armed guard against Arab vessels and other potential rivals.
30 Matthew, *Portuguese Trade*, p. 14. They were actually merchants from Cairo who wielded extraordinary influence between the 12th and 15th centuries on the spice trade. They constituted an "organization or corporation, an

organized body of merchants closely knit together, a collective group of men who associated themselves for the pursuit of a common commercial goal—trade in pepper and spices." State attempts to monopolize trade in Mamluk Egypt led to their decline and some came down to Calicut and settled for trading there.

31 For instance, the Venetians and other foreign merchants in Alexandria and other Muslim ports had enjoyed certain concessions right from 1238 concerning the solution of some cases arising among themselves without the interference of the Sultan.

32 Matthew, *Portuguese Trade*, p. 43.

33 Ibid., p. 209. Nevertheless they were not entirely dislocated and destroyed. A number of merchants from Mecca and the northern parts of the west coast of India who visited the ports on the Malabar Coast, especially Cochin, made use of new routes to evade the Portuguese guards. Similarly the route from Kanjirappilly to Tamil Nadu became important for the transportation of pepper on the backs of bullocks. Thus new trade routes developed on account of depredations of the Portuguese. Though the interference of the Portuguese caused the coastal trade to diminish, they could not interfere with the trade conducted on land routes.

34 Ibid., p. 102. For instance, Mahommad Macary was one of the principal merchants of Calicut who since 1513 helped the Portuguese in their trade at Calicut. The Portuguese officials in Cochin contacted Cherianina Merquar and Mamale Mercar, the great merchants of the locality to store pepper for the ships that arrived in the fleet of Lopo Soares. Mathias and Bragaida Taquatome were the main agents of the Portuguese in Kayamkulam and Quilon who supplied pepper and other commodities to the Portuguese.

35 Ibid., p. 104. This had to be done before the arrival of the ships which could not afford to wait in the ports for more than three to four months since the shipping depended on the monsoon winds. Moreover, the mode of payment partly in cash and partly in copper couldn't help the cultivators and even the Brahmin merchants in any way, as it wasn't possible for them to take copper to Cambay to sell it for a good price.

36 Ibid., p. 104. The harvesting time of pepper and other commodities fell outside the time of the arrival of the Portuguese ships, and therefore the spices had to be purchased in advance by paying cash. But the Portuguese officials weren't *fidalgos* so as to be entrusted with cash in advance.

37 Ibid., pp. 17–18. Chinese as well as Italian sources make mention of the way in which the brokers interfered between the sellers and purchasers and fixed the price. When the transaction was done, the broker got a good sum in the business.

38 Ibid., p. 210.

39 Walter De Gray Birch, ed., *The Commentaries of the Great Afonso Dalboquerque, Second Viceroy of India*, Translated from the Portuguese Edition of 1774, with notes and an Introduction by Walter De Gray Birch, London, The Hakluyt Society, 1875, p. 95.

40 Varadarajan, "Konkan Ports and Medieval Trade", pp. 13–16.

41 Meera Kosambi, "*The Konkan Port and European*: An Urban Perspective", *Medieval Deccan History: Commemoration Volume in Honour of PM Joshi, Popular Prakashan,* Bombay, 1996, p. 108.

42 Philip E. Steinberg, *The Social Construction of the Ocean*, Cambridge, Cambridge University Press, 2001, p. 22.

43 Ruby Maloni, "Portuguese Private Traders on the Coromandel Coast", *Proceedings of the Indian History Congress,* Vol. 73 (2012), pp. 311–17.

44 Sanjay Subrahmanyam, "Piero Strozzi, a Florentine in Portuguese Asia", *The Journal of European Economic History*, Vol. Xvi, No. 3 (1987), pp. 511–26.
45 Kenneth McPherson, *The Indian Ocean: A History of People and the Sea*, Oxford, Oxford University Press, 1996, p. 408.
46 Rila Mukherjee, "Maritime Order and the Eighteenth-Century Indian Ocean", in *Re-searching Transition in Indian History*, ed. by Radhika Seshan and Shraddha Kumbhojkar, Routledge, London, 2018, p. 111.
47 Holden Furber, *Rival Empires of Trade in the Orient, 1600-1800*, Vol. II, London, Oxford University Press, 1976, p. 410.
48 S. Arasaratnam, *Merchants, Companies and Commerce on the Coromandel Coast, 1650-1740*, Cambridge University Press, New Delhi, 1986, p. 114.
49 Tapan Ray Chaudhuri, *Jan Company in Coromandel, 1605-1690: A Study in the Interrelation of European Commerce and Traditional Economies*, The Hague, Antiqbook, 1962, p. 10.
50 Armando Cortesao, ed., *The Sumo Oriental of Tome Pires,* Vol. I, New Delhi, Madras, Asian Educational Studies, 1990, p. 86.
51 William Foster, ed., *The English Factories in India, 1624-29*, Oxford University Press, Oxford, 1909, p. 83.
52 J.E. Heeres, *Corpus Diplomaticum Neerlando Indicum*, Vol. 3, The Hague, Martinus Nijhoff, 1934, pp. 446–50.
53 W.H. Moreland, From Akbar to*: A Study in Indian Economic History*, London, Macmillan and Co. Ltd., 1923, pp. 156–58, where he has earliest mentioned Achyutappa as Malaya, as distinct from his brother Chinanna. See also Sanjay Subrahmanyam, *The Political Economy of Commerce: Southern India 1500-1650*, Cambridge, Cambridge University Press, 2004, p. 302.
54 Vijaya Ramaswamy, *Textiles and Weavers in South India*, New Delhi, Oxford University Press, 2006, p. 145.
55 Joseph J. Brenning, "Chief Merchants and the European Enclave of Seventeenth-Century Coromandel", *Modern Asian Studies*, Vol. 11, No. 3 (Cambridge University Press, 1977), pp. 323–24.
56 Subrahmanyam, *The Political Economy of Commerce*, p. 306.
57 Brenning, "Chief Merchants and the European Enclaves of Seventeenth-Century Coromandel", p. 32.
58 Chaudhuri, *Jan Company in Coromandel, 1605-1690*, p. 51.
59 Brenning, "Chief Merchants and the European Enclaves of Seventeenth-Century Coromandel", p. 326.
60 S. Arasaratnam, "The Dutch East India Company and Its Coromandel Trade 1700-1740", *Bijdragen tot deTaal-, and- en Volkenkunde*, Vol. 123, No. 3 (Leiden, 1967), p. 338.
61 Om Prakash, *The New Cambridge History of India, European Commercial Enterprises in Pre-Colonial India*, Cambridge, Cambridge University Press, 1998, p. 212.
62 Markus Vink, *Encounters on the Opposite Coast: The Dutch East India Company and the Nayaka State of Madurai in the Seventeenth Century*, Leiden, Boston, Brill Publication, 2015, p. 389.
63 M. Manickam, *Trade and Commerce in Pondicherry (A.D. 1701–1793*), Tellicherry, Institute for Research in Social Sciences and Humanities of MESHAR, 2001, p. 22.
64 Lotika Varadarajan, ed., *India in the 17th Century (Social, Economic and Political) Memoirs of Francois Martin* (1670–1690), Vol. 1, part 2, New Delhi, Manohar, 1981, pp. 593–95.
65 K.S. Mathew, *French in India and Indian Nationalism (1700 A.D-1963 A.D),* Vol. I, New Delhi, B.R. Publishing Corporation, 1999, p. 183.

66 J. Frederick Price and K. Rangachari, *The Private Diary of Ananda Ranga Pillai*, Vol. I, Superintendent, Govt. Press, 1904, pp. 42–44.
67 *The Private Diary of Ananda Ranga Pillai Diary*, Vol. VII, p. 245.
68 *The Private Diary of Ananda Ranga Pillai Diary*, Vol. II, p. 10.
69 Manickam, *Trade and Commerce in Pondicherry*, pp. 36–37.
70 Arvind Sinha, *The Politics* of *Trade*, Anglo-French Commerce on the Coromandel Coast, 1763-1793, New Delhi, Manohar Publication, 2002, pp. 90–91.
71 *The Private Diary of Ananda Ranga Pillai Diary*, Vol. III, p. 10.
72 *The Private Diary of Ananda Ranga Pillai Diary*, Vol. I, pp. 4–5, 305.
73 Ibid., p. 224.
74 *The Private Diary of Ananda Ranga Pillai Diary*, Vol. V, pp. 213, 299.
75 *The Private Diary of Ananda Ranga Pillai Diary*, Vol. I, p. 118.
76 Varadarajan, ed., *India in the 17th Century, Memoirs of Francois Martin*, 1670-1690, Vol. 1, Part 1, pp. 302–03.
77 Manickam, *Trade and Commerce in Pondicherry*, pp. 111–12.
78 *The Private Diary of Ananda Ranga Pillai Diary*, Vol. VII, p. 50.
79 *The Private Diary of Ananda Ranga Pillai Diary*, Vol. X, pp. 131, 306.
80 Mathew, *French in India and Indian Nationalism*, p. 31.
81 Sinha, *The Politics* of *Trade*, p. 102.
82 Prakash, *The New Cambridge History of India, European Commercial Enterprise in Pre-Colonial India,* p. 257.
83 Ibid., p. 258.
84 *The Private Diary of Ananda Ranga Pillai Diary*, Vol. I, pp. 104, 108–09.
85 Manickam, *Trade and Commerce in Pondicherry*, p. 143.
86 *The Private Diary of Ananda Ranga Pillai Diary*, Vol. III, pp. 296, 306.
87 Ibid., Vol. I, pp. 65, 104.
88 Manickam, *Trade and Commerce in Pondicherry*, p. 157.
89 Kautilya, *The Arthashastra*, ed. by L.N. Rangarajan, Penguin Classic India, 14 October 2000.
90 Vijay K. Seth, *The Story of Indian Manufacturing: Encounters with the Mughal and British Empires* (1498–1947), Springer, 29 September 2017, p. 42.
91 S.V. Puntambekar, "A Royal Edict, Translation of the Ajnapatra Marathi" (Reprinted from the *Journal of Indian History*, Vol. VIII, parts I and II), Chennai, 1929, p. 31.
92 A.R. Kulkarni, *Maharashtra in the Age of Shivaji*, Diamond Publications, Poona, 1969, p. 252.
93 N.G. Chapekar, "Peshwaichya Sawalit", Bharat Itihas Samsodhan Mandal Publication, Publication no. 34, Poona, 1937, pp. 2–10.
94 Mahajan, *Industry, Trade and Commerce during the Peshwa Period*, p. 89.
95 Ibid.
96 Ibid., p. 91.
97 Ibid.
98 Ibid.
99 Ibid.
100 Ibid.
101 Ibid., p. 92.
102 Chapekar, "Peshwaichya Sawalit", p. 39.
103 G.C. Vad and Kashinath Balkrishna Marathe, eds., *Selection from the Peshwa's Diaries*, Vol. VIII, Swai Madhavrav Peshwa, Deccan Vernacular Translation Society, Poona, 1911, p. 194.
104 Chapekar, "Peshwaichya Sawalit", p. 39.
105 Mahajan, *Industry, Trade and Commerce during the Peshwa Period*, p. 92.

106 Chapekar, "Peshwaichya Sawalit", p. 120.
107 G.C. Vad and D.B. Parasnis, eds., *Selection from the Satara Raja's and Peshwa Diaries,* Vol. II, Deccan Vernacular Translation Society, Poona, 1906, p. 12.
108 Mahajan, *Industry, Trade and Commerce during the Peshwa Period*, p. 93.
109 Ibid.
110 Ibid.

Bibliography

Original Sources Unpublished Documents

I) English

A) Bombay Secretariat (Mumbai)

1) The Secret and Political Department Diary ---Volume 18 A (1777 dup.)
2) The Secret and Political Department Diary ---Volume 19 (1778 dup.)
3) The Secret and Political Department Diary ---Volume 19 A (1778 dup.)
4) The Secret and Political Department Diary ---Volume 19 B (1778 dup.)
5) The Secret and Political Department Diary ---Volume 20 (1779)

B) India Office Records (Oriental and India Office Collections, British Library, London) (Duplicate Microfilms)

I/1/1-17 The French in India (Series Volume 1 to 17) (East India Company Records) 1664–1820.

1. I/1/1: 1664–1810 Miscellaneous Correspondence. Etc.
2. I/1/2: 1749–1759 Extracts from the East India Company's advices on the conduct of the French on the Coromandel Coast.
3. I/1/3: 1754–1755 Correspondence on the French in India.
4. I/1/4: 1752–1779 Copies of miscellaneous papers on the French in India.
5. I/1/5: 1771–1775 Proceedings of the Madras Government of French complaints about interruption to their commerce.
6. I/1/6: 1772–1797 Claims of the French, Dutch and Danes.
7. I/1/7: 1773–1776 Disputes with the French – I.
8. I/1/8: 1783–1785 Disputes with the French – II.
9. I/1/9: 1783–1786 Disputes with the French – III.
10. I/1/10 1884–1786 Disputes with the French – IV.
11. I/1/11: 1785–1788, Political negotiations between the English, the French, the Nizam of Hyderabad and Tipu Sultan of Mysore.
12. I/1/!2: 1782–1813 Miscellaneous letters and papers – I.
13. I/1/13: 1776–1804 Miscellaneous letters and papers – II.
14. I/1/14: 1810, Correspondence on the expedition against the French islands.
15. I/1/15: Miscellaneous, extracts on Labourdonnais from the Pondicherry archives.
16. I/1/16:

C) Orme Manuscripts

1) Volume 3.
2) Volume 14.
3) Volume 55

II) French

A) Archives du Ministere des Affaires Étrangères. (AMAE) (Unpublished Documents).

1) Fonds Angleterre – Volume 18
2) Fonds Asie - Volumes 4, 6, 7, 11, 16, 20.
3) Fonds Perse - Volume 5.

These are Memoires and Documents which are either copies or extracts (1668-1815).

Fonds Angleterre :

Vol.18 : -f.138.

Fonds Asie :

Vol.4:- f.4,6,7,11,16,20,165,166,167,167v-168,169-169v,173,174,174v,175,177v-178,180-180v,180-181v,185-191,186v,195-196,197-198,198v-202,204-204v,206-208.

Vol.6:- f.279.

Vol.7:- .f.,123-123v.

Vol.11 : - f.272v,304-310v.

Vol.16 : - f.323-326,354-355.

Vol.20 : -f.287-288v.

Fonds Perse ;

Vol.5 : - f.92-96,94v.

B) Archives du Ministere des Colonies. (Primary Documents)

1) Inde (Miscellaneous Documents which are either copies of extracts (1668-1817) – Cartons : 522, 536.

C) Archives Nationales.

1) Serie B – Volume 147 (Dispatches and Orders of the King).
2) Serie C² - Inde (General Correspondence) – 1666-92. These are letters written mostly by the Governors of Pondicherry to the Controller General, The Minister of Navy and the Minister for Foreign Affairs. There are also letters written by the Governors to the various Indian Princes and to the Heads of the French Comptoirs and vice-versa. The majority of these letters are original.

(A) 1st Series: Volumes 62,83,84,86,89,90,92,93,94,97,98,100,102,118,120,123,124,126,127,128,138,139, 140,141,142,144,146,148,152,153,155,156,157,160,162,163,164,166,167,169,172, 174,179,180,184,185.

(B) 2nd Series : Volumes 234 and 265.

SERIE B – VOL.147 (DISPATCHES AND ORDERS OF THE KING)

1. AN,B147,1772,f.1v-2v

2. AN,B147,1772,f.3
3. AN,B147,1772,f.5v-6
4. AN,B147,1777,f.222 & 229

SERIES--AN,C^2,62.

1. AN,$C^2$62,f.4-6
2. AN,$C^2$62,f.125
3. AN,$C^2$62,f.166
4. AN,$C^2$62,f.316-317
5. AN,$C^2$62,f.316v
6. AN,$C^2$62,f.330

SERIES—AN,C^2,83.

1. AN,$C^2$83,f.16v
2. AN,$C^2$83,f.144-149
3. AN,$C^2$83,f.153-157
4. AN,$C^2$83,f.153v-157
5. AN,$C^2$83,f.157-161
6. AN,$C^2$83,f.162-167
7. AN,$C^2$83,f.162-170
8. AN,$C^2$83,f.172v-175

SERIES – AN,$C^2$84.

1. AN,$C^2$84,f.138-151

SERIES – AN,$C^2$86.

1. AN. AN,$C^2$86,f.17v
2. AN,$C^2$86,f.78
3. AN,$C^2$86,f.80v-82
4. AN,$C^2$86,f.104
5. AN,$C^2$86,f.107v-108
6. AN,$C^2$86,f.108
7. AN,$C^2$86,f.128
8. AN,$C^2$86,f.135v-136
9. AN,$C^2$86,f.150
10. AN,$C^2$86,f.150v
11. AN,$C^2$86,f.184,186,187,188,199
12. AN,$C^2$86,f.277

SERIES – AN,$C^2$89.

1. AN,$C^2$89,f.234v-235
2. AN,$C^2$89,f.281

3. AN,C^{2}89,f.281-282v
4. AN,C^{2}89,f.299v-300

SERIES – AN,C^{2}90.

1. AN,C^{2}90,f.188v-189
2. AN,C^{2}90,f.201v-202
3. AN,C^{2}90,f.202

SERIES – AN,C^{2}92.

1. AN,C^{2}92,f.178-180

SERIES – AN,C^{2}93.

1. AN,C^{2}93,f.16
2. AN,C^{2}93,f.24-24v

SERIES – AN,C^{2}94.

1. AN,C^{2}94,f.66v-67

SERIES – AN,C^{2}97.

1. AN,C^{2}97,f.20-20v
2. AN,C^{2}97,f.84
3. AN,C^{2}97,f.88
4. AN,C^{2}97,f.261v
5. AN,C^{2}97,f.274v

SERIES – AN,C^{2}98.

1. AN,C^{2}98,f.6v
2. AN,C^{2}98,f.20v

SERIES – AN,C^{2}100.

1. AN,C^{2}100,f.102
2. AN,C^{2}100,f.169-171

SERIES – AN,C^{2}102.

1. AN,C^{2}102,f.252-257
2. AN,C^{2}102,f.260v
3. AN,C^{2}102,f.263v-264
4. AN,C^{2}102,f.266

5. AN,$C^2$102,f.293v-294
6. AN,$C^2$102,f.307

SERIES – AN,$C^2$118.

1. AN,$C^2$118,f.44v-48
2. AN,$C^2$118,f.254v-255
3. AN,$C^2$118,f.269-270

SERIES – AN,$C^2$120.

1. AN,$C^2$120,f.8v
2. AN,$C^2$120,f.8v-9

SERIES – AN,$C^2$123.

1. AN,$C^2$123,f.7-7v
2. AN,$C^2$123,f.7v-12
3. AN,$C^2$123,f.41-42
4. AN,$C^2$123,f.106v-107

SERIES – AN,$C^2$124.

1. AN,$C^2$124,f.11

SERIES – AN,$C^2$126.

1. AN,$C^2$126,f.218
2. AN,$C^2$126,f.228v-229v
3. AN,$C^2$126,f.263
4. AN,$C^2$126,f.365v-367

SERIES – AN,$C^2$127.

1. AN,$C^2$127,f.21

SERIES – AN,$C^2$128.

1. AN,$C^2$128,f.3v-9
2. AN,$C^2$128,f.48v-49v
3. AN,$C^2$128,f.66
4. AN,$C^2$128,f.209-212
5. AN,$C^2$128,f.238-239
6. AN,$C^2$128,f.261-261v

SERIES – AN,$C^2$138.

1. AN,$C^2$138,f.85

2. AN,$C^2$138,f.152-154v

SERIES – AN,$C^2$139.

1. AN,$C^2$139,f.57v
2. AN,$C^2$139,f.97
3. AN,$C^2$139,f.322-322v

SERIES – AN,$C^2$140.

1. AN,$C^2$140,f.103-104

SERIES – AN,$C^2$141.

1. AN,$C^2$141,f.46v
2. AN,$C^2$141,f.53-64

SERIES – AN,$C^2$142.

1. AN,$C^2$142,f.13-14

SERIES – AN,$C^2$146.

1. AN,$C^2$146,f.94

SERIES – AN,$C^2$148.

1. AN,$C^2$148,f.41-41v
2. AN,$C^2$148,f.164
3. AN,$C^2$148,f.234v-235
4. AN,$C^2$148,f.170-172

SERIES – AN,$C^2$152.

1. AN,$C^2$152,f.305

SERIES – AN,$C^2$155.

1. AN,$C^2$155,f.95-95v
2. AN,$C^2$155,f.110-113v
3. AN,$C^2$155,f.114v
4, AN,$C^2$155,f.115
5. AN,$C^2$155,f.118
6. AN,$C^2$155,f.147v-148,catalogue,I,p.100
7. AN,$C^2$155,f.157-161
8. AN,$C^2$155,f.265
9. AN,$C^2$155,f.292

SERIES – AN,$C^2$156.

1. AN,$C^2$156,f.20-20v
2. AN,$C^2$156,f.55-56v
3. AN,$C^2$156,f.87-92

SERIES – AN,$C^2$157.

1. AN,$C^2$157,f.73v

SERIES – AN,$C^2$160.

1. AN,$C^2$160,f.28-29
2. AN,$C^2$160,f.28v

SERIES – AN,$C^2$162.

1. AN,$C^2$162,f.126-128v
2. AN,$C^2$162,f.156-164v
3. AN,$C^2$162,f.157
4. AN,$C^2$162,f.157v
5. AN,$C^2$162,f.164

SERIES – AN,$C^2$163.

1. AN,$C^2$163,f.55
2. AN,$C^2$163,f.55-58v
3. AN,$C^2$163,f.59v-60
4. AN,$C^2$163,f.62v-63
5. AN,$C^2$163,f.64
6. AN,$C^2$163,f.86
7. AN,$C^2$163,f.86-86v
8. AN,$C^2$163,f.94
9. AN,$C^2$163,f.94v-95
10. AN,$C^2$163,f.102
11. AN,$C^2$163,f.129
12. AN,$C^2$163,f.131
13. AN,$C^2$163,f.137-137v
14. AN,$C^2$163,f.140-141
15. AN,$C^2$163,f.142-143
16. AN,$C^2$163,f.145v-416v
17. AN,$C^2$163,f.146v

SERIES – AN,$C^2$164.

1. AN,$C^2$164,pp.1-8,of the memoir

SERIES – AN,$C^2$165.

1. AN,$C^2$165,f.149

SERIES – AN,C^{2}166.

1. AN,C^{2}166,f.9v-10
2. AN,C^{2}166,f.12
3. AN,C^{2}166,f.51v-52
4. AN,C^{2}166,f.52v
5. AN,C^{2}166,f.63-76

SERIES – AN,C^{2}167.

1. AN,C^{2}167,f.107-108v

SERIES – AN,C^{2}169.

1. AN,C^{2}167,f.5-5v
2. AN,C^{2}167,f.17v-18,19
3. AN,C^{2}167,f.47-48
4. AN,C^{2}167,f.95-96v
5. AN,C^{2}167,f.100,102,106,108,111
6. AN,C^{2}167,f.102v-104v
7. AN,C^{2}167,f.115-118v
8. AN,C^{2}167,f.117v-118
9. AN,C^{2}167,f.121-122
10. AN,C^{2}167,f.122v-123
11. AN,C^{2}167,f.129-129v
12. AN,C^{2}167,f.129v-131v
13. AN,C^{2}167,f.149v
14. AN,C^{2}167,f.150-150v
15. AN,C^{2}167,f.177

SERIES – AN,C^{2}172.

1. AN,C^{2}172,f.22v
2. AN,C^{2}172,f.26v-27
3. AN,C^{2}172,f.34
4. AN,C^{2}172,f.142v,143-143v
5. AN,C^{2}172,f.153v
6. AN,C^{2}172,f.159
7. AN,C^{2}172,f.162v
8. AN,C^{2}172,f.164,165
9. AN,C^{2}172,f.169-169v
10. AN,C^{2}172,f.169v-170v
11. AN,C^{2}172,f.171
12. AN,C^{2}172,f.181-181v

SERIES – AN,C^{2}174.

1. AN,C^{2}174,f.24v-25

SERIES – AN,$C^2$179.

1. AN,$C^2$179,f.19
2. AN,$C^2$179,f.22
3. AN,$C^2$179,f.35v-36
4. AN,$C^2$179,f.61-62
5. AN,$C^2$179,f.70-70v
6. AN,$C^2$179,f.72
7. AN,$C^2$179,f.195-196v
8. AN,$C^2$179,f.199v-201v
9. AN,$C^2$179,f.216-217
10. AN,$C^2$179,f.225-226v
11. AN,$C^2$179,f.242
12. AN,$C^2$179,f.248v
13. AN,$C^2$179,f.253
14. AN,$C^2$179,f.253v-254
15. AN,$C^2$179,f.255-256
16. AN,$C^2$179,f.257-257v
17. AN,$C^2$179,f.276
18. AN,$C^2$179,f.280v

SERIES – AN,$C^2$180.

1. AN,$C^2$180,f.06

SERIES – AN,$C^2$184.

1. AN,$C^2$184,f.142

SERIES – AN,$C^2$185.

1. AN,$C^2$185,f.141

SERIES – AN,$C^2$265.

1. AN,$C^2$265,f.62-64

D) Archives de Versailles.

1) Volume .E. 3748 (Dupleix's letters to Bussy, 16th January 1751-19th October 1753)
2) Volume .E. 3750 (Dupleix's letters to Law and Bernier, January 1752 – 16th June 1752)
3) Volume .E. 3754 (Dupleix's letters to the army of Golkonda, 30th May 1752 – 28th February 1754)

I) Vol .E.3748.

1. AV,E3748,f.103
2. AV,E3748,f.116
3. AV,E3748,f.121
4. AV,E3748,f.122
5. AV,E3748,f.124

II) Vol .E.3750.

1. AV,E3750,f.46
2. AV,E3750,f.72v

III) Vol .E.3754.

1. AV,E3754,f.5v
2. AV,E3754,f.10v
3. AV,E3754,f.22-22v
4. AV,E3754,f.23-23v
5. AV,E3754,f.26v-29
6. AV,E3754,f.33v-37
7. AV,E3754,f.52v
8. AV,E3754,f.52v-53v
9. AV,E3754,f.20v
10. AV,E3754,f.54

E) Bibliotheque Nationale.

1) Nouvelles Acquisitions Francaises : Volume 8931 (Fonds Ariel-Dupleix)
2) Nouvelles Acquisitions Francaises : Volume 9156-57 (Duplexeslettres to the officiers of Karnataka army)
3) Nouvelles Acquisitions Francaises : Volume 9158 – 59 (Lettres from the officiers of the Deccan army)
4) Nouvelles Acquisitions Francaises : Volume 9358 – 61 (India in the 18th century : 1750-1762)

Bibliotheque Nationale : Nouvelles Acquisitions Francaises. Vol .8931

(Fonds Ariel- Dupleix)

Series BN,NAF,9156.(Dupleix's letters to the officers of the Karnatak army)

1. BN,NAF,9156,f.35-36v
2. BN,NAF,9156,f.108v
3. BN,NAF,9156,f.110v

Series BN,NAF,9157. .(Dupleix's letters to the officers of the Karnatak army)

1. BN,NAF,9157,f.409

Series BN,NAF,9158.(Letters from the officers of the Deccan army)

1. BN,NAF,9158,f.7-7v
2. BN,NAF,9158,f.13v
3. BN,NAF,9158,f.15v
4. BN,NAF,9158,f.39-40v
5. BN,NAF,9158,f.41-43
6. BN,NAF,9158,f.44-44v
7. BN,NAF,9158,f.48
8. BN,NAF,9158,f.49
9. BN,NAF,9158,f.91-91v
10. BN,NAF,9158,f.127
11. BN,NAF,9158,f.146
12. BN,NAF,9158,f.161
13. BN,NAF,9158,f.162v-63
14. BN,NAF,9158,f.164
15. BN,NAF,9158,f.174
16. BN,NAF,9158,f.204-204v
17. BN,NAF,9158,f.206v
18. BN,NAF,9158,f.214

Series BN,NAF,9159. (Letters from the officers of the Deccan army)

1. BN,NAF,9159,f.137v
2. BN,NAF,9159,f.137,138,139
3. BN,NAF,9159,f.139v
4. BN,NAF,9159,f.140
5. BN,NAF,9159,f.141-141v
6. BN,NAF,9159,f.144
7. BN,NAF,9159,f.145-146
8. BN,NAF,9159,f.148v,149v
9. BN,NAF,9159,f.158v-159
10. BN,NAF,9159,f.280
11. BN,NAF,9159,f.283
12. BN,NAF,9159,f.286
13. BN,NAF,9159,f.290
14. BN,NAF,9159,f.303v-304
15. BN,NAF,9159,f.304
16. BN,NAF,9159,f.370

Séries BN, NAF,9161.

1. BN, NAF,9161, f.150-161(11 pages)

Series BN,NAF,9356.

1. BN,NAF,9356,f.128
2. BN,NAF,9356,f.133v

Series BN,NAF,9357.

1.BN,NAF,9357,f.405.

Series BN,NAF,9358.(India in the 18th Century 1750-1762)

1.BN,NAF,9358,f.10
2.BN,NAF,9358,f.74
3.BN,NAF,9358,f.77
4.BN,NAF,9358,f.78

Series BN,NAF,9359. (India in the 18th Century 1750-1762)

1. BN,NAF,9359,f.19-22
2. BN,NAF,9359,f.28v
3. BN,NAF,9359,f.34-34v
4. BN,NAF,9359,f.37
5. BN,NAF,9359,f.37v-40
6. BN,NAF,9359,f.43,45,46
7. BN,NAF,9359,f.46v
8. BN,NAF,9359,f.50
9. BN,NAF,9359,f.57v
10. BN,NAF,9359,f.60v
11. BN,NAF,9359,f.61
12. BN,NAF,9359,f.80v
13. BN,NAF,9359,f.332

Series BN,NAF,9360. (India in the 18th Century 1750-1762)

1. BN,NAF,9360,f.16
2. BN,NAF,9360,f.94v
3. BN,NAF,9360,f.95
4. BN,NAF,9360,f.118v
5. BN,NAF,9360,f.172v
6. BN,NAF,9360,f.183v
7. BN,NAF,9360,f.207
8. BN,NAF,9360,f.237v-238
9. BN,NAF,9360,f.247
10. BN,NAF,9360,f.256v-257
11. BN,NAF,9360,f.289v
12. BN,NAF,9360,f.300v-302v
13. BN,NAF,9360,f.303,304

14. BN,NAF,9360,f.304-305v
15. BN,NAF,9360,f.310,311
16. BN,NAF,9360,f.311-312v
17. BN,NAF,9360,f.313,314,315
18. BN,NAF,9360,f.315v-322
19. BN,NAF,9360,f.324v-330
20. BN,NAF,9360,f.330v
21. BN,NAF,9360,f.333v

SERIES BN,NAF,9361. (INDIA IN THE 18TH CENTURY 1750-1762)

1.BN,NAF,9361,f.143,144,145,146

Published Documents

English

Dodwell, H., ed., *Calendar of the Madras Dispatches,(1744- 55)*, Madras Government Press, Madras, 1920.

Forrest, G.W., ed., *Selections from the Letters, Dispatches and other State Papers Preserved in the Bombay Secretariat, Maratha Series*, Government Central Press, Bombay, 1885.

Foster, W., ed., *English Factories in India, 1668-69*, Oxford Clarendon Press, London, 1927.

Gazetteer of the Bombay Presidency, Vol. XI-B, Kolaba and Janjira, Bombay, Government of Bombay, 1926.

Hatalkar, V.G., ed., *French Records*, Vol. I to IX, Maharashtra State Board for Literature and Culture, Bombay, 1978–1985.

Irvine, W., ed., *Storio de Mogor, Niccolao Manucci*, Vol. II, John Murray, London, 1907.

Martin, M., ed., *The Despatches, Minutes and Correspondence of the Marquess of Wellesly*, H. Ellen, London, 1837.

Paranjape, B.G., ed., *English Records on Shivaji*, edited by D.V.Kale, Shiva Charitra Karyalaya, Poona, 1931.

Price, F., Rangachari, K., eds.,*The Private Diary of Ananda Ranga Pillai*, Vol. I–XII, New Delhi, Asian Education Services, Reprint 1985.

Records of Fort St. George, *Diary and Consultation Book 1687-93*, Superintendent, Government Press, Chennai, 1913.

Records of Fort St. George, *French Correspondence*, Madras Government Press, Madras, 1914.

Sardesai, G.S., Sarkar, J.N., eds., *Poona Residency Correspondence*, Vol. I–VII, IX, edited by Dr. R.Singh, Government Central Press, Bombay, 1939–1951.

The Calendar of Persian Correspondence, Vol. V, VII, Calcutta, Imperial Record Department, 1930–1940.

The Gazetteer of the Bombay City and Island, Vol. I, Compiled under the Government of India Orders, Bombay, Times Press, 1909.

Thevenot, J.de, *Indian Travels of Thevenot and Careri*, edited by S.Sen, New Delhi, National Archives of India, 1949.

Varadarajan, L., ed., *India in the 17th Century, Social, Economic and Political (Memoirs of Francois Martin)*, Vol. I (Part I & II), Vol. II (Part I & II), New Delhi, Manohar, 1981.

Yule, H., *The Diary of William Hedges*, Vol. II, London, Hakluyt Society, 1888.

Dutch

Chijs, J.A.vander et al. ed., *Dagh-register Gehouden int Casteel Batavia Vant Passerende Daer Ter Plaetseals Als Over Geheel Nederlandts-India, 1624-1682*, 31 Vols, Batavia and the Hague, 1887–1928.

Kol. Archives. (Hague) Vols. 1122, 1123,1124, 1132, 1133, 1136,1137, 1142, 1143, 1144,1145, 1146, 1152, 1156, 1159, 1160.

Letter Books (Batavia) Vols. 1660-1, 16661-2, 1663-4, 1664-5, 1665-6, 1668-9, 1670-1, 1671-2, 1672-3, 1673-4, 1674-5, 1675-6, 1676-7, 1677-8, 1680-1, 1681-2,1682-3.

Colenbrander, H.T. ed., *Jan Pietersz Coen Bescheiden Omtrent Zijn Verblijf in Indiee*, 5 vols, the Hague, M. Nijhoff, 1919–1923.

Coolhaas, W.Ph. ed., *Generale Missiven van Gouverneurs-Generaal en Raden aan Heren XVII der Verenigde Oostindische Compagnie*, 6 vols, Rijks Geschiedkundige Publicatien, Grote Series nrs. 104, 112, 125, 134, 150, 164 and 193, the Hague, Martinus Nijhoff, 1960–1984.

Dam, P.V., *Beschryvinge van de Cost- Indische Compagnie, 1693-1701*, 7 vols, the Hague, M. Nijhoff, 1927–1954.

Heeres, J.E., ed. *Corpus Diplomaticum Neerlando-Indicum*, 5 vols, The Hague, 1907–1938.

Nationaal archief (Den Haag): Vereenigde Oostindische Compagnie archief: - NL-HaNA, VOC 1.04.02. inv. no. 8373. - NL-HaNA, VOC 1.04.02 inv. no 8919

Reconstruction of the Archives of the VOC Office, Correspondence with Indigenous, NA, 1.04.02, 1055, 1156,1227,1449, 24255Coromandel.

Reconstruction of the Archives of the VOC Office, Dagregisters en registers op dagregisters Algemene dagregisters, NA 1.04.02, 1321, Vengurla.

Portuguese

Albuquerque, A.de, Cartas de Affonso de Albuquerque, Lisboa, 1884-1935 Barros, Joao de, *Da Asia de…, dos feitos que os Portuguese fizeram no descubrimento e conquista dos mares e terras do Oriente[1], Decadas I to IV*, edited by Livraria Sam Carlos, Lisbon, 1974.

Bocarro, A., *Decada 13 da Historia da India*, Tomo, I and II, Academia Real das Sciencias de Lisboa, Lisboa, 1876.

Couto, D.do, *Da Asia de…, dos feitos que os Portuguese fizeram no descubrimento e conquista dos mares e terras do Oriente1, Decadas IV-XII*, Imprensa Nacional-Casa da Moeda, Lisboa, 1974.

Rivara, H.H., *Cunha, Arquivo Portuguese Oriental*, 6 vols. in 9 parts, Archivo Portuguez Oriental, Nova Goa, 1857–1876.

French

Délibérations du Conseil Supérieur de Pondichéry, Vol. III, Societie De L'Histoire De L'Inde Française, Pondicherry, 1914.

Gaudart, E., ed., *Catalogue des Manuscrits des Anciennes Archives de l'Inde française*, Tomes I (1922), II, Pondichéry, Bibliothèque colonial, Leroux, 1927.
La Politique de Dupleix d'après sa lettre a Saunders de 18 Février 1752 et son Mémoire du 16 Octobre 1753, Paris, 1927.
Lettres Edifiantes et Curieuses, écrites des Missions Etrangeres, Tome VIII, Lyon, 1829.
Martineau, A., ed.,*Lettres et Conventions des Gouverneurs de Pondichéry avec différents Princes Hindous (1666-1793)*, Pondichéry, 1911–1914.
Martineau, A., *Les Origines de Mahe de Malabar*, Paris, 1917.
Martineau, A., *Correspondance du Conseil Supérieur de Pondichéry et de la Compagnie*, edited by A.Martineau, Tomes III, IV,V, VI (2nd ed.), Pondicherry, Imprimerie Moderne.
Martineau, A., ed., *Le Journal de Bussy*, Paris, 1932.
Martineau, A., ed., *Mémoires de François Martin*, Vol. I, II, III, Paris, 1931.
Martineau, A., ed., *Jean Law de Lauristan, Mémoire sur quelques affaires de l'Empire Mongol, 1756-1761*, Forgotten Books, Paris, 1913.
Mémoire a Consulter et Consultation, pour le sieur de Bussy avec des Lettres de Bussy, Lally, etc., Paris, M. DCCC. LXVI, n.d.
Mémoire pour le Marquis de Bussy, Maréchal...contre les Syndics et Directeurs de la Compagnie de indes, Mémoire pour les Syndics cotre le Marquis de Bussy, Paris, M. DCC LXVII, n.d.
Sources de l'Historie de l'Asie et de l'Océanie dans les Archives et Bibliothèque françaises I & II, Bibliothèque Nationale, K.G. Saur, 1981.

Marathi

Anant, K., *Sabhasad Bakhar*,S.N.Joshi, ed., Oriental Book Agency, Poona, 1960.
Garge, S.M., ed., *British Riyasat*, Vols. I & II, Mumbai, Popular, 1988.
Garge, S.M., ed., *Marathi Riyasat*, Vols I & VIII, Mumbai, Popular, 1988.
Garge, S.M., ed., *Musalman Riyasat*, Vols. I & II, Mumbai, Popular, 1988.
Gopal, V., ed., *Modi Documents in the T. M. S. S. M. Library*, Tanjavur, Tanjavur Maharajah Serfoji's Saraswati Mahal Library, 1999.
Gopalan, S., *Bhonsle Vamsa Charitra, Marathi Historical Inscriptions in the Big Temple*, 2nd edition, Tanjavur, Thanjavur Saraswati Mahal Library, 1980.
Joshi, S.N., ed., *Krishnaji Anant Sabhasad, Virachita Chhatrapati Shri Shivajiraje Yanchi Bakhar*, Pune, Chitrashala Prakashn, 1960.
Kelkar, Y.N., *Vasaichi Mohim*, Diamond Publications, Poona, 1939.
Khare, G.H.,ed., *Aitihasik Sankirna Nibandha*, Vol. 10, Bharat Itihas Samshodhan Mandal, Pune, BISM, 1677.
Khare, G.H., ed., *Shjyacharitra Sahitya XIII*, Bharat Itihas Samshodhan Mandal, Poona, BISM, 1965.
Khare, V.V., ed., *Aitihasik Lekhasangraha*, Vol. VI, VII, Bharat Itihas Samshodhan Mandal, Pune, 1901–1926.
Mawji, P.V., and Parasnis, D.B., eds., *Kaifiyat, Yadi, Patern, etc.*, Sardesai, G.S., Kale, Y.M., Wakaskar, V.S., eds., Poona, Kavyetihasa Sangraha, 1930.
Parasnis, D.B., ed., *Pararashtranchya Darabaratil Marathyanche Vakil*, Bharat Itihas Samshodhan Mandal, Poona, 1923.
Parasnis, D.B., *Aitihasik Tipane, Part IV*,Itihas Sangraha, Pune, 1908.

Parasnis, B., ed., *Chinapattankadil Rajakarane*, Bombay, 1917.
Pisurlekar, P.S., ed., *Marathayanchya Itihasachi Sadahane*, (Portuguese Daftar Khand) Vols. I–III, Bharat Itihas Sanshodhak Mandal, Bombay, 1974.
Potdar, M., eds., *English East India Companicha Peshwe Darabarashi Pharshi Patravyavahar*, Poona, 1923.
Purandare, K.V., ed., *Purandhare Daftar*, Vol. I, Poona, 1929.
Rajawade, V.K., ed., *Marathayanchya Itihasachi Sadahane*, Vols. I, III, VI, X, XII, Pune, 1918.
Sardesai, G.S., Kulkarni, K.P., and Kale, ed., *Aitihasik Patravyavahar*, Poona, 1933.
Sardesai, G.S., ed., *Mhadji Shinde Hyanchi Kagad patre*, Gwalior, 1937.
Sardesai, G.S., ed., *Peshwa Daftar*, Vol. 24, 25, 28, 34, Bombay, 1930–1934.
Sardesai, G.S., ed., *Marathiyanchya Itihasachi Sadhane, Portuguese Daftar*, Vol. II, Bombay, 1974.
Vaidya, S.L., ed., *Vaidya Daftar*, Vol. 4, Poona, 1949.
Wad, G.C., Parasnis, eds., *Selections from the Satara Rajas and the Peshwas' Diaries*, Vol. I; Vol. V, Joshi, B.P., ed., Vol. VI, Marathe, Poona, Deccan Vernacular Translation Society, 1906–11.

Secondary Sources

Ahmed, A., *Indo-Portuguese Trade in Seventeenth Century (1600–1663)*, New Delhi, Gian Publishing House, 1991.
Aiyangar, K., *Ancient India*, Madras, Luzac & Company, 1911.
Alavi, S., *The Eighteenth Century in India*, New Delhi, Oxford University Press, 2002.
Alexander, K., Nairne, R., *History of Konkan*, New Delhi, Asian Educational Service, 1988.
Ali, M.A., *The Apparatus of Empire: Awards of Ranks, Offices and Titles to the Mughal Nobility (1574–1658)*, New Delhi, Oxford University Press, 1985.
Ali, M.A., *The Mughal Nobility under Aurangzeb*, New Delhi, Oxford University Press, 1997.
Altekar, A.S., *Rashtrakutas and their Times*, Poona, Poona Oriental Book Agency, 1934.
Anderson, P., *The English in the Western India*, Bombay, Smith and Taylor, 1854.
Appasamy, J., *Tanjavur Painting of the Maratha Period*, Vol. 1, New Delhi, Abhinav Publications, 1980.
Apte, B.K., *A History of the Maratha Navy and Merchantship*, Bombay, State Board for Literature and Culture, Government of Maharastra, 1973.
Arasaratnam, S., *Maritime India in the Seventeenth Century*, New Delhi, Oxford, 1994.
Arasaratnam, S., *Merchants, Companies and Commerce on the Coromandel Coast 1650–1740*, New Delhi, Oxford, 1986.
Baldeus, P., *A True and Exact Description of the Most Celebrated East-India Coasts of Malabar and Coromandel, and Also of the Isle of Ceylon*, Vol. 3, (Amsterdam, 1672) reprinted, New Delhi, AES, 2000.
Banaji, D.R., *Bombay and the Siddis*, Bombay, University of Bombay, 1932.
Banerji, R.N., *Economic Progress of the East India Company on the Coromandel Coast (1702–1746)*, Nagpur, Nagpur University, 1974.

Bernier, F., *Travels in the Mogul Empire A.D. 1656–1668*, edited by I.Brock, translated by A.Constable (Reprint Westminster 1891 edition), New Delhi, Asian Education Services, 1996.
Betham, R.M., *Marathas and Dekhani Musalmans*, Calcutta, Superintendent of Government Printing, 1908.
Bhandarkar, R.G., *Early History of the Deccan*, Calcutta, Bharatiya Publishing House, 1928.
Birch, G.W.de, *The Commentaries of the Great Afonso Dalboquerque, Second Viceroy of India: Volume I–IV*, London, Hakluyt Society, 2010.
Bowring, L.B., *Haider Ali and Tipu Sultan and the Struggle with the Musalman Powers of the South*, edited by W.W.Hunter (Ruler of India Series, Reprint Oxford 1893 edn.), New Delhi, Asian Education Services, 1998.
Boxer, C.R., *The Dutch Seaborne Empire, 1600–1800*, London, Hutchinson, 1965.
Boxer, C.R., *The Great Ship of Amacon: Annals of Macao and the Old Japan Trade 1555-1640*, Lisbon, Centro de Estudos Historicos Ultramarinos, 1959.
Boxer, C.R., *The Portuguese Seaborne Empire, 1415-1825*, London, Hutchinson, 1961.
Braudel, F., *Civilization and Capitalism 15th–18th Centuries: The Perspective of the World*, Vol. III, Britain, Harper & Row, 1984.
Broughton, T.D., *Letters Written in a Maratha Camp* (Reprint Westminster 1892 edn.), New Delhi, Asian Education Services, 1995.
Brown, C.P., *Memoirs of Hyder and Tipoo, Rulers of Seringapatam* (Reprint 1849 edn.), New Delhi, Asian Education Services, 1988.
Brown, W., *The History of Christian Missions of the Sixteenth, Seventeenth, Eighteenth and Nineteenth Centuries*, London, T. Baker, 1863.
Bruce, J., *Annals of the Honourable East India Company*, 3 vols, London, Black, Parry and Kingsbury, 1810.
Buchanan, F., *A Journey through Mysore, Canara and Malabar*, Vol III, Cambridge, Cambridge University Press, 1807.
Campos, J.J.A., *History of the Portuguese in Bengal*, Patna, Janaki Prakashan, 1979.
Carre, A., *The Travels of the Abbe Carre in India and the Near East from 1672 to 1674*, 3 Vols, translated & edited by C.Fawcett, New Delhi, Asian Education Services, 1992.
Carton, A., *Mixed-Race and Modernity in Colonial India: Changing Concepts of Hybridity Across Empires*, London, Routledge, 2012.
Champalakshmi, R, *Religion, Tradition and Ideology –Pre- colonial South India*, India, Oxford University Press, 2011.
Chandra, S., *Medieval India: From Sultanate to the Mughals, Part Two, Mughal Empire (1526–1748)* (Revised edn.), New Delhi, Har Anand Publications Pvt. Ltd., 2007.
Chatterjee, A., *Bengal in the Reign of Aurangzeb, 1658–1707*, Calcutta, Progressive Publishers, 1967.
Chaudhuri, K.N., *The Trading World of Asia and the English East India Company 1660–1760*, Cambridge, Cambridge University Press, 1978.
Chaurasia, R.S., *History of Medieval India: From 1000 A.D. to 1707 A.D.*, New Delhi, Atlantic Publishers & Dist., 2002.
Chitnis, K.N., *Socio-Economic History of Medieval India*, New Delhi, Atlantic (P) Ltd., 2002.
Commissariat, M.S., *A History of Gujarat*, Vol. II, Bombay, Orient Longmans, 1957.

Correia, L.Assis, *Portuguese India, Mumbai-Chaul-Vasai,1498-1739*, Goa, The Golden Press, 2009.

Cortesao, A., ed., *The Sumo Oriental of Tome Pires*, Vol. I, New Delhi, Asian Educational Studies, 1990.

Cronin Vincent, *A Pearl to India, the Life of Robert de Nobili*, New York, E.P. Dutton and Company, 1959.

Dale, S.F., *Indian Merchants and Eurasian Trade 1600–1750*, Cambridge, Cambridge University Press, 1994.

Danvers, F.C., *The Portuguese in India*, Vol. II, New Delhi, Asian Educational Services, 1992.

Das Gupta, A.&M.N.Pearson, ed., *India and the Indian Ocean 1500–1800*, New Delhi, Oxford University Press, 1987.

Das Gupta, A., *Indian Merchants and the Decline of Surat, c.1700–1750*, Germany, First published by Franz Steiner Verlag, Wiesbaden, 1979, Reprinted New Delhi, 1994.

Das Gupta, A., *The Merchants of Surat, c.1700–1750*, edited by E.Leach&S.N.Mu kherjee, Cambridge, Elites in South Asia, 1970.

Das Gupta, A., *Trade and Politics in 18th Century India*, edited by D.S.Richards, Oxford, Islam and the Trade of Asia, 1970.

Das, D., *Economic History of the Deccan from the First to the Sixth Century A.D.*, New Delhi, Mushiram Manoharlal, 1969.

Das, H., *The Norris Embassy to Aurangzeb (1699–1702)*, condensed and rearranged by S.C.Sarkar, Calcutta, K. L. Mukhopadhyay, 1959.

Debreuil, G., *Jeavou*, Pondicherry, Ancient History of the Deccan, 1920.

Desai, S.V., *Social Life in Maharashtra Under The Peshwas*, Bombay, Popular Prakashan, 1983.

Deshmukh, S., "Maratha Paintings" unpublished thesis, Marathwada University, 1986.

Dhabu, D.G., *Kulabkar Angre Sarkhel (Ansre Gharanachya Itihas)* (1st edn.), Bombay, Alibag, 1939.

Dodwell, H., ed. *The Private Diary of Ananda Ranga Pillai from 1736 to 1761*, Vol. IV, The Superintendent, Madras, Government Press, 1916.

Dodwell, H., *Dupliex and Clive: The Beginning of Empire*, New Delhi, Asian Education Services, 1989.

Douglas, J., *Bombay and Western India, Sampson Low*, London, Marston and Company, 1893.

Duarte, A., *Les premières relations entre les Français et les Princes indigènes dans l'Inde au XVIIe siècle (1666-1706)*, Jouve & C, Paris, 1932.

Duff, G., C.James,*A History of the Marathas, I & II*, Oxford, Oxford University Press, 1921.

Englishman, R., *Embassies and Foreign Courts, A History of Diplomacy*, London, G. Routledge & Co., 1855.

Eaton, R., *A Social History of The Deccan, 1300–1761: Eight Indian Lives (The New Cambridge History of India*), Cambridge, Cambridge University Press, 2008.

Farooqui, S.A., *A Comprehensive History of Medieval India: Twelfth to the Mid-Eighteenth Century*, New Delhi, Pearson Education India, 2011.

Faruqi, S.R., *Early Urdu Literary Culture and History*, India, Oxford University Press, 2001.

Firishta, M.Q., *Tarikh-i-Firishta*, 2 Vols, Lucknow, Naval Kishor, 1864–1865.
Furber, H., *Rival Empires of Trade in the Orient 1600–1800*, Vol. II, London, Oxford University Press, 1976.
Glamann, K., *Dutch Asiatic Trade 1620–1740*, The Hague, Copenhagen, 1958.
Gleig, Rev. G.R., *Memoirs of the Life of Warren Hastings*, Vol. II, London, R. Bentley, 1841.
Gokhale, B.G., *Surat in the Seventeenth Century: A Study in Urban History of Pre-Modern India*, Bombay, Popular Prakashan, 1979.
Gopal, A., "Shivaji's Forgotten Cousins", *Poona Digest*, August 1986.
Gordon, S., *Marathas, Marauders, and State Formation in Eighteenth-Century India*, New Delhi, Oxford India Paperbacks, 1998.
Gordon, S., *The Marathas, 1600–1818*, New Delhi, Cambridge University Press, 1993.
Gune, V.T., *The Judicial System of The Marathas*, Poona, Deccan College Postgraduate and Research Institute, 1953.
Gune, V.T., ed., *Bassein Campaign*, Panaji, Government Printing Press, 1979.
Gupta, U.D., (compiled by), *The World of Indian Ocean Merchant 1500–1800*, New Delhi, Oxford, 2001.
H.Castonnet des Fosses, l'Inde française au XVIIIe siècle, Paris, 1899
H.Castonnet des Fosses, L'Inde française Avant Dupleix, Paris, 1887.
Haidar, N.N.M.S., *Sultans of the South: Arts of India's Deccan Courts, 1323–1687*, New York, Metropolitan Museum of Art, 2011.
Haidar, N.N., M.Sardar, *Sultans of Deccan India, 1500–1700: Opulence and Fantasy*, New York, Metropolitan Museum of Art, 2015.
Haig, W., ed., *The Cambridge History of India*, Vol III, London, Cambridge University Press, 1928.
Haley, K.H.D., *The Dutch in the Seventeenth Century*, London, Thames &Hudson, 1972.
Hamilton, C.J., *The Trade Relations between England and India*, Delhi, Idarah-i-Adabyat-i-Delli, 1975.
Hasan, F., *State and Locality in Mughal India: Power Relations in Western India, c.1572–1730*, Cambridge, Cambridge University Press, 2006.
Hatalkar, V.G, tr & ed., *French Records: Relating to the History of Marathas*, Vol. VIII, Bombay, 1985.
Hatalkar, V.G, *Relations between the French and the Marathas (1668–1815)*, Bombay, University of Bombay Press, 1958.
Henri Froidevaux et A. Martineau, *Historie des Colonies françaises et de l'Expansion de la France dans le Monde*, Tome V, Societe de L'Histoire Nat'l, Paris, 1932.
Heyligers, A.J.M., *Press List of Ancient Dutch Records from 1657 to 1825 (Beschrijvende catalogus van de hele Hollandsche massa te Madras*, Madras State Archives, Madras, 1952.
Hunter, W.W., *A History of British India*, Vol. II, London, Longmans, 1900.
Irvine, W., *The Later Mughals*, I & II, Delhi, Low Price Publication, 2006.
Jain, D., G.Cardona, *The Indo-Aryan Languages*, Routledge, Florence Taylor and Francis Ann Arbor, 2007.
Joshi, V.V, *Clash of Three Empires (The Rise of the Maratha Nation)*, Allahabad, Kitabistan, 1941.
Jouveau-Dubreuil, D., Dupleix, Imprimerie de la Mission, Pondicherry, 1941.

Kadam, U.A., *History of the Marathas (French-Maratha Relations, 1668–1818)*, New Delhi, Sundeep Prakashan, 2008.
Kadam, V.S, *Maratha Confederacy. A Study of its Origin and Development*, New Delhi, Munshiram Manoharlal Publishers Pvt Ltd, 1993.
Kaepplin, P., *La compagnie des Inde Oriental et Francois Martin*, A Challamel, Paris,1908.
Kail, O.C., *The Dutch in India*, New Delhi, Macmillan India Ltd., 1981.
Kakodkar, P.R., *Portuguese and the Marathas*, Bombay, State Board for Literature and Culture, 1975.
Kamlapur, J.N., *The Deccan Forts: A Study in the Art of Fortification in Mediaeval India*, Bombay, Popular Book Depot, 1961.
Kantak, M.R., *The First Anglo-Maratha War 1774–1783*, Bombay, Popular, 1993.
Karim, A., *Murshid Quli Khan And His Times*, Dacca, Dacca Asiatic Society of Pakistan, 1963.
Keene, H.G.*Madhava Rao Sindia*, Oxford, Clarendon Press, 1891.
Kelakara, N.C., Apte, D.V., *English Records on Shivaji 1659–1682, Part I, Shiva Charitra Karyalaya*, Poona, Shivaji Tercentenary Memorial Series, 1931.
Kent, E.F., *Converting Women: Gender and Protestant Christianity in Colonial South India*, New York, Oxford University Press, 2004.
Khafi, K., *Muntakhab-ul-Lubab*, edited by A.Maulvi Kabir-ud-Dīn, Vol. I&II, Asiatic Society of Bengal,1869.
Khare, V.V., *Nana Fadnavis, Yanche Charitra*, Varada Prakashan, 1892.
Kincaid and Parasnis, *History of the Maratha People*, London, Oxford University Press, 1931.
Krishna, B., *Commercial Relations between India and England*, London, Routledge, 1924.
Krishna, B.l, *Shivaji the Great*, Vol. I–IV, Bombay, The Aryan Book Depot, 1932–1940.
Kruijtzer, G.*Xenophobia in Seventeenth-Century India*, Leiden, Leiden University Press, 2009.
Kulkarni, A.R, *History in Practice: Historians and Sources of Medieval Deccan Maratha*, New Delhi, Books and Books, 1993.
Kulkarni, A.R., *Medieval Maratha Country*, Pune, Diamond Publications, 2008.
Kulkarni, A.R, *Maharashtra in the Age of Shivaji*, Poona, Deshmukh & Co., 1969.
Kulkarni, A.R, *The Marathas*, Pune, Diamond Publication, 2008.
Kulkarni, A.R, *Ajnapatra*, Pune, Mansanman, 2003.
Kulkarni, A.R., *Explorations in the Deccan History*, New Delhi, Pragati Publication and ICHR, 2006.
Kulkarni, GT, *The Mughal Maratha Relations: Twenty Five Fateful Years, 1682–1707*, Poona, Deccan College Post-Graduate Research Institute, 1983.
Kulkarni, M., *Nana Phadnavis Ani Marathi Rajya Prashasan*, Pune, Diamond Publication, 2004.
Kumar, R., *Maratha Military Systems*, Delhi, Commonwealth Publishers, 2004.
L.Herman, *Historie de la Rivalité des Français et des Anglais dans l'Inde*, Hachette Livre, Paris, 1852.
Lafont, J.M., "Reminiscences (The French in India)", *The Indian National Trust for Art and Cultural Heritage*, New Delhi, Munishiram Manoharlal, 1986.
Lane-Poole, S., *Aurangzib And the Decay of the Mughal Empire*, Delhi, Atlantic Publishers and Distributors Pvt Ltd, 1991.

Lombard, D., J.Aubin, eds., *Asian Merchants and Businessmen in the Indian Ocean and the China Sea*, Delhi, Oxford University Press, 2000.

Low, C.R., *History of the Indian Navy (1613–1863)*, Vol. I, London, R. Bentley and son, 1929.

Lyall, A., *The Rise of the British Dominion in India*, London, J. Murray, 1898.

M.Collin de Bar, Histoire de l'Inde ancienne et moderne ou l'Industan, Tome II, Paris, 1814.

M.G.Ranade, *Rise of the Maratha Power and other Essays and Gleanings from Maratha Chronicles*, edited by K.T.Telang, Published by T.V.Chidambara, Bombay, University of Bombay, 1961.

M.Gentil, *Memoires sur L'Industan ou Empire Mogol*, Paris, 1822.

M.M.D.L.T, *Historie d'Ayder-Ali Khan ou Nouveaux Mémoiressur l'Inde.*

Macdonald, A., *Memoir of the Life of the late Nana Fadnavis*, Bombay, American Mission Press, 1927.

MacDougall, P., *Naval Resistance to Britain's Growing Power in India, 1660–1800: The Saffron Banner and the Tiger of Mysore*, Vol. 10, Woodbridge, Boydell & Brewer Ltd, 2014.

Mahajan, T.T., *Shivaji and His Diplomats*, Delhi, Commonwealth Publishers, 1997.

Mahajan, T.T., *Industry, Trade, and Commerce During Peshwa Period*, Jaipur, Pointer Publishers, 1989.

Majumdar, R.C., V.G.Dighe, ed., *The History and Culture of the Indian People: The Maratha Supremacy*, Vol. VIII, Bombay, Bharatiya Vidya Bhavan, 1977.

Malcom, J., *Political History of the India*, Vol. I, London, John, Murray, 1826.

Malleson, G.B., *History of the French in India, from the founding of Pondichery in 1674 to the capture of that place in 1761*, London, W.H. Allen & Co. Limited, 1893.

Malleson, G.B., *Final French Struggles in India*, London, W.H. Allen & Co. Limited, 1884.

Malleson. Col., *Dupliex and the Struggle for India: By the European Nations*, Clarendon Press, Oxford, 1899.

Malleson. Col., *Lord Clive and the Establishment of the English in India*, Clarendon Press, 1900.

Maloni, R., *European Merchant Capital and the Indian Economy (Surat Factory Records1630-1668)*, New Delhi, Manohar Publications, 1992.

Manickam, M., "Trade and commerce in Pondicherry (A.D. 1701–1793)", PhD Thesis, Pondicherry University, 1995.y, ,

Manucci, N., *Storia do Mongor, 1653, 1708, William Irwin(ed.) Vol. II*, London, John Murray, 1907.

Marguerite, V.L., *Le Vieux Pondichéry (1673–1815)*, Paris, 1936.

Marshall, P.J., ed., *Oxford in India Readings: Themes in Indian History: The Eighteenth Century in Indian History*, New Delhi, Oxford University Press, 2003.

Martin, R.M., *The , History, Antiquities, Topography and Statistics of Eastern India, Ist Indian edition*, Vol. III, London, W. H. Allen and Co., 1838.

Martineau, A., *Bussy et l'Inde française*, Société **Française** d'Histoire d'Outre-mer, Paris, 1935.

Martineau,A., *Dupleix et l'Inde française*, Vol. I–IV, Paris, 1920.

Mate, M.S, *Maratheshahi Vastushilp*, Pune, Continental Publishers, 2008.

Mathew, KS and Chandra, S., ed., *Ship-building and Navigation in the Indian Ocean Region AD 1400–1800*, Delhi, Munshiram Manoharlal Publishers Pvt. Ltd., 1997.

Mathew, KS., ed., *French in India and Indian Nationalism (1700A.D. - 1963 A.D.)*, 2 Vols, New Delhi, B.R.Publishing Corporation, 1999.
Mathew, K.S., *Portuguese and the Sultanate of Gujarat*, Delhi, Mittal Publications, 1986.
Mathew, K.M., *History of the Portuguese Navigation in India*, Delhi, Mittal Publication, 1988.
Mathew, K.S., *Portuguese Trade with India In The Sixteenth Century*, Delhi, Manohar,1983.
Mathew, K.S., ed., *Indian Ocean and the Cultural Interactions, A.D 1400–1800*, Pondicherry, Pondicherry University, 1996.
McPherson, K., *TheIndian Ocean: AHistoryofPeopleandtheSea*, New York, Oxford University Press, 1993.
Metcalf, B.D., T.R.Metcalf, *A Concise History of Modern India*, Cambridge, Cambridge University Press, 2006.
Mhamai, S.K., *The Sawants of Wadi*, New Delhi, Concept Publishing House, 1984.
Michell, G.M.Z., *Architecture and Art of the Deccan Sultanates*, Vol. 1, Cambridge, Cambridge University Press, 1999.
Moreland, W.H., *From Akbar to Aurangzeb: A Study in Indian Economic History*, London, Macmillan and Co. Ltd, 1923.
Nadakarni, R.V., *The Rise and Fall of the Maratha Empire*, Bombay, Popular Prakashan, 1966.
Nagraju, S, *Buddhist Architecture of Western India*, Delhi, Agam Kala Prakashan, 1981.
Naik, J.V, *The Foundation of Swarajya, in Shivaji and Swarajya*, Delhi, Orient Longman, 1975.
Narwane, M.S., *Forts of Maharashtra*, New Delhi, APH Publication Corporation, 1995.
Nayeem, M.A., *External Relations of the Bijapur Kingdom (1489–1686 A.D.)*, Hyderabad, Bright Publishers, 1974.
Nightingale, P.,*Trade and Empire in Western India: 1784–1806*, Cambridge, Cambridge University Press, 1970.
O'Malley, J.W., *The First Jesuits*, Harvard University Press, Cambridge, 1993.
Oaten. E.F., *European Travellers in India during the 15th, 16th, & 17th Centuries*, New Delhi, Asian Education Services, 1991.
Orme, R., *A History of the Military Transactions of the British Nation in Indostan*, Vol. I–III, London, Printed for F Wingrave, 1803.
Owen, S., *India on the Eve of the British Conquest*, London, W.H. Allen, 1872.
P. Cultru, *Dupliex ses plans politiques; sa disgrace*, Paris, 1901.
Pagadi, S.S, *Shivaji*, Delhi, National Book Trust, 1983.
Paniker, K.A., *Medieval Indian Literature: Surveys and Selections*, New Delhi, Sahitya Akademi, Elgant Printers, 1997.
Panikkar, K.M., *Asia and Western Dominance: A Survey of the Vasco da Gama Epoch of AsianHistory 1498-1945*, New York, John Day Company, 1954.
Pathan, Y.M, *Marathi Bhakriti Parsiche Swarup*, Aurangabad, Marathawada University, 1973.
Paul, K., *La Compagnie des Indes Orientales et François Martin*, Paris, 1908.
Pawar, A.G., *Maratha History Seminar Papers*, Kolhapur, Shivaji University, 1971.

Pearse, Col. H., *Memoir of the Life and Military Services of Viscount Lake Baron Lake of Delhi and Laswaree, 1744–1808*, London, W. Blackwood and Sons, Edinburgh and, 1908.

Pearson, M.N., *The Portuguese in India*, Cambridge, Cambridge University Press, 1987.

Pechel, S., *An Historical Account of the Settlement and Possession of Bombay by the English East India Company and of the Rise and Progress of the War with the Maratha Nation*, London, W. Richardson, for J. Robson, 1781.

Pillai, M.S., *Rebel Sultans: The Deccan from Khilji to Shivaji*, New Delhi, Juggernaut Books, 2018.

Pissurlencar, PS., *Portuguese Mahratta Relations*, translateed by ShriT.V.Parvate, Bombay, Maharashtra State Board for Literature and Culture Mantralaya, 1983.

Pissurlencar, P.S., *Portuguese Marathe Sambandha*, Pune, Poona University, 1967.

Pol, B. Van Der, *The Dutch East India Company in India: A Heritage Tour through Gujrat*, Malabar, Coromandel and Bengal, United Kingdom, Parragon Books, 2014.

Prakash, O., *The Dutch Factories in India 1617–1623: A Collection of Dutch East India Company Documents Pertaining to India*, Delhi, Munshiram Manoharlal, 1984.

Prakash, O., *The New Cambridge History of India: European Commercial Enterprise in Pre Colonial India*, Cambridge, Cambridge University, 1998.

Prakash, O., *The Dutch Factories in India 1617–1623, A Collection of Dutch East India Company Documents Pertaining to India*, New Delhi, Munshiram Manoharlal, 1984.

Price, J.F., H.Dodwell, ed., *The Private Dairy of Ananda Ranga Pillai*, Vols I, II, IV, VII, Madras, the Superintendent, Government Press, 1904–1928.

Radwan, A.B., *The Dutch in Western India, 1601–1632, A Study of Mutual Accommodation*, Calcutta, Firma KLM Private Ltd, 1978.

Rafael, V.L., *Contracting Colonialism: Translation and Christian Conversion in Tagalog Society Under Early Spanish Rule*, Durham and London, Duke University Press, 1993.

Rajamanickam, S.S.J., *The First Oriental Scholar*, Thirunelveli, De Nobili Research Institute, 1972.

Rajwade, V.K., *Chobhakrit Ushaharan*, Bharat Itihas Samshodhak Mandal Annual Report (Ahwal) Shake 1833, 1920.

Ramaswamy, V., *Walking Naked: Women, Society, Spirituality in South India*, Shimla, Indian Institute of Advanced Study, 2007.

Ramaswamy, V., *Textiles and Weavers in Medieval South India*, New Delhi, Oxford University Press, 2006.

Ranade Anuradha, K., *Socio –Economic Life of Maharashtra (1100–1600 A.D.)*, New Delhi, Serials Publications, 2009.

Ranade, M.G, *Rise of the Maratha Power*, Delhi, Ministry of Information and Broadcasting, 2012.

Ray, A., *Adventurers, Landowners and Rebels Bengal, c.1575- c.1715*, New Delhi, Munshiram Manoharlal Pvt Ltd., 1998.

Ray, A., *The Merchant and the State:The French in India(1666–1739)*, Vol I, New Delhi, Munshiram Manoharlal Publishers, 1996.

Ray, J.K., *Aspects of India's International Relations, 1700 to 2000: South Asia and the World*, India, Pearson Education, 2007.

Raychaudhuri, T., I.Habib, eds., *The Cambridge Economic History of India*, vol. I: c.1200-c.1750, Cambridge University Press, New Delhi, 2004.
Raychaudhuri, T., *Jan Company in Coromandel, 1605-1690: A Study in the Interrelation of European Commerce and Traditional Economies*, The Hague, Antiqbook, 1962.
Richards, J.F., *Mughal Administration in Golconda*, Oxford, Clarendon Press, 1975.
Roberts, P.E., *History of British India*, Oxford, Oxford University Press, 1930.
Roe, T., J.Fryer, *Travels in India in the 17th Century* (Reprint 2nd 1875 edn.), New Delhi, Asian Education Services, 1987.
Rothermund, D., *Asian Trade and European Expansion in the Age of Mercantilism*, New Delhi, Manohar, 1981.
Roy, A.C., *A History of Mughal Navy and Naval Warfare*, Calcutta, The World Press, 1972.
Roy, K., *War, Culture and Society in Early Modern South Asia, 1740–1849*, Vol. 3, New York, Taylor & Francis, 2011.
Sahai, B., *Indian Shipping: A Historical Survey*, Publications Division, Ministry of Information and Broadcasting, Government of India, New Delhi, 1996.
Sardesai, G.S, *The Main Currents of Maratha History*, Calcutta, M.C Sarkar & Sons, 1926.
Sardesai, G.S., *New History of the Maratha, Vol. I, II, III*, Bombay, Phoenix Publications, 1957–1958.
Sardesai, G.S., *Peshwa Nanasaheb*, G.M. Mahadev & Co., Bombay, 1929.
Sardesai, G.S., *Shivaji Souvenir*, Bombay, K.B., Dhawale, 1927.
Sardesai, H.S., *Shivaji, the Great Maratha*, Vol. I–IV, New Delhi, Cosmo Publications, 2002.
Sarkar, J.N., *The History of Bengal: Muslim Period 1200–1757*, Vol. II, Patna, Academica Asiatica, 1973.
Sarkar, Sir J., *House of Shivaji*, Calcutta, Orient Blackswan Private Limited, 1940.
Sarkar, Sir J., *Shivaji and his Times*, Calcutta, Orient Longman Ltd., 1929.
Sastri, K.A.N., *A History of South India*, Madras, Oxford University Press, 1976.
Sastri, K.A.N., R.Champakalakshmi, *A History of South India: From Prehistoric Times to the Fall of Vijayanagar*, Oxford, Oxford University Press, 1997.
Sen, S.N., *Administrative System of the Marathas*, Calcutta, Ananda Press and Publication Pvt. Ltd., 1925.
Sen, S.N., *The Military System of the Marathas*, Calcutta, Orient Longmans Pvt. Ltd., 1959.
Sen, S.P, *The French in India 1763-1816*, 2nd ed., Delhi, Munshiram Manoharlal, 1971.
Sen, S.N., *Early Career of Kanhoji Angria and Other Papers*, Calcutta, University of Calcutta, 1941.
Sen, S., *Foreign Biographies of Shivaji*, Calcutta, Book Co., 1927.
Seth, V.K, *Ascent and Decline of Native and Colonial Trading: Tale of Four Indian Cities*, India, SAGE Publications, 2008.
Seth, V.K.*The Story of Indian Manufacturing, Encounter with Mughal and British Empire*, New Delhi, Ane Books, 2017.
Sewell, R., *A Forgotten Empire (Vijayanagar) A Contribution to the History of India*, London: Swan Sonnenschein &Co Ltd, 1924.

Shamasastry, R., ed., *Arthashastra by Kautilya*, Varanasi, Chaukhamba Surbharati Pakashan, 2010.
Sharma, S.R., *Mughal Empire in India, Part II*, Bombay, Karnatak Printing Press, 1934.
Sharma, S.R, *The Founding of Maratha Freedom*, Bombay, Oriental Longman, 1964.
Shastry, B.S., *Studies in Indo-Portuguese History*, Bangalore, IBH Prakashana, 1981.
Sherwani, H.K., P.M.Joshi, *Medieval Deccan, 1295–1724*, Vol. I, Hyderabad, Published under the Authority of the Govt. of Andhra Pradesh, 1973.
Shirgaonkar, V.S., *Eighteenth Century Deccan, Cultual History of the Peshwa*, New Delhi, Aryan Books International, 2010.
Shrivastavya, B.K., ed., *The Angreys of Kolaba in British Records 1719 A.D. To 1884 A.D*, Poona, Aitihasik Gaurav Granth Mala, 1950.
Silva Gracias, F.da, *HealthandHygieneinColonialGoa, 1510–1961*, No. 4, New Delhi, Concept Publishing Company, 1994.
Sinha, A., *The Politics of Trade: Anglo-French commerce on the Coromandel Coast 1763-1793*, New Delhi, Manohar Publication, 2002.
Sinha, N.K., *Haider Ali*, Calcutta, A. Mukherjee & Co., 1941.
Smith,V., *Early History of India* (4th edn.) Oxford, Clarendon Press, 1924.
Smith, V.A., *The Oxford History of India*, Oxford, 1923.
Sorokhaibam, J., *Chhatrapati Shivaji: The Maratha Warrior and His Campaign*, New Delhi, Books India Pvt Ltd, 2013.
De Souza, T.R., *Medieval Goa: A Socio-Economic History*, New Delhi, Concept Publishers, 1979.
Sridharan, K., *A Maritime History of India*, Delhi, Publications Division, 1965.
Srinivasachari, C.S., *Ananda Ranga Pillai, The "Pepys" of French India*, Madras, Varadachary & Co., 1940.
Steensgard, N., *The Asian Trade Revolution of the Seventeenth Century: The Decline of Caravan Trade*, Chicago, The University of Chicago Press, 1974.
Steinberg, P.E., *The Social Construction of the Ocean*, Vol. 78, Cambridge, Cambridge University Press, 2001.
Stephen, S.J., *Pondicherry under the French: Illuminating the Urban Landscape 1674–1793*, Delhi, Primus Books, 2018.
Stephen, S.J., *Portuguese in the Tamil Coast: A Historical Explorations in Commerce and Culture, 1507–1749*, Pondicherry, Navajyothi Publishing House, 1998.
Stephen, S.J., ed., *The Indian Trade at the AsianFrontier*, New Delhi, Gyan Publishing House, 2008.
Stewart, C., *History of Bengal*, London, Cambridge University Press, 1813.
Strandberg,E., *The Modi Documents from Tanjore in Danish Collections*, Wiesbaden, Franz Steiner Verlag, 1983.
Subrahmanyam, S., *The Political Economy of Commerce: Southern India, 1500–1650*, Cambridge, Cambridge University Press, 2004.
Subramanian, L., *Indigenous Capital and Imperial Expansion (Bombay, Surat and the West Coast)*, New Delhi, Oxford University Press, 1996.
Subramanian, L., ed., *The French East India Company and the Trade of the Indian Ocean*, New Delhi, Munshiram Manoharlal Publishers, 1999.
Subramanyam, K.R., *Maratha Rajas of Tanjore*, Delhi, Asian Educational Services, 1988.

T.Hamont, *Dupleix d'après sa correspondance inédite*, Paris, 1881.

T.Hamont, *La Fin de l'empire française aux Indes*, Paris, 1887.

Tandon, R.K., *European Adventurers and Changes in the Indian Military System*, Amsterdam University Press, 2009.

Tavernier. J.B, *Travels in India, trans.* by V. Ball, London, Oxford University Press, 1889.

Toy, S., *The Strongholds of India*, London, Heinemann Educational Publisher, 1957.

Valentia George, *Viscount, Voyages and Travels to India, Ceylon, The Red Sea, Abyssinia and Egypt; In the Years 1802–1806*, 4 Vols, (Reprint London 1811 edn.), New Delhi, Asian Education Services, 1994.

Valle, P.D., E.Grey, ed., *The Travels of Pietro Della in India*, 2 Vols, (Reprint London 1892 edn.), New Delhi, Asian Education Services, 1991.

Varadarajan, L., ed., *India in the 17th Century (Social, Economic and Political) Memiors of Francois Martin (1670–1690)*, Vol. 1, part 2, Delhi, Manohar, 1985.

Vardachari, K.C., *Aivars of South India*, Bombay, Bhartiya Vidya Bhavan, 1966.

Vink, M.P.M., *Encounters on the Opposite Coast: The Dutch East India Company and the Nayaka State of Madurai in the Seventeenth Century*, Leiden, Brill Publication, 2015.

Walls, A.F., *The Missionary Movement in Christian History*, New York, Orbis Books publications, 1996.

Weber,H., *La Compagnie française des Indes (1604–1875)*, Paris, 1904.

Wilks, Col. M., *Historical Sketches of the South of India*, London, Longman, 1817.

Winius, G.D.&P.M.Vink, *Marcus, The Merchant-Warrior Pacified: The VOC (The Dutch East India Company) and Its Changing Political Economy in India*, Oxford, Oxford University Press, 1991.

Yazdani, G., ed., *The Early History of the Deccan in Two Volumes*, the Authority of the Government of Andhra Pradesh, Oxford University Press, 1960.

Zupanov, I., *Disputed Mission: Jesuit Experiments and Brahmanical Knowledge in Seventeenth-century India*, New York, Oxford University Press, 1999.

Articles

Alam, I., "The Dutch East India Company Trade at Vengurla in the seventeenth century", *Proceedings of Indian History Congress*, Vol. 64 (646–666) 2003.

Apte, B.K., "The Maratha Weapons Of War", *Bulletin of the Deccan College Post-Graduate and Research Institute*, Vol. 19, No.1/2, Deccan College of Post Graduate and Research Institute, Poona, 1958.

Apte, B.K, "The Contents of Maratha Nationalism", *Proceedings of Indian History Congress*, Vol 16, 1953.

Arasaratnam, S. "The Dutch East India Company and its Coromandel Trade 1700–1740", *Bijdragen tot del Taal – Land – en Volkenkunde*, Vol. 123, No. 3, Leiden, 1967.

Askari, S.H., "Mughal Naval Weakness and Aurangzeb's Attitude Towards the Traders and Pirates on the Western Coast", *The Journal of Bihar Research Society*, Vol. XL VI, Jan–Dec., 1960. Available at http://worldhistoryconnected .press.illinois.edu/12.1/forum_delagarza.html. Accessed on 4 March 2016.

Barua, P., "Military Developments in India 1750–1850", *Journal of the Royal Society of Arts*, Vol. 78, No. 4049 (599–616), Oct. 1994.

Bellarykar, N., "Dutch-Maratha (i.e. VOC-Angre) Naval Battle of 1754: Multiple Aspects of a Little-discussed but Important Incident", *Prag Samiksha*, 49–66, February 2018.

Bellarykar, N., "Dutch-maratha relations and the Porto-Novo affair" *Quarterly of the Bharat Itihas Sanshodhan Mandal*, Vol. 1–4 (57–71) Pune, June 2015– April 2016.

Bhattacharya, B., "Porto Novo and Shipping in the Bay of Bengal in the Mid-18th Century", International Conference on Shipping, Factories and Colonisation, edited by J.Everaert and J.Paramentier (103-118) Brussels, 1994.

Burman, J.J.R., "Shivaji's Myth and Maharashtra's Syncretic Traditions", *Economic Political Weekly*, Vol. 36, No. 14–15, 07 Apr, 2001.

Carson, P., "Christianity, Colonialism and Hinduism in Kerala: Integration, Adaptation or Confrontation?", in *Christians and Missionaries in India*, edited by R.EFrykenberg, Cambridge, Cambridge University Press, 2003.

Chandra, M., "The history of the Indian Costume from the 1st Century A.D. to the Beginning of the 4th Century A.D. to the Beginning of the 4th Century A.D.", *Journal of Indian society of Oriental Art*, Vol. VIII, 2017, pp. 185–224.

Chaudhuri, K.N., "The Portuguese Maritime Empire, Trade and Society in the Indian Ocean during the sixteenth Century", *Portuguese Studies*, Vol. 8, Special Issue supported by the Comissão Nacional para as Comemorações dos Descobrimentos Portugueses, Modern Humanities Research Association, 1992.

Chavan, K., M.Painting, *Bulletin of the Deccan College Post-Graduate and Research Institute*, Vol. 58/59, 1998–1999.

David, N.L., "Marco Della Tomba and the Brahmin from Banaras *Missionarie*, Orientalists and Indian Scholar's", *The Journal of Asian Studies*,Vol. 65, Feb. 2006.

de la Garza, A., "Command of the Coast: The Mughal Navy and Regional Strategy", *World History Connected*, Vol. 12, No. 1, February 2015.

Deshpande, A., "Limitations of Military Technology: Naval Warfare on the West Coast, 1650–1800", *Economic and Political Weekly*, XXVII, April 25, 1992.

Dighe, V.G , "The Edlabad Meeting of the Peshwa and the Nizam", *Proceedings of the Indian History Congress*,Vol. 13, 1950.

Elias, J.J., "Sufism", *Iranian Studies*, Vol. 31, No. 3–4 (595–613) *A Review of the Encyclopaedia Iranica* (Summer - Autumn, 1998).

Ferguson, D, "The Settlements of the Danes at Tranquebar and Serampore" *Journal of the Royal Asiatic Society of Great Britain and Ireland*, Vol. 30, Jul 1898, pp. 625–629.

Fernandes, W.., "Jesuit Contribution to Social change in India (16th–20th centuries)", in T.R.De Souza, C.Borges, eds., *Jesuits in India, A Historical Perspective*, Goa, Xavier Centre for Historical Research, 1992.

Frykenberg, R.E.,"On the Study of Conversion Movements: An Analytical and Research Perspective", *The Indian Economic and Social History Review*, Vol. XVII, 1980.

Ghurye, G.S., "Features of the Caste System", in *Social Stratification*, edited by D.Gupta, New Delhi, Oxford University Press, 2004.

Gracias, F.D.S. "The Impact of Portuguese Culture on Goa", *Goa and Portugal: Their Cultural Links*, Vol. 7, 1997, pp. 41–51.

Hefner, R.W., "Introduction: World Building and the Rationality of Conversion", in *Conversion to Christianity: Historical and Anthropological Prospective on a*

Transformation, edited by R.W.Hefner, Berkley, University of California Press, 1993.

Indrani Ray, "India in the Asian Trade in the 1730's- An 18th century French Memoire", Proceedings of the Indian History Congress, 34th Session, 271–290, Chandigrah, 1973.

Jain Kirti, "Boat Building and the Son Kolis of the Raigad District, Maharastra", *Marine Archaeology*, Vol. 4, July1993.

Jha, M., "Locating The Space for Sudras in Medieval Bhakti (A.D. 600–1400)", *Proceedings of the Indian History Congress*, Vol. 66, New Delhi, 2005–2006, pp. 379–393.

Joseph, J.B., "Chief Merchants and the European Enclaves of Seventeenth Century Coromandel", *Modern Asian Studies*, Vol. 11, No. 3, Cambridge University Press, 1977, pp. 321–340.

Joshi, G.B., "Caste Conflicts of the Brahmins in 18th and 19th Centuries Maharashtra", *Proceedings of the Indian History Congress*, Vol. 43, 1982, pp. 418–423.

Kadam, U.A, "French Maratha Relations: India in the 17th century" Marathanchya Itihasache Pehelu', *Dr. Appasaheb Pawar Lecture Series, Vol.II, French-Maratha Relations: India in the 17th Century*, editd by M.A.Lohar, Shivaji University, Kolhapur, pp. 83–111, 2012.

Kadam, U.A., "Maratha History: A Quest for Regional Identity", in *Medieval India Problems and Possibilities*, edited by, R.Seshan, Pune, Rawat Publications, 2006.

Kadam, U., "Fragments of Maratha History, LusoDutch presence in the Deccan", Proceedings of Akhil Maharashtra Itihas Parishad, 21th National Session Volume: 21 2013.

Kadam, U., "The Whole Universe is my Home': Bhakti in Medieval Maharashtra", in '*Looking Within Looking Without: Exploring Households in the Subcontinent Through Time', Essays in Memory of Nandita Prasad Sahai,* edited by K.Roy, Primus, New Delhi, 2015.

Kail, O.C., "Dutch Commercial & Territorial Influence in India", *Journal of the Asiatic Society of Bombay*, 43–44, 1968–1969.

Kantak, M.R, "The Political Role of Different Hindu Castes and Communities in Maharashtra in the Foundation of Shivaji's Swarajya", *Bulletin of the Deccan College Research Institute*, Vol. 38, No. 1/4, Pune, 1978–79.

Keller-Lapp, H., "Who is the Real Sovereign of the Ursulines of Pondicherry?", *French Colonial History*, Vol. 13, Michigan University Press, 2012.

Khan, I., "Unpublished Documents Relating to English East India Company's Trade in Gujarat, 1669–82", Proceedings, Indian History Congress, 52"d Session, 1991–1992.

Kishwa, M., R.Vanita, "Poison to Nectar", *Manushi*, Vol. 50–51, New Delhi, 1989.

Kosambi, M.. "The Konkan Ports and European Dominance: An Urban Perspective", *Medieval Deccan History: Commemoration Volume in Honour of PM Joshi, Popular Prakashan, Bombay*, Vol. 1996 (108–123), 2001.

Krishnamurty, B., "French Trade in India", *Proceedings of the Indian History Congress*, 1983.

Kulkarni, A.R., *Medieval Maratha Country*. Pune, Diamond Publications, 2008. "Protection to Salt Industry By Shivaji." Proceedings of the Indian History Congress, 24:188–190. JSTOR, 1961.

Kulkarni, A.R., "Social Relations in the Marat ha country in the Medieval Period", *Proceedings of the Indian History Congress*, Vol. 1, 1970.
Kulkarni, G.T., "Deccan (Maharashtra) Under the Muslim Rulers From Khaljis to Shivaji : Study in Interaction", *Bulletin of the Deccan College Post-Graduate and Research Institute*, Vol. 51/52, Professor S.M Katre, Felicitation Volume (501–10), 1991–92.
Levi, S., "The Indian Merchants Diaspora in Early Modern Central Asia and Iran", *Iranian Studies*, vol. 32, No. 4, 1999 pp. 483–512.
Lotika, V., "Francois Martin", Proceedings of the Indian History Congress, Baroda, 1976.
Luba Zubkova, "Dravidian Studies in the Netherlands Part I (1605–1690s) Pioneers of Orientalism at the VOC", *International Institute for Asian StudiesNews Letter*, Vol.. 35, 2004.
Majumdar, S., "The Dense Desolate Pathway: Routes of Bhakti in Medieval Indian Literature", *Sahitya Akademi*, Vol. 35, No. 3 (149), 1992.
Malekandathil, P., "Religious Rhetoric, Mercantile Strategies and a Community in Revolt: A Study on the Conflicts between the St. Thomas Christians and the Portuguese Padroado", *Negotiating Religion: Perspectives from Indian History*, edited by R.P.Bahuguna, R.Dutta and F.Nasreen, New Delhi, Manohar, 2012.
Maloni, R.. "Portuguese Private Traders On The Coromandel Coast (16th And 17th Centuries)", *Proceedings of the Indian History Congress*, Vol. 73 (311–317), 2012.
Manilal, K.S., "Hortus Malabaricus and the Ethnoiatrical Knowledge of Ancient Malabar", *Ancient Science of Life*, Vol. 4, No. 2, Calicut, 1984.
Mark, I.K., Governor Joseph Francois Dupleix-His Religious Policy, *Proceedings of the Indian History Congress*, Vol. 38, 1977.
Mohan, J.., "British and French Ethnographies of India: Dubois and his English Commentators", *French Colonial History*, Vol. 5, Michigan State University Press, 2004.
Moosvi, S. "The Mughal Empire and The Deccan—Economic Factors and Consequences", In *Proceedings of the Indian History Congress*, Vol. 43 (365–382) 1982.
Moraes, G.M., "Maratha Portuguese war of 1683–84", *The Journal of the University of Bombay*, Vol. 11, No. 4, January, 1943.
Muhammad, A.K., "Some Notes on the Bahmani Dynasty", *Journal of the Asiatic Society of Bengal*, Vol. 73, No. 1 (463), 1904.
Mukherjee, R., "Maritime order and the Eighteenth-Century Indian Ocean", *Re-searching Transition in Indian History*, edited by R.Seshan, S.Kumbhojkar, London, Routledge Publication, 2018.
Naik, B.S., "European Trade and Politics in Medieval South Canara", *ProceedingsoftheIndian History Congress*, Vol. 69 (361–372), 2008.
Nisha, T.M., Dr P.Jayasudha., "Portuguese Architecture in India-The Architectural Scenario of Manapad, an Indian Coastal Village", *Indian Journal Of Scientific Research*, Vol. 14, No. 1, 2017.
Odegard, E., "A Company of State. The Dutch East India Company and the Debates on the Company-State in Asia, 1660s-1690s", in *Mechanisms Of Global Empire Building*, edited by A.Polonia Catia Antunes (127–144), Centro de Investigação Transdisciplinar Cultura, Espaço & Memória (Publisher), Leiden, 2017

Pande, R., "The Bhakti Movement: An Interpretation", *Proceedings of the Indian History Congress*, Vol. 48, Goa University, Bambolim, 1987.
Pendse, S., "The Dutch Factory at Vengurla", *International Journal of Maritime History*, Vol. 30, No. 4 (724–732), 2018.
Puntambekar, S.V., trans., "A Royal Edict of the Principles of State Policy and Organisation", *Journal of Indian History*, Vol. VIII, No. Parts I and II, Madras, 1929.
Ramaswamy, "Vijaya, Rebels-Conformist? Women saint in Medieval South India", Anthropos, 1992 Bd. 87, H. 1./3, pp. 133-146.
Rao, V.N., S.Subrahmanyam, "History and Politics in the Vernacular: Reflections on Medieval and Early Modern South India," in *History in the Vernacular*, edited by R.Aquil and P.Chaterjee (25–65), Permanent Black, 2008.
Ray, A. "French-Golconda Relation Between 1671 and 1681: Problems of Attitudes and Resources over St. Thome and Masulipatnam", *Studies in History of the Deccan: Medieval and Modern: Professor AR Kulkarni Felicitation*, Vol. 2002.
Robinson, R., "Some Neglected Aspects of the Conversion of Goa: A Socio-historical Perspective", *Sociological Bulletin*, Vol. 42, No. 1/2, Sage Publication, 1993.
Saswadkar, P.L. "The Siddis' tyranny Over the Hindus in 18th Century Konkan", *Proceedings of the Indian History Congress*, Vol. 37 (223–229). JSTOR, 1976.
Seethalakshmi, V., Marathas of Thanjavur and Land Grants, *IOSR-JHSS*, Vol 20, No. 3, Ver. II (36–37), March 2015.
Sen, A.P., "Unruly Hinterlands and Settlement Histories of the Deccan Plateau", *Rachel Carson Center Perspectives*, edited by S.Krishnan, C.L.Pastore, S.Temple, Vol. 3 (55–60), 2015.
Setu Madhavrao Pagadi, "Maratha-Nizam Relations: Nizam-Ul-Mulk's Letters", *Annals of the Bhandarkar Oriental Research Institute*, Vol. 51, No.1/4 (93–121), 1970.
Shejwalkar, T.S, "An Unrecorded Kanara Campaign by the Marathas", *Bulletin of the Deccan College Post-Graduate and Research Institute*, Vol. 4, No. 3. (204–207), 1943. JSTOR, www.jstor.org/stable/42929316
Shejwalkar, T.S., "Shivaji's raid on Basrur", *Bulletin of the Deccan college Post-Graduate and Research Institute*, Vol. 4, No. 2, 1942, pp. 135–46.
Subrahmanyam, S., "Um Bom Homem de Tratar Piero Strozzi: A Florentine in Portuguese Asia, 1510–1522", *Journal of European Economic History*, Vol. 16, No. 3, 1987, pp 511–26..
Teixeira, M.C., "Portuguese traditional Settlements, a result of cultural Miscegenation", *Traditional Dwellings and Settlements Review, Journal of the International Association for the Study of Traditional Environments*, Vol. 1, No. 2, Spring 1990.
Thompson, V.M., "Frenchmen prior to Dupliex", *Dupliex and His Letters, 1742–1754*, Ballou, New York, 1933.
Varadarajan, L., "Konkan Ports and Medieval Trade", *Indica*, Vol. XXII, No. I, Bombay, Heras Institute of Indian History and Culture, St. Xavier Institute, March 1985.
Varkey, J., "The Significance of Mahe in Eighteenth-century French India", *Proceedings of the Indian History Congress*, Vol. 58 (295–302), JSTOR, 1997.
Velmuragan, R., "The upper caste and lower caste Christians in Pondicherry during the eighteenth century", *Proceedings of the Indian History Congress*, Vol. 60, Aligarh, 1999, pp. 456–459.

Zelliot, E., "Chokhamela Anand Eknath: Two Bhakti modes of legitimacy for modern changes", *Tradition and Modernity in Bhakti Movement*, edited by J.Lele, Leiden, E.J. Brill, 1981.

Zupanov, I.G., "Conversion Historiography in South Asia; Alternate Indian Christian Counter-Histories in Eighteenth century Goa", *The Medieval History Journal*, Vol. XII, No. 2, 2009, pp 303–325 .

Periodicals

1. Bengal, Past and Present, Vol. XVI.
2. Indian Historical Records Commission Proceedings, Vol. 17, 19, 20, 22 26 28 & 29.
3. Indica, Vol. 8, Bombay, 1971.
4. Indica, Vol. 9, Bombay, 1972.
5. Modern Review, No. 74, 1943.
6. Proceedings of the Indian History Congress, 1945.
7. Revue Historique de l'Inde française, Vol. II & V, Pondicherry.
8. Sahyadri, No. 9, 1947.
9. The Quarterly of the Bharat Itihas Samsodhak Mandal, Poona, 1923.

Appendix

GENEALOGY OF THE BHOSALE FAMILY

Maloji

Shahaji
(1595–1664)

Sambhaji

Shivaji
(1630–1680)

Ekoji OR Venkoji

Sambhaji
(1657–1689)

Rajaram
(1670–1700)

Shahu
(1682–1749)
Ramraja (adopted)
(1750–1777)

Shivaji I
(son of Tarabai)

Sambhaji
(son of Rajasbai)

Ramraja (adopted to Satara)
(b. 1726)

Shahu Raje (younger) (adopted)
(coronation 11, December 1777, d. 3 May 1808)

|
Pratapsinh Raje (coronation 16 May 1808, dethroned 30 Aug. 1839, d. 4 Oct. 1848)
|
Shahaji Appasaheb (brother of Pratapsinh) (5 Sept. 1839, d. 5 April 1848)
|
End of Maratha Kingship (1 May 1849)

GENELOGY OF THE BHATT PESHWA FAMILY

Balaji Vishwanath
(Peshwaship 17 Nov. 1714, d. 2 April 1720)
|
Bajirao (Elder)
(Peshwaship 17 April 1720, d. 28 April 1740)
|
Balaji Bajirao alias Nanasaheb
(Peshwaship 15 June 1740, d. 13 June 1761)
|
Madhavrao (Elder)
(Peshwaship 20 July 1761, d. 18 Nov. 1772)
|
Narayanrao (younger brother of Narayanrao)
(Peshwaship 13 Dec. 1772, d. 30 August 1773)
|
Sawai Madhvarao (son of Narayanrao)
(Peshwaship 28 May 1774, d. 20 August 1795)
|
Bajirao Raghunath (Bajirao II)
(Peshwaship 5 Dec. 1796, Bajirao surrenders on 4 June 1818, d. 28 Jan. 1851)
|

End of Peshwaship
(4 June 1818)

CHRONOLOGY OF EVENTS

Events relating to the Marathas, Portuguese, Dutch, English, French, Mughals and others from 1600 to 1818

Year	*Date*	*The Marathas*	*The French*	*The Mughals, the Portuguese, the English, the Dutch, etc.*
1600	December 31			The English East India Company was formed.
1602	March 28			The Dutch East India Company was formed.
1628	August			The Portuguese East India Company was established.
1630	February 19	Birth of Shivaji the Great.		
1632				The Mughal Emperor deprives the Portuguese of their possessions in Bengal.
1653–54				Shivappa Nayak of Bednur captures the Portuguese forts in Karnatak.
1659	August 16			Portuguese Viceroy reports Shivaji's complete possession of south Konkan.
1661				The Marathas attacked Goa.
1663				The Portuguese request Shivaji to mark an officer with whom correspondence can be established in important matters. By 1663 the Dutch dethrone the Portuguese from the Malabar Coast.
1664	August 27		The French East India Company was formed.	
1665				The Portuguese hand over the island of Bombay to the British.
1666	March 29		La Boullaye le Gouz and Bebber arrive at Surat.	
1666	September 4		The French obtain a firman from the Emperor to open a factory at Surat.	

(*Continued*)

Year	*Date*	*The Marathas*	*The French*	*The Mughals, the Portuguese, the English, the Dutch, etc.*
1666	November 17			Portuguese signs treaty with the Mughals.
1667	November 19–22			Shivaji attacked Goa because the Portuguese were not allowing practice of any other religion than Christianity.
1667	December 5			Shivaji concludes a treaty with the Portuguese Viceroy.
1667	December 11			Confirmation of the treaty by Shivaji, which was signed on 5 December 1667.
1668	February 13		Francois Caron arrives at Surat as Director of the Company.	
1668	December	Shivaji grants a firman to the French to open a factory at Rajapur.		
1669	January 17		Francois Martin arrives at Calicut.	
1670				Maratha Portuguese sign a friendship treaty. One of the provisions of this treaty was that the Portuguese would mediate between the Marathas and the Siddis.
1670	October 3–5	Shivaji sacks Surat for the second time.		
1674	January		The French establish themselves at Pondicherry.	
1674	June 6	Shivaji crowns himself as King (Chhatrapati).		

1674	September 23		The French capitulate at St.Thome.	
1675	April 6		Francois Baron's interview with Sherkhan.	
1675	May 16			Shivaji captures Ponda fort.
1676	September 24		The French storm the fortress of Valadour.	
1677	May 31	Jinji surrenders to Shivaji.		
1677	July 6	Shivaji defeats Sherkhan.		
1677	July 17	Treaty signed between Shivaji and Sherkhan.	Pondicherry passes under Maratha rule.	
1680	April 3	Shivaji dies.		
1683				Sambhaji attacks the Portuguese at Chaul & Goa.
1683	October			Sambhaji victorious against the Portuguese.
1683	November			Sambhaji retires from Goa.
1685	February 23			Marathas attack Bardez.
1689	January 9	The French obtain a firman from the Marathas to fortify Pondicherry.		
1689	March 11	Shambhaji assassinated by the Mughals.		
1689	November 15	Rajaram arrives at Jinji.		

(Continued)

Year	*Date*	*The Marathas*	*The French*	*The Mughals, the Portuguese, the English, the Dutch, etc.*
1690	June		Customs and other revenues of Pondicherry ceded to the French in return for a loan of Rs.10,000 by the Marathas.	
1690	September 15			The English purchase the fort of Tegnapatam (Fort St. David) from Rajaram. The Mughals besiege Jinji.
1693	August 27	Rajaram sells Pondicherry to the Dutch.		
1693	September 8		Pondicherry capitulates to the Dutch.	
1698	February 7			Jinji surrenders to the Mughals.
1699	March 16		Pondicherry restored to the French.	
1700	March 2	Rajaram dies.		
1701	January 21		A Council established at Pondicherry.	
1706	December 31		Francois Martin dies.	
1707	February 20			Emperor Aurangzeb dies.
1708	January 12	Shahu coronated as King of Marathas.		
1722	January 9			Bajirao signs a peace treaty with the Portuguese at Varsoli.
1722	August 16		Dupleix arrives at Pondicherry as Councillor.	
1724				Nizam-ul-Mulk becomes Viceroy of the Deccan.

1726	August 21		Lenoir becomes Governor of Pondicherry.	
1731	August 28		Dupleix becomes Director at Chandernagore.	
1735			Duma becomes Governor of Pondicherry.	
1736	August 17		Duma obtains a firman from the Emperor to coin money at Pondicherry.	
1739	February 14		The French occupy Karikal.	
1739	March 1			Marathas capture Ponda fort and the fort of Usagaon.
1739	May 5	Bassein capitulates to the Marathas.		
1740	May 19			Dost Ali killed in a battle with the Marathas.
1740	May 25			Dost Ali's family takes shelter at Pondicherry.
1740	June 25	Balaji Bajirao alias Nanasaheb becomes Peshwa.		
1740	August	Treaty signed between the Marathas and Safdar Ali.		
1740	September 1			Safdar Ali and Chanda Sahib arrive at Pondicherry.
1741	March 26	Chanda Sahib made prisoner by the Marathas.		

(Continued)

Year	*Date*	*The Marathas*	*The French*	*The Mughals, the Portuguese, the English, the Dutch, etc.*
1742	January 14		Dupleix becomes Governor.	
1742	August			Safdar Ali assassinated.
1746	November 4			Battle of Adyar.
1748	April 25			Emperor Muhammad Shah Shah dies.
1748	April 28			Ahmad Shah becomes Emperor.
1748	May 21			Nizam-ul-Mulk dies.
1748	June–October 17		Siege of Pondicherry raised by the English.	
1749	August 3			Nawab Anwar-ud-din killed in the battle of Ambour.
1749	December	King Shahu dies.		
1750	September 12		Bussy captures Jinji.	
1750	December 16			Nazir Jang assassinated: Muzaffir Jang declared Viceroy of Deccan.
1751	February 14			Muzaffir Jang assassinated; Salabat Jang proclaimed Viceroy of Deccan by Bussy.
1751	April 3	Treaty of Pangal signed between Balaji and Salabat Jang.		
1751	November 23			Salabat Jang declares war against the Peshwa.
1751	December 1	Battle of Parner; the Marathas retire before the accurate firing of the French artillery.		

1751	December 3		Bussy launches a surprise attack on the Maratha camp.	
1751	December 10	Battle of Malthan; honours with the Marathas.		
1751	December 14	The Marathas capture the fort of Trimbak.		
1752	January 17	Treaty of Ahmednagar signed between the Peshwa and Slabat Jang.		
1752	April			Ramdas Pant assassinated; Sayyad Lashkar Khan becomes Diwan.
1752	June 13		The French capitulate at Trichinopoly.	
1752	August			Ghazi-ud-din arrives at Barhanpur.
1752	September			Ghazi-ud-din arrives at Aurangabad.
1752	October 16			Ghazi-ud-din dies being poisoned.
1752	November 24	Treaty of Bhalki signed between the Peshwa and Salabat Jang.	Treaty of alliance between the Peshwa and Bussy.	
1752	December 24			The Mughal army revolts; refuses to march to the Karnatak.

(*Continued*)

Year	*Date*	*The Marathas*	*The French*	*The Mughals, the Portuguese, the English, the Dutch, etc.*
1753	End of February		Bussy leaves for Masulipatam for reasons of health.	
1753	June 15		Bussy returns post-haste to Hyderabad.	
1753	September 13	The Peshwa stations a Vakil at Bussy's camp.		
1753	End of November		Bussy returns to Aurangabad.	
1753	December 9	Bussy sends presents on the occasion of the marriage of the Peshwa's second son Madhavrao.		
1753	December			Sayyad Lashkar Khan resigns; Shah Nawaz Khan becomes Diwan.
1754	January		Bussy obtains the release of the two brothers of Salabat Jang.	
1754	January 22		A conference at Sadras begins between the French and the English delegates.	
1754	End of February	Raghuji Bhosale invades the Nizam's territory.		

1754	June 2			Ahmed Shah disposed; Alam Gir II becomes Emperor.
1754	April 10	Peace signed between Raghuji and the Nizam.		
1754	June 7		Bussy leaves Hyderabad for the Circars.	
1754	August 2		Godeheu arrives in India.	
1754	October 11		Truce signed between the French and the English.	
1754	October 15		Dupleix leaves for France.	
1755	January		Bussy returns to Hyderabad.	
1755	January 11		Treaty signed between the French and the English in India for 18 months.	
1755	February 14	Raghuji Bhosale dies.		
1755	April		De Leyrit becomes Governor of Pondicherry.	
1755	April 7	Murrarao seeks Bussy's co-operation in a conspiracy against the Peshwa.		The Mughal army led by Bussy arrives before Shrirangapatan.
1755	December		Bussy receives a proposal from the Emperor for a French detachment.	

(Continued)

Year	*Date*	*The Marathas*	*The French*	*The Mughals, the Portuguese, the English, the Dutch, etc.*
1755	July	Balaji seeks Bussy's assistance against Tulaji Angre.		
1755	December	Balaji repeats his demand for French Troops.		
1756	January 20	The Peshwa arrives before Savnur.		
1756	February 14	Tulaji Angre surrenders to the Peshwa.		
1756	End of April	Peace concluded between the Peshwa, Murarrao and the Nawab of Savnur.		
1756	Beginning of May		Bussy dismissed by the Nizam.	
1756	June 14		Bussy arrives at Char-Minar.	
1756	June–August		Bussy's famous defence at Char-Minar.	

1756	August 30		Bussy reinstated at the Nizam's Court.	
1756	November		Bussy leaves for the "Circars".	
1757	June 23			Battle of Plassey; Siraj-ud Daulah defeated and killed.
1758	February		Bussy arrives at Aurangabad at the Nizam's urgent call.	
1758	May 11		Hyder Jang, Bussy's Diwan assassinated.	Shah Nawaz Khan assassinated.
1758	July 18		Bussy finally leaves Hyderabad.	
1759	March 4			Surat captured by the English.
1760	January 22		Bussy made prisoner by the English.	
1761	January 14	The Marathas routed at the Panipat by Ahmed Shah Abdali.		
1761	January 16		Pondicherry surrenders to the English.	
1761	June 23	The Peshwa Nanasaheb dies.		
	July 20	Madhavrao becomes Peshwa.		
1761	September 3		Chevalier de Mouhy arrives at Goa.	
1761	December 9	Queen Tarabai dies.		

(Continued)

Year	*Date*	*The Marathas*	*The French*	*The Mughals, the Portuguese, the English, the Dutch, etc.*
1762	April 4		Comte de Maudave arrives at Negapatam.	
1762	July 7			Salabat Jang made prisoner by Nizam Ali.
1762	September 16			Salabat Jang assassinated.
1763				Portuguese conquer Ponda Panchmahal from the Marathas.
1763	February		Treaty of Paris signed between the England and the France.	
1764	October 23			Battle of Buxar; the English defeat the Emperor, Shuja-ud-daulah, Nawab of Audh and Mir Kasim, Nawab of Bengal.
1765	April 11		Law de Lauriston arrives at Pondicherry.	
1765	August 12			The English acquire the Diwani of Bengal.
1767	August			War commences between Haider Ali and the English.
1769	April			Peace concluded between Haider and the English; honours with Haider Ali.
1770	December 15	The Marathas capture Etawah.		
1770	December			The Emperor seeks Maratha protection.
1771	February 10	The Marathas take possession of Delhi.		
1771	February 24		Huguel joins Haider Ali.	
1772	January 6			Shah Alam enters Delhi and occupies the throne under Maratha protection.

1772	January	Madhavrao proposes Franco-Maratha alliance to Law.	
1772	October 13		Mostyn arrives at Poona as English Resident.
1772	November 18	Peshwa Madhavrao dies.	
1772	December 13	Narayanrao becomes the Peshwa.	
1773	January	Treaty signed between Mahadji Shinde and Chevalier to expel the English from Bengal.	
1773	August 30	Peshwa Narayanrao assassinated.	
1773	September 17		The English capture Tanjore.
1773	October 10	Raghunathrao alias Raghoba becomes Peshwa.	
1774	April 18	Sawai Madhavrao born.	

(*Continued*)

Year	*Date*	*The Marathas*	*The French*	*The Mughals, the Portuguese, the English, the Dutch, etc.*
1774	May 28	Sawai Madhavrao receives robes of Peshwaship.		
1774	October 26			Warren Hastings becomes Governor General.
1774	December 28			The English capture Salsette.
1774	End of 1774	Council of the Regency of the Barbhais formed.		
1775	March 6			Treaty of Surat signed between the English and Raghoba against Poona Darbar.
1775	Middle of April	The Marathas propose an alliance to the French against the English.		
1776	March 1	Raghoba proposes a treaty to Braincourt.		
1776	July 4			War of American Independence declared.
1776	September 19		St. Lubin sets sail for India.	
1777	January 8		Marquis de Bellecombe becomes Governor of Pondicherry.	

1777	March 16		St. Lubin arrives at Chaoul.	
1777	April 26		St. Lubin arrives at Purandhar.	
1777	June 18	Treaty of Commerce signed between the Marathas and the French.		
1777	September 1		Pascal de Santy arrives at Surat with packets for Europe.	
1778	March			War declared between England and France.
1778	March 25	Revolution at Poona; Moroba assumes power.		
1778	May 13	The Peshwa's proposal for the French troops against the English.		
1778	July 10			The English capture Candernagore.
1778	July 11	Moroba arrested and imprisoned.		
1778	July 12		St. Lubin leaves Poona for Daman.	

(Continued)

Year	*Date*	*The Marathas*	*The French*	*The Mughals, the Portuguese, the English, the Dutch, etc.*
1778	October 18		Pondicherry capitulates to the English.	
1778	November 3		Briancourt made prisoner by the English.	
1779	January		St.Lubin leaves Daman for Europe.	
1779	January 13	The Marathas force the English to capitulate at Wadgaon.		
1779	March 19			Col. Braithwaite captures Mahe.
1779	April	Raghunathrao escapes to Surat.		
1779	June		St. Lubin arrives at Mecca.	
1780	January 11			The Portuguese, in accordance with the treaty of 11 January 1780, with the Marathas, secured the Nagar Haveli province.
1780	February 13			The English capture Ahmedabad.
1780	February 26	Treaty of alliance signed between the Marathas and Haider Ali.		
1780	May 11			The English capture Kalyan.
1780	July 1		St. Lubin arrives at Malta.	

1780	July 20			Haider Ali enters the Karnatak.
1780	August 4			Capt. Popham captures Gwalior.
1780	End of October		St. Lubin arrives at Versailles.	
1780	December 12			The English capture Bassein.
1781	February	The Marathas make proposals for a French alliance against the English.		
1781	March 24			Col. Camac defeats Mahadji Shinde.
1781	April 15	The Marathas force Gen. Goddard to retreat from Khandala.		
1781	July 1	Mahadji defeats Col. Muir.		Gen. Coote defeats Haider at Porto-Novo.
1781	August 7			Battle of Polilur; Haider Ali defeated.
1781	September 9		Montigny and Piveron de Moriat arrive at Goa.	
1781	September 27			Battle of Sholinghur; Haider Ali defeated.
1781	October 13	Truce signed between Mahadji and Col. Muir.		
1781	November 5		Montigny arrives at Poona as French Resident.	
1781	December		Piveron arrives at Haider's camp near Chittoor.	

(*Continued*)

Year	*Date*	*The Marathas*	*The French*	*The Mughals, the Portuguese, the English, the Dutch, etc.*
1782	January 25		The French squadron arrives in the Gulf of Bengal.	
1782	February 9		D'Orves dies; Suffern becomes the C-in-C of the French Naval forces.	
1782	February 17		Naval battle near Madras between the French and the English squadrons; indecisive.	
1782	February 21		The French squadron arrives before Pondicherry.	
1782	March 10 & 11		French troops under Duchemin land at Porto-Novo.	
1782	April 3			Tipu Sultan captures Cuddalore, assisted by the French.
1782	April 12		Second action between the French and English squadrons near Trincomallee; indecisive.	
1782	May 17	Treaty of Salabai signed by Mahadji and Col. Anderson.		
1782	May 31		Bussy arrives at the Isle of France.	

1782	June 6			Hastings signs the Treaty of Salabai.
1782	End of June	The Marathas make fresh proposals to the French for an alliance.		
1782	July 6		Third action between Suffren and Hughes; Suffren fails to capture Negapatam.	
1782	July 26		Grand interview between Suffren and Haider Ali.	
1782	July 31		De Launay, Bussy's envoy, received at a Darbar by Haider Ali.	
1782	August 12		Duchemin dies; Hoffelize assumes command	
1782	August 31		Suffren captures Trincomallee.	
1782	September		Fourth battle between Suffren and Huges; indecisive.	
1782	December 7			Haider Ali dies.
1782	December 18		Bussy leaves the Isle of France.	
1782	December 20	Nana Padhnavis affixes his signature to the Treaty of Salabai.		
1782	December 29			Tipu Sultan ascends the throne of his father.

(Continued)

Year	*Date*	*The Marathas*	*The French*	*The Mughals, the Portuguese, the English, the Dutch, etc.*
1783	February 10	Peshwa Sawai Madhavrao married.		
1783	March 10		Bussy arrives at Trincomallee.	
1783	April 8	Maratha flotilla captures English vessels.		
1783	April 17		Bussy arrives at Cuddalore.	
1783	April 30			Tipu Sultan recaptures Bednur from the English.
1783	June 13–30		Battle between the French and the English; Suffren triumphs.	
1783	July	Raghoba surrenders to Haripant Phadke at Dhodap.		
1783	December 11	Raghoba dies at Kopergaon.		
1784	Early		De Boigne enters Mahadji's service.	
1784	March 11			Peace signed between Tipu and the English.
1784	November 14	Vakil-i-Mutalak conferred on Mahadji by the Emperor.		

1785	January 7		Bussy dies at Pondicherry.	
1785	February 5			Hastings leaves India.
1785	May		Souillace arrives at Pondicherry as Governor General.	
1785	June 19		Souillac's fresh proposal to Franco-Maratha relations.	
1785	October 10		Souillac leaves India for the Isle of France.	
1786	March 3			Mallet arrives at Poona as Resident.
1786	August 8		Godard arrives at Poona.	
1786	September 7		Godard leaves Poona.	
1786	September 22			Cornwallis becomes Governor-General.
1787	Middle of February	Peace signed between the Marathas and Tipu.		
1787	July 22			Tipu's Ambassador leave for France.
1788	May 13		Montigny retires from Poona.	
1790	June 1	Tripartite treaty signed at Poona.		
1790	December 12			War begins between Tipu Sultan and the allies.
1792	February 11			Peace signed between Tipu Sultan and the allies.
1793	October 20			Cornwallis retires from office.
1794	February 12	Mahadji dies.		
1795	March 11	Battle of Kharda; Nizam Ali defeated.		

(*Continued*)

Year	*Date*	*The Marathas*	*The French*	*The Mughals, the Portuguese, the English, the Dutch, etc.*
1795	December		De Boigne retires.	
1796	October 27	Sawai Madhavrao dies.		
1796	December 6	Bajirao II becomes Peshwa.		
1798	April 26			Lord Morington arrives in India.
1798	October 22		French regiments at Hyderabad disbanded.	
1799	May 4			Tipu Sultan dies on the battle field.
1800	March 13	Nana Fadnavis dies.		
1802	December 31	Treaty of Bassein signed by Bajirao the Second with the English.		
1803	August 7	War begins between Daulatrao Shinde and the English.		
1803	December 30	Daulatrao Shinde sues for peace; Perron's regiments disbanded.		

1805	July 30		Lord Wellesley resigns.
1818	June 3	Bajirao surrenders to Malcom; end of the Maratha Confederacy.	

Portuguese Governors

Date	Name of Governor
4 November 1509–September 1514	Afonso de Alburquerque
8 September 1514–September 1518	Lopo Soares de Albergaria
8 September 1518–January 1522	Diogo Lopes de Sequeira
22 January 1522–September 1524	D. Duarte de Menezes
17 January 1525–February 1526	D. Henrique de Menezes
February 1526–November 1529	Lopo Vaz de Sampaio
18 November 1528–September 1538	Nuno da Cunha
3 April 1540–May 1542	D. Estevao da Gama
8 May 1542–1545	Martim Afonso de Sousa
10 September 1545–1548	D. Joao de Castro
6 June 1548–June 1549	Garcia de Sa
13 June 1549–November 1550	Jorge Cabral
16 June 1555–September 1558	Francisco Barreto
19 February 1564–September 1564	Joao de Mendonca
9 December 1573–September 1576	Antonio Moniz Barreto
September 1576–August 1578	D. Diogo de Menezes
March 1581–September 1581	Fernao Teles de Menezes
May 1588–1591	D. manuel de Sousa Coutinho
June 1607–1609	Fr. Aleixo de Meneses
1609	Andre Furtado de Mendonca
1619–1622	Fernao de Alburquerque
1639–1640	Antonio Teles de Meneses
23 August 1655–14 January 1656	Rodrigo Lobo da Silveira, Count of Sarzedas
14 January 1656–22 May 1656	Manuel Mascarenhas Homem
1686–1690	D. Rodrigo da Costa
1690–January 1691	D. Miguel de Almeida
January 1717–October 1717	Fr. Sebastiao de Andrade Pessanha
July 1723	Cristovao de Melo (Interim Governor)
1768–1774	Joao Jose de Melo
1774	Filipe de Valadares Sotomaior (Interim Governor)
1774–1779	D. Jose Pedro da Camara (governor and Caption General of India)
1779–1786	D. Frederico Gulherme de Sousa Holstein (Governor and Captain General of India)
1786–1794	Francisco da Cunha e Meneses (Governor and Captain general of India)

1794–1806	Francisco Antonio da Veiga Cabral da Camara (Governor and Captain General of India)
1826–1830	D. Manuel Francisco Zacarias de Portugal e Castro
1835	Bernardo Peres da Silva
1835	D. Manuel Francisco Zacarias de Portugal e Castro
1835	Joaquim Manuel Correia da Silva e Gama
1836–1837	Bernardo Peres da Silva
1837–1839	Simao Infante de Lacerda de Sousa Tavares
1839	Jose Antonio Vieira da Fonseca
1839–1840	Manuel Jose Mendes
1840–1842	Jose Joaquim Lopes Lima (Interim Governor)
1842–1843	Francisco Xavier da Silva Pereira
1843–1844	Joaquim Mourao Garcez Palha
1844–1851	Jose Ferreira Pestana
1851–1855	Jose Joaquim Januario Lapa
1855–1865	Antonio Cesar de Vasconcelos Correia
1864–1870	Jose Ferreira Pestana
1870–1871	Januario Correia de Almeida
1871–1875	Joaquim Jose Macedo e Couto
1875–1877	Joao Tavares de Almeida
1877–1878	Antonio Sergio de Sousa
1878–1882	Caetano Alexandre de Almeida e Albuquerque
1882–1886	Carlos Eugenio Correia da Silva
1886	Francisco Joaquim Ferreira do Amaral
1886–1889	Augusto Cesar Cardoso de Carvalho
1889	Joaquim Augusto Mouzinho de Albuquerque (Interim Governor)
1889–1891	Vasco Guedes de Carvalho e Meneses
1891	Francisco Maria da Cunha
1891–1892	Joao Manuel Correia Taborda (Interim Gocernor)
1892–1893	Francisco Teixeira da Silva
1893–1894	Rafael Jacome de Andrade
1894	Joao Manuel Correia Taborda (Interim Governor)
1894–1895	Elesbao Jose de Bettencourt Lapa
1895–1896	Rafael Jacome de Andrade
1896–1897	Joao Antenio de Brissac das Neves Ferreira (Interim Governor)
1897	Joao Manuel Correia Taborda (Interim Governor)
1897–1900	Joaquim Jose Machado
1900–1905	Eduardo Augusto Rodrigues Galhardo
1905–1907	Arnaldo de Novais Guedes Rebelo
1907–1910	Jose Maria de Sousa Horta e Costa
1910–1917	Francisco Manuel Couceiro da Costa (Governor General)
1917	Francisco Maria Peixoto Vieira (Interim Governor General)
1917–1919	Jose de Freitas Ribeiro (Governor General)
1919–1920	Augusto de Paiva Bobela da Mota (Interim Governor General)

1920–1925	Jaime Alberto de Castro Morais (Governador General)
1925	Francisco Maria Peixoto Vieira (Interim Governor General)
1925–1926	Mariano Martins (Governor General)
1926	Tito Augusto de Morais (Interim Governor General)
1926–1927	Acurcio Mendes da Rocha Dinis (Interim Governor General)
1927–1929	Pedro Francisco Massano de Amorin (Governor General)
1929	Acurcio Mendes da Rocha Dinis (Interim Governor General)
1929–1930	Alfredo Pedro de Almeida (Governor General)
1930–1936	Joao Carlos Craveiro Lopes (Governor General)
1936–1938	Francisco Craveiro Lopes (Interim Governor General)
1938–1945	Jose Ricardo Pereira Cabral (Governor General)
1945–1946	Paulo Benard Guedes (Interim Governor General)
1946–1947	Jose Ferreira Bossa (Governor General)
1947–1948	Jose Alves Ferreira (Interim Governor General)
1948–1952	Fernando de Quintanilha e Mendonca Dias (Governor General)
1952–1958	Paulo Benard Guedes (Governor General)
1958–1961	Manuel Antonio Vassalo e Silva (Governor General)

Dutch Governors in India

Date	**Name of the Governor**
1610–1614	Pieter Both
1614–1615	Gerard Reynst
1615–1619	Laurens Reael
1619–1623	Jan Pieterszoon Coen
1623–1627	Pieter de Carpentier
1627–1629	Jan Pieterszoon Coen
1629–1632	Jacques Specx
1632–1636	Hendrik Brouwer
1636–1645	Anthony van Diemen
1645–1650	Cornelis van der Lijn
1650–1653	Carel Reyniersz
1653–1678	Joan Maetsuycker
1678–1681	Rijkloff van Goens
1681–1684	Cornelis Speelman
1684–1691	Johannes Camphuys
1691–1704	Willem van Outhoorn
1704–1709	Joan van Hoorn
1709–1713	Abraham van Riebeeck
1713–1718	Christoffel van Swoll
1718–1725	Hendrick Zwaardecroon
1725–1729	Mattheus de Haan

1729–1732	Diederik Durven
1732–1735	Dirk van Cloon
1735–1737	Abraham Patras
1737–1741	Adriaan Valckenier
1741–1743	Johannes Thedens
1742–1750	Gustaaf Willem baron van Imhoff
1750–1761	Jacob Mossel
1761–1775	Petrus Albertus van der Parra
1775–1777	Jeremias van Riemsdijk
1777–1780	Reinier de Klerk
1780–1796	Willem Alting
1796–1801	Pieter Gerardus van Overstraten
1801–1805	Johannes Siberg
1805–1808	Albertus Wiese
1808–1811	Herman Willem Daendels
1811	Jan Willem Janssens
1811–1816	Under British rule
1816–1826	G.A.G.Ph. Baron van der Capellen
1826–1830	L.P.J. Burggraaf du Bus de Gisignies / Hendrik Merkus de Kock
1830–1833	Graaf van den Bosch
1833–1836	J.C. Baud
1836–1840	D.J. de Eerens
1840–1841	C.S.W. Graaf van Hogendorp
1841–1844	P. Merkus
1844–1845	Jhr J.C. Reijnst
1845–1851	J.J. Rochussen
1851–1856	A.J. Duijmaer van Twist
1856–1861	C.F. Pahud
1861–1866	L.A.J.W. Baron Sloet van de Beele
1866–1872	P. Mijer
1872–1875	J. Loudon
1875–1881	J.W. van Lansberge
1881–1883	F. s'Jacob
1883–1888	O. van Rees
1888–1893	C. Pijnacker Hordijk
1893–1899	jhr. C.H.A. van Wijck
1899–1904	W. Rooseboom
1904–1909	Johannes Benedictus van Heutsz
1909–1916	A.F.W. Idenburg
1916–1921	J.P. Graaf van Limburg Stirum
1921–1926	D. Fock
1926–1931	jhr. A.C.D. de Graeff
1931–1936	jhr. B.C. de Jonge

1936–1942	Alidius Warmoldus Lambertus Tjarda van Starkenborgh Stachouwer
1942, 1945–1948	Hubertus Johannes van Mook
1948–1949	Louis Beel
1949	A.H.J. Lovink

French Governors and Officials in India:

1674	**French territory**
Jan 1760–1765	British occupation
1778–1783	British occupation
1793–1816	British occupation
2 May 1954	Chandernagore transferred to India
1 Nov 1954	Pondicherry transferred to India

Governors (from 1948, Commissioners)

Date	**Name of Governor**
1699–31 Dec 1706	François Martin (b. 1634–d. 1706)
Jan 1707–Jul 1708	Pierre Dulivier (1st time)
1708–1712	Guillaume André d'Hébert (1st time)
1712–1717	Pierre Dulivier (2nd time)
1717–1718	Guillaume André d'Hébert (2nd time
Aug 1718–11 Oct 1721	Pierre André Prévost de La Prévostière (b. ...–d. 1721)
1721–1723	Pierre Christoph Le Noir (1st time) (acting)
1723–1726	Joseph Beauvollier de Courchant
1726–1734	Pierre Christoph Le Noir (2nd time)
Nov 1734–1741	Pierre-Benoît Dumas (b. 1668–d. 1745)
1742–1754	Joseph François Dupleix (b. 1697–d. 1763)
Aug 1754–1754	Charles Robert Godeheu de Zaimont (acting)
1754–1758	Georges Duval de Leyrit
1758–Jan 1760	Thomas Arthur, comte de Lally-Tollendal (b. 1702–d. 1766)
1765–1766	Jean Law de Lauriston (1st time)
1766–1767	Antoine Boyellau
1767–1777	Jean Law de Lauriston (2nd time)
1777–1782	Guillaume-Léonard de Bellecombe, seigneur de Teirac (b. 1728–d. 1792)
1783–1785	Charles Joseph Pâtissier, marquis de Bussy-Castelnau (b. 1718–d. 1785)
1785	François, vicomte de Souillac (b. 1732–d. 1803)

Oct 1785–1787	David Charpentier de Cossigny (b. 1740–d. 1801)
Oct 1787–1789	Thomas, comte de Conway (b. 1733–d. *c.*1800)
Oct 1789–1792	Camille Charles Leclerc, chevalier de Fresne
1792–1793	Dominique-Prosper de Chermont (b. 1741–d. 1798)
Sep 1816–Oct 1825	André Julien, comte Dupuy
Oct 1825–19 Jun 1826	Cordier (1st time) (acting)
19 Jun 1826–Aug 1828	Philippe Panon, vicomte Desbassayns de Richemont (b. 1774–d. 1840)
Aug 1828–10 Apr 1829	Cordier (2nd time) (acting)
10 Apr 1829–3 May 1835	Auguste Jacques Nicolas Peureux de Mélay
3 May 1835–Apr 1840	Hubert Jean Victor, marquis de Saint-Simon
Apr 1840–1844	Paul de Norquer du Camper
1844–1849	Louis Pujol
1849–1850	Hyacinth Marie de Lalande de Calan
1851–1852	Philippe Achille Bédier
1852–1857	de Verminac Saint-Maur
1857–1863	Alexandre Jean Baptiste de Verminac Durand d'Ubaye
1863–1871	Napoléon Joseph Louis Bontemps
1871–1875	Pierre Aristide Faron
1875–1878	Adolph Joseph Antoine Trillard
1878–1881	Léonce Laugier
1881–1884	Julien Théodore Drouet
1884–1886	Étienne-Antoine-Guillaume Richaud (b. 1841–d. 1889)
1886–1888	Louis Evenor Édouard Manès
1888–1889	Georges Jules Piquet
1889–1891	Louis Hippolyte Marie Nouët
1891–1896	Léon Émile Clément Thomas
1896–1898	Louis Jean Girod
1898–1902	François Pierre Rocher
1902–1904	Victor Louis Marie Lanrezac
1904–1905	Jean-Baptiste Philémon Lemaire
1905–1906	Joseph Pascal François
1906–1908	Gabriel Louis Angoulvant (b. 1872–d. 1932)
1908–1909	Adrien Jules Jean Bonhoure (b. 1860–d. 19...)
1909–1910	Ernest Fernand Lévêcque
1910–1912	Pierre Louis Alfred Duprat
1912–1918	Alfred Albert Martineau (b. 1857–d. 1941)
1918–1926	Louis-Martial-Innocent Gerbinis (b. 1871–d. 1954)
1926–1928	Pierre Jean Henri Didelot

1928–1931	Robert Paul Marie de Guise
1931–1934	François-Adrien Juvanon
August 1934–1936	Léon Solomiac (b. 1873–d. 1960)
1936–1938	Horace Valentin Crocicchia
1938–1945	Louis Alexis Étienne Bonvin (b. 1886–d. 1946)
1945–1947	Nicolas Ernest Marie Maurice Jeandin
1947–1949	Charles François Marie Baron
1949–1950	Charles Chambon
1950–1954	André Ménard

Index

For Product Safety Concerns and Information please contact our EU representative GPSR@taylorandfrancis.com
Taylor & Francis Verlag GmbH, Kaufingerstraße 24, 80331 München, Germany

www.ingramcontent.com/pod-product-compliance
Ingram Content Group UK Ltd.
Pitfield, Milton Keynes, MK11 3LW, UK
UKHW020143200926
475702UK00005B/887
9781032427164